U.S. Naval Gunfire Support in the Pacific War

U.S. Naval Gunfire Support in the Pacific War

A Study of the Development and Application of Doctrine

Donald K. Mitchener

andarta books
an imprint of the University Press of Kentucky

Brécourt Academic

Published by Andarta Books
An imprint of The University Press of Kentucky

Scholarly publisher for the Commonwealth,
serving Bellarmine University, Berea College, Centre College of Kentucky, Eastern Kentucky University, The Filson Historical Society, Georgetown College, Kentucky Historical Society, Kentucky State University, Morehead State University, Murray State University, Northern Kentucky University, Spalding University, Transylvania University, University of Kentucky, University of Louisville, and Western Kentucky University.

Editorial and Sales Offices: The University Press of Kentucky
663 South Limestone Street, Lexington, Kentucky 40508-4008
www.kentuckypress.com

Cataloging-in-Publication data available from the Library of Congress

ISBN 978-1-94-966812-4 (hardcover : alk. paper)
ISBN 978-1-94-966814-8 (pdf)
ISBN 978-1-94-966813-1 (epub)

This book is printed on acid-free paper meeting the requirements of the American National Standard for Permanence in Paper for Printed Library Materials.

Manufactured in the United States of America.

ASSOCIATION of UNIVERSITY PRESSES

Member of the Association of University Presses

To the two most important women in my life:
Eula W. Mitchener, my grandmother, who raised me,
and Rebecca A. Mitchener, my wife, who completes me.

Contents

Preface

Naval gunfire support (NGS) is a topic that has been given only limited treatment separate from all the other components of amphibious operations. This work is an attempt to begin to rectify this general oversight. It is not, and is not meant to be, an exhaustive treatment of every aspect of naval gunfire support in every theater of operations during the Second World War. The focus is on the Central and Western Pacific, the areas where the original American amphibious warfare doctrine that was developed by the United States Navy and Marine Corps was most purely applied. The description and analysis of the use of NGS in other theaters will be undertaken in future works.

The author's purpose in producing this work is two-fold. First, to provide other scholars with a description of the basic American doctrine for the use of NGS in amphibious operations that is based upon a close reading of the relevant Fleet Training Publications and the various documents issued during the war to update those publications. Second, to address a number of questions concerning the development and application of that doctrine that have been debated, hotly at times, over the years since the war: did the American NGS doctrine change during the course of the war; if it changed, what were those changes; and did the Americans consistently apply the doctrine in the operations under consideration? It is expected that the conclusions reached after addressing these questions will provide fuel for further debate and analysis about a most important aspect of amphibious warfare during World War II.

Chapter 1

Why Naval Gunfire Support?

> "[The preliminary bombardment was i]ncredible! I'd never seen such firing in my life! The big guns from the ships and rockets! Then the airplanes came in and bombed and strafed. A little bit later on, they came in and dropped napalm bombs on the base of Suribachi. . . . [The bombardment] seemed to be pretty destructive. I didn't see how much of anything could live through it."[1]

> "When we got up on deck before we went to get on the tractors, the island was just a mass of dust. We thought: 'My God! There's nothing left!'"[2]

But there *was* something left, much more than met the eyes of observers on that February morning in 1945. Unfortunately for the over 60,000 Marines slated to take part in Operation Detachment, the majority of Japanese defensive installations on Iwo Jima survived the American bombardment and the island's defenders protected by them would exact a high price in exchange for their dutifully sacrificial extermination.

Richmond Kelly Turner, a naval officer heavily involved in planning and conducting the United States' Central Pacific offensive against the Japanese during World War II, had very definite opinions about the effectiveness of that offensive. He believed that the amphibious warfare doctrine used by the United States in the Pacific was adequate to meet the challenge of breaching the prepared defenses of the Japanese. He also believed that the doctrine *did not change in any substantial way* during the course of the war. According to Turner, what appeared to be changes in the doctrine were, in fact, simply changes in the techniques used to implement it.[3] Was this indeed the case? Is it possible to show that it was not?

---

[1] David Peake, interview by Ronald E. Marcello, 9 October 1994, interview OH 1041, transcript, University of North Texas Oral History Program, pp. 9 and 10.

[2] Lloyd Gossell, interview by Ronald E. Marcello, 12 March 2001, interview OH 1394, transcript, University of North Texas Oral History Program, p. 37.

[3] George C. Dyer, *The Amphibians Came to Conquer: The Story of Admiral Richmond Kelly Turner*, Vol. I (Washington, DC: GPO, 1969), p. 224.

According to Dyer, Turner believed that the pre-World War II amphibious doctrine could be summarized as follows: "(1) The place chosen for landing amphibious troops must be favorable from the naval point of view, so that the landing craft can land easily; and the terrain in the rear of the chosen beach must be favorable from the Landing Force point of view, so

A work dedicated to demonstrating all of the changes in doctrine that occurred during World War II as the United States Navy and Marine Corps put their existing amphibious warfare doctrinal views to the test over the period of 1941 until 1945 would run to several hundred pages, the reading of which would be a most tedious exercise for the average reader. Perusing written doctrine can diminish the flexibility of even the supplest of minds and studies of it tend to have the same effect. Such a long and mind-numbing exercise is not necessary in this case, however. One does not have to show every example of change in order to prove that Turner's general assessment was not accurate. The reason this is so is that if he were mistaken in a particular case, then any conclusions drawn by him in which that case played an integral part would also be suspect if not mistaken as well. Turner's assessment was a broadly-based general one that admitted no exceptions. This study will examine Turner's statement in light of the application of one component of the amphibious warfare doctrine followed by the American sea services during World War II—the use of naval gunfire support. By demonstrating doctrinal change in this one component, it will be shown that Turner's assessment was flawed and that the accuracy of his conclusions was compromised.

The parameters of this inquiry need to be narrowed further beyond just the selection of a doctrinal component upon which to concentrate. Here, again, length and complexity of the finished product are considerations. There is a more substantive one as well, however. The author's main interest is in the ability of naval gunners to perform a function that the writers of the U.S. doctrine believed them capable of performing: supplying support for an amphibious assault before the attacking force's organic field artillery was in a position to do so. Supplying this support required gunners aboard ship to engage targets with a level of precision

---

the attack can move away from the beach area. (2) The naval gun and the airplane must be used to control the sea and air at the objective area, to reduce or eliminate enemy resistance in the chosen landing beach area, and to assist the Landing Force in moving out of the beach area to its objectives. (3) The Landing Force early objectives must be far enough away from the chosen landing beach to remove the landing beach from the field of enemy artillery fire. (4) The logistic support of the Landing Force via a reasonably secure line of communications must build up rapidly so as to free the Fleet for further movement. (5) As soon as the action ashore changes from amphibious warfare to land warfare, the Army relieves the Marines. . . ."

Dyer continued: "All of these things were of course subject to all the over-riding General Principles of War, such as surprise, landing where and when the enemy wasn't immediately expecting you, and the only part of this general doctrine which I would say that was changed markedly in the war was the fifth one. The Army got into amphibious warfare in a big way, and in the earliest stage—at Guadalcanal, they didn't relieve the Marines as soon as I thought the doctrine called for. . . . Of course during Guadalcanal, I can't say we had a secure line of communications, or that at Okinawa we had control of the air all the time. But that didn't change the doctrine. We just were temporarily unable to carry it out." Dyer, *The Amphibians Came to Conquer,* Vol. I, pp. 224–25.

for which their previous naval gunnery training had not prepared them. It is consequently the preoperational training and planning and the execution of the various bombardments up to the point when fire control parties were being activated ashore that will be the focus of what follows. In other words, the emphasis in this study is on the period when the gunners and gunnery officers aboard support vessels were virtually on their own, with additional help being supplied only by mostly Navy-supplied aircraft spotters and with minimal help from anyone on land. Operations against the following objectives will serve as a basis for this analysis: Betio Island in Tarawa Atoll; Roi-Namur in Kwajalein Atoll; Saipan and Guam in the Mariana Islands; Peleliu in the Palau Islands; and Iwo Jima. Turner oversaw amphibious planning and execution for all of these save one—the operation to take Peleliu. The author will show that naval gunfire doctrine did indeed evolve, contrary to Turner's assessment, and that United States naval and Marine officers selectively applied the evolving doctrine. In addition, he will show that American amphibious warfare planners working in the Central Pacific, under pressure to keep operations going at an accelerated tempo so as to keep the Japanese off balance and believing enemy aircraft and submarines to be a real and present threat, often put together operations in such a way as to preclude the most efficient use of the massive naval gunfire support that experience showed to be necessary for the reduction of the evolving enemy defenses. Succinctly put, doctrine and techniques evolved, but American strategy and planning, at times, worked to defeat both.

Most Americans of the World War II generation, not being students of naval and military history, came to see amphibious warfare as a Second World War development and the United States Marine Corps as its chief practitioner. Was this hybrid military/naval specialty new at the time the Americans began their march to the Home Islands? Such was hardly the case. Men have used ships to transport soldiers to battle since the time of the ancient Greek wars, and the Japanese themselves applied an amphibious doctrine of their own as they expanded their Empire out into the Pacific.[4] Was the United States Marine Corps a hardened amphibious force of longstanding when it began its counterattack against the Japanese in late 1942? Although the Corps has existed since the eighteenth century, it did not specialize in amphibious warfare until the early twentieth century. Marines served aboard ship in the Age of Sail as small arms marksmen in the rigging during a naval battle, as members of a ship's landing party when necessary, and as seagoing policemen who enforced discipline and order aboard ship. They continued to perform the latter two functions after the transition to steam and added service as

[4] E. B. Potter, ed., *The United States and World Sea Power* (Englewood Cliffs, NJ: Prentice-Hall, 1955), pp. 10–11; Allan R. Millett, "Assault from the Sea: The Development of Amphibious Warfare between the Wars—the American, British, and Japanese Experience," in Williamson Murray and Allan R. Millett, eds., *Military Innovation in the Interwar Period* (New York: Cambridge University Press, 1996), pp. 64–70.

imperial constabulary troops after the Spanish-American War. Battles with the Navy and Army that at times threatened its continued existence forced the Marine Corps to look for a mission that it could claim as its own. This is one of the most important reasons for the Corps' concentration during the 1930s on the development of a workable amphibious warfare doctrine.[5]

How did the mission and the accompanying doctrine evolve?[6] Using the changes that affected naval gunfire support doctrine as a framework for a chronology, its evolution over the years 1900–1945 can be divided into four periods: 1900–1933, 1934–1 August 1943, 2 August 1943–February 1944, and March 1944–October 1945. The first of these periods, by far the longest of the four, witnessed the creation of the Advanced Base Force and its evolution into the Fleet Marine Force. The job of the Advanced Base Force was to take and defend bases as part of a naval campaign, the emphasis being on the Western Pacific Ocean and a war with Japan. The objective in mind was to use naval forces to project American power across the vast Pacific. Naval gunfire support doctrine, such as it existed during the second half of this period, was rooted in concepts derived from World War I artillery doctrine and was tempered by the lessons derived from the Gallipoli operation of 1915.

The second period began with the completion of the first version of the *Tentative Manual* and ended with the promulgation of Change 3 of *FTP* [Fleet Training Publication] *167, Landing Operations Doctrine, U.S. Navy, 1938*. The authors of the *Tentative Manual* thought that the majority of ships' gunfire was needed only until the landing force's field artillery could get ashore. Consequently, most gunfire support ships were not expected to remain on station very much past H-hour. The danger of possible air, surface, or submarine attack was too great to keep them there any longer than what was considered essential for the initial battle on the beaches. The emphasis during this period was on surprising the enemy and then overwhelming his forces in the immediate area of the beach so that lodgment of the landing force could be achieved. Significant destruction of the enemy's emplacements was considered to be too difficult to accomplish and, if attempted, would endanger the naval vessels engaged in the process by tying them for too long a period of time to the area of the invasion. The object was to bombard for a short time and then to leave the area for open water. To the naval mind, nothing was more important than the security of the ship.

The third period, 2 August 1943–February 1944, encompassed the evolution of doctrine from the promulgation of Change 3 of *FTP 167* until just after the

[5] Allan R. Millett, *Semper Fidelis: The History of the United States Marine Corps*, rev. ed. (New York: The Free Press, 1991), pp. 26–51, 115–286, and 319–43.

[6] This paragraph is a summary of the argument that is made in the text that follows this introductory chapter. Citations for the secondary sources and primary evidence that support the various parts of the argument will be given at the proper time within the text.

capture of Roi-Namur in the Marshall Islands. Change 3 contained many doctrinal ideas first found in the *Tentative Manual,* but there were differences as well. The most prominent example of the conservation of earlier doctrine was an insistence that destruction of enemy emplacements over anything more than a small area was impossible. This point of doctrine would change as a result of Navy and Marine Corps experience in the Gilbert Islands in November of 1943. The assault of Betio Island, Tarawa Atoll, in the Gilberts was the first time that the two services were able to test their amphibious warfare doctrine in an attack against a heavily defended beach. The difficulties encountered by the 2nd Marines in going ashore on Betio led to the conclusion that destruction, not neutralization, was necessary if landing force casualties were to be kept to an acceptable level. The capture of Roi-Namur in February of 1944 convinced the two services that the lessons of Tarawa were effective and that they had been absorbed and properly implemented.

The last period, March 1944–October 1945, encompassed the evolution of doctrine from the aftermath of the capture of the Marshall Islands to the promulgation by the Marine Corps Schools at Quantico, Virginia, of *Amphibious Operations—Naval Gunfire Support* [PHIB-11]. This document, although not a U.S. Navy publication, was an accurate statement of American naval gunfire doctrine as it existed at the end of the war. Its publication is a fitting place to end an analysis of the use of naval gunfire by the United States' sea services in support of amphibious operations during World War II. The authors of PHIB-11 state that *FTP 167* was the "current standard operating doctrine for amphibious warfare," an indication that the Navy did not issue any substantial official written changes to the document during the war.[7]

Attempts have been made over the years to analyze the use of naval gunfire in the Central Pacific during World War II. Donald M. Weller, the Fifth Amphibious Corps naval gunfire officer for the Iwo Jima operation, has addressed this topic in various post-war writings from the 1950s and 1970s, as have Jeter Isely and Philip Crowl in their analysis of the Marine Corps and American amphibious doctrine in

---

[7] Marine Corps Schools, *Amphibious Operations—Naval Gunfire Support,* PHIB-11 (Quantico: Marine Corps Schools, 1945), p. 3.

The Navy's decision not to update the written doctrine post-1 August 1943 might be the basis of Turner's comment that doctrine did not change during the war, but such a decision is not evidence of doctrinal stagnation. Changes did occur, the shift of emphasis from neutralization to destruction after Tarawa being just one example. PHIB-11 contains no doctrinal statements to the contrary, but a statement emphasizing the preference of neutralization over destruction, like the one found in *FTP 167* Change 3, is not present.

The offices of the Commander-in-Chief of the U.S. Fleet and Chief of Naval Operations did not update *FTP 167,* but the Commander-in-Chief Pacific Fleet did issue two Confidential Letters (PacFlt Conf. Ltr. 13CL-44 and PacFlt Conf. Ltr. 38CL-45) that updated naval gunfire doctrine for the Pacific Fleet. It was not until PHIB-11 was published that the changes made during the war were incorporated into a service-wide publication.

the Pacific published in 1951. Weller wrote in 1977 of changes in American doctrine and of changes in Japanese defenses. He also listed reasons why naval gunfire could not address those defenses adequately. His emphasis was on the ability of United States naval forces to obliterate Japanese defensive structures and he correctly pointed out that American firepower forced the Japanese to concede the beach to their enemy by late 1944 and 1945. He did not, however, address directly the question of how effective the new Japanese strategy was in offsetting the power of American naval gunfire in support of assaulting troops. Isely and Crowl, writing within six years of the end of the war, documented what they perceived to be doctrinal change on the part of the Americans, but they were even more reticent than Weller to address the question of the efficacy of the new Japanese defensive tactics. Their book, which is still recognized as the standard interpretation of its subject, contains a number of errors and misinterpretations, particularly regarding the history of the early development of amphibious doctrine and the relationship between the Navy/Marine Corps' doctrine and the doctrine developed by the United States Army.[8]

Unlike these previous studies, the present work addresses directly the question of whether or not naval gunfire support was effective and, where it was not, what were the reasons for its inefficacy. A concise statement of the consensus among United States naval and Marine Corps historians concerning the effectiveness of naval gunfire in support of amphibious operations in World War II can be found in PHIB-11:

> [The effectiveness of naval gunfire doctrine] is undeniable. Naval gunfire, through its ability to neutralize a landing beach by leisurely saturation bombardment, permitted the Allies to invade beaches of their own choice with greatly reduced losses. It enabled them to put troops ashore on islands and in areas far more heavily defended than ever before in all history. The complete reversal of Japanese tactics is sufficient testimony. Early in the war they adopted, wherever possible, the policy of repulsing the invasion at the water's edge. But the tremendous weight of naval gun-

[8] Donald M. Weller, *Gunfire Support of Amphibious Operations: Past, Present, and Future* (Dahlgren, VA: Naval Surface Weapons Center, 1977). Jeter A. Isely and Philip A. Crowl, *The U.S. Marines and Amphibious War: Its Theory and Its Practice in the Pacific* (Princeton: Princeton University Press, 1951). Isely and Crowl's work is still considered the "bible" of World War II Pacific Theater amphibious warfare analysis, especially by historians who write from a naval or Marine background. Adrian R. Lewis, in his book *Omaha Beach: A Flawed Victory* (Chapel Hill: University of North Carolina Press, 2001), argues that the United States Army in the European Theater of Operations did not employ Navy/Marine Corps amphibious doctrine. Its doctrine, according to Lewis, was an amalgamation of U.S. Army, U.S. Navy, and British thought, not simply *FTP 167* "put between Army covers," as some have described it.

> fire, properly coordinated with aerial bombardment, defeated this stratagem at Tarawa, the Marshalls, and elsewhere. It had the effect of forcing the enemy to yield an undefended beachhead, or one defended by fire at the most. They yielded not because of surprise or stealth, but by design because the landing zone was untenable to them. Thereafter, they shifted their tactics. The battle doctrine of the 32nd Army at Okinawa instructed them to give up the beach without a contest, and to pin their hopes on defeating the Americans in the subsequent engagement inland. The results are a matter of history—a history underlined by the development of naval gunfire as a supporting weapon.[9]

The basic truth of this statement as to the results of the operations mentioned is beyond question. Those results are, as the document states, "a matter of history." There are a number of problems with the authors' conclusions, however. First, the authors of the *Tentative Manual* and everyone who worked on the doctrine after them placed great faith in the ability of naval gunfire to overcome practically any defenses an enemy might present them. This faith proved not to be justified in every case. Second, the authors of PHIB-11 mention Tarawa and the Marshalls as two operations that validated the doctrine. This conclusion is based upon a fundamental misinterpretation of the evidence. The doctrine tested at Tarawa was not the doctrine documented in PHIB-11; American experience in the Gilberts changed it, and the Marshalls operation only proved that the doctrine worked against an enemy whose defenses were insufficient. Third, the authors of PHIB-11 represent the Okinawa operation as the ultimate proof of their contention that naval gunfire was at least one of the most significant factors in making the Japanese change their defensive tactics. It is granted that naval gunfire did influence Japanese thinking and practice, but the assaults on Saipan, Guam, and Okinawa were undertaken against objectives that were large enough to give the Japanese a choice as to tactics. In other words, the options offered to the Japanese by the changes in size and topography of the islands also must be taken into account—they did not have to meet the Americans at the shoreline as they had to do on the small atolls.

The authors of PHIB-11 do not mention one very important operation, however. All of the basic principles of naval gunfire doctrine as they had been developed by the time this operation was undertaken were followed, but the results cannot be seen as neatly validating the authors' conclusions. This operation was the invasion of Iwo Jima. General Kuribayashi, the Japanese commander on Volcano Island, recognized that the tremendous power of U.S. naval gunfire support precluded the meeting of the American forces on the beach and driving them back into the sea. He would, therefore, have to attempt to defeat the invaders through

---

[9] PHIB-11, p. 4.

attrition. The defensive scheme he chose—a defense in depth designed to bleed the enemy assault forces to the point of exhaustion and, hopefully, cause the United States to have second thoughts about continuing on to the Home Islands of Japan—was one that effectively neutralized the American firepower advantage beyond the landing beaches. Kuribayashi was almost successful in another regard. The losses incurred by United States forces on Iwo Jima gave the Americans pause, but the outcome of the war was all but inevitable by February of 1945, and Kuribayashi's sacrifice ultimately did not stave off defeat.

While there is no way to foresee the future with accuracy, the Japanese should have embarked upon the road to war more trepidatiously than they did. They predicated success in that war upon several premises, and it was the failure of many in positions of leadership within Japan to recognize the strategic realities of the late 1930s and early 1940s that doomed their enterprise almost from the start. First, they assumed that they could recreate the quick victories of earlier conflicts like the 1894–95 war with China and the 1904–05 war with Russia, ensuring that their limited supplies of important commodities such as oil and rubber would not hinder them. Second, they assumed that Germany would be victorious in its war with Great Britain and the Soviet Union, and that the United States would be distracted by having to deal with a powerful Nazi state that dominated Europe. Third, they assumed that the United States lacked the moral fiber to fight back against Japan—"superior culture and spirit" giving the Japanese an edge that the Americans would not dare to challenge. Finally, they assumed that once Japan had pushed the American military forces out of the Western Pacific, the emperor's army and navy would hold the line against U.S. attempts to push back. The Americans, having to deal with Germany, would eventually acquiesce, allowing Japan to keep her conquests. If Germany lost, however, there was really no way for Japan, alone, to win. Japanese success was therefore dependent upon German success. For most of 1941, Germany seemed unstoppable, so such a dependency was not regarded as a liability at the time Japan made the decision for war. Once events began to turn against Hitler, however, the misguided strategic nature of such a plan became apparent. In the end, every one of their strategic assumptions proved wrong, and the Japanese found themselves in a war that they were not properly prepared to fight and they most likely could not win.[10]

One final question: why should a study of the use of naval gunfire in a war that ended so long ago be considered important? After all, the weapons, techniques,

---

[10] Ronald M. Spector, *Eagle Against the Sun: The American War with Japan* (New York: The Free Press, 1985); Gerhard L. Weinberg, *A World at Arms: A Global History of World War II*, 2nd ed. (Cambridge: Cambridge University Press, 2005); H. P. Willmott, *Empires in the Balance: Japanese and Allied Pacific Strategies to April 1942* (Annapolis: Naval Institute Press, 1982); and Akira Iriye, *The Origins of the Second World War in Asia and the Pacific* (London: Longman, 1987).

and doctrines of the United States armed forces have changed over the years and the present-day strategic picture is vastly different. Put simply, it is important because the lives of thousands of young men were dependent upon the successful application of the doctrine developed by the United States Navy and Marine Corps to get them ashore across the hostile beaches of the Pacific, and many of them lost their lives when certain parts of that doctrine proved inadequate or were applied improperly. A lesson for the present is there, though one must look past the trappings of history in order to see it. The same generic mistakes are still made today. The present generation of naval and Marine Corps leaders should be able to see in this story the results of the misinterpretation of strategic and tactical realities. Given our technology, understanding of the enemy, and resources at the time, did our armed forces produce the most effective doctrine, and if they did not, what were the reasons for their failure? To begin answering these questions, let us look first at the state of the doctrine at the beginning of the war.

Chapter 2

Doctrine, the *Tentative Manual*, and *FTP 167*

The United States Marine Corps as an institution, in conjunction with officers of the United States Navy who provided important input to the process, undertook the development during the 1930s of a doctrine for the execution of amphibious assaults. This doctrine was originally promulgated as the *Tentative Manual for Landing Operations* in 1934. It was reissued in revised form as the *Tentative Landing Operations Manual, 1935* on 9 July 1935. This revision was updated and released for limited Navy and Marine Corps use on 21 June 1937 as *Landing Operations Doctrine, U.S. Navy, 1937.* On 25 November 1938 the Navy released what proved to be the final general revision of the doctrine that was undertaken prior to the beginning of World War II, which they entitled *Landing Operations Doctrine, U.S. Navy, 1938* (*FTP 167*).[1] Three modifications were incorporated into this document prior to the beginning of the Central Pacific Campaign in November of 1943: Change 1, promulgated 2 May 1941; Change 2, promulgated 1 August 1942; and Change 3, promulgated 1 August 1943. Each of these modifications reflected experience gained by the Navy and the Marine Corps in trying to implement the amphibious warfare doctrine described within the pages of *FTP 167* in Fleet Landing Exercises 6 and 7 of early 1941 and the Solomons operation of 1942–1943.[2]

American naval and Marine commanders relied upon this doctrine as they worked to plan and train forces for the assault of Tarawa Atoll in late 1943. As

[1] Kenneth J. Clifford, *Amphibious Warfare Development in Britain and America from 1920 to 1940* (Laurens, NY: Edgewood, 1983), pp. 103–05. A note as to the proper title of *FTP 167* is in order. A number of secondary sources give the meaning of the abbreviation "F.T.P." as "Fleet Tactical Publication." This is incorrect. First of all, the title page of the original 1938 version of *FTP 167,* and every version thereafter, clearly states that the manual is the work of the Office of Naval Operations, Division of Fleet Training. Yes, the manual contains information about tactics, but its ultimate purpose is to provide a basis for the training of forces in the accepted doctrine for the carrying out of amphibious assaults. Second, according to the *Glossary of U.S. Naval Abbreviations* (OPNAV 29-P1000), 5th Edition (Washington, DC: GPO, 1949), there is one—and only one—meaning for the abbreviation "F.T.P." during World War II—Fleet Training Publication.

[2] Clifford, *Amphibious Warfare,* pp. 107 and 208–14.

stated earlier, Kelly Turner insisted until his death that the doctrine never changed in any substantial way during the war, that any perceived doctrinal changes were really just changes in techniques used in its implementation. How accurate was his assessment? The answer to this question cannot be ascertained, however, until a proper analytical foundation has been laid. The cornerstone of this foundation must be an accurate understanding of the place of doctrine in early 20th century American naval thinking. How did the U.S. Navy view the concept of "doctrine" going into World War II? A pivotal event in the development of the American attitude concerning naval doctrine is the Sampson-Schley controversy that followed the Spanish-American War. At the heart of this controversy were two naval flag officers, Rear Admiral William T. Sampson and Commodore Winfield Scott Schley. Supporters of these two men sniped at one another in public over which of them was ultimately responsible for the American victory in the U.S. vs. Spanish fleet engagement off Santiago, Cuba, in 1898. The debate, which went on for several years and only ended by order of President Theodore Roosevelt, left a lasting impression on American naval officers of the time. The controversy was most profoundly influential regarding the issue of doctrine. An aversion to "airing the Navy's dirty laundry in public" developed in the minds of officers. This aversion was so powerful that the Navy chose to squelch open and frank public discussions of all differences of opinion, even going to the point of purging the term "doctrine" from the vocabulary of Navy men for years afterward and causing a whole generation of officers to claim that "doctrine," as such, did not exist in the United States Navy.[3]

Chester W. Nimitz, Raymond A. Spruance, and Richmond Kelly Turner, the three men most responsible for guiding the Navy during the war in the Central Pacific, all graduated from the Naval Academy during the first decade of the 20th century. Their formative years as midshipmen and junior officers were shaped by the superficially anti-doctrinal American naval culture of the time.[4] Doctrine,

[3] James J. Tritten, *Naval Doctrine . . . From the Sea* (Norfolk: Naval Doctrine Command, 1994), p. 1; Wayne P. Hughes, *Fleet Tactics: Theory and Practice* (Annapolis: Naval Institute Press, 1986), p. 30; E. B. Potter, ed., *Sea Power: A Naval History*, 2nd edition (Annapolis: Naval Institute Press, 1981), p. 185.

[4] Though many of these men were able to put this embarrassment behind them, some of them actually enjoying the discomfort it caused older officers above them in the ranks—Midshipman Chester W. Nimitz was not one of them. According to Nimitz's biographer, E. B. Potter, the scandal was a traumatic experience for the young cadet. As Potter wrote: "[Nimitz] made a vow then and there that, if ever he was in a position to prevent it, there would be no washing of the Navy's dirty linen in public. The shock of the Sampson-Schley controversy may indeed have been at the root of Nimitz's later almost obsessive discretion." E. B. Potter, *Nimitz* (Annapolis: Naval Institute Press, 1976), p. 53. "Dirty linen" included, in the minds of naval officers of the time, vigorous differences of opinion concerning proper principles and doctrines.

however, did not disappear. As James Tritten, an historian specializing in the development of naval doctrine, describes it: "Doctrine was driven into the formal tactical publications, read primarily by the professional officer, as well as taking root in the unwritten, but extremely powerful, form of shared experiences derived from service at sea, exercises, and war college courses. Doctrinal debate took place mainly in the wardroom and the classroom—not primarily on the pages of professional journals."[5]

This was the environment in which the "doctrines" of the Navy began to take shape prior to World War I.

What exactly is "doctrine?" This is an important question, for which there is no precise answer. No two authorities agree on the exact meaning of the word.[6] The best place to start for the purposes of this study is the presently accepted Department of Defense (DOD) definition: "Fundamental principles by which the military forces or elements thereof guide their actions in support of national objectives. It is authoritative but requires judgment in application."[7] This definition, though more broad in its connotations, agrees with what Clausewitz wrote: "Principles, rules, regulations, and methods are . . . indispensable concepts to or for that part of the theory of war that leads to positive doctrines; for in these doctrines the truth can express itself only in such compressed forms."[8] He continues, relating the development of doctrine most closely to the tactical level of war: "Those concepts will appear most frequently in tactics, which is that part of war in which theory can develop most fully into positive doctrine."[9] Before one leaves too quickly the study of what Clausewitz has to say about doctrine, believing that he places his *imprimatur* upon the development and strict adherence to doctrinal orthodoxy, one should also read what he says under the heading "A Positive Doctrine is Unattainable":

> Given the nature of the subject, we must remind ourselves that it is simply not possible to construct a model for the art of war that can serve as a scaffolding on which the commander can rely for support at any time. Whenever he has to fall back on his innate talent, he will find himself outside the model and in conflict with it; no matter how versatile the code, the situation will always lead to the consequences we have already alluded

[5] Tritten, *From the Sea*, p. 1.

[6] Hughes, *Fleet Tactics*, p. 30.

[7] U.S. Department of Defense, *Dictionary of Military Terms* (New York: Arco Publishing, 1988), p. 117.

[8] Carl von Clausewitz, *On War*, Michael Howard and Peter Paret, eds. and translators (Princeton: Princeton University Press, 1976), p. 152.

[9] Ibid.

> to: *talent and genius operate outside the rules, and theory conflicts with practice* [italics in original].[10]

In these words can be seen one of the origins of the DOD definition's concept of judgment in application.

The U.S. Navy of the early 20th century developed an understanding of doctrine along these lines, perceiving a close relationship between doctrine and tactics as well as doctrine and training. Wayne P. Hughes, Jr. describes these relationships and the resulting naval understanding of doctrine in his study of the fleet tactics of the United States Navy. To use his description, by itself, as a basis for an historical understanding of early 20th century American naval thought would be anachronistic, but his comments are enlightening nevertheless and can be used as a starting point for discussion:

> Doctrine is the commander's way of controlling his forces in writing, before military action. Doctrine enunciates policies and procedures that govern action. In its broad sense, doctrine is what is taught as "right behavior"—"rules upon which we act spontaneously and without orders for the accomplishment of a mission," wrote Admiral Harry E. Yarnell. In its stringent sense, doctrine is mandatory behavior; it must be obeyed. Either way, high levels of command want coherence of policy for control, while tactical levels want procedures for cooperative effort. These are merely matters of emphasis. Two points about doctrine must be remembered: it is vital, and it must not become dogmatic.

Hughes wrote that "Doctrine may also be thought of as every action that contributes to unity of purpose. Doctrine isn't [*sic*] what is written in the books; it is what warriors believe in and act on. . . . Doctrine is greater than tactics in that it encompasses command structure and communication. It is less than tactics in that it can establish no more than procedures that enable and enhance the execution of tactical choice on the battlefield." He continued that

> In the execution of good doctrine there is always tension between conformity and initiative. . . . There is a measure of entropy in all doctrine. With too little entropy there is order and understanding but no initiative. With too much entropy there is creativity and change but no order. . . . Doctrine is the basis for training and for the measurement of the achievement of training standards. . . . Tactical doctrine is the standard operating procedure that the creative commander adapts to the exigencies of battle. . . . Doctrine is . . . the standard the tactical analyst uses to evaluate the new

[10] Ibid., p. 140.

> against the old. . . . In sum, doctrine must be whole and firm but not dogmatic. It must leave room for men of freewheeling genius, for such will be the aces of the next war. But it must never surrender control, because control is the prerequisite of concerted action.[11]

Doctrine, tactics, and training are, therefore, interrelated and must be seen as such. In addition, just like Clausewitz, Hughes stressed the importance of leaving room for the "man of genius." In this regard, the use of judgment in the application of doctrine, Hughes also agrees with the DOD definition.

Clausewitz's comment on the relationship between principles and doctrine is most significant. Early 20th century American naval thinkers were unclear as to the proper relationship between the two. For Clausewitz, principles, amongst other things, "[lead] to positive doctrines." In other words, a doctrine is not a principle. Rather, doctrine relies upon and is created with principles in mind. Lieutenant Commander Dudley W. Knox wrote an article for the United States Naval Institute *Proceedings* in 1915 regarding the Navy's reluctance, after the Sampson-Schley controversy, to debate doctrine in a public forum. In his article, Knox addressed this question of principles versus doctrine in these words:

> One meaning of doctrine is a "principle" or "body of principles," but that is not the sense in which it is employed when applied to the art of war by European military forces. Some military writers and translators have caused great confusion by using the term as a synonym for principles. Military doctrines are beliefs or teachings which have been reasoned from principles; that is, they flow from principles as a source. They are intended to be general guides to the application of mutually accepted principles, and thus furnish a practical basis for co-ordination under the extremely difficult conditions governing contact between hostile forces.

---

[11] Hughes, *Fleet Tactics,* pp. 28–31. The 1942 edition of the U.S. Naval War College's volume entitled *Sound Military Decision* contains the following description of "doctrine" on pp. 16 and 17: "Military doctrine, in its broad sense, is a digest of the accepted beliefs of the military profession. In a narrower sense a military doctrine may be confined to the views of a single commander on a specific subject. The object of military doctrine, however, is always to furnish a basis for mutual understanding to the end that prompt and harmonious action by subordinate commanders may ensue without the necessity for referring every problem to superior authority before taking action. . . . Doctrine thus provides a basis for action in possible situations when, for whatever reason, precise instructions have not been issued." Hughes' comments reflect a similar view concerning the relationship between doctrine and practice.

Knox continued, writing that

> A principle is a "fundamental truth as a basis of reasoning; the cause, source or origin of anything." Obviously, there is a great difference between a principle and a military doctrine, notwithstanding that they are related. It has been aptly said that the difficulty with fundamental principles lies not in their comprehension but in their application. Under any given circumstances fundamental principles might be correctly applied in a number of materially different ways, depending upon the varieties of doctrines held. Furthermore, in war the number of possible acceptable solutions to a situation is increased not alone by the number of possible applications of the several principles involved, but as well by the variations in the relative importance which may be assumed for each.[12]

Knox appears to follow Clausewitz's conception of the distinction and relationship between the two. Hughes shows a similar understanding of this relationship:

> [T]here is a distinction between military principles . . . and the actions that derive from them. Tactics change, but that does not preclude the search for tactical principles, and if there are strategic principles, that does not mean that strategies do not change. Strategies as well as tactics are influenced by "weapons made by man." . . . Throughout the hierarchy of enlightenment, from Truth, which the epistemologists say exists but is never known with certainty, to principles, which express our contemporary vision of Truth, to policy and doctrine, which are programs for concerted action based on principles, and finally to strategic or tactical decisions, which are individual actions guided by policy and doctrine—throughout this hierarchy, error creeps in. . . .[13]

The continuity of thought between these two naval authors over a 71-year interval as to the proper relationship between principles and doctrine, and their recognition that naval officers make mistakes in their understanding of that proper relationship, is instructive.

What of the Marine Corps? Did Marine officers contemporary with Knox agree with his assessment of the relationship between these two very important concepts? Major John H. Russell, a future Commandant of the Marine Corps, wrote an article in 1916 in which he contended that the Corps needed to develop

[12] Dudley W. Knox, "The Role of Doctrine in Naval Warfare," *Proceedings* 41 (March/April 1915), pp. 334–35.

[13] Hughes, *Fleet Tactics,* pp. 140–41.

a policy and doctrine for itself beyond the simplistic idea of "cooperation with the Navy." As part of his argument he stated:

> It is well understood by military men of the present time that the Art of War has its theories and its principles, otherwise it would not be an art. It follows that it also has the application of its principles or Doctrine. The common acceptation of the word doctrine makes it synonomous [*sic*] with principle. This is not true. A principle is a fundamental truth. A military principle is a fundamental truth arrived at by a study of the military history of wars and adapted to the circumstances and characteristics not only of the military organization but of the nation it represents. Napoleon has aptly said: "The principles of war are those which have directed the great leaders and of which history has transmitted to us the main facts." The word "Doctrine," as applied to military life, means a teaching that provides for a "mutual understanding" among the commissioned personnel of a military organization. In plain words "team work." Military doctrine is born of military principles. It is the application of principle. A principle cannot be wrong, it is a fact. A doctrine, on the other hand, may be wrong. As it becomes ripened by experience or to suit new conditions, it is altered. It is thus, at first, tentative and gradually built up by a process of evolution. The historical study from which we derive certain principles is nothing more or less than an estimate of the Situation. The principles deduced represent our decision. Having once made a decision it becomes necessary to put it into execution, in other words to apply the principles. This is true military Doctrine.[14]

Russell, as can be seen, agreed with Knox as to the relationship between principles and doctrine. His ideas, along with those of others, would eventually serve as the point of departure for those wishing to create a mission for the Marine Corps that thoroughly differentiated the Corps from both the Navy and the Army.

What does this seemingly pedantic differentiation between the terms "principle" and "doctrine" have to do with the use of naval gunfire in support of amphibious operations in World War II? Turner's statement that what appeared to be

[14] John H. Russell, "A Plea for a Mission and Doctrine," *Marine Corps Gazette* 1 (June 1916), p. 115. The "estimate of the Situation" to which Russell refers was a part of the analytical process taught at the Naval War College. The first step in preparing a plan of action was to analyze all the relevant data—your ship's position, the enemy's position, what was known about the enemy's capabilities relative to your own, etc . . . —and then to begin planning based upon this reasoned foundation. Russell viewed the historical study undertaken by military and naval thinkers as the equivalent of this "estimate of the Situation." Historical study lays a foundation for the derivation of principles just as the "estimate of the Situation" lays the foundation for solid planning and proper action.

changes in the doctrine during the war were actually changes in the techniques used to apply the doctrine—that the doctrine itself was proved valid and remained essentially unchanged—supplies the connection. Once again, was Turner correct in this assessment? Reading or even hearing the rumor of a civilian presuming to analyze the actions and conclusions of a professional naval officer would have brought a most profanely worded objection from Turner. No amount of apologetic explanation would have warmed him to the idea of what he would see as a blatantly ignorant and conceited effort. Before embarking upon a critique of Turner's statement, therefore, the author wishes to make it clear that he is keeping in mind Clausewitz's caution to the critics of military matters and decisions: "A critic should never use the results of theory as laws and standards, but only—as the soldier does—as aids to judgment. If, in tactics, it is generally agreed that in the standard line of battle cavalry should be posted not in line with but behind infantry, it should nevertheless be foolish to condemn every different deployment simply because it is different. The critic should analyze the reasons for the exception. He has no right to appeal to theoretical principles unless these reasons are inadequate."[15]

The author's goal is not to show that Turner and his subordinate commanders were wrong in their tactics. An opinion as to the better use of gunfire support in particular situations will be hazarded from time to time, but producing such opinions is not the purpose of this study. The goal is to show that naval gunfire doctrine did change and that a problem that plagued many Navy men of his time, an imperfect understanding and use of terminology, was the reason for Turner's inability to recognize that change.

The third official modification of *FTP 167* contains a statement that shows just how mistaken Turner was concerning this seemingly pedantic point. In discussing techniques, the writers state:

> The techniques herein described have been developed in training and tested, most of them in combat. They offer a solution to the problems, and are presented for use when desired or for use when no other technique is prescribed by competent authority. It must be borne in mind that a technique is designed for a certain type of equipment; and that any change in equipment may render a technique obsolete. *Technique is not doctrine; the responsibility of the commander for prescribing a suitable*

[15] Clausewitz, *On War*, p. 158. An example of Turner's reaction to the attempts of others to analyze his and the Navy's contributions to the development of amphibious warfare doctrine and practice can be found on pages 202 and 203 of Dyer's biography of Turner. The "Princeton History Group" to which Turner refers in the letter quoted by Dyer is the team that produced Isely and Crowl's *The U.S. Marines and Amphibious War.*

> *technique for an operation and of training the components of his Force in the execution of the technique is doctrine* [emphases added].[16]

In other words, the writers of Change 3 understood the connections between both techniques and doctrine and training and doctrine. The comment is rendered in an almost off-handed way and might be missed if a researcher is not engaging in a careful reading of the document. The significance of the statement is that someone involved in the Change 3 revision of *FTP 167* understood the relationship between training and doctrine and that combat experience in the Solomons showed that modifications were necessary. As the writers allude, change in technique is not, in itself, a change in doctrine. A change in the training methods for the implementation of a new technique, however, is a change in doctrine. Hence, many changes in technique required a change in doctrine because they required a modification in the training process. This was not true in every instance because some techniques can be absorbed into standard operating procedures without having to modify the training process materially. However, when such modifications had to be made, they were by definition changes in doctrine. This point will be addressed further concerning the assault on Tarawa Atoll.

The U.S. Navy was not alone in its penchant for terminological misapprehension, however. Jeter Isely and Philip Crowl, in their study of the Marine Corps' practice of amphibious warfare during World War II, provide an excellent example of imprecise vocabulary on the part of Marines of the era. This was the use of "neutralization" when the speaker or writer meant "destruction."[17] They are right to point out this mistake. They also rightly conclude that American Marines and naval gunfire experts believed prior to Tarawa that shore targets can only be neutralized and that destruction was out of the question. An example of this belief is found in a report by Rear Admiral Francis W. Rockwell concerning operations over 11–29 May 1943. Rockwell wrote that "[i]t is the opinion of Commander Amphibious Force, Pacific Fleet, that naval gunfire may be expected to neutralize but not destroy enemy installations."[18]

---

[16] Marine Corps University Archives (hereinafter MCUA), Quantico, VA, Historical Amphibious File (hereinafter HAF) 638, Department of the Navy, *FTP 167, Landing Operations Doctrine, U.S. Navy, 1938,* Change 3 (hereinafter *FTP 167* with Change 3), p. 131.

[17] Jeter A. Isely and Philip A. Crowl, *The U.S. Marines and Amphibious War: Its Theory and Its Practice in the Pacific* (Princeton: Princeton University Press, 1951; reprint, Quantico: Marine Corps Association, 1988), p. 232 (page citations in the present volume are to the reprint edition). The authors' treatment of this inconsistent use of terminology on the part of contemporary Marines will be treated in greater detail in chapter 3.

[18] Eisenhower Library, Walter Bedell Smith Collection of World War II Documents, 1941–1945, Box 47, File 1, United States Navy, *Notes on Amphibious Warfare, No. 2,* pp. 5-9 and 5-10.

Isely and Crowl's attempt at clearing up the confusion concerning these two terms is commendable, but at the same time they are also an example of and are partly responsible for perpetuating the confusion of the two terms that Knox and Russell tried so hard to differentiate properly: "principle" and "doctrine." The best example of this confusion on their part is found on page 582 of *The U.S. Marines and Amphibious Warfare:*

> At the war's beginning, United States forces had at their disposal a body of tactical principles forming a basic amphibious doctrine which the test of war proved to be sound. This doctrine was first set forth by the Marine Corps in 1934 and officially accepted by the Navy in 1938. An examination of these first statements of tactical principles for employment in amphibious war reveals that for the most part they stood up well and, with slight modifications, were as valid throughout the war as when written.
>
> This is not to say that the war in the Pacific taught no new amphibious lessons. Such a proposition would be absurd on the face of it, and the foregoing chapters of this volume should be sufficient to disprove it completely. But the modifications wrought between 1942 and 1945 in the art of amphibious warfare did not seriously affect underlying principles.[19]

Obviously, Isely and Crowl are not referring to the lists of "principles of war" referenced above by Hughes. They refer, instead, to the lesser principles that govern thought on a lower plane than that occupied by high-blown theory. The only tactical principles about which this present study is concerned are those relating to naval gunfire in support of amphibious operations, and there was really only one of these: naval guns can be used in place of land-based artillery in support of an assault against a well-defended beach. This principle was itself an example of how fluid even fundamental concepts can be. Orthodox thought prior to the early 1930s was that, as Nelson put it, "a ship's a fool to fight a fort." The Allied debacle at Gallipoli in 1915 seemed to prove the "Truth" of this idea to the satisfaction of many British and American military theorists. Marine Corps and Navy thinkers in the early 1930s, however, studied the Gallipoli operation carefully and thoroughly and determined that this seemingly self-evident truism was wrong, that ships can fight forts if the power of naval guns is harnessed and controlled properly. Isely and Crowl are therefore correct, in this particular instance, when they say that principles did not change. The Americans began the war believing that naval guns could take the place of artillery and they ended the war convinced that such was the case.

Doctrine, however, is a different story. As Knox and Russell explained in their articles, doctrine provides guidance for the right and proper way to apply principles.

[19] Isely and Crowl, *U.S. Marines and Amphibious War,* p. 582.

The writers of the naval gunfire support chapters of both the *Tentative Manual* and *FTP 167* began with the aforementioned principle and they developed a doctrine for how it should be applied. This doctrine included an emphasis on the neutralization, not complete destruction, of enemy emplacements in order to allow assaulting troops enough time to establish themselves ashore. Massive quantities of ordnance poured onto enemy positions over a short time, just before the landing, were supposed to numb the defenders to the point where their effective resistance during the first critical minutes of the assault was severely impaired. Precision fire, while discussed by Marines and sailors, was deemed to be unnecessary. Tarawa taught that this point of doctrine was incorrect. Precision *was* necessary, *along with* massive quantities of ordnance. The doctrine was changed and the "lessons of Tarawa" provided naval gunfire planners with a new doctrinal template for the rest of the Central Pacific Campaign.

The Development of Naval Gunfire Doctrine

The focus of this chapter is the development of the naval gunfire component of American amphibious warfare doctrine as it is recorded in the following documents: *Tentative Manual, 1935; FTP 167;* Change 1 of *FTP 167;* and Change 3 of *FTP 167.*[20] Before beginning an analysis of the evolution of this one component, however, a quick outline of all the components is in order so that the reader can understand how the one fits into the whole. The *Tentative Manual, 1935* divides amphibious operations into six major parts. These six parts are as follows: command relationships, naval gunfire support, aircraft support, the ship-to-shore movement, securing of the beachhead, and logistics. The first of these components consists of the command procedures for and the organization of both the landing and the naval forces involved in the assault. Both procedures and organization are deemed integral to the efficient practice of proper command and control in the carrying out of an operation. The senior flag officer commanding the naval attack force should be in overall command of the operation, thus ensuring naval control at the point of contact with the enemy. This overall commander should have two officers subordinate to him, the commanders of the landing force and of the naval support force. The landing force is responsible for carrying out the assault of the beach and then conducting operations once it has been established ashore. It also should provide troops for reconnaissance of the beach and for the delivery of sup-

[20] Many secondary sources describe Change 1 of *FTP 167* as a complete revision of the original manual and leave it at that. As far as chapter 5 is concerned, this statement is true. A comparison of the two versions of chapter 5 shows that the basic doctrine remained the same. The changes are few and doctrinally immaterial. Since this is the case and Change 1 was the version of chapter 5 used by the U.S. Navy and the Marine Corps at the beginning of World War II to late 1943, the original 1938 version of chapter 5 is ignored and all comparisons to *FTP 167* with Change 3 are based upon *FTP 167* with Change 1.

porting fire from small arms and assigned boat guns while the assault forces are embarked in landing craft on their way to the beach. The naval support force should: provide reconnaissance adequate for the successful completion of the assault mission; protect the landing operation from enemy naval forces; provide and man the landing craft that carry the landing force to the shore; support the landing operation using naval gunfire and other methods; and provide for signal communications between ships and the shore.[21]

The second major doctrinal component is the provision of naval gunfire support. The authors of the *Manual* recognize that one of the biggest problems that will be encountered in projecting military power ashore from ships is providing adequate support for the landing at a time prior to the establishment of the landing force's field artillery units on the beach. The main question they address in relation to this problem, consequently, is how naval guns can be used as a replacement for organic artillery during this critical period. They deem inadequately controlled naval gunfire to be worse than no support at all, however, so they also address the problems associated with the establishment of proper fire control methods and the placement of properly trained spotters and liaison officers ashore.[22]

The use of aircraft in support of an amphibious operation is the third major doctrinal component addressed in the *Manual.* Aircraft should be assigned four basic tasks, each one tied to a particular stage of the assault. Prior to the beginning of the operation, aircraft should be responsible for providing the visual and photographic reconnaissance needed to prepare an overall plan of attack and a scheme of maneuver for the forces put ashore.[23] They should then be responsible for providing cover over the transports and landing craft at the point of embarkation and all the way through the ship-to-shore movement, the most critical part of which is the assault landing.[24] As the boat waves approach to within 1,000 yards of the shoreline, they should then provide airborne fire support in lieu of the lifting naval gunfire.[25] Finally, they should be responsible, in conjunction with gunfire support ships, for providing the troops ashore with fire support until such time as field artillery can be landed and brought to bear on enemy positions.[26]

---

[21] MCUA, Historical Amphibious Files, Box 1, HAF 6, Department of the Navy, *Tentative Landing Operations Manual, 1935* (hereinafter *Tentative Manual, 1935*), pp. 42–43.

[22] Gunther E. Rothenberg, "From Gallipoli to Guadalcanal," in Merrill L. Bartlett, ed., *Assault from the Sea: Essays on the History of Amphibious Warfare* (Annapolis: Naval Institute Press, 1983), p. 179; E. B. Potter and Chester W. Nimitz, eds., *Sea Power: A Naval History* (Englewood Cliffs, NJ: Prentice-Hall, 1960), p. 632.

[23] *Tentative Manual, 1935*, p. 189.

[24] Ibid., pp. 190–91.

[25] Ibid., p. 192.

[26] Ibid., p. 193.

The movement of landing craft from transport ships to the beach lies at the very heart of an amphibious operation. It is, as it were, the *raison d'être* for the entire doctrine. The authors of the *Manual* insist that the only way to provide the best chance for troops to be moved successfully from offshore transports to the beach is to plan the operation with precision and to exercise effective control of landing craft during their movement to shore.[27] The method they choose to use in organizing and managing landing craft requires the employment of control, picket, and guide boats that are to be positioned in such a way as to conduct the landing craft through the precisely planned stages of the ship-to-shore movement.[28] So that maximum control of the operation both at the point of embarkation and at the point of landing on the beach can be maintained, it is determined that one—and only one—fully self-sufficient infantry battalion, reinforced with artillery and other arms, be loaded onto each transport.[29] The authors also specify the preferred organization of men and equipment within each landing craft and the best arrangement for boat waves as they make their way ashore.[30]

The fifth component of the doctrine is the securing of the beachhead once the troops have landed. The authors describe the techniques that are necessary for the survival of the landing force between the time during which it is solely reliant upon naval gunfire support and the point at which its own field artillery can take over from naval guns. They also address the problems associated with establishing communications between units ashore and units still afloat, as well as those affecting the provision of services and supplies to the landing force. The solution for the problem of providing these services and supplies is the establishment of a beach party, under the command of a naval officer titled a beachmaster. The beachmaster is given the responsibility of controlling both the movement of boats to the shore and the unloading of supplies and equipment from them. A second group, termed the shore party, is then to control the movement of the unloaded supplies from the beach to the supply dumps and from there to the front lines.[31]

The final component of the doctrine is logistics. The authors of the *Manual* cover most of the mundane topics one expects to encounter in a discussion of this important but far from scintillating topic. In the midst of their discussion, however, they put forward one concept that is especially worthy of note. It is a concept that revolutionized the way in which the Navy supported amphibious assaults, though it would take a lot of hard combat experience before naval planners truly understood its importance. This revolutionary idea is known as combat unit loading, and

[27] Ibid., p. 82.

[28] Ibid., p. 127.

[29] Ibid., p. 67.

[30] Ibid., pp. 84–134.

[31] Ibid., pp. 51–55.

its basic tenets are simple. First, all cargo loading should be tailored to the requirements of the landing force. Second, in addition to one assault battalion and its landing boats, each transport should also carry that battalion's equipment. Third, the battalion's equipment should not be stowed haphazardly, but should be loaded on the transport with the immediate needs of the assaulting troops in mind—the most-needed items upon going ashore loaded at the top of the holds for easy access and items for use later in the assault stowed below them. These very logical ideas provided a solution to many of the problems associated with the adequate supply of necessary equipment and ammunition to the landing force at the time those items were most needed.[32]

Such are the essential aspects of the overall doctrine as set forth in the *Tentative Manual, 1935* and also in *FTP 167.* These six components provided the basic framework for amphibious assault planning in the Pacific Ocean Areas Theater throughout the Second World War. They did not exist in their original 1935 form, however, even at the beginning of the Central Pacific Campaign in late 1943. Changes had been made, some before the U.S. became involved officially in the war, and this is particularly true for the second component. To show how this evolution took place over time, an analysis of the three major statements of naval gunfire doctrine that were published prior to the Gilberts operation will be presented. The wholesale reorganization of the naval gunfire chapter in Change 3 of *FTP 167* makes a one-to-one comparison difficult, so an artificial analytical structure has been imposed. Each subsection of the analysis will begin with a description of one aspect of naval gunfire support doctrine as it existed in the *Tentative Manual, 1935.* This statement will be followed by a description of the evolution of that aspect of doctrine in Change 1, where relevant, and in Change 3.[33]

The authors of the *Tentative Manual* were faced with many problems to which they were expected to find workable solutions. How best to sustain an assault from the sea without recourse to field artillery was just one of those problems. The necessity of backing an assault with adequate artillery support was made abundantly clear to both the United States Army and the Marine Corps during World War I. The authors use the knowledge of artillery support that the Marines acquired in the heat of combat during that earlier conflict as their point of departure. Paragraphs 20 and 21 of the *Manual* are an example of the extent to which the "Great War" influenced the thoughts of the writers in this regard. On these pages is information that was to be used by planners in determining the amount of artillery required for a given assault mission. The authors begin by offering a logical foundation for the planning process—a classification system for defenses and formulae

---

[32] Ibid., pp. 266–67.

[33] Chapter 5, the naval gunfire chapter in both the *Tentative Manual, 1935* and *FTP 167,* was not revised in Change 2 of the latter. This is why only Change 1 and Change 3 of *FTP 167* are referenced in this analysis.

for the use of artillery in countering them. The system is very straightforward: defenses are either "weak," "average," or "strong." Allotments of artillery are theoretically calculated accordingly: a "weak" allotment (one 4-gun battery per fifty yards of front) against hastily dug entrenchments and relatively poor morale; an "average" allotment (one 4-gun battery per thirty-seven yards of front) against well-constructed entrenchments behind some barbed wire; and a "strong" allotment (one 4-gun battery per twenty-eight yards of front) against well-organized resistance consisting of concrete machine gun emplacements and shelters. One 4-gun battery per forty yards of front is reported to have been a workable rule of thumb by the end of World War I.[34]

The writers use an "average" defense in making their calculations. This means that they assume that a prospective enemy will be occupying well-constructed earth works and will be reasonably strong in relation to the front he is defending.[35] The strength and armament of a defender relative to that of an attacker also bears directly on determining artillery support requirements.[36] An attacker, according to the theory, has two definite advantages over a defender: initiative and relative mobility. The ability to move about while a defender remains in place gives an attacker a choice of objectives when determining at what time and at what place to strike. The greatest advantage in having a choice of objectives is that an attacker has the opportunity to assail a position where a defender is not prepared adequately.[37]

The authors of the *Manual* report that a change in the tactical use of artillery occurred during World War I, and the emphasis they place on this reported change will prove to have a profound effect on how naval gunfire will be used in support of amphibious operations early in the course of the next war. According to the authors, long artillery barrages prior to an infantry attack were the usual practice up until and including part of 1917. The last year of the war, however, saw the development of a tendency toward the use of short, extremely intense bombardments that were delivered immediately prior to the launching of an attack. The *Manual's* authors deem the rapid fire of naval guns to be well-suited to delivering this type of short, intense bombardment. In addition, the relatively economical ammunition requirements for providing such barrages seemed to be at least a partial solution to the perceived problem of limited warship magazine capacities.[38] Even though a description of World War I land artillery doctrine is dropped from Change 3 of *FTP 167,* vestiges of the "short and intense" bombardment theory can still be seen in the planning and execution of naval gunfire support of the landings

[34] *Tentative Manual, 1935,* p. 155.

[35] Ibid., p. 156.

[36] Ibid.

[37] Ibid.

[38] Ibid., pp. 155–56.

at Tarawa a scant three months after the promulgation of this final official version of the 1938 descendant of the *Manual*. The Second Marine Division would pay a heavy price for the Navy's continued reliance on this "lesson" from the First World War.

Analysis of the Doctrine

The following five sections provide an analysis of naval gunfire doctrine and are divided into five major categories: the organization of D-day for the purpose of planning naval gunfire support; the classification of fires; the characteristics of naval guns, ammunition, ships' batteries, and naval vessels; the organization of fire support groups; and the organization and use of shore fire control parties.

Organization of D-day[39]

The *Tentative Manual, 1935* and Change 1 of *FTP 167* are very vague concerning the organization of D-day. References to time are relative rather than exact with the one exception being recommendations as to the most effective fire schedule for the prescribed bombardment immediately preceding the landing.[40] Change 3 of *FTP 167* introduces a much more exact organization, in three phases, that coordinates naval gunfire with the activities of the landing force. During Phase I, from H-3 to approximately H-1, the landing force is supposed to be offloading from transports to landing craft and forming boat waves for the movement toward the assault beaches. In Phase II, from approximately H-1 to H-hour, the landing craft are supposed to execute the ship-to-shore movement of the landing force. Finally, in Phase III, the assault units of the landing force are supposed to be ashore and advancing inland. This last phase is supposed to begin at H-hour and continue until naval gunfire is no longer needed. Field artillery of the landing force can usually begin to take over fire missions from the naval gunfire support forces at about H+2, but the authors of Change 3 deem it a rare occurrence for artillery to completely relieve naval gunfire of responsibility for fire support by the end of D-day.[41]

[39] The term "D-day" has become associated in the minds of many Americans with the invasion of Normandy on 6 June 1944. There was no such particular association in the jargon of military planners during the Second World War. "D-day" simply referred to the day on which an amphibious landing was to occur. "H-hour" was the hour designated for it to begin. Different designations were used at times, usually when operations so closely overlapped one another that using the same terms in reference to multiple landings would cause confusion.

[40] Eisenhower Presidential Library, Walter Bedell Smith Collection of World War II Documents, 1941–45, Box 38, Department of the Navy, *Fleet Training Publication 167, Landing Operations Doctrine, U.S. Navy, 1938,* Change 1 (hereinafter *FTP 167* with Change 1), p. 121.

[41] *FTP 167* with Change 3, p. 115.

How the authors of Change 3 tie this system of organization into the planning of fire missions will be described in the next section.

Classification of Fires

There are still many questions to be addressed even after a commander has organized D-day along the proper lines specified in doctrine. The authors of the *Manual* recognize that complete destruction of a major percentage of enemy personnel, weapons, and equipment is generally beyond the capabilities of the attacking force, but a volume of fire sufficient at least to cause the enemy to cease-fire and take cover should be provided. This volume of fire should be maintained for a long enough period of time so as to reduce the enemy's morale such that the attacking infantry can overcome him. A dependence upon the psychological effect of bombardment on morale makes it difficult to determine exactly how much artillery is necessary to produce the desired effect. One still should make an estimate, however, and go forward with planning fire missions for the landing.[42] The *Manual,* in discussing the decisions associated with providing an adequate volume of fire on the beach, states:

> Probably the most difficult decision in formulating the scheme of maneuver is that pertaining to the frontage which can be effectively covered by the fire of the available ships, and it is here that the judgment and responsibility of the commander is put to the severest test. In deciding this question, consideration must be given to: First, *The devastating effect of the fire of relatively few machine guns when firing under advantageous conditions;* Second, *That an attack against such weapons has little chance of success unless adequately supported by artillery;* Third, *That a landing operation cannot be stopped and resumed at the will of the commander, and, as a rule, only one chance for success will be offered* [emphasis in original].[43]

The authors here demonstrate an understanding of the magnitude of the challenge before them and the importance of the use of artillery in meeting that challenge. They also demonstrate that they are aware of the false sense of security that the presentation of formulae for the "proper" use of artillery against given defenses can create. They state that, unlike World War I theorists, they have made no attempt to provide planners with any "absolute" formulae for determining the amount of naval artillery support that is necessary for a given assault situation, and they admit that such formulae are impossible to derive.[44] Consequently, they relate

[42] *Tentative Manual, 1935,* p. 155.

[43] Ibid., p. 25.

[44] Ibid., p. 156.

detailed descriptions of what they view as the seven types of fire support roles that naval gunnery can be expected to fulfill during the course of an amphibious assault without tying the descriptions to anything that can be used as the basis for meaningless, possibly dangerous, calculations. These seven missions are: supporting fires, counter-battery, interdiction, destruction, harassing fires, counter-ship, and fires on targets of opportunity.[45]

They deem the first type of mission, support for the troops going ashore, to be the most immediately important of the seven. The three main purposes of these all-important supporting fires in an amphibious assault are as follows: to cause the enemy to cease-fire and take cover, to inflict losses on him while doing so, and to reduce his combat efficiency so that the attacking infantry can overcome him. Two types of supporting fires should be employed for these purposes in the execution of an amphibious landing. Termed close- and deep-support, each type contributes materially to the success of the assault and should be properly and sufficiently planned for and executed in order to provide the attacking troops with the artillery backing they need for the successful completion of their mission.[46]

Close-supporting fires should be delivered on that part of the enemy force that is to be attacked immediately upon troops getting ashore. The target objectives of close-supporting fires should be the enemy personnel encountered on the beach and, more importantly, the enemy weapons that are most dangerous to the attacker's initial landing force. Since close-supporting fires destroy the enemy's ability to defend against the attacker's initial assault at the time when the latter is in his most vulnerable position, then they should receive top priority in the assignment of both guns and ammunition. This type of gunfire support is the most difficult for naval guns to deliver, however, due to their low angle of trajectory.[47] Consequently, every effort should be made to compensate for the deficiencies of naval gunfire as early in the assault as is practicable. This should be done through the use of aircraft, boat guns, the guns of inshore support vessels, and the tanks and artillery of the landing force.[48]

The authors consider direct aim to be the only acceptable method of sighting and delivering close-support fire from naval vessels. Use of this method limits naval guns to the delivery of fires on the beach prior to the landing and, after the landing has been affected and fire has been lifted inland, to areas visible from the sea. Offshore fire support groups, given the task of providing close-supporting

[45] Ibid., p. 148.

[46] Ibid.

[47] Naval guns and ammunition were designed to engage naval surface targets, not targets on shore. See section below on "Characteristics of Naval Guns, Ammunition, Ships' Batteries, and Naval Vessels" for an explanation of why this was so and how it affected the naval gunfire support mission.

[48] *Tentative Manual, 1935*, p. 148.

fires for the initial landing, should be assigned a particular, definite target area that includes a section of the beach and a specified depth inland. While gunfire support needs to cover all of the target area, the plan of fire should pay particular attention to those areas where the enemy is known or is suspected to be. Proper fire distribution should be maintained, this being best undertaken through the assignment of a particular target area to each ship in a fire support group. Use of the time-sector method will ensure that no part of a target area will be left uncovered for any length of time. Ships firing both main and secondary batteries should work target areas over with both of them and should open rapid fire at frequent intervals in order to maintain an element of uncertainty on the part of the enemy.[49]

Close-supporting fires should reach a density equivalent to sixteen 75mm shells per minute per 100-yard square in order to achieve the three objectives listed above. This is especially true of fire delivered immediately prior to the beginning of the assault. This density should be maintained on the enemy's defenses at the beach and, if possible, as far inland as the forward slopes of any terrain features from which small arms fire might be expected.[50] The final burst of fire just prior to the troops going ashore should be as intense as possible. It should start before the landing craft are within effective small-arms range of the shore and it should continue until the boats are about to make the dash to the beach. Gunners should vary their firing patterns so that the enemy cannot determine when he should take cover.[51]

Deep-supporting fires should be used to extend the coverage of close-supporting fires at the time of the initial amphibious assault. They should also to be used to cover machine guns, mortars, artillery, and other weapons being used by the enemy to provide overhead fire from rear positions in support of his own front line. The writers believe these fires to be effective at reducing the activity and combat efficiency of enemy troops in rear positions that are to be assaulted later. They also believe them to be disruptive of the enemy's command, communications, and observation systems.[52] Targets particularly suitable for naval gunfire in the deep-supporting role, given the preceding considerations, include: the edges of woods; the tops of hills; any masonry buildings, fences, or hedgerows in the area; and any other topographical features easily identifiable and assumed to be organized for defense.[53] Sufficient density can rarely be attained over this entire target area because the size of the space over which the deep-supporting bombardment should be spread is too large to allow for

---

[49] Ibid., p. 178.

[50] Ibid., p. 160. The sixteen 75mm shells per minute per 100-yard square rule of thumb was developed based upon World War I artillery experience.

[51] Ibid., p. 162.

[52] Ibid., p. 148.

[53] Ibid., pp. 180–81.

thorough coverage. Available deep-supporting fire, therefore, should be concentrated upon particularly important enemy positions. The writers believe that the relatively long dispersion pattern of naval ordnance will many times allow for the collateral delivery of deep-supporting fire in conjunction with the delivery of close-support fire to the beach area. Consequently, ships do not necessarily have to be assigned specified deep-support missions prior to the landing of the assault troops. Deep-support missions, however, do need to be assigned to particular ships or specified batteries of battleships and cruisers once the assaulting troops go ashore and begin to advance inland.[54]

Targets for the initial uplift of gunfire inland from the beach should be determined in advance. The distance of the initial uplift depends upon a number of factors. These factors include range, visibility, the slope of the ground, the direction of fire in relation to the advance of troops, the type of guns being used, the sea conditions at the time of the uplift, and whether or not the area on which the fire is to be delivered is visible from the firing ships. The targets for the initial uplift should be no farther inland than is necessary for the safety of the troops, with the preceding factors taken into account. The fire of inshore support ships, aircraft, boat guns, infantry weapons, and the field artillery of the landing force initially should cover the gap between the beaches and the area being shelled in deep support. Infantry weapons and field artillery can only be used effectively once they are landed, so priority should be given to getting them ashore as soon as practicable. Using them, the assaulting force can then make every effort to cover as thoroughly as possible the ground between the beach and the target area for the first lift. Tentative targets should be prescribed for the second and third lifts, but these target lists should be modified relative to actual battle conditions as the assault progresses.[55]

The second major fire mission described in the *Tentative Manual, 1935* is counter-battery. Counter-battery fire is delivered on enemy artillery positions for two purposes: first, causing the enemy artillery to cease-fire and second, inflicting losses on personnel and materiel.[56] Effective counter-battery requires fire on specific targets rather than on a general area. Theoretically, the number of naval guns necessary to silence an enemy artillery battery is the number necessary to produce the required density (sixteen 75mm shells per minute per 100-yard square) on target given the pattern of the particular guns used at the given range. One can reduce the amount of counter-battery fire on a target by half once the battery is silenced. This can be accomplished either by reducing the rate of fire or by assigning some of the guns that began the fire mission to other targets.[57] Enough ammunition

---

[54] Ibid., pp. 163–64.

[55] Ibid., pp. 181–82.

[56] Ibid., p. 148.

[57] Ibid., p. 164.

should be allotted so that supporting naval guns can begin delivery of counter-battery before the landing boats arrive within range of the targeted shore batteries. This fire should continue during the critical stages of the operation, ceasing only when the missions can be taken over by field artillery.[58] Demonstrations by boats without troops can be made on the flanks of the landing beach in order to cause enemy artillery fire to disperse over a larger area and also in order to get enemy batteries to open up so that they can be located and destroyed.[59]

Each ship in a counter-battery group should be assigned a definite area of target responsibility prior to the landing operation. Assigning ships in this way reduces confusion as to responsibility for a previously unknown target that might begin firing during the execution of the landing. It is desirable that each ship be able to take under fire all of the targets within its area of responsibility simultaneously.[60] In addition to the method mentioned above, there are a number of suggested ways to locate enemy artillery batteries. These include: aerial observation and photography; observation from surface craft and submarines; information from intelligence reports; information from prisoners captured by patrols; ground observation after the landing; flash and sound ranging stations; and information from front line troops after the landing.[61] All located enemy batteries should be assigned counter-battery fire from naval guns. Once again, the authors stress that fire should be opened on located batteries and emplacements *before* landing boats come within range of them and *before* they open fire on the boats. Additional naval guns should open fire immediately upon any enemy artillery batteries not previously located that fire upon the landing force. Targets should be fired on in rotation if there are too many of them to be taken under fire simultaneously. Provision should be made as well for the shifting of ships and target areas if necessary. The usual method of controlling counter-battery fire is through aircraft spotting. Each firing ship should have a spotting plane and radio frequency assigned to it alone. Indeed, where practicable, each ship should have two or more planes so that two or more targets can be fired upon simultaneously and so that each of the ship's gun groups can be controlled continuously.[62]

Interdiction fire, the third major fire mission, should be delivered on points or areas in order to deny their use to the enemy. Characteristic targets include roads used for the movement of enemy reserves or supplies and the areas where the enemy is involved in some observable undertaking. Examples of points that should receive interdiction fire that are randomly listed by the authors of the *Manual*

[58] Ibid., p. 165.

[59] Ibid., pp. 165 and 183.

[60] Ibid., pp. 182–83.

[61] Ibid. Radar would be added to this list later in the war.

[62] Ibid., pp. 183–84.

include crossroads, demonstrable places of assembly, railroad stations, detraining points, defiles, bridges, and fords.[63] The authors deem a density of eight 75mm shells per minute per 100-yard square, maintained for a five-minute period, sufficient to stop movements overland. A density of sixteen 75mm shells per minute per 100-yard square or greater should be maintained as long as the enemy is in a vulnerable position in order to stop movement and inflict the maximum possible losses upon him. They estimate that bursts equivalent to eight or fewer rounds of 75mm per minute per 100-yard square every five to fifteen minutes thereafter to be sufficient to keep the enemy immobilized.[64] Direct observation or plane spot should be used to control the execution of interdiction fire, though the job can be assigned to shore-based fire control parties on occasion. There seldom will be enough ammunition aboard the gunfire support ships to allow for interdiction fires over an entire general target area. Consequently, interdiction fire should be limited to those types of targets that can be assumed to be important to the enemy for the moving of reserves and supplies. Interdiction can be accomplished by either firing on targets as they appear or, when observation is impossible, by the firing of bursts at irregular intervals over an extended period. The second method, though indirect, can produce the desired results, but direct observation is much preferred. To keep the enemy from being able to avoid losses by way of a practicable detour around the damage inflicted upon him by the interdiction fires, roads and railways should also be covered.[65]

Fires for destruction, the fourth major fire mission according to the authors of the *Tentative Manual, 1935,* should be delivered in order to render a material target useless to the enemy. They require a heavy expenditure of ammunition and, therefore, they should be called for only when there is a reasonable expectation that complete destruction can be obtained. Targets for destruction fires during landing operations should be of limited area and, preferably, should be visible from the sea. Randomly selected examples of such targets include particularly dangerous machine guns and anti-boat guns, buildings located in the immediate vicinity of the landing, important bridges, and coastal and field artillery that are located close to the shoreline being assaulted.[66] The authors understand that the amount of ammunition necessary to destroy a given target varies according to a number of factors. These factors include the nature of the object to be destroyed, the accuracy of the fire being delivered, the caliber and type of shell being used, and the degree of destruction required. In order to be effective, fires for destruction should be delivered at the shortest possible range for as long a period as is

[63] Ibid., p. 149.

[64] Ibid., p. 165.

[65] Ibid., p. 184.

[66] Ibid., p. 149.

necessary to achieve the degree of destruction required. The authors emphasize that one material target that is *not* to be taken under fire by naval guns for the purposes of destruction is barbed wire. To cut a significant breach in any barbed wire that is located on the invasion beach requires an amount of ammunition that is most prohibitive. Other methods, therefore, should be used to accomplish the task.[67] The writers do not deem any special rules of performance to be necessary since fires for destruction should be executed by direct observation.[68]

The last three types of major fire missions are not covered in the *Tentative Manual, 1935* with the thoroughness of the first four described. Harassing fires are defined as fires delivered during a relatively quiet period. They are meant to interfere with the enemy by alerting him unnecessarily, and thereby lowering his morale and efficiency. Ranging shots preliminary to bombardment are deemed to have some harassing effect. Harassing fires should be used with care, however, because they have a tendency to accustom the enemy to artillery fire, thus decreasing their morale effect.[69] Fires on targets of opportunity are supporting fires delivered on any suitable target that appears within a specified area. Supporting ships and groups that have been assigned this mission should keep their assigned areas under observation and should open fire on targets when they present themselves. Randomly selected examples of such targets include enemy troops that are forming for a counterattack, enemy work parties, enemy troop and train movements, enemy batteries of artillery that have not been observed previously, enemy troops preparing or occupying a defensive position not previously located, and any seemingly important activity within an assigned area. The targets for this class of fires are, generally, the same as those for counter-battery and interdiction. Consequently, ships engaged in the two latter fire missions should usually be assigned the mission of firing on targets of opportunity as well.[70] The last type of fire mission, counter-ship, is delivered on enemy ships that attempt to interfere with the landing operation. If the strength of the naval attack force permits, these missions should be assigned to ships that are not directly engaged in fire missions against shore targets.[71]

Change 1 of *FTP 167* follows the *Tentative Manual's* classification of fires rather closely. Change 3 of *FTP 167* defines the various types of fire missions in similar terms to the *Tentative Manual,* but it introduces a more detailed classification system. In this system, fire missions are classified according to five basic criteria: the effects sought, the forms taken, whether or not they are prearranged, the tactical

[67] Ibid., p. 165.

[68] Ibid., p. 184.

[69] Ibid., p. 149.

[70] Ibid.

[71] Ibid., pp. 149–50.

purposes sought, and the method of fire control needed to complete them. Fires for purposes of neutralization and destruction fall under the classification of effects sought. The means of achieving them, concentrated fire to achieve neutralization and point fire to achieve destruction, are the two categories of forms recognized.[72] Classification according to prearrangement is broken down as follows: fire delivered on a time schedule; fire delivered on prearranged locations but only when called for; and fire on targets of opportunity, a category that takes care of any targets not covered by the first two forms of prearranged fires.[73]

Here is a good place to address a significant difference between the *Tentative Manual* and *FTP 167* regarding equivalencies between field artillery and naval gunfire. Beginning with the original 1938 version, *FTP 167* states in Paragraph 510 that there are no field artillery terms that correspond exactly to the naval gunfire terms "close" and "deep" support. This statement takes the place of the *Tentative Manual's* Paragraph 10 in which a number of field artillery terms are discussed. Change 3 of *FTP 167* goes even further than the original version and Change 1 by dropping the reference to field artillery terms all together. The most interesting, and important, difference is not that of mere form, however. The *Tentative Manual* actually addresses a terminological problem already mentioned in this study. In Paragraph 10 (sub-paragraphs d and e), the writers state:

> d. In the field artillery, "destruction" indicates the intensity of the fire rather than a distinct fire mission. In a landing operation, it will practically never be possible to increase to destructive intensity any considerable part of the fires. The usual procedure will be to assign a ship or ships to a specific destruction mission on a designated target of limited extent. For this reason, the term "destruction" has been utilized to indicate a specific fire mission.
>
> e. Field artillery employs the term "neutralization" quite extensively. As defined in the field artillery, this term means fire delivered for the purpose of causing severe losses, preventing movement or action, and in general, destroying the combat efficiency of enemy personnel. It varies from an effect which is a little short of annihilation to one which merely causes personnel to take cover. On account of the broad application of the term, as to the effect produced by neutralization fires, the term is not generally used in this manuel [*sic*] in connection with naval gunfire. In discussing fire missions, an attempt is made to give a more specific description

[72] *FTP 167* with Change 3, p. 113.

[73] Ibid., p. 114.

> of the effect it is desired to produce with a given class of fire and a given amount of ammunition.[74]

In other words, the writers decide that the field artillery usage of the term "neutralization" is so imprecise as to be completely useless if not misleading. Consequently, they choose not to employ it. The naval and Marine officers involved in the preparation of Change 3 of *FTP 167* chose to reintroduce the term. Marine spotters, with a background in field artillery, are essentially set up for confusion as a result. The terminological gaffe criticized by Isely and Crowl is almost an inevitable result, therefore.

Change 3's classification of fires according to tactical purposes sought covers the most important categories of offensive fires listed in the *Tentative Manual's* system, introduces some new ones, and integrates all of them into the new D-day organization described earlier. The first tactical purpose sought is preparation. The authors define it as intensive fire delivered on the landing beaches and adjacent areas during the approach to shore of the leading wave's landing craft. It falls under Phase II of the D-day organizational plan. The second tactical purpose sought is close support. They define the term, along the same lines as the *Tentative Manual,* as fires placed on enemy troops, weapons, or positions that, because of their proximity to friendly units ashore, present the most immediate threat to those supported units. These fires fall under Phase III. Deep-support fires fulfill the third tactical purpose sought. They are defined as the more distant fires furnished in support of an operation. They are distinguished from fires of more direct and immediate benefit to the front line assault troops. Examples given include fires against enemy artillery, enemy reserves, and on critical points or areas in order to deny the enemy the use thereof. Deep-supporting fires, unlike preparation and close support, can be delivered during all three phases of D-day. The last category is termed "special missions." These missions are deep-supporting fires for which large caliber naval guns are especially suited. Targets for these "special missions" are cities, airfields, seacoast batteries, and permanent fortifications. The majority of these missions are to be undertaken during Phases I and II.[75]

The last of Change 3's classification criteria, the method of fire control, separates fires according to whether or not the fall of shot can be seen from the firing ship. Direct fire control can be used when fires are delivered on a target that is visible from the ship providing the gunfire support. Indirect fire control should be used when fires are delivered on a target that is not visible from the ship. Spotting of the fall of shot can be undertaken from the firing ship in cases of direct fire control, but fall of shot should be observed either by plane spotters or spotters on the shore in cases of indirect fire control.[76]

---

[74] *Tentative Manual, 1935,* p. 150.

[75] *FTP 167* with Change 3, pp. 114 and 115.

[76] Ibid., p. 114.

Characteristics of Naval Guns, Ammunition, Ships' Batteries, and Naval Vessels

The differences in organization between the *Tentative Manual, 1935,* Change 1 of *FTP 167,* and Change 3 of *FTP 167* are evident in the treatment of fire missions classification, but more substantial differences really come to the fore when comparing their treatments of the characteristics of naval guns, ammunition, ships' batteries, and naval vessels. From a superficial perspective, the first major difference between the first two manuals and the third is in the decidedly naval tone taken in Change 3 as opposed to the more Marine Corps/artillery tone evident in the *Tentative Manual* and Change 1. Change 3, in other words, describes naval matters in terms understandable to naval officers, placing emphases on characteristics of ships and naval guns that a Marine would not necessarily recognize as requiring emphasis. This section of the analysis will begin, as in all cases in this chapter, with a statement of the general doctrine as set forth in the *Tentative Manual, 1935* and then taken over into Change 1 of *FTP 167.* It will conclude with a statement of the much more detailed doctrine set forth in Change 3 of *FTP 167.*

The authors of the *Tentative Manual* recognize seven factors as important when determining the suitability of naval gunfire for supporting shore operations: muzzle velocity and trajectory of naval ordnance, dispersion, the various types of shells and fuses, direct fire, indirect fire, ammunition supply, and mobility of ships relative to land-based artillery.[77] They stress that all of these factors and the advantages and disadvantages of each regarding the suitability of naval guns as a replacement for field artillery should be weighed together and understood. The advantages should be exploited to the greatest extent possible and measures should be taken to compensate for the disadvantages.[78]

The differences between naval guns and ammunition and land-based artillery is a most important and quite vexing problem to be addressed. Naval service ammunition, when fired, produces higher muzzle velocities than equivalent field artillery ammunition. High muzzle velocities cause heavy erosion of gun tubes and produce a flatter trajectory than that produced by field artillery ammunition. This flat trajectory makes naval guns much less effective than field artillery in sweeping reverse slopes and in engaging defiladed shore batteries. The authors point out that the effectiveness of naval guns when used in these roles can be increased by using reduced charges, selecting firing positions on the flank or in the rear of the reverse slopes, or by having the ships engaging defiladed targets stand off at greater ranges.[79] Planners always need to keep these limitations in mind when using naval gunfire in place of field artillery, but they should not forget that the high muzzle

---

[77] *Tentative Manual, 1935,* p. 151.

[78] Ibid.

[79] Ibid., p. 152.

velocity of naval ordnance is of great effect on forward sloping terrain. The authors believe that the demoralizing effects of high velocity ordnance are readily apparent and can be put to effective use against targets on forward slopes.[80]

The relatively large dispersion of naval gunfire makes it less useful in the role of close support of infantry than equivalent calibers of field artillery.[81] Dispersion of naval guns is greater in range than it is in deflection, but it is possible to overcome this problem to a certain extent by having ships fire from flanking positions. There is a danger, however, of the entire pattern being displaced laterally as well as in range in situations where suitable aiming points are not available.[82] The terminal ballistics of naval ordnance is not the only characteristic that should be considered, though. Common and armor-piercing naval shells are not well-suited for use in the support of landings for a number of reasons. The delayed fuses used with these munitions and their small bursting charges relative to the same caliber of field artillery makes them less effective than some other types of shells against the targets most likely to be encountered during an amphibious landing, especially enemy personnel who are not under cover.[83] Common and armor-piercing shells with delayed fuses can be used with good effect against concrete emplacements and masonry walls, but they are still not the best choice. Flat nose, anti-aircraft, and bombardment shell types compare favorably with field artillery projectiles and, therefore, should be used in most supporting fire situations.[84]

Naval gunfire is especially useful in support of landings where the ability of naval gunners to deliver rapid accurate fire on visible targets can be used to the maximum possible extent. The authors of the *Manual* exhibit knowledge of the importance of extremely close-range support when they state: "In planning the support of a landing, full advantage should be taken of this characteristic by having certain supporting ships, under cover of the fire of offshore ships, stand close inshore and engage the enemy beach defenses at short ranges."[85] Yet again, the authors emphasize that the fire from enemy machine guns, automatic rifles, other infantry small arms, and anti-boat guns that are located on or in the immediate vicinity of the landing beaches pose the greatest danger for the troops coming ashore. These enemy weapons can deliver direct, aimed fire on the landing boats and the troops that disembark from them.[86] It is difficult to locate these weapons accurately because they do not usually open fire until the landing boats are close

[80] Ibid.

[81] Ibid.

[82] Ibid.

[83] Ibid.

[84] Ibid.

[85] Ibid.

[86] Ibid., p. 153.

to the beach. This is the point in the operation at which offshore vessels either cease firing or lift their fire inland.[87] To counter this threat, inshore vessels should stand in and close on the beach as the depth of water permits, watching for the enemy to open fire. Protected by counter-battery fire from offshore groups, these inshore vessels can maintain supporting fire closer to the landing boats and disembarking troops.[88]

The writers are confident that naval guns can get the job done effectively when the spotters aboard ship can see their targets, but their confidence declines significantly when they consider targets that are not within sight. They recognize that naval guns are not well-suited for the delivery of indirect fire for two important reasons. First, naval guns are fired from essentially unstable platforms. Second, the position of these platforms changes in relation to the target and any established aiming points.[89] These difficulties can be compensated for, to an extent, by selecting well-defined aiming points on the beach that are suitably located relative to targets as well as by providing gunners with continuous aerial or terrestrial observation.[90] Boats or buoys can be anchored for the purpose of providing suitable aiming points if such do not exist on shore. In addition, markers can be set up onshore once the landing force is established.[91] Aircraft can be assigned particularly difficult indirect fire missions where possible. The need for the use of indirect fire is not as great when attacking small islands or a peninsula because such objectives allow maneuvering ships to take positions easily from which they can attack targets using direct fire.[92]

Solving the problem of what ammunition to use is a significant step in the right direction, but not being able to deliver that ammunition will make the entire exercise moot. Ensuring an adequate supply of the proper ammunition for the support of a landing operation is a serious problem in its own right because the magazine capacity aboard naval vessels is limited and combatant vessels must carry sufficient common and armor-piercing ordnance aboard to enable them to engage an enemy fleet if necessary.[93] The writers believe that this problem can be addressed in a number of ways. First, obsolete vessels and converted merchantmen can be used in gunfire support roles to the maximum extent possible. These ships are not expected to contribute to the protection of the fleet, thus allowing them the luxury of filling their magazines with bombardment ammunition. Second, landing boats

[87] Ibid.

[88] Ibid.

[89] Ibid.

[90] Ibid.

[91] Ibid.

[92] Ibid.

[93] Ibid.

can be provided with a powerful armament of their own. Finally, the assault artillery of the landing force can be put ashore as early as possible so as to relieve the naval forces of the responsibility of supporting the operation by gunfire.[94]

The last factor to be considered when determining the suitability of naval gunfire for supporting shore operations, according to the authors of the *Tentative Manual, 1935,* is the mobility of ships relative to land-based artillery. The greater relative mobility of ships gives naval gunfire a degree of flexibility in the support of landings that is very desirable and it offers the planners of an amphibious assault several options. First, supporting vessels can stand in with the landing boats to allow for the engagement of beach defenses at short range. Second, the fire of several ships can be concentrated in support of successive landings on different beaches. Third, the mobility of ships offers a wide choice as to firing positions for the execution of given fire missions. Finally, the ability of ships to move around offshore provides the landing operation with some protection from enemy submarines, aircraft, and shore artillery.[95] The authors insist that the personnel in charge of developing the scheme of maneuver and of planning the fire support for an operation should seek to maximize all these advantages of ship mobility.[96]

The information in the *Manual* concerning the general characteristics of naval guns and ammunition is essentially the same as that found in Change 1 and Change 3 of *FTP 167.* Change 3, however, reflecting its more naval-oriented approach, goes into greater detail concerning certain characteristics of both of these and also discusses something that neither the *Tentative Manual* nor Change 1 include in their coverage of this component of the doctrine: the characteristics of ships' batteries and of naval vessels. The definition, according to Change 3, of what constitutes a battery aboard a ship is twofold: first, a naval battery consists of two or more guns of the same caliber on the same ship that can be directed from the same fire control station; second, keeping the first part of the definition in mind, a naval gunfire support battery consists of the number of guns responding to one control and bearing on one target.[97] Generally speaking, the number of guns contained in a battery determines the type of mission that can best be fulfilled by that battery. When firing against personnel targets for the purpose of neutralization, a minimum of four guns is needed to produce the necessary volume of fire quickly enough and to cover the entire target area simultaneously. Batteries of fewer than four guns are not to be assigned close or deep-support missions under normal conditions, but exceptions can be made in emergencies. The use of batteries of more than six guns usually results, for smaller calibers at least, in the unnecessary expenditure of

[94] Ibid.

[95] Ibid., pp. 153–54.

[96] Ibid., p. 154.

[97] *FTP 167* with Change 3, p. 117.

ammunition. When firing against material targets for the purpose of destruction, one to three guns in one turret per target will suffice. The authors deem more guns per battery desirable, however, when firing against large area targets and "special mission" targets (e.g. airfields, cities, large supply dumps, and docks) where fine adjustments are not required.[98]

The sophistication of a battery's fire control technology determines if that battery can be used for indirect fire or if it should be restricted to direct fire. Batteries furnishing close-support fires have to be equipped with the most modern fire control installations. These installations are capable of firing on targets without reference to an aiming point. Batteries that are not equipped with modern fire control installations can be used in close support if they are located aboard ships that are providing support for combat units that are moving parallel to the shoreline. These ships have to be moving parallel to the supported troops, firing across the infantry front onto generally visible targets. Even though the most modern fire control installations and navigational instruments make unobserved fires on large areas practicable, these instruments should not be relied upon if the unobserved target area is near friendly troops.[99]

The number and types of batteries aboard a ship are irrelevant, however, if those batteries can not be brought to bear on the enemy in an effective way. A ship's draft, speed, and maneuverability are the key characteristics that determine just how close to the shore and to enemy coastal battery positions it can take station in order to place ordnance on a target. The ships that are best suited for engaging targets at close range near a beach are those that are of relatively shallow draft, which travel at high speeds, and that can turn quickly. These types of ships can provide preparation fires for the landing of the assault waves of the landing force and can provide cover for heavier, less maneuverable ships. They can also engage coastal batteries.[100]

The magazine capacity of a ship determines how long it can be employed in support of operations ashore. Generally, fifty percent of a ship's magazine capacity should be set aside for shore target ammunition when that ship is designated to provide fire support. The reservation of fifty percent of a ship's ammunition for surface engagements ensures that the bombardment groups are capable of fleet defense if necessary. Of the fifty percent reserved for shore bombardment, close- and deep-support ships should reserve at least one half for targets of opportunity during Phase III. Ships assigned to close-support duty for a battalion or to deep-support duty for a regiment should have sufficient reserve ammunition to engage at least fifteen targets of opportunity during Phase III. Destroyers assigned as a group in close support should have a combined magazine capacity that will allow

---

[98] Ibid.

[99] Ibid. This, of course, is "modern" relative to 1943.

[100] Ibid.

them to provide the necessary supply of shore target ammunition. Regardless of the proportions of ammunition kept on hand, the writers point out, ships are not very effective at deep support unless aerial spotting with suitable communication between the aircraft and the supporting ships is available. Consequently, effective deep support requires more than just consideration of ballistics and logistics.[101]

The number and type of fire support batteries aboard a ship determines which echelons of a landing force a ship can support. A ship with only one battery can support only one unit, either in close support of a battalion or in deep support of a higher echelon. A ship with two or more batteries, depending on the estimated strength of the enemy's defenses, can provide effective close support for a battalion with one or two of its batteries while providing deep support to that same battalion's parent regiment. There is a caveat here, however. The same ship is not to provide close support to battalions of different regiments, nor is the same ship to be assigned deep support of one regiment and close support of battalions of a different regiment. The reasons why the effective support of widely separated units is not considered practicable are twofold: first, there are great difficulties involved in providing firing positions suitable for engaging widely separated targets; second, providing effective liaison and communications between widely separated units is highly problematic.[102]

After having addressed the problems associated with getting into firing position and then being able to place ordnance on target, the problem of maximizing damage to the enemy is taken up. Change 3 of *FTP 167* provides a more detailed list of acceptable naval projectiles for the purposes of bombardment than did either the *Tentative Manual* or Change 1. Naval projectiles are classified according to their effectiveness for neutralization, from most effective to least, as follows: anti-aircraft projectiles set to burst above the ground; high capacity projectiles with superquick fuses; anti-aircraft projectiles set to burst on impact; high capacity projectiles with short delay fuses; common naval projectiles; and, finally, armor piercing rounds. The relative effectiveness of these same projectile types for the destruction of fortifications upon a direct hit is the inverse of the order given in this list.[103]

Naval guns can also be classified according to their effectiveness in performing the various gunfire support roles. Five-inch guns can be used for most close-support missions because of their high rate of fire, small pattern, and suitable angle of fall. Five-inch/38-caliber and six-inch guns have the requisite range, rate of fire, and small pattern for use in deep support of echelons up to and including the division. Six-inch guns are especially suited for counter-battery against all enemy field

---

[101] Ibid.

[102] Ibid. See also the section of this chapter on fire control party liaison.

[103] Ibid., p. 118. See chapter 3 for a discussion of the problems inherent in the adoption of the term "neutralization" by the authors of *FTP 167* with Change 3.

artillery in range of a landing area. Large-caliber guns of eight inches and above have rates of fire that are too slow and patterns that are too large to allow them to be used in close support. Consequently, they are classified tactically as deep-support weapons. They are best used against long-range targets such as cities and airfields as well as in the destruction of major, permanent fortifications regardless of range. In addition, if six-inch guns are not available, eight-inch guns can be used in long-range counter-battery. Guns of all classifications are suitable for use in preparation for a landing with coverage of the objective split in one of two ways: either five-inch guns can be used to bombard the beach itself and larger calibers used on adjacent areas, or the heavier calibers can be used in the early period of preparation and the lighter calibers in the later period.[104] Based upon this analysis of naval guns, the authors of Change 3 classify the standard naval batteries used in naval gunfire support as follows: four 5″/25-caliber for close support; four 5″/38-caliber for close and deep support; six 6″/47-caliber for close and deep support; and nine 8″/55-caliber for deep support and "special missions."[105] The number of guns in a battery can vary from this standard according to the way in which a particular ship is equipped.[106] The standard target areas for each of these standard naval batteries, based upon the size of the normal patterns of the guns that compose each of them, are as follows: 5″/25-caliber and 5″/38-caliber, 150 yards; 6″/47-caliber, 250 yards; and 8″/55-caliber, 400 yards.[107]

Naval guns and batteries do not exist on their own, however. They are attached to platforms, and these platforms come in a variety of different configurations. Each configuration, or ship type, exhibits certain advantages and disadvantages relating to their use in naval gunfire support missions. The three major ship types described in Change 3 of *FTP 167* are destroyers, cruisers, and battleships. Destroyers are particularly well-suited for preparation in Phase II because of their shallow draft, high speed, and excellent maneuverability, and they are well-suited for providing close support in Phase III, particularly for units involved in combat at the shoreline. They can stand close inshore, ahead of and on the flanks of the boat waves, placing accurate fire on beach area targets at close range. Destroyers have only one control, however, regardless of the number of guns on board, so they are limited as to the number of targets a single ship can engage. Consequently, one destroyer by itself can not be assigned as a close fire support group as normally would be the case with cruisers and battleships.[108]

---

[104] Ibid.

[105] Ibid., p. 119.

[106] Ibid., p. 118.

[107] Ibid., p. 119.

[108] Ibid., pp. 120 and 121.

Cruisers can be used in both close and deep support. Their ability to use airplane spot as well as their adequate radio communications facilities and control systems—usually consisting of two controls for the main batteries and two for the anti-aircraft batteries—allow them to use their five-inch batteries for close support and their main batteries for deep support. Light cruisers are preferable to heavy cruisers because of the greater utility of six-inch guns over eight-inch guns in the naval gunfire support role. Cruiser magazine capacity allows them to participate in preparation with both five-inch and main batteries, if necessary, while being able to reserve adequate ammunition for close and deep support in later phases.[109] Battleships are treated like very large heavy cruisers as far as naval gunfire support is concerned. They are generally classified as deep support ships because of their depth of draft and the size of their main armament, but their five-inch batteries make them ideal for close support where hydrographic conditions permit them to approach close to shore.[110]

Change 3 goes into detail as to the fire support requirements for D-day. It breaks down these requirements according to batteries, ammunition, and ships. Regarding batteries, sufficient numbers are to be assigned during Phase I to perform several missions: to neutralize and maintain neutralization of known and suspected enemy guns that are capable of effectively firing on the transport area; to neutralize enemy observation, disrupt his communications, and to neutralize his field artillery positions, bivouac areas, outposts, and other forward garrisons; and to execute any necessary "special missions." During Phase II, the number of batteries assigned should be sufficient to: neutralize all beach defenses; continue engagement of coastal batteries; and engage field artillery batteries that are in position to lay fire on beach areas. The emphasis during Phase III should be the proper support for a given echelon of the landing force. First, there are to be sufficient batteries assigned to provide necessary close support for each assault battalion. Second, there are to be sufficient batteries assigned to provide necessary deep support for each assault regiment and division.[111] Keeping in mind the fifty-fifty split described above, each support group should be provided sufficient ammunition of suitable types to engage each target on the time schedule twice over, with an equal amount reserved for targets of opportunity.[112]

In summary, then, the number and types of ships sufficient to provide the necessary batteries for each phase of an assault and the necessary ammunition for those batteries should be provided. Included in this calculation should be an adequate number of the following ship types: highly mobile ships, such as destroyers

---

[109] Ibid.

[110] Ibid., p. 120.

[111] Ibid., p. 122.

[112] Ibid.

or their equivalent, that can be used to cover the assault waves in close to the beach; cruisers for close support for battalions and deep support to regiments and divisions; and battleships or heavy cruisers for "special mission" requirements.[113] Fire support requirements have to be met from an organizational standpoint as well as from the standpoint of firepower, however. With this in mind, Change 3 provides a standard for proper support that is much clearer than anything stated in the *Tentative Manual* or Change 1. According to this standard, four to eight destroyers, two light cruisers, and one heavy cruiser or battleship should support each assault regiment and one heavy cruiser or battleship should be added for each landing force division.[114]

Organization of Fire Support Groups

Mention has been made in numerous places thus far of groups of ships being used in naval gunfire support, but the only details provided have been about individual gun and ship types. What is the recommended organization of these groups and what is their function in providing gunfire support for landing operations? According to the authors of the *Tentative Manual,* ships should be organized into task entities known as fire support groups. Each of these groups should be assigned one or more fire missions within its area. The number of fire support groups that should be organized for any given landing operation is dependent upon the number and types of firing ships, the scheme of maneuver adopted for the landing, the number and types of fire missions, and the hydrography of the waters adjacent to the landing area.[115] The flagship of the attack force commander is not to be assigned a fire support mission, *per se.* If its fire is needed, it can best serve by reinforcing the fires of other ships in addition to providing fire on targets of opportunity. Fire support groups executing close- and deep-supporting fires should be assigned to support specific units of the landing force (e.g., a battalion or a division). The commanders of both the landing force unit and its assigned support group should work out gunfire support plans jointly. Within the limits of the ammunition allowance, fire should be delivered on the targets that are agreed upon. Once the operation begins, requests for fire should be transmitted to ships through fire control parties on the beach. The exact types of fire missions that the fire support groups should be expected to perform for specified units of the landing force are to be clearly defined during the planning stages of the operation. These specified missions, however, are not to preclude the execution of other fire missions in an emergency.[116]

---

[113] Ibid.

[114] Ibid.

[115] *Tentative Manual, 1935,* p. 166.

[116] Ibid., p. 168.

There are a number of factors to be considered when determining what types of ships to assign to fire support groups. First, these ships are to carry enough guns and suitable ammunition to carry out their designated fire missions. These missions are to be undertaken according to the following priorities: close-supporting fires, deep-supporting fires, counter-battery, interdiction, and, finally, other fire missions including counter-ship and fires on targets of opportunity. Second, consideration should be given to maintaining a uniformity of ship types within each group. Taking this step permits the maintenance of normal fleet organization, thereby facilitating the proper maneuvering of ships and the more efficient control of fire. Third, attention should be paid to the equalization of ammunition consumption and gun barrel erosion from ship to ship within a fire support group. Fourth, the scheme of maneuver adopted for the landing should be considered and ships assigned accordingly. Fifth, the hydrography of the waters adjacent to the landing area should be considered, especially as it relates to the ability to get deep-drafted vessels in close to the beach. Sixth, the number of subordinate units of the landing force to be supported should be determined and separate gunfire support groups should be assigned to each of them accordingly. Finally, the maximum number of targets that can be taken under fire by ships in a gunfire support group should be determined so that the group can be matched to a target area efficiently.[117]

Flanking fire should be used whenever possible. Positioning ships to deliver flanking fire gets them out of the way of the ship-to-shore movement and allows them to fire on reverse slopes and defiladed areas more accurately. It also allows boats to approach closer to shore before supporting fires have to be lifted. All direct fire should be delivered from as close in as possible since accuracy increases as range decreases. In assigning fire support areas for the delivery of counter-battery fires and fires on reverse slopes, however, care should be taken that sufficient range is maintained to ensure proper angle of fall needed to reach the target. The authors assume that a range sufficient to produce an angle of fall of twenty-five degrees will allow ships to reach all enemy weapons employed in beach defense. Mortars and airplanes should be used to reach those positions that remain defiladed from ships' guns. Reduced charges should be used to increase angles of fall, to permit a greater range of weapons choices, and to reduce gun barrel erosion.[118]

There should be enough ammunition on board the inshore fire support ships to maintain their maximum rate of fire during the approach of the boats to the shore and to cover the flanks of the initial inland advance. Inshore ships, therefore, are not to be required to reinforce the fire of offshore ships if such reinforcement does not allow them to fire at their maximum rate during this period. The best situation is one in which both the inshore and offshore fire support groups are

[117] Ibid., pp. 166–67.

[118] Ibid., pp. 169–70.

capable of delivering the required density of fire on the beach, the offshore ships lifting fire upon approach of the boats to the beach and the inshore groups continuing to fire on targets until the boats are right at the point of beaching. Inshore vessels at a range of 1,000 yards or less are much more accurate in their delivery of ordnance on targets than are offshore groups. Their increased accuracy allows for an equivalent amount of damage without having to supply as great a density over the whole target area.[119]

Inshore fire support groups are to open fire either just before or immediately after the offshore groups cease fire. They can reinforce offshore group fires while both are engaged in their missions, but they should take over the target area once the offshore group lifts inland or ceases fire. Inshore support ships are not to use the time-sector method of bombardment because the period for landing troops on the beach is too short. Instead, they are to fire upon the beach at their maximum rate and cease fire when the landing craft approach close to the shore. Well-trained observers are to be aboard vessels involved in inshore fire support. These observers are to work in tandem with the fire control and gun groups in order to bring heavy fire down upon an observed target as quickly as possible. Machine guns and anti-boat guns should be considered the most important targets at this stage of the assault. Fire should be maintained over the whole target area if no observable targets present themselves.[120]

Inshore support ships are to watch for enemy flanking fire coming from positions located in the target areas of other ships that are masked from the direct fire of the ship responsible for that area. A ship that has the ability to place direct fire upon such a target should do so, regardless of whether or not the target is in its area of responsibility. Inshore support ships should continue to lay fire ahead and on the flanks of the landing party. They are not to cease fire because of an inability to see aiming points. Provision should be made to continue delivery of fire using indirect methods in case smoke and dust hamper visibility in the target area.[121] Offshore supporting groups should execute deep-supporting fires once the approach of the landing boats to the shore forces them to lift their fire off of the beach. Other ships specially designated for the purpose are to augment the offshore supporting groups in the accomplishment of their fire missions.[122] Deep-supporting fires are to be concentrated on important enemy positions such as areas known or estimated to contain enemy troops and key enemy defensive positions along the axis of the main

[119] Ibid., p. 163.

[120] Ibid., pp. 178–79.

[121] Ibid., p. 180. This is an interesting point of doctrine given the problems with visibility encountered at Tarawa and the complaints made by so many naval officers after that operation about the lack of visibility and the effect those visibility problems had on the effective delivery of naval gunfire support.

[122] Ibid.

attack. As in the case of ships providing close-supporting fires, efforts should be made to select firing positions for ships involved in deep-supporting fires that will allow the latter to lay fire by direct observation. Allowing these ships to fire in this way gives them the best chance of approximating the characteristics of close-supporting fires. Deep-supporting fires should be controlled by plane spot or by fire control parties ashore if fire by direct observation is not possible.[123]

The ships providing gunfire support for the amphibious assault should be assigned to fire support areas offshore. These fire support areas should be located such that they do not interfere with the transport area or the movement of the boats to the beaches, but care should be taken that their locations not jeopardize the effectiveness of the support ships in carrying out their fire missions. Close-supporting fires being executed best by direct observation, the fire support areas should be located such that the need for indirect fire is kept to a minimum. In line with this necessity, ships firing on small islands and peninsulas should position themselves so that they can undertake fires on reverse slopes and some counter-battery fires by means of direct observation. In order to economize ammunition as well as observation planes, as well as to ensure that fire is brought to bear on targets as rapidly as possible, ships that are assigned to interdiction missions should be positioned, whenever practicable, such that their targets can be kept under continuous, direct observation from the ship.[124]

A fire support area should be large enough to allow for the maneuvering of the ships assigned thereto. It should also be large enough to give the commanders of the fire support groups assigned to it a reasonable amount of latitude in selecting suitable firing runs. Firing runs should allow for the maximum number of guns to be laid on a target at one time. They also should allow for the minimum amount of adjustments of range and deflection during the firing. In other words, the target should bear on the ship's beam at the center of the run, the run being fairly straight and long enough so as not to require frequent turns during the progress of the firing.[125] It is very important that firing ships not be made to turn at critical times during their runs and that fire be delivered from the most effective position in those runs while presenting the least amount of danger to the landing craft and other ships. Consequently, the position of ships in their firing runs should be closely coordinated with the firing schedule and with the position of the landing craft.[126] Since delays are bound to occur during the execution of a landing, however, fire support ships should not open fire until the leading boats are in the position prescribed by the attack force commander. Individual ship commanders

---

[123] Ibid., p. 182.

[124] Ibid., p. 169.

[125] Ibid., p. 170.

[126] Ibid., p. 173.

should not go strictly by the time schedule! Neither should that schedule be constructed around a particular hour of the day or a portion thereof. It should be flexible, playing off the time when the landing craft actually begin their run toward the beach.[127]

Once again, Change 1 of *FTP 167* follows the *Tentative Manual* rather closely. The most obvious difference between the two is in Change 1's specification that second line combatant ships and suitable Coast Guard vessels should be used to execute fire support missions wherever possible in order to release first line combatant ships for fleet action.[128] Change 3 contains much of the same information as the earlier documents concerning the basic concepts of fire support group organization, but it goes into greater detail as to the classification of those groups and the most effective groupings of ship types within them. It classifies fire support groups as close-support, deep-support, and "special." One close-support fire group should be assigned to each assault battalion and one deep-support group should be assigned to each assault regiment. An additional deep-support group should be assigned to each assault division if it is determined that such additional support is needed. The "special" support groups should be assigned as necessary, their principal use coming, as to the timing of the assault, during the preparation phase and being, in relation to the assault as a whole, against targets classified as "special" from a tactical standpoint.[129]

Change 3 of *FTP 167* treats one of the concepts concerning the assembling of ships in fire support groups differently than does the *Tentative Manual* and Change 1. That concept is the simplicity of control. The earlier documents recognize the advantages of keeping the use of fire control as simple as possible, but they do not stipulate a solution to the problem, *per se.* Change 3 is more direct: "By reason of simplicity of communication and fire control it is desirable that only one ship constitute a fire support group whenever practicable."[130] Destroyers, as explained above, are capable of simple communication and fire control, but because they have only one control, they are too limited in the number of targets that can be engaged by a single ship.[131] Regarding ship types, the authors of Change 3 use the same classification system they used before in discussing general characteristics of naval vessels, this time with an eye toward how best to use the vessels in fire support groups. The authors deem light cruisers in general to be the "ideal component" of close fire support groups and six-inch light cruisers and eight-inch heavy cruisers to be "preferable" for the deep support of regiments. Battleships, on the

[127] Ibid., pp. 173–74.

[128] *FTP 167* with Change 1, p. 123.

[129] *FTP 167* with Change 3, p. 122.

[130] Ibid.

[131] See also the section of this chapter concerning the limitations of destroyers in this capacity.

other hand, are to be reserved as divisional deep support and for use as "special" fire support groups. Destroyers, according to the authors, are especially well-suited for use in "special" fire support groups, for participation in preparation fires, and for providing fire on targets of opportunity on the flanks of the assault. It is suggested that it can even be desirable to use several destroyers as a close-support group rather than one cruiser, the destroyers being used in rotation in answering calls from the shore fire control parties.[132]

Organization and Use of Shore Fire Control Parties

Ships' fire control parties should perform two functions according to the writers of the *Tentative Manual, 1935:* they should provide liaison between a supporting ship or fire support group and the unit of the landing force for which they are providing support, and they should spot ships' gunfire from control vessels and observation stations located ashore.[133] The most desirable setup would be to have a fire control party from each ship in a group firing close- and deep-supporting missions situated on the beach or group of beaches being supported. The participation of all ships involved in the fire missions allows for greater flexibility in the execution of fires on several targets because two or more observation stations would be occupied simultaneously.[134] To simplify matters, however, a fire support group that has been given the task of supporting two or more beaches can designate one ship to provide a fire control party on a particular beach that can act for the entire group.[135]

The composition of each fire control party should be as follows: one fire control officer, one spotter with necessary recorders, and a small detail of communications personnel. The fire control officer is the person who acts as a liaison with the units of the landing force being supported. Both he and the commander of the attached supporting field artillery elements usually take up a position with the senior landing force unit commander on his assigned beach. A chief fire control officer should be designated to act as liaison officer where two or more fire control parties are operating on the same beach. The spotting details are ideally to take up positions at the field artillery observation posts.[136] The fire control parties for offshore fire support groups should be stationed initially aboard control vessels in order that they might provide assistance in the control of fires on the beach, but

---

[132] *FTP 167* with Change 3, pp. 122–23.

[133] *Tentative Manual, 1935,* p. 184.

[134] Ibid., pp. 184–85.

[135] Ibid., p. 185.

[136] Ibid.

provision should be made for landing these parties in time for them to perform their duties ashore.[137]

The doctrine concerning fire control parties as related in Change 1 of *FTP 167* is practically the same as that in the *Tentative Manual* with one minor and one major exception. First, it stipulates that the communication detail of the fire control parties be equipped with a portable radio, two field telephones, and approximately a mile of wire so that a spotter can take a position quite distant from the radio set.[138] Second, it provides greatly detailed instructions as to how fire control parties should be used and trained, even down to a discussion of the equipment for and the carrying out of training on board ship.[139]

Change 3 of *FTP 167* drops this highly detailed exposition and goes back to the more succinct treatment of the *Tentative Manual.* The similarity with the earlier document ends there, however. There is a significant difference between the doctrine promulgated in Change 3 and the one espoused in both of its earlier incarnations. These differences concern two components: first, the liaison between the naval support groups and the landing force, and second, the separation of the naval gunfire liaison officer from the fire control party. The earlier version of the doctrine provides for one-way liaison from the landing force units to the firing ships by way of an officer who, in most instances, is also in command of a fire support party. Change 3 puts in place an additional liaison, from the fire support group to the supported infantry commander, and separates the liaison officer ashore from responsibility for any one particular fire support party. Change 3 stipulates that the naval gunfire support officer (the naval officer sent to the commander of the unit of the landing force being supported) should be qualified in naval gunnery and should have complete information as to the characteristics of the ships composing the gunfire support group from which he came. He should also have some knowledge of the fire support areas his group has been assigned. The landing force officer (the Marine or Army officer sent from the landing force to the ships providing fire support) should have complete knowledge of the scheme of maneuver that has been planned for the assault forces and of information from the intelligence annex and subsequent reports concerning the enemy's situation ashore.[140] This dual liaison system, according to the authors of Change 3, provides the best method of coordinating fire between the firing ships and the supported units during Phase III of D-day, the period in which unforeseen tactical situations would most likely arise that would require a modification of the prearranged firing plan.[141]

[137] Ibid.

[138] *FTP 167* with Change 1, p. 135.

[139] Ibid., pp. 135–37.

[140] *FTP 167* with Change 3, p. 123.

[141] Ibid., p. 130.

The fire control party described in Change 3 is different from the one described in the two earlier versions of the doctrine. First, there is a change in the title given to the group. They are no longer "ships' fire control parties" but "shore fire control parties." Second, rather than the vague references to "the units of the Fleet Marine Force being supported" that are found in the *Tentative Manual,* Change 3 stipulates that one shore fire control party should be organized for each assault battalion of the landing force. What is more, they should act under the instructions of the battalion commander. Third, the composition of the fire control party is slightly different: an officer who acts as spotter, a non-commissioned officer who acts as his assistant and who is capable of adjusting fires if necessary, a private who acts as the instrument operator, and a detail of communications personnel.[142]

This, then, was the basic United States naval gunfire support doctrine as it existed the day Marines went ashore on Betio Island. How was this doctrine applied in that operation? Did American experiences at Tarawa lead to further modifications of the doctrine and, if so, what were those modifications? Answers to these questions require a close look at what happened on the day when the name "Tarawa" became engraved indelibly in the chronicle of Marine Corps history.

---

[142] Ibid., p. 123.

Chapter 3

Operation Galvanic

Introduction: The Sacrifice of Duty

It had already been a long and trying morning and it did not look like it was going to get any better. Lieutenant Colonel Herbert R. Amey had so many things on his mind, and complications were adding to the list. Having to deal with transferring his battalion landing team from transports to landing craft in the open ocean off Tarawa Atoll would have been difficult enough under the best of circumstances, but the Japanese were not helping matters with their periodic shelling. The transports had to move to a different position, creating a chaotic condition that cost precious time, but all that had been worked out and things were beginning to get back on track. Now, at 08.24, the first waves of amphibian tractors (LVTs or landing vehicles, tracked) were leaving the line of departure and heading for the beach, but they were behind schedule and they were falling further and further behind as they churned on. Things were not going exactly according to plan.

Amey waited in his LCM (landing craft, medium), taking in what was going on as the first three waves of his landing team (LT), 2nd Battalion of the Second Marines, made their way in their LVTs toward their smoke-shrouded objective, Beach Red Two, just to the west of the pier. The Navy had talked of pounding the island so hard that the Marines would be able to waltz right in and take it from the Japanese without hardly firing a shot. Amey was suspicious of such a boast, but he held out hope in the back of his mind that it would happen that way—that is until the leading elements of his landing team reached the reef.

Anti-boat and machine gun fire ripped into his men as they crossed the reef in their amphibian tractors, and there was nothing their commanding officer could do but watch. He had to get into this fight—provide some leadership—but he had to wait until it was time for his wave of landing craft to leave the line of departure. Lieutenant Colonel Walter I. Jordan, an observer from the Fourth Marine Division, could see the wrinkles of concern on Amey's face, and Jordan understood all too well why they were there. Some of those wrinkles disappeared as the LCM started toward the island, but the task was not about to get any easier, and Amey knew it. He tried to get a better view of the beach ahead as the landing craft made its way forward, but the smoke and dust made observation very difficult.

Suddenly, his thoughts were yanked away from his pinned down men on the beach and back to his own little group. With a loud grating crash, the LCM came to a halt on the reef. It would go no farther. He and the other battalion commanders knew that there was a possibility that LCVPs (landing craft, vehicle and personnel) and LCMs might not be able to get over the reef. Now he was faced with irrefutable proof that they would not. He had to get ashore, regardless. His men were being torn to pieces and he had to get to them. Two empty LVTs that were heading back to the transports passed nearby. Amey flagged them down and had his command post group offloaded into them. Neither of the LVTs was big enough to carry everyone, so Amey and Jordan got into one with thirteen other officers and men while the rest got into the other tractor with Major Howard Rice, LT 2/2's executive officer. Heavy enemy fire forced Rice's LVT westward, away from Red Two, but Amey's tractor was able to stay on course. There appeared to be something in the water ahead, but it did not matter—they had to reach the beach so he could set up his command post and begin directing his Marines in the midst of this nightmare. The LVT tried to barrel through the obstacle, but it came to a halt about 200 yards from the shore as it became entangled in what turned out to be barbed wire. Now was the time when he could begin leading by example. Amey ordered his men over the sides of the tractor. Only a short distance through shallow water and he would be there, on the beach. Waving his pistol toward the island, he yelled to his men, "Come on! Those bastards can't stop us!"

Lieutenant Colonel Herbert R. Amey fell where he stood, killed by a Japanese machine gun bullet that tore into his throat. His experience on the bloody shores of Betio Island can be seen as symbolic of the frustrations and torments the Second Marine Division would have to face and surmount over the seventy-six hours of agony that was the Battle of Tarawa. Mistakes were made during that battle and lives were lost because of those mistakes. The Navy and Marine Corps had spent the interwar period attempting to address every foreseeable problem associated with attacking a fortified position from the sea. Tarawa was the first test of the amphibious warfare doctrine the Naval Services had produced, and it proved to be a most unforgiving one.[1]

---

[1] James R. Stockman, *The Battle for Tarawa* (Washington, DC: Historical Section, HQMC, 1947), pp. 16–17; Henry I. Shaw, Jr., Bernard C. Nalty, and Edwin T. Turnbladh, *History of U.S. Marine Corps Operations in World War II*, Vol. III, *Central Pacific Drive* (Washington, DC: Historical Branch, HQMC, 1966; reprint, Nashville: The Battery Press, 1994), p. 60 (page citations in the present volume are to the reprint edition); Martin Russ, *Line of Departure: Tarawa* (Garden City, NY: Doubleday, 1975), pp. 83–84; Joseph H. Alexander, *Utmost Savagery: The Three Days of Tarawa* (Annapolis: Naval Institute Press, 1995; reprint, New York: Ivy Books, 1995), p. 128. Two slightly different versions of the Amey quote are found in Russ and Alexander. Russ quotes Amey as saying "These bastards . . ." while Alexander quotes him as saying "Those bastards. . . ." Dates provided in this work are those traditionally given in U.S. accounts of the battles unless otherwise specified.

The Amphibious Assault of Tarawa Atoll

The troops of Combat Team 2, Second Marine Division (Reinforced), began to debark at 03.55 on the morning of 20 November 1943 from the transports of Task Group 53.1, climbing down cargo netting into waiting LCVPs for subsequent transferal to LVT(1)s and LVT(2)s. Before the Marines could complete debarkation, however, the Navy had to address an unanticipated complication. A strong current carried the transports too far south, placing the ships within easy range of shore batteries on Betio and causing them to mask Fire Support Area 1. The fire support vessels had to be unmasked so that they could begin the vitally important job of destroying enemy defenses prior to the Marines going ashore and the transports needed to be moved out of range of the Japanese guns. Commander of the Southern Landing Force (CTF 53), Rear Admiral Harry W. Hill, aboard the Pearl Harbor veteran USS *Maryland* (BB-46), addressed this problem by halting debarkation at 04.31 and ordering the whole transport group to move north to its proper position.[2] This unplanned shift caused some confusion. LCVPs already loaded with troops had to try to keep up with the larger vessels to which they had been assigned as those ships traveled through the open ocean at night. Some of the LCVPs became separated in the darkness and time was lost as these strays were rounded up.[3] The transports resumed debarkation of troops once they were in the correct position. They were joined at 04.15 by LSTs (landing ship, tank) loaded with LVT(2)s. These ships disgorged their amphibian tractors and troops from the attack transports then transferred into them. Organizing the first waves of LVTs threw the time schedule off even further.[4]

---

[2] Shaw et al., *Central Pacific Drive,* p. 53; U.S. National Archives and Records Administration (hereinafter NARA), Record Group (hereinafter RG) 127, USMC Geographic Files, Box 26, File A3–1, TF 53 Operational Report, Tarawa, Gilberts, Commander Task Force 53, Report of Tarawa Operations, 13 December 1943, Enclosure A, p. 8 (hereinafter CTF 53 Operations Narrative). Stockman states on page 11 of *The Battle for Tarawa* that the transports reached Transport Area Baker at 03.20 instead of Area Able and that, when the problem of position was discovered, TRANSDIV 4 (temporary) moved north to Area Able and completed debarkation. He is not specific as to the time at which debarkation resumed. A perusal of several ships' action reports shows that there is no consensus as to the exact times involved. Shaw et al., *Central Pacific Drive* accepts the times recorded in CTF 53's report as being accurate. The present author does as well. One correction is necessary, however. Shaw et al., *Central Pacific Drive* cites page 18 of CTF 53's report for the times related in their narrative. The record shows that the chronology for 20 November begins on page 7 and that the relevant times for this narrative are related on page 8.

[3] Shaw et al., *Central Pacific Drive,* p. 53.

[4] NARA, RG 38, Box 545, 5th PhibFor Groups, 12–22–43, Commander Group Two, Fifth Amphibious Force, Forwarding of Action Reports, 9 January 1944, Enclosure A, Commander Task Group 53.1 (Commander Transportation Division 18) Report on Tarawa Operations, p. 1; Stockman, *The Battle for Tarawa,* p. 12.

The Japanese had been quiet while all of this was going on, but shore batteries began opening up on the invaders at 05.07. Fire support vessels attempted to neutralize the Japanese emplacements until 05.42, at which point Hill called for a cease-fire to allow for a scheduled air strike against the beachhead.[5] The air strike was not delivered on time, however, possibly as a result of a misunderstanding as to whether it was to take place at dawn or at sunrise, and Hill was unable to contact the pilots in order to reschedule. Regardless of why it did not occur at the proper time, the approximately thirty minutes during which the fire support ships waited for the air attack allowed the Japanese to fire on the transport area unmolested.[6] The fire support vessels resumed firing at 06.00, only to have to stop once again for ten minutes when the belated air strike finally came in at a few minutes before 06.15.[7] The resumption of fire at 06.20, after the delivery of the air strike, signaled the official beginning of the Phase I pre-landing bombardment.[8]

At sunrise, 06.12, the minesweepers USS *Pursuit* (AM-108) and USS *Requisite* (AM-109) began clearing the entrance to the lagoon under cover of smoke generated from pots carried by LCVPs. Aboard *Pursuit* to act as a guide was a Lieutenant Forbes of the New Zealand Navy, a man familiar with the waters around Tarawa Atoll. Waiting in the wings until a path had been swept through the mines were USS *Ringgold* (DD-500) and USS *Dashiell* (DD-659). The destroyers, from their positions just outside the entrance to the lagoon, temporarily silenced Japanese guns that fired on the minesweepers while the latter were doing their job.

---

[5] Stockman, *The Battle for Tarawa,* p. 12; Shaw et al., *Central Pacific Drive,* p. 53.

[6] Stockman, *The Battle for Tarawa,* p. 12; Shaw et al., *Central Pacific Drive,* pp. 53–54; Colonel Merritt A. Edson, in a letter to Colonel Gerald C. Thomas, stated that "Due to the diversion of the Carrier Group for the Rabaul strike while we were in the rehearsal area, there was never any opportunity for a conference between Admiral Montgomery and anyone from the Southern Attack Force. The NGF plan provided for an airstrike from 0545 to 0615, the latter hour being designated in the plan as W-Hour, and the time that the first phase of naval bombardment was to begin. The Carrier Group interpreted W-Hour as the time the air strike was to begin instead of the end, with almost disastrous results. During this half hour period, the Jap shore batteries opened up on the transports which were only about 10 to 12 thousand yards off and had free shooting, since Admiral Hill did not consider it advisable to continue naval gunfire with the momentary expectation of an air strike arriving. Luckily the Japs did not hit any of our transports although they got several near misses." Library of Congress, Manuscript Division, Edson Papers, Box 5, File 40, Letter from Merritt A. Edson to Gerald C. Thomas, 13 December 1943 (hereinafter Edson–Thomas Letter, 13 December 1943), p. 1.

[7] Stockman, *The Battle for Tarawa,* p. 12; Shaw et al., *Central Pacific Drive,* p. 54; CTF 53 Operations Narrative, p. 30; NARA, RG 127, USMC Geographic Files, Box 26, File A5–1, TG 53.4 AR, Commander Task Group 53.4, Action Report, Period 17–22 November 1943, 25 December 1943, p. 4 (hereinafter TG 53.4 AR).

[8] Shaw et al., *Central Pacific Drive,* p. 54.

Pursuit began marking the line of departure, the assault lanes, and any shoals that might present a danger to other ships or small craft after she had completed her minesweeping duties. Meanwhile, *Requisite* left the lagoon in order to guide the destroyers inside. The entry of *Ringgold* and *Dashiell* was too much for the previously silenced Japanese gunners to tolerate. Shells began to fall around the destroyers as they came through the cleared passage. One dud slammed into *Ringgold* on her starboard side below the waterline and penetrated to her after engine room. Lieutenant W. A. Parker, the ship's Engineering Officer, plugged the hole in the hull with his shoulder until more suitable materials could be found. Another dud ricocheted off of the number 5 tube of *Ringgold's* forward torpedo mount, barreled through sickbay, and finally came to rest in her emergency radio room. She opened fire on the gun position from which the shelling was believed to originate, and within a few moments a brilliant explosion lit up the early morning sky. Her shells apparently had found the enemy battery's ammunition supply.[9]

Pursuit, after completing the work of setting up for the ship-to-shore movement, took position at the line of departure at 07.15 and turned on a 24-inch searchlight. She would act as a beacon, guiding the LVTs through the dust and smoke already kicked up by the naval and air bombardment. Tracking the waves of amphibious tractors by radar, her commander reported to CTF 53 that they were twenty-four minutes behind schedule and would not be able to land at the appointed H-hour of 08.30. The pilot of one of *Maryland's* spotter planes, Lieutenant Commander Robert A. Macpherson, also reported that the tractors were

[9] Ibid., pp. 54–55; MCUA, Box 4, Folder 11, Commanding Officer USS Pursuit, Report of Action against Gilbert Islands Galvanic Operation, 6 December 1943, pp. 1–3 (hereinafter CO USS Pursuit AR); CTF 53 Operations Narrative, p. 32; NARA, RG 313, Box 70, File A1 (241), Commanding Officer USS Ringgold, Action Report, 1 December 1943, pp. 9–11 (hereinafter CO USS Ringgold AR); Theodore Roscoe, *United States Destroyer Operations in World War II* (Annapolis: United States Naval Institute, 1953), p. 385; the Commanding Officer of *Ringgold,* Commander T. F. Conley, Jr., described the plan for how his ship was to participate in this action as follows: "Hypo hour was originally set at 0830. At H-90 (0700), the RINGGOLD and DASHIELL were to precede the landing craft into the lagoon at Tarawa, passing through a channel swept and marked by the U.S.S. REQUISITE and U.S.S. PURSUIT, and firing at targets of opportunity as desired. RINGGOLD and DASHIELL were then to close the beach to machine gun range, and were to fire prearranged fire from H-35 (0755) to H-5 (0825), strafing the beach with machine guns during this period. From H-5 (0825) to H (0830), all surface fire was to cease while planes strafed the beach area. At H hour, the first wave was to land. From H plus 20 (0850), RINGGOLD and DASHIELL were to fire interdiction fire; upon completion of interdiction fire they were to fire at targets of opportunity, and remain available for call fire. One especial duty was to destroy any personnel attempting to escape from Betio Island to Bairiki Island." CO USS Ringgold AR, p. 9.

not going to meet the schedule. Hill, having few options from which to choose, radioed all units to postpone H-hour until 08.45.[10]

The problems with the transports and LVTs and the confusion over the timing of the air strike made for a bad start to the Admiral's day. The day was only beginning, however. Compounding his troubles was a communications problem to which there was no immediate solution. This problem's origin can be traced back to the decision to use as his command ship a vessel that was also scheduled to take part in the preliminary bombardment. The concussion resulting from the firing of *Maryland's* sixteen-inch main guns caused damage to her radio equipment. Though repairs were made and the radios began to function once again, intermittent outages plagued Hill throughout the operation. It was one of these outages that had kept him from contacting the planes of the air strike that had been scheduled for 05.42. Another one now kept him from notifying the pilots of a second air strike due to coincide with the planned H-hour that the assault had been postponed. Hill received information from Macpherson that the LVTs had finally reached the line of departure and, based upon information that the amphibian tractors were capable of 4–4½ knots, the task force commander once again rescheduled H-hour, this time for 09.00.[11] Why had the LVTs of the assault waves fallen behind schedule? There were three principal reasons: first, the shift in transport anchorage early on the morning of 20 November caused them to start out late from the very beginning; second, the drivers of the LVT(2)s had joined the task force at Tarawa and had not taken part in the rehearsals for the operation, consequently leaving them unfamiliar with agreed upon signals, speeds, and load limitations; finally, the faster LVT(2)s had to dress on the slower LVT(1)s, the older model not being capable of maintaining even four knots when fully loaded.[12]

Just as Hill was making this change in plans known to the units of the task force, the air strike that had been scheduled to occur immediately before the landing began to rip and pound the shoreline. All well and fine, except that the LVTs were still approximately forty minutes out from shore. *Maryland's* radios were in working order at the time, however, and Hill was able to contact the carrier pilots. He called off their strafing attacks and rescheduled them for between 08.55 and 09.00. The task force continued to bombard the landing beach on Betio right up until that time. At 08.55 the bombarding ships lifted their fire off of the beach in order to allow the planes to make their strafing runs and, at 09.00, the bombardment came to a halt with the exception of the destroyers firing from the lagoon.[13]

---

[10] Shaw et al., *Central Pacific Drive*, p. 55; CO USS Pursuit AR, pp. 3 and 4.

[11] Shaw et al., *Central Pacific Drive*, pp. 54 and 55.

[12] Ibid., p. 52; Isely and Crowl, *U.S. Marines and Amphibious War*, pp. 227–28. See below concerning the acquisition of LVT(2)s.

[13] Shaw et al., *Central Pacific Drive*, p. 55.

The preliminary bombardment did not destroy all of Betio's defenses. The enemy's most powerful guns—the eight-inch coastal defense rifles—had been specifically targeted along with many of the dual-purpose anti-aircraft mounts and anti-boat guns. These very dangerous weapons were effectively silenced. On the other hand, the majority of the Japanese concrete pillboxes and the emplacements that were protected by layered coconut logs and sand remained undamaged by either bombs or naval shells. The island commander, Rear Admiral Keiji Shibasaki, had done his job well in this regard.[14] Based upon reports from POWs, it would appear that the preliminary bombardment had achieved notable success in only one area. The rain of shells and bombs had disrupted the enemy's communications by destroying the wire that had been run between positions. The destruction of their hardwired communication network forced the Japanese to rely upon messengers, most of whom were either killed or forced to stay under cover. Consequently, few messages got through to their destinations. This was a factor that contributed greatly to a breakdown in command and control.[15]

The Betio defenders began shelling the LVTs as the tractors made their way from the line of departure to the reef surrounding the island. These first shells were set to burst over the tractors in order to shower the Marines inside with shrapnel. The bursting charges of these shells were too powerful, however, and the resulting fragments of metal were no larger than grains of sand. No significant casualties resulted from these airbursts or from the long-range fire of Japanese machine guns located on Betio. Defensive fire increased significantly as the LVTs crossed the reef, but troop casualties remained low and few of the amphibious tractors failed to reach the beach.[16]

First Lieutenant William D. Hawkins and his 2nd Scout-Sniper Platoon approached the smoke-enshrouded ruin of what was once the peacefully idyllic island of Betio at about 08.30. Hawkins and his unit were tasked with clearing the Japanese from a long pier on the lagoon side of the island. Extending from the shoreline to the reef, this pier allowed access to Betio regardless of tidal conditions. American forces would need it for logistical reasons later in the operation, but the main concern here at the beginning was its use by the enemy as a position from which to spray enfilading fire onto the approaching waves of amphibian tractors. There was a seaplane ramp that ran from the pier over the reef to the lagoon and it is here that Hawkins and a small portion of his unit landed at 08.55. These were the first American troops to set foot on what would be remembered henceforth simply as "Tarawa."[17]

---

[14] Ibid., pp. 55–56.

[15] Ibid., p. 56.

[16] Shaw et al., *Central Pacific Drive,* pp. 56–57; Stockman, *The Battle for Tarawa,* p. 15.

[17] Shaw et al., *Central Pacific Drive,* p. 57.

Hawkins led the way from his platoon's LCVP, jumping onto the seaplane ramp and charging up it toward the pier. Engineer Second Lieutenant Alan G. Leslie, Jr., and four other Marines followed close behind him. After he and the others had secured the ramp, Hawkins called for the rest of his platoon to join them. As his men began to transfer from their boat to the ramp, however, enemy fire began to slam into the pier around some gasoline drums that were stored there. Hawkins ordered his Marines back into the LCVP while he, Lieutenant Leslie, and the four scouts who were already with him began to advance toward the shore. The engineer carried a flamethrower, and he hosed down everything that looked like a place where the enemy might hide. Hawkins and the four scouts, meanwhile, made sure that no Japanese were left alive to fire upon the rest of the platoon. Leslie actually set a part of the pier ablaze in his zeal to flush out the Japanese, burning a gap in it that would cause problems later when trying to move supplies ashore. Future logistical difficulties were not foremost in the minds of Hawkins and his scout-snipers, however. Their task was to ensure the safety of their fellow Marines in the approaching assault waves—whatever it took.[18]

Major John F. Schoettel's 3/2 was the first assault battalion to reach its assigned beach, going ashore on Red One beginning at 09.10. Company I landed on the extreme right while Company K landed on the extreme left, on the boundary of Beaches Red One and Red Two. This boundary happened to coincide with a Japanese strongpoint that was in a position to pour flanking fire onto Company K as that unit attempted to gain the protection of the coconut log barricade located a few yards inland. Company K was responsible for tying into the unit on the extreme right of Red Two. The company's commander could not locate any Marines to his left, so he made contact with Company I but made no attempt to advance toward Red Two. These two assault companies lost over one half of their men over the next two hours of the battle. Company L of 3/2 and the battalion mortar platoon were only slightly more fortunate. Boated in LCVPs rather than LVTs, they suffered approximately thirty-five percent casualties wading toward Red One after their landing craft grounded on the reef.[19]

Major Henry P. Crowe's 2/8 reached Beach Red Three at 09.17. Fire from the destroyers in the lagoon, which was kept up until 09.10, forced the Japanese to remain under cover. The seven minutes between the cease-fire and 2/8's landing were insufficient for the defenders to recover before the Marines were upon them. Two of the battalion's LVTs made their way through a gap in the beach barricade and were able to unload their troops at the airstrip. The remaining LVTs stopped at the log barrier, unloaded, and returned to the control boats in the lagoon. Fewer

[18] Ibid.

[19] Ibid., p. 59.

than twenty-five of the 552 men in the first three waves assaulting Red Three became casualties during the landing.[20]

Lieutenant Colonel Amey's 2/2 faced the most violent opposition of all the assault battalions on D-day. Company F and most of Company E landed on Red Two at 09.22. One platoon of Company E was driven off course by machine gun and anti-boat fire and was forced to land on Red One. Company G followed the first two by only three minutes, but even with its additional weight given to the assault, 2/2 could only carve out a beachhead approximately fifty yards deep. Battalion casualties were very heavy, with Company F alone losing approximately one half of its strength.[21]

The first three assault waves encountered water depths across the reef that varied from three feet to only a few inches. Standard landing craft (LCVPs and LCMs) drafted approximately four feet or more of water, so they were barred from access to the beachhead. Infantrymen and pack howitzer crews either transferred to LVTs or were forced to wade the 400–500 yards from the reef to the beach under the strain of the weight of their weapons and the withering enemy fire from the island. Tanks had to attempt the trip from reef to beach under their own power, their crews hoping against hope that they would not sink into potholes and drown their engines in the process.[22] The men who waded ashore from the reef suffered the largest number of casualties on D-day at Tarawa. Tactical organization broke down as they attempted to advance in the face of what seemed to be certain annihilation; the movement ashore became more a battle for survival than a coordinated amphibious assault.[23]

Battalion command groups faced major, seemingly insurmountable problems in coming ashore. Boated in landing craft that were divided up between the third and fourth waves, the commanders and their staffs were among those who had to wade to shore from the reef. Major Crowe, on Red Three, encountered the least trouble. Lieutenant Colonel Amey's death severely compromised command and control of his battalion at a key point in the operation and Major Schoettel, while surviving the ordeal, was not able to get ashore over Red One until late in the afternoon. Shortly after 09.59, while he was still hung up on the reef, Schoettel radioed a reply to a message from regimental commander Colonel David M. Shoup ordering him to land his reserve over Red Two and attack westward. His stark statement: "We have nothing left to land."[24]

---

[20] Ibid.

[21] Ibid., pp. 59 and 60.

[22] Ibid., pp. 59–60.

[23] Ibid., p. 60.

[24] Ibid., pp. 60–61.

Colonel Shoup also encountered major problems in going ashore. Not being able to continue past the reef, he commandeered an LVT that was carrying wounded back from the beach and, after having the wounded transferred to his own LCVP, started for shore on the left half of Red Two. The LVT came under intense fire as it neared the beach. Shoup and his command group went over the side of the tractor and waded toward the central pier. According to Shoup, "From then on it was a matter of getting from the pier on down. You could say my CP [command post] was in the boat, then in the LVT, and then on the pier on the way in, but there was very little business conducted." Upon reaching the beach, Shoup determined just how much of Red Two was in 2/2's possession and then set up his CP. By the time he and his command group had done this, it was approximately 12.00.[25]

At 09.58, during Shoup's exchange with Schoettel over the landing of the battalion commander's reserve, the colonel ordered his regimental reserve, Major Wood B. Kyle's 1/2, to land on Red Two and attack westward in order to help 3/2 in their battle on Red One. This plan was slow to develop due to a shortage of LVTs. Only enough tractors could be found at that time to transport Companies A and B of 1/2. Heavy fire from the right side of Red Two forced some of the tractors carrying these two companies, comprising a total of four officers and 110 men, to veer off and land on Red One. The rest of the LVTs landed on Red Two and helped expand the beachhead there. It was not until the next morning that all of Kyle's command was landed.[26]

At 10.18, Second Marine Division commander Major General Julian Smith committed one of his two divisional reserve battalions to the battle, the 3/8 commanded by Major Robert H. Ruud. Tactical control was given to Shoup at 11.03 and the colonel ordered 3/8 to land on Red Three in support of Major Crowe's 2/8. Ruud's first four waves were cut to pieces as his men tried to make their way from the reef to the shore. Shoup halted the landing of the battalion after the fourth wave and the remaining units stayed at the end of the central pier until ordered in at approximately 15.00. All of 3/8's surviving Marines were ashore by 17.30. Ruud, on Shoup's orders, then deployed one of his companies to plug a gap between 2/8 and 1/2. Company K was already attached to Crowe's 2/8, having arrived in the first waves of 3/8's landing. It remained attached to 2/8 throughout the rest of the battle.[27]

The operation lost momentum after the initial assault waves had gained a toehold on the island. LVT losses mounted as the battle progressed. It was these losses, more than anything else, that slowed the attack down as the afternoon wore on. Many reserve elements had to go in aboard LCVPs and, like the men in the

[25] Ibid., p. 61, Shoup quote from Shoup interview with Captain James R. Stockman, 26 May 1947, quoted in source.

[26] Ibid.

[27] Ibid., p. 62.

fourth and fifth waves of the assault, they were forced to wade ashore under fire. The battle raged just inshore from the beach, so those men who survived the 400–500 yard gauntlet between the reef and the beach had to enter combat immediately upon emerging from the water. Command and control for the reserves coming ashore under these conditions was virtually impossible at the battalion and even at the company level. Much of the burden of continuing the assault fell upon individual Marines. These men kept pushing forward, trying to get ashore and under cover despite all that the Japanese tried to do to stop them.[28]

Observation of what was happening on the beach and inland was very difficult. The pre-invasion naval bombardment and air strikes had raised a pall of dust and smoke over the island and subsequent action continued to contribute to it. Only parts of the island were visible at any one time, even from the air, so that neither Julian Smith aboard *Maryland* nor Colonel Shoup in the thick of the battle ashore could either directly or indirectly observe more than an ever-changing and miniscule part of the operation as it unfolded. Continuing communications problems, both with the radios used by the Marines on the island and with the radios aboard *Maryland,* ensured that command and control at all levels was difficult.[29]

Colonel Shoup set up his CP approximately thirty yards inland on Red Two, right up against a Japanese pillbox that still contained approximately twenty-five live Japanese. Sentries were posted at the entrances to the pillbox to keep the enemy from emerging.[30] The regimental commander began to have a better idea of what he was dealing with by noon on D-day. He was able to contact his subordinates, finding out from them what they needed in order to make progress against the enemy. He then began to call for medical supplies, ammunition, and air support, the most critical items requested.[31]

Major Michael P. Ryan, commander of Company L 3/2, consolidated his company's beachhead on Red One using a conglomerate command made up of pieces of several units. His "provisional company" consisted of elements from all the companies of 3/2, four platoons and part of the headquarters company from 2/2, and the four officers and 110 men from 1/2 who had been driven off course while attempting to land on Beach Red Two. Major Rice, Lieutenant Colonel Amey's executive officer, had also ended up on Red One and he brought with him the only usable radio to be found in the vicinity of their beachhead. This radio was the only

---

[28] Ibid., pp. 62–63.

[29] Ibid., p. 63. The radio sets used by the Marines were not properly waterproofed. When they got wet, which was inevitable as the Marines went ashore, they would not work properly until they had dried out. These problems with radios aboard ship and on the island were major contributors to the lack of adequate coordination of air and naval gunfire. See Isely and Crowl, *U.S. Marines and Amphibious War,* pp. 241–42.

[30] Stockman, *The Battle for Tarawa,* p. 36.

[31] Shaw et al., *Central Pacific Drive,* p. 63.

link Ryan had with Colonel Shoup's CP. Ryan and the Marines under his command cleared an area 500 yards deep and 150 yards wide during the afternoon of D-day. Not having enough men to hold all of this ground, however, they had to pull back approximately 200 yards and dig in when night came. Two medium tanks out of six that attempted to make the crossing from the reef to the beach reached Red One by 11.30. Both of them contributed to Major Ryan's advance that afternoon. One was destroyed during the battle while the other, only its bow machine gun operational by that time, was placed in a position to protect the beachhead flank during the night.[32]

Medium tanks and also artillery landed on Red Two by the end of D-day. Three tanks that had originally gone ashore on Red Three crossed over to Red Two and supported 2/2 as it advanced toward the runway of the airfield. The tanks rolled up to the openings of the Japanese pillboxes and fired their 75mm main gun into them at point-blank range. Two of the tanks were knocked out, but one of these was retrieved on the morning of D+1.[33] Artillery arriving on Red Two was originally meant for Red One. Lieutenant Colonel Presley M. Rixey was the commander of this artillery, 1st Battalion 10th Marines (1/10). As a member of Shoup's CP group, Rixey had landed before noon while his 75mm pack howitzers and their crews awaited further orders at the line of departure. Shoup and Rixey decided that Red One was too hot a beach for landing artillery, so they ordered the guns ashore on Red Two. One section from Battery A and one from Battery B were transferred to LVTs for a dusk landing. Three sections from Battery C were also ordered to land, but they had not transferred to LVTs and had to make the trip to the beach in LCVPs. When their landing craft hit the reef, the gun crews had to wade ashore along the side of the pier loaded down with their dismantled pack howitzers, the largest element of which weighed 225 pounds. Not reaching shore until after dark, the five sections of 1/10 had to wait until dawn to get into position and to contribute to the battle.[34]

Elements of Major Crowe's 2/8 penetrated all the way to the interior of the triangle formed by the island's runway and taxi strip after coming ashore over Red Three. His men encountered a Japanese strongpoint on their left flank, located at the base of the pier. Seventy Marines from 3/8 were sent into the triangle to hold that section of the line. A group of Marines from various battalions were found to be taking shelter under the pier. Their weapons had been either lost or ruined by immersion in saltwater. These Marines were led ashore, rearmed, and sent into battle on 2/8's left flank.[35] Major Crowe's men attempted throughout D-day to

---

[32] Ibid., pp. 64–65.

[33] Ibid., p. 65.

[34] Ibid.; Stockman, *The Battle for Tarawa,* pp. 27–28; Alexander, *Utmost Savagery,* p. 15.

[35] Shaw et al., *Central Pacific Drive,* p. 65.

advance beyond the fortifications just inland of the pier. Once past these fortifications, the battalion was to turn eastward and attack along the narrowing "tail" of the island. Crowe used four medium tanks to support his advance, but the Japanese positions were too strong. Enemy gunners disabled one tank, another was accidentally destroyed by an American dive bomber, and a third was destroyed when it drove into an excavation used by the Japanese as a fuel dump. Only one tank was able to contribute to the fight for long, even though an enemy shell damaged it during the course of the battle.[36]

The landing of 3/8 left Julian Smith with only one landing team in reserve, 1st Battalion 8th Marines. If he committed 1/8 to the battle, the only units he would have left in reserve would be elements of the 10th Marines (artillery), the 18th Marines (engineers), division Special Troops, and Service Troops.[37] He decided that he had no choice but to commit 1/8, so he requested that the 6th Marines be withdrawn from corps reserve and given over to his command. Admiral Hill concurred with his decision. He contacted V Amphibious Corps commander Major General Holland M. Smith at 13.31 with the request and approval was received within the hour from Assault Force Commander Rear Admiral Richmond Kelly Turner. While awaiting word from the corps commander, Julian Smith began making plans for assembling his support group into provisional battalions for use ashore.[38]

At 13.43 division command ordered Colonel Elmer E. Hall, CO of the Eighth Marines, to proceed with his Regimental Headquarters and his remaining landing team, 1/8 under the command of Major Lawrence C. Hays, Jr., to the line of departure and await further orders. Julian Smith asked Colonel Shoup where best to land 1/8, but the commander of the Second Marines did not receive the message. Hall's HQ and 1/8 remained at the line of departure throughout the afternoon of D-day waiting for Shoup's instructions. Finally, at 16.25, Julian Smith ordered Hall to land on the north shore of the most eastern end of Betio at 17.45. The landing team was then to attack to the northwest in support of 2/8's and 3/8's battle on Red Three. Like Shoup, however, Hall did not receive these orders. Division command did not discover until midnight that Hall and his men were still afloat at the line of departure awaiting word to go ashore.[39]

At 12.30, Colonel Shoup sent Lieutenant Colonel Evans F. Carlson off to *Maryland* in order to inform Julian Smith of CT 2's plan for the conquest of Betio. Carlson had been assigned as an observer for Operation Galvanic and he had been present with Shoup all morning long. Balky communications made it necessary

---

[36] Ibid., pp. 65–66.

[37] Ibid., p. 66.

[38] Ibid., p. 65.

[39] Ibid., pp. 66–67.

for the combat team commander to send Carlson as a messenger. Shoup's plan was to attack southward, unite the beachheads, and then make one last advance to take the island. He instructed Carlson to inform division command of this plan and to tell them that reserves needed to be landed on Red Two to support this effort. As the two men parted, Shoup told Carlson "You tell the general and the admiral that we are going to stick and fight it out."[40] Carlson reported to General Smith aboard *Maryland* at 18.00. After leaving Shoup at approximately 12.30, he had spent time shuttling several LVT-loads of Marines to the island and returning with casualties who were put aboard LCVPs at the reef and then taken back to waiting transports. The combat team commander knew of Carlson's actions and approved them. When this work was completed, Carlson left his LVT at the reef and boarded an LCVP for transport to *Maryland*.[41]

Division command informed Assistant Division Commander Brigadier General Leo D. Hermle, on board the USS *Monrovia* (APA-31), early in the afternoon of D-day that he needed to prepare his CP group for landing. At 13.43, Hermle was ordered to go to the end of the central pier, determine how the operation was progressing, and then to report back to Julian Smith. Hermle attempted to raise Shoup on the radio as he approached the pier, trying to determine the location of CT 2's command post, but he was unsuccessful. At 17.40, he reported reaching the pier and that he was under heavy fire. His attempts to radio reports of the action ashore to division command, however, were thwarted by the aggravating communications failures that continued to plague the Tarawa operation.[42] Hermle was able, nonetheless, to establish intermittent radio contact with Shoup and Crowe from his position at the pier. He was informed that the Marines ashore desperately needed water and ammunition. Enough men were available in the immediate vicinity of Hermle's position, members of 3/8 who had gathered under the pier for protection, for the general to organize parties for carrying supplies inland. Tenuous to begin with, his radio link with the embattled commanders ashore failed at approximately 19.30.[43]

Hermle needed to locate Shoup's command post and he also needed to know where the combat team commander wanted to land the reserves, so at 19.30 he sent Major Rathvon McClure Tompkins and Captain Thomas C. Dutton to track down Shoup and his command group. Tompkins and Dutton made it to Shoup, found out the information, and finally made it back to Hermle to report their findings at 03.45. The general could not relay this information to Julian Smith because of communications problems, however, so he and his party went back into the

[40] Ibid., p. 67; quote from same source.

[41] Ibid., pp. 67–68.

[42] Stockman, *The Battle for Tarawa*, p. 25; Shaw et al., *Central Pacific Drive*, p. 68.

[43] Stockman, *The Battle for Tarawa*, p. 26; Shaw et al., *Central Pacific Drive*, p. 68.

lagoon and boarded *Ringgold* to use her radio. Word that Shoup wanted Major Hays' 1/8 landed near the central pier on Red Two was radioed to *Maryland* at 04.45.[44] At 05.10 Hermle radioed Shoup informing him of the recommendations he had made to division. A few minutes later Hermle received instructions from Julian Smith that he was to remain aboard *Ringgold* and to come aboard *Maryland* when the destroyer reached her. When he arrived, Hermle was informed that the division commander had radioed an order to him at 17.50 instructing him to take command of the troops ashore and to report when he had established his command post. Hermle had not received the message—the victim of another communications failure—and Colonel Shoup remained in command of operations on Betio for another day.[45]

Strategic and Operational Objectives for Galvanic

Admiral Ernest J. King, Commander-in-Chief of the United States Fleet (Cominch) and Chief of Naval Operations (CNO), succinctly presented the orthodox explanation for why the Gilbert Islands were assaulted by the United States in November of 1943 in his first report on the conduct of the war to Frank Knox, Secretary of the Navy, dated 27 March 1944: "The Gilbert Islands are a group of coral atolls lying athwart the equator. They had been held by the British up to the outbreak of war in December 1941, when they were seized by the Japanese. Their location is of great strategic significance because they are north and west of other islands in our possession and immediately south and east of important Japanese bases in the Carolines and Marshalls. The capture of the Gilberts was, therefore, a necessary part of any serious thrust at the Japanese Empire."[46] The connection between the Gilberts and the Marshalls was not as obvious to American planners during early 1943 as King's statement would make it appear, however. The road to Tarawa was a convoluted one, and no one knew that better than King himself.

Two of the first questions military planners have to ask themselves after a basic strategy has been ironed out are what are the necessary objectives for the carrying out of the strategy and what is the nature of each of those objectives. The nature of an objective includes its location and basic geography. The Gilbert Islands are situated between 03°30' N 173°00' E and 03°00' S 177°00' W, which places them approximately 2,400 miles southwest of Hawaii and 2,800 miles northeast of Australia. The Japanese occupied Tarawa Atoll, the principal objective in Operation Galvanic, on 24 December 1941. Its location, 1°30' N 173°00' E, is approximately

---

[44] Shaw et al., *Central Pacific Drive,* p. 68.

[45] Stockman, *The Battle for Tarawa,* p. 26.

[46] Ernest J. King, *U.S. Navy at War, 1941–1945: Official Reports to the Secretary of the Navy by Fleet Admiral Ernest J. King, U.S. Navy* (Washington, DC: United States Navy Department, 1946), p. 71.

2,390 miles southwest of Pearl Harbor. A coral atoll that is triangular in shape, its eighteen-mile-long northeastern side is oriented northwest to southeast and is composed of forty-two islands and islets. Its base, to the south, is twelve miles long, composed of five islands and runs roughly east to west. The northwest side of the lagoon is 12½ miles wide and is not bounded by islands, but it is protected by a submerged reef that has only a single one-mile-wide gap located 3½ miles north of Betio Island. The main objective for the assault of Tarawa, Betio is a coral sand island that is 800 yards wide at its west end. It tapers to a point over a length of approximately 3,800 yards. These dimensions give it an area of 291 acres, equal to approximately one-third of New York City's Central Park.[47] How did this insignificant little speck in the far-flung reaches of the Pacific Ocean come to garner so much attention from the American Joint Chiefs and the United States Navy and Marine Corps? To understand the process whereby their attention came to be focused on such a miniscule objective one must look back beyond the point King, in his letter to Knox, indicates as the beginning. One must, in fact, go back to the earliest years of the 20th century.

The military establishment of the United States is given a number of responsibilities during peacetime. One of the most important of these responsibilities is the development of contingency plans that are to be implemented when the use of military force is deemed necessary by the civilian authorities. The famous Orange plans of the period 1906–1939 are examples of such planning by the United States armed forces. "Orange" was the codename for the possible enemy against whom the plan was to be used. That possible enemy, in this case, was Japan. At the heart of most of the Navy's versions of the various Orange War Plans was a thrust across the Central Pacific through two island groups of the Japanese Mandate: the Marshalls and the Carolines. Use of the British-owned Gilberts as a staging area for such a movement into the Mandate was suggested and discussed from time to time, but the perceived strategic and tactical realities dictated by an Orange war always argued against their use. The idea, accordingly, was dropped each time. It was not until mid-1941, when Franklin D. Roosevelt became interested in entering into a Lend-Lease arrangement that allowed the United States to use British Central and South Pacific islands as bases, that the possibility of going at the Marshalls from the Gilberts once again became an item for discussion.[48] In addition to

[47] Gordon L. Rottman, *World War II Pacific Island Guide: A Geo-Military Study* (Westport, CT: Greenwood Press, 2002), pp. 332–34.

[48] Edward S. Miller, *War Plan Orange: The U.S. Strategy to Defeat Japan, 1897–1945* (Annapolis: Naval Institute Press, 1991), pp. 105 and 247. The Navy's version of War Plan Orange went through several evolutions from the time it was first conceived until it was disestablished as a possible national war plan in July of 1941. The chief identifying characteristic of Orange was that it was offensive in nature. There were at times two competing basic plans, one calling for a quick thrust, usually to rescue American forces besieged in the Philippines,

Roosevelt's interest, some of the staff members of the Navy War Plans Division (Op-12) in May of 1941 considered using the idea of possible operations in the Gilberts as a lure to lead the aggressive newly-appointed Commander-in-Chief of the Pacific Fleet (CinCPac), Admiral Husband E. Kimmel, away from his insistence on operating the fleet in the dangerous Wake-Eniwetok region. The lure did not work, so the idea of operations from or through the Gilberts was once again dropped.[49]

After 7 December, as the Japanese ran the United States and her Allies out of one position after another in Asia and the Pacific, the production of viable plans for a war with Japan began in earnest. Admiral King believed that the three primary objectives for the United States during this early stage of the war were: first, to secure and hold the Hawaiian Islands; second, to support Australia and New Zealand (King's term was "Australasia"); and third, to advance northwestward into Japanese-held territory from bases in the New Hebrides.[50] The staff of Op-12, with King's objectives in mind, prepared an outline of a campaign against Japan and presented it to him in mid-April 1942. The plan depicted an advance against Japan in four stages:

> (a) *First Stage,* in which we are now engaged, envisages building up forces and positions in the Pacific Theater and particularly in the South Pacific and Southwest Pacific for the purpose of holding these areas, and in preparation for launching an ultimate offensive against the Japanese; and for supporting the fleet forces operating there. During this stage the amphibious forces necessary to carry

---

followed by attacks on Japan, the other calling for a longer, step-by-step movement across the Pacific, rolling the Japanese back as the American Pacific Fleet captured advanced bases and projected its power all the way to the shores of the Home Islands. It was the second of these iterations that eventually provided the theoretical framework for the Navy's Central Pacific Campaign during World War II, proving that the basic plan was viable. See Miller, *War Plan Orange,* chapters 8–23 and 28–30.

[49] Ibid., pp. 247–48. Miller, in chapter 21, discusses the argument within the pre-war United States Navy over the importance of Wake Island. Concomitant with this argument was a disagreement over whether a possible Orange war should be prosecuted along a northern route, through the northern part of the Mandate, or a southern route. Wake was important in the northern route strategy. Kimmel was one of those who believed in the northern route. He insisted on operating the Pacific Fleet in the area near Wake, which the U.S. controlled, and Eniwetok, which was part of the Japanese mandate. Operations in those waters were considered to be too provocative toward the Japanese by the more cautious proponents of the southern route strategy, hence the reason for the attempt to lure Kimmel away from Wake.

[50] Grace Person Hayes, *The History of the Joint Chiefs of Staff in World War II: The War Against Japan* (Annapolis: Naval Institute Press, 1982), p. 138.

> on this offensive will be assembled in the areas and trained; . . . available air, amphibious and naval forces will take minor offensive action against enemy advanced positions and against exposed enemy naval forces for purposes of attrition. . . .
>
> (b) The *Second Stage* as now envisaged involves a combined offensive by United States, New Zealand and Australian amphibious naval and air forces through the Solomons and New Guinea to capture the Bismarck Archipelago and the Admiralty Islands. Heavy attrition attacks would then be undertaken against the enemy forces and positions in the Caroline and Marshall Islands.
>
> (c) The *Third Stage* involves seizure of the Caroline and Marshall Islands and the establishment there of Fleet and air advanced bases.
>
> (d) The *Fourth Stage* involves an advance into the Netherlands East Indies or, alternatively, into the Philippines whichever offers the more promising and enduring results.[51]

Stage Three reflected the Orange plans' Central Pacific agenda. It once again neglected the Gilberts in favor of a thrust directly into the Mandates, but King took out some insurance just in case a bold thrust proved to be unworkable. During the same month in which the Op-12 plan was brought to him for approval, he requested the British government's permission to occupy any British or Dominion islands in the Pacific as might be required in the course of the war. He made this request through Field Marshal Sir John Dill, the head of the British liaison delegation in Washington. This "blanket authority," as it is described in memos exchanged between King and Dill, cleared the way for current Navy planners to entertain other options in addition to those already contemplated by their predecessors.[52]

The next step along the path to Galvanic was taken at the Casablanca Conference in January 1943. In meetings between the United States Joint Chiefs of Staff and the British Imperial Chiefs of Staff from late 1941 to early 1943, the two groups found that they had different opinions as to the relationship between the European and Pacific components of the war. The American Joint Chiefs were dedicated to the Arcadia resolution to make Germany the first priority in the war, but Admiral King was especially insistent that the Pacific not become a forgotten backwater area during the buildup to the anticipated invasion of continental Europe. King was adamant that the Japanese should not be allowed to consolidate their positions nor, most importantly, should they be allowed to initiate any significant offensive action against the Allies. The American and British planners at Casablanca disagreed as to exactly how such an objective should be met and the Americans became very

[51] Quoted in Hayes, *History of the JCS in WWII*, p. 139, italics in original.

[52] Hayes, *History of the JCS in WWII*, p. 139.

frustrated with what some of them saw as British intransigence. Finally, the U.S. Joint Staff Planners (JPS) drew up a study that sketched their overall plan for Pacific operations in 1943 and they began to circulate this study, under the title CCS 153, among both the Combined Chiefs and their planning staffs after 15 January. Enclosure B of the study dealt with projected operations in Burma, operations with which the British would have to be involved. Given the fact that they would have to supply men and materiel in Burma, thus taking away from commitments in both Europe and the Mediterranean, the British disagreed with the plan put forward in Enclosure B.[53]

Enclosure A, on the other hand, did not cause them as much immediate anxiety. It dealt with the Pacific, an area the Americans tended to view as the responsibility of the United States alone. Knowing that the British were ever skittish as to American intentions, the JPS grounded "A" on four specified assumptions:

> . . . that the ultimate objective of the basic global strategy is to bring the war to a successful conclusion at the earliest practicable date, that in gaining this objective efforts must be made toward the destruction of the economic and military power of all our adversaries at a rate exceeding their power of replacement, that Germany is recognized as the primary, or most powerful and pressing enemy, and that the major portion of the forces of the United Nations are to be directed against Germany insofar as it is consistent with the overall objective of bringing the war to an early conclusion at the earliest possible date.[54]

These assumptions made it clear that America still considered Germany the main enemy, but they also served notice to the British that such a determination was not the only factor to consider. The ultimate goal for the Americans was to bring the entire war to a close at the earliest practicable date. They did not believe that leaving the Japanese alone in order to concentrate solely on Germany would accomplish that goal. Japan had to be contained and controlled, but within the limits set by the "Germany first" agreement.

With what they saw as the ultimate goal in mind, then, the JPS suggested that the Allies undertake the following operations in the Pacific: "(a) Seizure and consolidation of United Nations forces in the Solomon Islands, Eastern New Guinea up to Lae Salamaua peninsula, New Britain-New Ireland (Rabaul) area; (b) Seizure and occupation of Kiska-Agattu (Western Aleutians); (c) Seizure and occupation

---

[53] Ibid., pp. 283–84.

[54] CCS 153 (Revised), included in the collection *World War II Inter-Allied Conferences,* Casablanca Conference, Vol. 1; Casablanca, Morocco, 14–23 January 1943 (Washington, DC: Joint History Office, 2003) (hereinafter Casablanca Conference Papers), pp. 4–5; quoted and discussed in Hayes, *History of the JCS in WWII,* p. 284.

of Gilbert Islands, Marshall Islands, Caroline Islands, up to and including Truk. It is planned that these operations will be undertaken subsequent to Rabaul; (d) Extension of occupation of New Guinea up to approximately the Dutch border. This will be an extension of the Truk campaign for the second part."[55]

After much discussion and argument amongst themselves over several days, the Joint Chiefs of Staff prepared a basic plan for the conduct of operations in the Pacific in 1943 that was based on the JPS suggestions. In general, the Allies could:

(a) Keep Japan from further expansion, and from consolidating and exploiting her current holdings.
(b) Maintain the vital Midway–Hawaii line (key to New Zealand).
(c) Secure the line of communications to Australia and New Zealand.
(d) Block enemy approaches to Australia: (1) from the Northward via Rabaul; (2) from the Northwestward via the Malay barrier.
(e) Attain positions which menace enemy line of communication with the Dutch East Indies, the Philippines, and the South China Sea.
(f) Open the line of communications with China via Burma—in order to make use of Chinese geographical position (as to attack enemy line of communication in Formosa Straits and along the coast of China, perhaps to bomb Japan).
(g) Make ready to support Russia in case of war with Japan.
(h) Continue and intensify attrition of enemy strength by land, air, and sea (including submarine) action.[56]

The paper also listed seven different offensives the Japanese could undertake during 1943 and counterbalanced each, point by point, with possible Allied offensives. Possibility number three could be an attack against the Midway–Hawaii line. The Japanese had already tried to do this in June of 1942 and had failed, but that did not mean that they might not try it again. The reverse offensive for the United States would be against the Truk–Guam line via Wake and the northwest Marshall Islands. Such an attack would be very useful because it would allow the Americans to retain the initiative, it would help prevent the possible Japanese offensive, and it would draw enemy forces away from the Rabaul area. The fourth possible Japanese offensive could be an attack against the Hawaii–Samoa–Fiji–New Caledonia line. Such an attack would endanger the line of communications to Australia and New

[55] CCS 153 (Revised), pp. 6–7; quoted and discussed in Hayes, *History of the JCS in WWII*, pp. 284–85.

[56] CCS 168, included in Casablanca Conference Papers, pp. 95–96; quoted and discussed in Hayes, *History of the JCS in WWII*, pp. 299–300.

Zealand and, as such, had to be countered. The Solomons campaign that began in August 1942 made such an offensive unprofitable for the Japanese except by way of the Gilbert and Ellice Islands toward Samoa. To oppose such a move, the Allies would need to advance on the Samoa–Jaluit line via the Gilbert and Ellice Islands. A successful offensive from the Gilberts in the direction of the Marshalls would secure the line of communications to Australia and New Zealand and would also draw Japanese forces away from Rabaul. Admiral King explained the Joint Chiefs' plan to the Combined Chiefs of Staff on 22 January and it was included in the final report sent for approval to President Roosevelt and Prime Minister Churchill. The two leaders signed the report on 23 January and the Casablanca Conference came to an end.[57]

King, once back in the States, tried to get moving on the Casablanca Conference's allowance for an advance into the Gilberts. He sent a request to Commander-in-Chief of the Pacific Fleet and Pacific Ocean Areas Admiral Chester W. Nimitz (CinCPac and CinCPOA) and Commander of the South Pacific Area Admiral William F. Halsey on 9 February for comments concerning operations in the Gilbert and Ellice Islands. Both men begged off attacking the Gilberts in early 1943, mostly because the United States had not built up enough forces in the Pacific at that time to undertake such a major operation.[58] Later, on 21–23 February, King met with Nimitz in San Francisco for one of their periodic conferences concerning the war in the Pacific. King asked his Pacific Fleet commander if he thought that the Japanese would attack Samoa from the Gilberts by way of the Ellices and, before Nimitz could really answer, he suggested that CinCPac could check this threat by going ahead and taking the Gilberts before the Japanese had a chance to mount an offensive from them. Nimitz once again countered King's suggestion by saying that the United States was not in a position as of yet to mount a full-scale offensive against the Japanese in the Central Pacific. Besides, he could not hold the Gilberts at that point, even if he could take them away from the Japanese, because they were within range of enemy land-based aircraft flying out of the Marshalls. Nimitz then reminded King that he had landed Marines on Funafuti Atoll in the Ellices and was building an airstrip there to block just the type of move by the Japanese that concerned the Joint Chiefs. King reluctantly agreed that the time was not ripe for beginning the Central Pacific Campaign, but he stressed to Nimitz the importance of keeping the initiative against the Japanese and that the forces allocated by the Combined Chiefs to the Pacific had to be used in order to justify their allocation.[59]

---

[57] Hayes, *History of the JCS in WWII*, pp. 300–01.

[58] Ibid., pp. 310–11.

[59] E. B. Potter, *Nimitz* (Annapolis: Naval Institute Press, 1976), p. 237; Ernest J. King and Walter Muir Whitehill, *Fleet Admiral King: A Naval Record* (New York: W. W. Norton, 1952; reprint, New York: Da Capo Press, 1976), pp. 430–32 (page citations in the present volume are to the reprint edition).

That was where the question of the Gilberts stood until the Pacific Military Conference that was held in Washington, DC, over 12–28 March 1943. One point of discussion at that conference concerned what to do about South Pacific naval assets while General MacArthur's forces in the Southwest Pacific were securing the Huon Peninsula on New Guinea. On 21 March, Admiral King suggested during a meeting of the Joint Chiefs of Staff that ran concurrently with the conference that these naval assets be used somewhere else rather than being made to sit around until MacArthur could complete his operation against Huon. His suggestion was to use them against the Gilberts and Marshalls. Nimitz's representatives at the conference, led by Rear Admiral Raymond A. Spruance who was CinCPac's Chief of Staff at the time, stated that the Pacific Fleet commander wanted first to make sure that Hawaii was secure before beginning any operations in the Central Pacific. To that end, Spruance suggested, part of the fleet in the South Pacific should be brought back into Hawaiian waters. Nimitz, Spruance went on, wanted to take both the Gilberts and the Marshalls eventually in order to remove the threat from Hawaii, but operations against both island groups would prove unprofitable unless they were continuous. Neither Spruance nor Nimitz believed that forces on hand in the Pacific as of March 1943 could sustain such operations.[60]

The Joint Chiefs continued to ponder the question of what would be the best course of action in Nimitz's theater even after the Pacific Military Conference ended. Also, the Chiefs stepped up efforts to send as many troops and as much materiel to the Pacific as the "Germany first" commitment would allow. The Joint War Plans Committee (JWPC) ordered its Rainbow Team of planners to prepare "an outline plan for advancing into the MARSHALLS, a study of the requirements for the operations recommended, and recommended target dates for initiating the operations." The Rainbow Team's report was sent to the Joint Staff Planners on 10 June 1943 with the caveat that no specific operations should be undertaken until the effect of each of them on all other operations was considered. Regarding approaching the Marshalls through the Gilberts, the Rainbow Team suggested that to do so would alert the Japanese before the main blow against the Marshalls could be landed. Alerting the enemy would allow him to disperse his aircraft over a wide area, providing him with a defense in depth while U.S. forces were in a strategically weak position. Therefore, attacking the Gilberts first was not a good idea.[61]

The Joint Staff Planners took the Rainbow Team's recommendations under advisement. The latter's opinion concerning the Gilberts did not upset anyone too badly—no one, least of all the Army, wanted to invade the Gilberts unless such an

---

[60] Hayes, *History of the JCS in WWII*, pp. 327–28; Thomas B. Buell, *The Quiet Warrior: A Biography of Admiral Raymond A. Spruance* (Boston: Little, Brown, 1974; reprint, Annapolis: Naval Institute Press, 1987), pp. 177–78 (page citations in the present volume are to the reprint edition).

[61] Hayes, *History of the JCS in WWII*, p. 416.

action was absolutely necessary. The preferred plan for taking the Marshalls, dubbed "Plan A," continued to be a direct assault on Kwajalein, Wotje, and Maloelap. The Joint War Plans Committee, nevertheless, presented an alternate "Plan B" on 18 June. The JWPC recommended in this alternate plan—despite the Rainbow Team's warnings to the contrary—that American forces advance toward the Marshalls from the south through the Gilberts if adequate forces could not be found to carry out Plan A. The first assaults would be against Tarawa Atoll and Nauru, an island 380 miles to the southwest of Tarawa and not a part of the Gilberts chain. The planners did stress, however, that this alternative was "definitely inferior to the MARSHALLS operation," referring to the preferred assault on Kwajalein-Wotje-Maloelap. The Joint Chiefs of Staff liked the idea of boldly thrusting into the heart of the Marshalls and, having determined by this time that a two-pronged approach—through the Central Pacific under Nimitz and from the Southwest Pacific under MacArthur—was the best strategy for the war against Japan, they sent Nimitz orders to implement the preferred plan with a target date of 15 November 1943.[62]

Resources and Plans for the Assault of Tarawa

Nimitz got to work producing detailed plans for the implementation of the JCS directive. Spruance had reservations about the Joint Chiefs' conception of the proposed operation, however, and he immediately raised questions about a number of its particulars. These questions led him to conclusions similar to those reached by the Joint Staff Planners. As the Chief of Staff studied the situation more and more closely he determined that the preferred plan was unworkable. He believed that the North African and Solomons campaigns demonstrated conclusively that accurate aerial reconnaissance was absolutely necessary to ensure success in amphibious operations. Such reconnaissance could not be made of the Marshalls in 1943, however, because the United States did not possess airfields close enough to the target islands from which the reconnaissance could be staged. Carrier-based planes could not carry cameras that were capable of providing the needed coverage or the necessary photographic detail at that point in the war, so Spruance concluded that a preliminary operation needed to be inserted in the JCS's plan. In his opinion, that preliminary operation should target the Gilbert Islands. Thomas Buell, in his biography of Spruance, provides an interesting synopsis of the reasoning his subject followed in choosing to suggest a course of action that was at odds with the Joint Chiefs' directive:

> American aircraft would reconnoiter the Gilberts from airfields in the Ellice and Phoenix islands, less than a thousand miles to the east-southeast of the Gilberts.

---

[62] Hayes, *History of the JCS in WWII,* pp. 421–24; Buell, *Quiet Warrior,* p. 180.

> Land-based aircraft on these same islands could provide air support to the amphibious assault troops, and air reinforcements could be provided from air bases in the Hawaiian Islands and the South Pacific.
>
> The Gilberts would provide experience for later assaults in the Marshalls. Spruance dreaded using inexperienced troops in a major operation against the heavily defended Marshall Islands. Instead he wanted an objective that was tough enough to try the Americans but not so tough that they would suffer heavy losses—or perhaps even lose the battle. Thus the Gilberts would be a "training ground" in preparation for the greater battles to come.
>
> Most important, the physical objectives had to be strategically valuable. The Gilberts fit the bill by providing bases for an assault against the Marshalls, the ultimate objective. Gilbert airfields would provide both air reconnaissance and air support; Gilbert lagoons would provide the fleet anchorages; Hawaii-South Pacific lines of communication, passing nearby, would be strengthened and improved.[63]

Nimitz did not agree with Spruance at first, but the logic of his Chief of Staff's idea became clearer as the difficulties inherent in carrying out the JCS plan became more and more obvious. He requested a change of objectives in mid-July and the Joint Chiefs sent back their approval on 20 July 1943. The name given to the new "preliminary" operation was Galvanic and its target date was the date originally set for the beginning of the Marshalls operation, 15 November.[64]

Nimitz had not wasted time during the first half of 1943 while waiting for the Chiefs to make up their collective mind concerning overall strategy. He was reasonably sure by early spring that his superiors would authorize him to begin operations in the Central Pacific in the near future and that, along with their authorization, would come many new ships to strengthen the Pacific Fleet. With these possibilities in mind, then, he began to consider whom to name as commander of the striking arm of this expanding armada. The man he chose was Rear Admiral Raymond A. Spruance. Spruance had already proved himself as a sea-going commander in the Battle of Midway in June of 1942 and had earned Nimitz's personal respect while in his present position at CinCPOA headquarters. Nimitz believed that Spruance was fully capable of taking on major command responsibilities, and the newly-created

[63] Buell, *Quiet Warrior*, pp. 181–82.

[64] Ibid., p. 182; Galvanic was the codename for the overall Gilberts operation. The assault of Tarawa was given the codename Longsuit, but usage over time has gravitated to using Galvanic in reference to Tarawa as well as the Gilberts operation in general. See usage in NARA, RG 127, USMC Geographic Files, Box 29, File A7–19, 2nd Marine Division, Report of Operations, Galvanic, Tarawa, Second Marine Division, Report on Gilbert Islands—Tarawa Operation, 23 December 1943, p. 1.

Central Pacific Force (eventually renamed the Fifth Fleet) would give Spruance the chance to demonstrate to others that this belief was not misplaced.[65] With the additional responsibilities came a promotion to Vice Admiral, and Spruance sat down in mid-June to consider who he wanted on his command team. Having no amphibious experience himself, he needed someone proficient in the practical aspects of amphibious warfare to organize and direct the most important component of a naval force whose job was to project power from the sea onto land. The man he chose for the job was Rear Admiral Richmond Kelly Turner. Turner was an old friend who had left the position of head of Op-12 in the spring of 1942 to take command of amphibious forces in the South Pacific. With that experience under his belt, Spruance believed him to be the right man for the job. An irascible perfectionist and a workaholic, Turner began to whip his new command into shape once it was established on 24 August 1943.[66]

Spruance then had to determine who he wanted as commander of his landing force. The Navy wanted the Marine Corps to provide the majority of troops in the Central Pacific Campaign, so Spruance believed that a Marine general officer was the logical choice for this command. He had first met Marine Major General Holland M. Smith at Culebra in the Caribbean in early 1941 when Smith, as a Brigadier General, was the commander of Marines in the Atlantic Fleet under then-Rear Admiral Ernest J. King. Spruance was very impressed with Smith at that time. The two men met occasionally during the early course of the war and Spruance, when he began to contemplate the ground forces command question, had only one man in mind for the job. Smith was just as passionate about amphibious perfection as was Turner. He was also exceptionally prickly when it came to the subject of Navy-Marine Corps relations. Smith and Turner would have to work together closely in planning and carrying out each and every Central Pacific operation involving the Fifth Fleet. Their strong personalities clashed often, sometimes violently, but, as Smith later wrote, " . . . our partnership, though stormy, spelled hell in big red letters to the Japanese." Smith eventually established his command, composed of the Second Marine Division and part of the 27th Infantry Division along with various reinforcing elements, on 4 September 1943 under the title V Amphibious Corps.[67]

---

[65] Ibid., pp. 167–85; according to Buell, *Quiet Warrior,* p. 188, the ships were designated "Fifth Fleet" at this time while all the manpower and related assets under Spruance's command—Navy, Marine Corps, and Army—were designated "Central Pacific Force" collectively. In 1944, dropping the latter title and referring to the entire command simply as the "Fifth Fleet" simplified this arrangement.

[66] Shaw et al., *Central Pacific Drive,* p. 25.

[67] Ibid.; Buell, *Quiet Warrior,* pp. 95–96; quote from Holland M. Smith and Percy Finch, *Coral and Brass,* (New York: Charles Scribner's Sons, 1948; reprint New York: Bantam Books, 1987), p. 102 (page citations in the present volume are to this reprint edition).

The command structure and the list of objectives underwent a number of changes during the early planning stages of the operation. Problems encountered at Guadalcanal had led to a doctrinal change concerning the relationship between the commander of the naval assault forces and the commander of the landing force in an amphibious operation. These changes had been adopted and promulgated prior to the point at which planning for Galvanic began. Spruance's staff, however, chose not to take cognizance of them. This apparent neglect of doctrinal change provided Holland Smith with a nasty surprise upon his reporting for duty as V Amphibious Corps commander. He found that he had been placed in a subordinate position to Turner in every respect within Spruance's command structure. Smith, after vociferously stating his displeasure with this arrangement, was able to prompt Spruance to reconsider. Turner remained the top amphibious commander during training and during the approach to the beach, but Smith would be Turner's equal in the echelon of command during the planning phase of the operation and once the troops had been lodged ashore.[68]

The new landing force commander also argued for a change in one of the objectives. He suggested the substitution of Makin Atoll in the Gilberts group for Nauru Island. The hydrographic and terrain features of Nauru, not to mention its strong defenses and distance from the primary target at Tarawa, made taking the island a foreboding proposition in Smith's estimation. Also, he did not believe that V Amphibious Force had access to enough assets at the time to boat and transport the two reinforced divisions along with the necessary garrison and construction echelons that would be necessary to carry out simultaneous but essentially disconnected assault landings against two well-defended islands. He did believe, however, that there were enough assets on hand for the Second Marine Division (reinforced) to assault Betio Island in Tarawa Atoll and for the 165th Regimental Combat Team (RCT) of the 27th Infantry Division to assault the lesser target of Butaritari Island in Makin Atoll at the same time. He found both Turner and Spruance surprisingly sympathetic to his concerns, Spruance himself already having entertained doubts as to the strategic sense of attacking two such widely separated objectives simultaneously. Nimitz was reluctant to bring up the suggested change with King in their 25 September meeting in Honolulu, but Cominch, after some discussion, agreed to the exchange. Nimitz, taking action upon this reorientation of objectives, set the date for the landings as 19 November 1943. A month later, he postponed the landings to 20 November in order to make sure that a sufficient force of carriers would be available and present.[69] Julian Smith, commanding general of the Second Marine Division, was alerted in August of 1943 that his unit would be part of the Gilberts offensive. The division, which had been participating in the mopping up of Guadalcanal, was transferred from I Amphibious Corps to

[68] Isely and Crowl, *U.S. Marines and Amphibious War*, p. 202.

[69] Ibid., p. 203; Buell, *Quiet Warrior*, pp. 197–98; Potter, *Nimitz*, pp. 253, 255.

V Amphibious Corps in mid-September. Julian Smith and his staff conferred with Holland Smith at Pearl Harbor in early October and then established a liaison between their respective headquarters.[70]

Julian Smith had to overcome a very difficult command problem early on as he worked to prepare his division for the upcoming assault. The commander of the Second Marines, Colonel William M. Marshall, either suffered a nervous breakdown during the rehearsal for the operation or developed a very bad working relationship with Smith and his Chief of Staff Colonel Merritt A. Edson. Either way, Marshall had to be replaced. Though not an insurmountable setback, a change of command at that level at such a critical time was definitely problematic. Fortunately for Smith and the division there was someone who would prove to be a more than adequate replacement. Lieutenant Colonel David M. Shoup had helped to plan the assault in his capacity as Second Marine Division Operations Officer. Julian Smith summarily promoted Shoup to Colonel and gave him the job of putting his own plan into action.[71] The plan called for the landing of three Battalion Landing Teams (BLTs) abreast while holding one BLT in reserve. The beach was divided up into sections, west to east, and the assault of each section was the responsibility of a given BLT. Beach Red One, the farthest west, was the responsibility of Major John F. Schoettel's 3rd Battalion 2nd Marines, while Beach Red Two, the center section, was to be taken by Lieutenant Colonel Herbert R. Amey's 2nd Battalion 2nd Marines. The job of assaulting the section farthest to the east, Beach Red Three, was given to Major Henry P. Crowe's 2nd Battalion 8th Marines. The 1st Battalion 2nd Marines, Major Wood B. Kyle commanding, was held back as regimental reserve.[72] Shoup's Second Marines were reinforced with medium tanks from Company C of I Marine Amphibious Corps (IMAC) Tank Battalion, a special weapons group from the 2nd Marine Defense Battalion, various combat and shore party engineers, eight shore fire control and air liaison parties, various medical and service units, and one battalion of 75mm pack howitzers.[73]

The Eighth Marines were to act as division reserve at Tarawa, but siphoning off its 2nd Battalion to strengthen the Second Marines in assault left Julian Smith with only two battalions to fall back on in case of trouble.[74] What is worse, the division itself had already been weakened as a result of the decision by Holland Smith to

[70] Isely and Crowl, *U.S. Marines and Amphibious War,* p. 204.

[71] Alexander, *Utmost Savagery,* p. 102; Howard Jablon, *David M. Shoup: A Warrior against War* (Lanham, MD: Rowman and Littlefield, 2005), pp. 41–42.

[72] Alexander, *Utmost Savagery,* p. 3.

[73] Isely and Crowl, *U.S. Marines and Amphibious War,* p. 206; Shaw et al., *Central Pacific Drive,* p. 64.

[74] Isely and Crowl, *U.S. Marines and Amphibious War,* p. 206.

use the Sixth Marines (reinforced) as his corps reserve for the entire Galvanic operation. This decision decreased the potential assault troop strength at Tarawa by one third. As it turned out, the Sixth Marines' parent unit, the Second Marine Division, did eventually use them at Tarawa, but Julian Smith was not able to plan for their use in the assault of Betio because of their status as corps reserve.[75] Doctrine taught that a three-to-one advantage over defenders was necessary when attacking a defended beach. Holland Smith's depletion of the Second Marine Division's assault strength gave Julian Smith only an estimated two-to-one advantage over the Japanese defenders on Betio, a ratio with which the division commander was not comfortable. Left with no options and no freedom of action, Julian Smith requested that his orders be drawn up reflecting that these decisions were not his. The Fifth Amphibious Corps commander obliged him.[76]

Holland Smith, his opinion informed by the totality of his experiences in the Central Pacific, stated in his post-war memoirs that "[t]he secret of amphibious warfare is concentration of your forces and meticulous co-ordination of all elements, plus as much naval gunfire and air bombardment as you can pour into enemy positions."[77] Planning for Galvanic was not, however, dominated by considerations that Smith and others retrospectively came to see as most important. Instead, the overarching concern in the minds of Pacific theater naval commanders was the completion of the attack with the utmost speed once it was launched. Nimitz and Spruance anticipated a violent reaction from Japanese bases in the Marshalls and they believed that the only way to minimize the consequences of such a reaction was to complete the operation with dispatch.[78] In their minds, this perceived need for strategic surprise argued against a heavy preliminary aerial and naval gunfire bombardment. Therefore, rather than concentrating on the ultimate objective over a period of time before the day of the assault, air and naval gunfire preparation would be spread over several possible objectives, thus keeping the Japanese guessing up to the very end.[79] The Americans were unaware in 1943, however, that their operations in the Solomon Islands had drained Japanese naval and air strength from the Central Pacific. By the time of the Gilberts offensive, the

---

[75] Ibid., pp. 203–04.

[76] Ibid., p. 205. This statement takes into account the concept of the use of naval gunfire as a force multiplier. Julian Smith, in his discussions with H. M. Smith concerning the number of Marines the Second Marine Division could have for the assault on Betio, never viewed naval gunfire as a substitute for the expected three-to-one troop advantage. For him, it was a question of manpower alone.

[77] Smith and Finch, *Coral and Brass*, pp. 124–25.

[78] Isely and Crowl, *U.S. Marines and Amphibious War*, p. 200.

[79] Ibid., p. 201.

Japanese did not have sufficient assets in place to reinforce their Central Pacific garrisons.[80]

Not knowing this, the Americans considered strategic surprise to be necessary. They also believed that it was at least partially obtainable. Achieving tactical surprise ashore, however, was not believed to be worth the invading troop losses that would be incurred. To attempt it would mean not allowing for any bombardment prior to the actual assault, and such a practice was condemned on a doctrinal as well as an empirical level. It was decided, therefore, to squeeze as much bombing and naval gunfire as possible into the period between sunrise and H-hour, thus providing for the artillery support needed by the assault forces and for the protection from naval counterattack required by the naval planners.[81] In keeping with this compromise, the assault forces of Combat Team 2 would go ashore on Betio Island after their objective had received less than three hours of air and naval gunfire preparation.[82]

Another difficult problem that needed to be addressed was how to get the troops ashore. Julian Smith, Merritt Edson, and David Shoup decided that the amphibious tractors (LVTs) the Marine Corps had been using to carry supplies to beaches and inland to supply dumps could be modified to allow them to be used tactically. This decision was an innovation. Seventy-five LVT(1)s of the 2nd Amphibian Tractor Battalion, veterans of service at Guadalcanal, were given additional armor and armament so that they could better stand up to the punishment they would receive as they approached the defended beach of Betio. These seventy-five would not be enough, however. Julian Smith located fifty newer LVT(2)s in San Diego and he convinced Holland Smith to get them transferred to the Second Marine Division for use against Tarawa. The tractors were shipped to American Samoa in LSTs where the members of a special amphibian tractor company newly formed by the Second Marine Division met them. These fifty LVT(2)s joined up with the division on D-day morning at Tarawa, not having had time for tests or rehearsals.[83] Even with these additional tractors, however, there were only enough LVTs to lift approximately one half of Combat Team 2 to the beach. With these

[80] Ibid., pp. 200–01. John Prados, in his work *Islands of Destiny: The Solomons Campaign and the Eclipse of the Rising Sun* (New York: New American Library, 2012), goes beyond the traditional case as presented by Isely and Crowl. He argues that the Solomon Islands Campaign was the true turning point of the war in the Pacific. Although Prados' scholarly methodology is suspect and his works are written for a popular audience, there is some truth to his argument. The deterioration of Japanese capabilities and the beginning of the build-up of American strength can both be traced directly to what happened in the Solomons from August of 1942 to November of 1943.

[81] Ibid., pp. 201–02.

[82] Ibid., p. 204.

[83] Ibid., p. 208; Alexander, *Utmost Savagery*, pp. 62–65.

numbers in mind, Julian Smith decided that the first three waves of assault troops would be given the LVTs while the remaining two waves, made up mostly of reinforcing elements, would be boated in LCVPs.[84] As it turned out, the first three waves were indeed able to get over the reef without having to worry about the level of the water—the LVTs did their job in that regard.

The Americans prepared themselves as best they could in anticipation of a tough fight, but they had had no experience so far in the Pacific War to which the coming battle could be compared.[85] Admiral Shibasaki created on Betio a defensive system that he believed would defeat the Marines at the water's edge. Under his command were approximately 3,000 effective combat troops and approximately 1,500 construction laborers, mostly Koreans. He set all of them to work emplacing twenty coastal defense guns along the shore of the island, ranging from 80mm to eight-inch in size, and building concrete tetrahedrons along the reef. These obstacles were designed to force landing craft into routes that would be swept by the smaller coastal defense guns, automatic cannon, and machine guns. In addition to these weapons, the defenders also had ten 75mm mountain howitzers, six 70mm guns, nine 37mm field pieces, at least thirty-one 13mm machine guns, an undetermined number of 7.7mm machine guns, several dual-purpose anti-aircraft weapons, and the 37mm guns of seven light tanks. To top all of this off, Shibasaki had his men string a double-apron of barbed wire between the reef and the beach and all along the beaches as well. In case the attackers were able to establish a beachhead, the admiral had a log fence constructed just inland of the shoreline and he had anti-tank ditches and other obstacles positioned such that the attacking force could be contained along a thin strip of sand and wiped out.[86]

---

[84] Isely and Crowl, *U.S. Marines and Amphibious War,* p. 210; Alexander, *Utmost Savagery,* pp. 61–63.

[85] See MCUA, Operation Galvanic, Tarawa, Box 2, Folder 5, Second Marine Division, "Estimate of the Situation—Gilberts," 5 October 1943, and "Supplementary Estimate of the Situation," 25 October 1943. In these documents, Merritt Edson shows that the Second Marine Division had some idea of what they would be up against. Also see MCUA, Operation Galvanic, Tarawa, Box 2, Folder 1, ICPOA Bulletin #30–43, Enemy Positions, The Marshalls-Gilberts Area, Vol. III, Gilbert Islands, 5 May 1943.

[86] Shaw et al., *Central Pacific Drive,* p. 50; MCUA, Operation Galvanic, Tarawa, Box 5, Folder 1, JICPOA Translation Item #3616-A, B, C, D.—Tarawa Organization Tables and Map as included in Gilbert Area Defense Force Opord #12–43, 8 December 1943. This JICPOA document is the translation of a Japanese document captured on 21 November 1943 at Makin. It lists the units assigned to Tarawa Atoll, their primary duties, and their principal weapons, vehicles, and boats. It also includes a map of Betio showing placement of weapons.

Naval Gunfire at Tarawa: The "Lessons" Learned

The assault on Betio provided the Navy and Marine Corps with the first complete real-world test of the amphibious warfare doctrine the United States sea services had developed during the 1930s. All six of the doctrine's components received a thorough review both before and after 20 November 1943, but this was especially true of naval gunfire. *FTP 167* with the Change 3 modifications presented the concept of "artillery from the sea," the substitution of naval guns for the attacking troops' organic artillery, as the solution to the problem of supplying those troops with the artillery support they so desperately needed during the early phases of an amphibious assault. Did the crucible of Tarawa simply purify and burnish what was an essentially correct theory or did it leave it a smoking, rejected cinder?

The first step in answering this question is to look at the Naval Gunfire Support Plan developed for the operation. A copy of the Marine Corps' version of this plan, designated Annex Baker to Corps Operation Plan No. 1–43, was attached to Holland Smith's Fifth Amphibious Corps Action Report. According to this plan, naval gunfire at Betio was to be divided into three phases. These phases are described as follows:

> Phase I—Prearranged neutraliztion [*sic*] and counter-battery fires delivered mainly by the heavy ships at moderately long range. For knocking out heavy turret guns, it may be necessary for heavy ships to close the range to 2000 or 3000 yards, and to employ AP projectiles.
>
> Phase II—Close support [*sic*] fires mainly by cruisers and destroyers at close range just before H-hour to support landings.
>
> Phase III—Call fires on targets of opportunity controlled by Shore Fire Control Parties after they have landed (not earlier than H plus THIRTY, but continuing possibly for one or more days). Continued slow neutralization fire on target areas 400 to 800 yards or more from the nearest troops.[87]

As far as how these fires should be carried out, the plan specified that "[f]iring will be deliberate at all times, though a somewhat more rapid rate will be required just before H-Hour when maximum neutralization must be effected to support landings."[88] Further instructions concerning what the Marine Corps considered to be

[87] NARA, RG 127, USMC Geographic Files, Box 26, File A6–2, VAC AR Enc. A, Oper. Plan 1–43, Gilberts, Commanding General, V Amphibious Corps (CG VAC), VAC Operation Plan No. 1–43, 13 October 1943, Annex Baker, Naval Gunfire Support Plan (hereinafter VAC NGF Plan), p. 1.

[88] Ibid. In today's parlance, this would be more accurately referred to as a suppression mission. Navy and Marine Corps usage of the word "neutralization" was very broad during World War II.

proper firing techniques were promulgated to the commanders of the ships participating in fire support missions. These instructions stated:

> Ship speed should be as low as practicable, especially during Phases II and III, mere steerageway being the best. Unnecessary course reversals shoud [*sic*] be avoided. For scheduled fires, the firing should be spread out equally throughout the time allotted, and, where an area is specified, spread equally throughout the area. Many duds may result if the trajectory is flat, unless trees are present to burst the projectiles. Pill boxes [*sic*] can best be destroyed by plunging fire at fairly high angles. For firing against personnel in the open, a percentage of the 5″ should be times-fuzed [*sic*], set so that NO bursts are higher than 75 feet above the ground.[89]

A comparison of this plan to Chapter 5 of *FTP 167* with Change 3 modifications shows that it conforms substantially to the doctrine as specified in October of 1943.[90]

The plan for scheduled fires was based upon the three-phase structure as presented in VAC Operation Plan 1–43. The two most important time benchmarks were designated as “W-hour” and “H-hour.” “W-hour” was the time when the first scheduled air bombardment of the morning was to end and the Phase I bombardment was to begin. “H-hour” was the time when the first troops were to set foot ashore. According to the Second Marine Division’s Operation Order No. 14, the original time line was as follows:

> 0545–0600 Air bombardment
>
> 0600 W-hour (beginning of Phase I bombardment)
>
> 0600–0715 General naval gunfire shore bombardment
>
> 0715–0730 Air bombardment
>
> 0730–0745 Ships fire on targets of opportunity (Time adjustment period)
>
> 0745 Beginning of Phase II bombardment (0740 boats cross line of departure)
>
> 0745–0805 Beach preparation
>
> 0805–0810 Ships fire on targets of opportunity (Time adjustment period)
>
> 0810–0825 Beach preparation

[89] Ibid., p. 2.

[90] *FTP 167* with Change 3, Paragraph 506.b, Figure 1, p. 115.

0825–0830 Aircraft strafe beaches. No gunfire on landing beaches.

0830 H-hour[91]

As described in the story of the D-day related above, Hill was not able to keep to this schedule. What went wrong? The answer to that question requires a more detailed description of the movements and actions of the naval gunfire support ships on the morning of 20 November.

The fire support ships, with the exception of the light cruiser USS *Santa Fe* (CL-60) and the destroyer USS *Gansevoort* (DD-608), were operating in their assigned fire support areas by 04.00. *Santa Fe* and *Gansevoort* cruised to the south of Betio, independent of the organized fire support groups, making sure that no Japanese aircraft took off from the airfield on the island. The battleships *Maryland,* USS *Tennessee* (BB-43), and USS *Colorado* (BB-45) had standing orders to lay counter-battery fire on any shore guns that opened up prior to the beginning of the carrier air strikes scheduled to commence at 05.45 and *Santa Fe* was directed to begin firing on the airfield intermittently if any ship should have to engage in counter-battery fire.[92]

The Japanese on Betio sent up a red signal flare from the south shore of the island at 04.41 and the order went out for the heavy ships of Fire Support Section 1, *Tennessee* and USS *Mobile* (CL-63), to get into position to deliver counter-battery fire when needed. At 05.07 shore batteries began firing slowly and erratically on the fire support ships surrounding the island and on the transport area. *Colorado* opened up on target areas at the center of Betio while *Maryland* took a two-gun 8″ battery on the southwest tip of the island under fire, knocking it out after delivering ten four-gun 16″ salvos. Other heavy ships also delivered fire on enemy gun positions in their sectors of responsibility resulting in large explosions and numerous fires.[93]

Admiral Hill ordered the cease-fire at 05.42 in anticipation of a carrier air strike, but the strike did not begin at its scheduled time of 05.45. Hill did not know at the time why it was late, but he did not have long to worry about the problem because, at 05.48, another situation presented itself that required his immediate attention. The transports reported at that time that they were under fire from Betio, with USS *Zeilen* (APA-3), *Virgo* (AKA-20), *La Salle* (AP-102), and *Thuban* (AKA-19) reporting very close near misses from heavy guns located on the eastern and northwestern tips of the island. Hill decided that he needed to resume counter-battery fire, regardless of the status of the scheduled air strike, so the heavy gunfire support ships opened up once again at 06.00. *Colorado* took the shore batteries on the eastern tip

[91] MCUA, Operation Galvanic, Tarawa, Box 2, Folder 3, Second Marine Division, Operation Order No. 14, Gilbert Islands—Tarawa, 25 October 1943, p. 19.

[92] CTF 53 Operations Narrative, p. 30.

[93] Ibid.

of the island under fire, *Maryland* opened up on the barracks area on the northern shore, and *Tennessee* blasted the batteries on the northwestern tip. Hill, needing to start the Phase I bombardment as soon as possible and not knowing where the carrier aircraft were, designated 06.13 as the new W-hour, but he had to cancel this order when the aircraft showed up at 06.12. He then reset W-hour for 06.20.[94]

Phase I, in accordance with this new W-hour, began at 06.20. The plan for this phase provided for the complete coverage of Betio by naval gunfire with heavy concentrations on enemy strongpoints. Battleships opened fire at 10,000–15,000 yards on the most strongly defended points of the island—the eastern, northwestern, and southwestern tips—closing to 2,000–6,000 yards. Cruisers followed the battleships at twenty to thirty minute intervals, also closing the range as Phase I progressed. Destroyers screened the larger ships during this phase and delivered some fire of their own against enemy batteries as they came close inshore. At 07.35, Phase I ended and Hill took stock of his situation. As far as he could determine, fires appeared to have been delivered accurately and the schedule carried out as planned with the exception of the necessary time adjustments. Large explosions littered the island with debris all during the bombardment and burning wreckage generated an immense volume of smoke. The amount of smoke was so great that ships to the west of the island had to fire on targets using radar control during most of the period.[95]

Rear Admiral Howard F. Kingman, commander of Battleship Division Two, describes the target acquisition problems: "Soon after Phase I bombardment started, BETIO Island was shrouded in a pall of dust and smoke which prevented observation from shipboard. All ships experienced great difficulty in spotting own fall of shot and therefore walked salvos around with arbitrary spots to cover thoroughly the assigned target area."[96]

In other words, the smoke and dust forced the crews of the gunfire support ships to substitute concentration fire for the "deliberate" point fire called for by the Marines. Concentration fire, according to doctrine, is "the form used for neutralization." The Marines needed point fire for destruction. Though the Navy meant to supply this type of support, they would not be able to do so from quite early in Phase I. This meant that most of the targets pinpointed on their maps of Betio could not and, consequently, were not directly engaged by naval gunfire prior to

[94] Ibid., pp. 30–31.

[95] Ibid., p. 31. U.S. Navy ships had been equipped with radar since the late 1930s. The radar mentioned in the records of the Betio assault could only be used to acquire basic range information when firing at land-based objectives. It could not pinpoint specific targets. The comments made by the various commanders concerning naval gunfire at Tarawa are, in essence, complaints that the smoke and dust required them to rely upon a method of targeting that forced them to provide area coverage rather than direct fire.

[96] TG 53.4 AR, p. 5.

the Marines hitting the beach. Proof of this lack of success on the part of the scheduled fire of Phase I is seen in Hill's report that the Japanese continued to fire on the transports and the fire support ships all during Phase I (06.20–07.35) and that the 5.5″ coast defense batteries in the northwestern sector of the island were firing as late as 06.58. Ships took individual shore batteries under fire at their own discretion and at the direction of higher command in an attempt to silence these guns.[97]

The minesweeper *Requisite* and the destroyers *Ringgold* and *Dashiell* entered the lagoon at 07.00. Japanese shore batteries immediately took these ships under fire and the destroyers answered with heavy counter-battery fire, but, even with the hail of 5″ shells they threw out, large caliber coastal defense guns on the eastern tip of the island were still firing as late as 07.24. *Ringgold* reported heavy fire from these guns, along with others located behind Beaches Red Two and Red Three, and *Maryland, Tennessee,* and the destroyer USS *Russell* (DD-414) directed fire on these positions to silence them. The heavy fire support ships outside the lagoon took up their stations for Phase II, an unanchored stationary position off the western shore of Betio, at 07.35. The fire support destroyers screened the heavier ships to seaward. From this area, the larger ships could provide enfilading fire onto the assault beaches. All ships continued counter-battery fire until the commencement of Phase II at 07.45. Hill officially confirmed H-hour for 08.30 at this point and announced the designated time to all hands.[98]

Phase II required the fire support ships to concentrate on the landing beaches (Red One, Two, and Three) on the north (lagoon side) of Betio. Fighter aircraft were scheduled to strafe these beaches from 08.25 until the first Marines landed, but a delay in getting the first assault wave to the line of departure necessitated pushing H-hour to 08.45. *Ringgold,* not having the best of days, announced at 07.45 that she had received a hit from a Japanese shell that damaged her port engine, knocking it out, and she later reported that she had been hit by three duds, two of which impacted the destroyer below the waterline. The heavy cruiser USS *Indianapolis* (CA 35) left Fire Support Area 2 at 08.19 to take position astern of the heavy cruiser USS *Portland* (CA-33) at the western end of Betio. Meanwhile, *Maryland* positioned herself astern of *Colorado* in the same area and began pumping fifteen minutes worth of fire into the area immediately adjacent to Beach Red One.[99]

---

97 *FTP 167* with Change 3, Paragraph 505.b.1, p. 113; CTF 53 Operations Narrative, p. 31.

98 Ibid. Firing enemy batteries needed to be visible from fire support ships in order for the naval gunners to take them under effective counter-battery fire.

99 Ibid., pp. 31–32. *Ringgold's* CO reports only two hits by duds, only one of which hit below the waterline. He is consistent in his AR when describing both the damage below the waterline and the repairs made after the action—only one hit below the waterline and only one hole repaired below the waterline. CO USS Ringgold AR, pp. 10–13.

Hill reset H-hour to 09.00 at 08.31 because the first wave of LVTs did not reach the line of departure until 08.23. Fighters began to strafe the landing beaches at 08.25, having not received communication of another change in H-hour, and Fire Support Section 4 (*Ringgold* and *Dashiell*) ceased fire until Hill's air officer and staff cleared the aircraft out of the way. Scheduled fires had to be adjusted with the new H-hour in mind, so Hill set them to begin again at the new H-20. Ships were to fire on targets of opportunity until then. Enemy guns continued to fire as late as 08.35 from the area to the west and inland of Beach Red One and from positions just up from the eastern tip of Betio. Destroyer *Russell* took the latter under fire and battleship *Tennessee* the former.[100]

Fire Support Ships ceased fire at 08.55 to allow for the belated strafing of the landing beaches by fighter aircraft. A heavy blanket of smoke and dust had settled over Betio, obscuring the observation of potential targets and generally making it extremely difficult for both airborne and shipboard spotters to perform their jobs. The call went out over all communications systems at 09.00 that H-hour had arrived, but the minesweeper *Pursuit* and a number of observation aircraft announced that the first assault wave was still fifteen minutes out from shore. Hill determined that the inability of observers to see where rounds were landing precluded the use of close support naval gunfire, so he called a cease-fire for all ships but ordered that aircraft continue to strafe the beaches so as to neutralize Japanese defenses along the north shore of Betio for as long as possible. *Ringgold* and *Dashiell* continued to fire on gun positions to the west and inland of Beach Red One until 09.16, however, because there were reports of a great deal of enemy fire streaming out of this area onto the approaching LVTs. The first assault troops finally set foot on the north shore of Betio at 09.10, technically marking the dividing point between Phases II and III.[101]

What did the Marine Corps think of the naval gunfire doctrine and techniques that were used at Tarawa? Since Marines were integrally involved in the process of amphibious warfare doctrinal development during the 1930s, one would assume that they were relatively pleased with its form by November 1943. Such an assumption would be right for the majority of officers in the corps at the time, but there were exceptions. One of these exceptions was Merritt A. Edson, Julian Smith's Chief of Staff. Edson's opinions are significant for the reason that he was intimately familiar with the Second Marine Division planning process prior to the Gilberts operation. As such, his thoughts should at least be noted. In a letter Edson wrote to Colonel G. B. Erskine, Holland Smith's Chief of Staff, on 11 November 1943, he made it known that he did not place too much faith in naval gunfire support of amphibious operations:

[100] CTF 53 Operations Narrative, p. 32.

[101] Ibid.

> The fact still remains that previous experience in the Solomon Islands and at Attu especially, has not indicated that naval gunfire and aerial bombardment has been particularly effective. From personal observation at Tulagi, Guvutu and Guadalcanal, this preliminary bombardment did not destroy a single Japanese defensive installation, nor, to the best of my knowledge, kill a single Jap. . . . It is true that this bombardment had an indeterminate morale effect on the troops, which I believe will occur. We all realize that in the GALVANIC operation we are getting more aerial bombardment and a much greater amount of naval gunfire support on a comparatively restricted area than has ever been thrown into a similar area in the past. We fully expect that this bombardment will have a disastrous effect upon Japanese installations. No one can predict, however, just how disastrous that effect will be until after H-hour on the target date. Having no real yardstick to go by, it seems best to us, and to me personally, that we should base our estimate upon past experience rather than upon an unknown future component. After D-day, GALVANIC, we will have something that we can definitely figure upon in our next show and I can assure you that it will then be taken into account and get its proportionate weight.
>
> You will note that in this Estimate [of the situation on Betio] we have given naval gunfire and aerial bombardment credit for taking ou[t] the larger caliber guns. I also hope that this bombardment will take out emplaced machine guns which, after all, are perhaps the most dangerous weapon from our standpoint, but until troops hit the beach without encountering such machine gun fire, I still am of the opinion that some automatic weapons will still be operating at H-hour.[102]

Edson was clearly not one of those who trusted the Navy's promise to obliterate Japanese resistance on the island. Did he see the events of 20 November as having proved his fears to be justified? Fortunately, he later communicated his conclusions regarding the Tarawa operation to Colonel Gerald C. Thomas, Chief of Staff at I Marine Amphibious Corps. Historians' speculation, then, is not necessary. Thomas had served with Edson in the First Marine Division on Guadalcanal and the two men were old friends. Concerning the effectiveness of naval gunfire, Edson wrote:

> Naval gunfire did just about what I expected. It silenced most of the coastal defense guns and heavy AA guns and took out some of the medium AA guns. It did comparatively little damage to the [machine

[102] Library of Congress, Manuscript Division, Edson Papers, Box 5, File 40, Letter from Merritt A. Edson to G. B. Erskine, 11 November 1943, p. 1. This letter refers to Edson's Estimate of the Situation—Gilberts, 5 October 1943.

> gun] emplacements and covered beach defenses, which are most dangerous to us. Admiral Hill took his ships in within 1,500 yards of the beach as he promised to do and had two destroyers inside the lagoon, one of which [*Ringgold*] received 3 hits, but none of which exploded. Bombardment just prior to landing was extremely heavy. During most of the bombardment, as a matter of fact, the smoke and dust was so thick after the initial salvos that the fire was in the nature of area fire, and a great deal of ammunition, in my opinion, was wasted by falling short or completely going over the island. I believe that next time a slower and more deliberate rate of fire, except for the final barrage just prior to hitting the beach, may give better results.[103]

Edson was not the only person to hold such opinions of the results of the Tarawa bombardment. Similar ideas can be found in many of the lists of recommendations and criticisms that were generated by both naval and Marine officers after the completion of operation Galvanic. Brigadier General J. L. Underhill, who served as an observer from the newly-formed Fourth Marine Division, was one such person. He stated in the report of his observations that "[t]he bombardment [of Betio], both air and naval gun, was said to be aimed at 'destruction approaching obliteration,' and with such a shock effect that resistance would be light."[104] Did the Navy achieve such a level of destruction? Underhill did not think so. He went on to say in his report:

> The amount of naval gunfire and air bombardment prior to H-Hour was said to be greater per square unit of ground than previously given in preparation for a landing operation. Nevertheless, it did not prevent very heavy resistance. This is not a condemnation of it for it was excellent and without it the assault would have failed. It is recommended that for future similar operations no less a concentration (proportional to ground covered) be used. A greater concentration is urged, particularly on the immediate beach revetments facing the landing beach and on pill boxes [*sic*] from which flanking fires can be placed along the beach and and

[103] Edson–Thomas Letter, 13 December 1943, p. 2. Once again, the number of hits reported on the destroyer is at odds with *Ringgold* CO Conley's tally. Edson's letter to Thomas is dated twelve days after Conley's CO USS *Ringgold* AR and ten days prior to Hill's CTF 53 Operations Narrative. Roscoe describes the action in the same terms as Conley in his *United States Destroyer Operations in World War II.* It appears that both Hill and Edson were working from the same set of data and that that set was not accurate in its description of the damage done to *Ringgold.*

[104] MCUA, Operation Galvanic, Tarawa, Box 3, Folder 2, Brigadier General J. L. Underhill, USMC, Observations on the 2d Marine Division operations, Tarawa, n.d., p. 1.

> [*sic*] obstacles or cross fires on boats coming in. Direct hits of 500 lb. bombs on some of the larger concrete dugouts had no effect beyond chipping off a corner or disturbing the sand on top. Direct hits by 16″ guns (apparently) on the top of one of the heavy covered emplacements did no effective damage.[105]

The difficulties encountered in taking Betio and the high percentage of casualties suffered by the Second Marine Division in doing so stunned Navy and Marine Corps planners and commanders. Recommendations for improvement were routinely included in After Action Reports, but Tarawa begged for an especially thorough post-operational examination. There were literally hundreds of recommendations from every level of command. Some, like the idea put forward by the Executive Officer of *Ringgold*, while heartfelt, were not helpful. He stated: "With an island such as Betio, it might be possible at high tide to drive the defenders inland by use of waves created by destroyers steaming at high speed near the ocean side reef. I have read of these islands being swept by tidal waves—it might be possible to drown them in their foxholes or shelters."[106] Such flights of fancy aside, the lists of recommendations were studied and certain ideas were recognized as logical and certain changes as necessary. These ideas, when written down in a form that could be easily understood and digested, became the legendary body of doctrinally influential wisdom known as the "Lessons of Tarawa."

One of the people responsible for establishing these "lessons" as the standard against which plans for all future operations would be judged was the man in command of Task Force 53 at Tarawa, Rear Admiral Harry Hill. He, like Holland Smith, Kelly Turner, Julian Smith, and just about every other commanding officer in the entire Fifth Amphibious Force, generated a list of these "lessons" and had his staff pour over the Action Reports of every subordinate commander in his Task Force in order to glean as much pertinent information from them as possible. Hill's close associations with every facet of the operation and his presence, in overall command, on D-day at Betio lend his comments special weight. As such, they need to be described in detail. The focus of this work being naval gunfire support, let us look at the naval gunfire recommendation component of his report, the first section of which is a summary of the whole. In that summary he states the following:

> 1. That immediate steps be taken to construct, at home base areas, dugouts, pillboxes and bomb proof shelters duplicating those found on [Betio] Island, and that aerial and naval gunfire bombardment

[105] Ibid., p. 8.

[106] NARA, RG 127, USMC Geographic Files Box 31, File A37-1, USS Ringgold AR, 21 October–2 December 1943, Executive Officer, USS Ringgold, Comments on Landing at Tarawa, 1 December 1943, p. 32.

be conducted on these for training and determination of effectiveness of bombardment methods and ammunition. . . .

2. That fire support ships and shore fire control parties be assigned well in advance, in order to permit essential joint training in the delivery of call fire.
3. That fire support ships be strongly impressed with the necessity for delivering fire at close ranges for effective bombardment.
4. That landing plans definitely provide for destroying automatic weapons and small caliber batteries remaining in action after assault waves have landed.
5. That, in event of a pre-dawn approach, fire should commence as soon as earliest light permits and before the transport area can be taken under fire by shore batteries.
6. That naval gunfire must not be discontinued during delivery of aerial bombing strikes. . . .
7. That a method be devised for rendering anti-boat mines safe for the passage of assault waves to the beach. . . .
8. That the bombardment allowance of ammunition be increased and include AP projectiles; that a bombardment allowance of common projectiles be established and made available for 5″/38 and 5″/25 batteries. Percentages of ammunition types must depend upon a study of the problem, but in general the delay action fuze will be required during all bombardment phases except Phase TWO. . . .
9. That, if fire support ships can be assigned early, the initial fire support plans outline only in broad form the overall bombardment effect desired, the general areas to be covered, and the type and amounts of ammunition to be expended for its accomplishment. That the details of fire schedules and their coordination with maneuvers required, track charts, and other details of section and individual ships problems, be delegated to Fire Support Section Commanders for planning and solution.
10. That gunfire support plans for future bombardment of enemy held islands similar to [Betio] embody the following:
    (a) Five general phases of bombardment as follows: (1) Initial counter-battery fire against known strong points [*sic*] using HC and AP projectiles, and commencing at ranges producing an angle of fall of 15 degrees; (2) General area bombardment using HC and AA common projectiles delivered at ranges between 10,000 and 5,000 yards; (3) Destruction of heavy defenses, pillboxes, and dugouts along the landing beaches by

slow, accurate, and deliberate fire, using AP and common projectiles. This fire is to be delivered at close ranges using pointer fire if practicable; (4) Heavy concentration fire at close range on landing beach areas during the boat approach; (5) Delivery of call fire by ships assigned after H hour [*sic*].

(b) Use of a rolling barrage system of fire rather than radical shifting of target areas during area bombardment.

(c) Restriction of air burst firing for use only as a weapon of opportunity against exposed personnel.

(d) Maximum use of 40[mm] batteries whenever range and other conditions permit and control of those batteries by 5-inch gun directors if fire control installation permits.

(e) Stationing of close fire support ships in a favorable position relative to the landing beaches, and at closest safe navigation range, so as to provide their continuous observation of assault boat waves, permitting these ships to decide at what time their fire must be ceased for safety of landing personnel.

(f) Destruction of hulks, latrines, and similar potential machine gun nests located in favorable beach enfilading positions.

(g) Plans for local supply of destroyer and light cruiser replacement ammunition, and depth charges.

(h) Readiness for immediate shift to radar controlled gunfire during all phases of bombardment except [numbers] 3 and 5 [of paragraph 10 (a) above].[107]

Being a summary, the above-listed points are made succinctly without much additional comment. Hill elaborates on a number of issues brought up in this list, however, in the next section of his report. The most important of these issues are the following: the coordination of the air strikes with naval gunfire support; the need to try to fool the Japanese as to the pattern of gunfire support coverage; the expenditure of ammunition during the pre-landing bombardment; the overall effectiveness of the support provided by naval guns; and, finally, the accuracy of naval gunfire. It was the first of these problem areas that produced many of the difficulties that stood in the way of the timely execution of Phases I and II of the bombardment plan on

[107] CTF 53 Operations Narrative, NGF Supplement, n.d., Naval Gunfire Support, Summary of Recommendations, pp. 41–42. It is important to note that Hill recommends the use of a rolling barrage in 10(b). Historians tend to credit Donald Weller for being the first to think about incorporating such a rolling barrage as part of his NGF plan for Iwo Jima. The idea, as this evidence shows, was not original to Weller.

the morning of 20 November 1943. Hill alluded to these difficulties in the sixth of his summarized recommendations, referring the reader to other pages of his report for a more detailed treatment. On those pages he recommended that the following "conclusions be used as a basis for coordinating air and gunfire support in future bombardments of enemy held islands similar to [Betio]":

1. Air bombardment, like surface bombardment, failed to destroy the defenses it was delivered against unless a direct hit was made. It had, however, two advantages: rapidity of delivery after called for, and high morale effect on own troops.
2. Plans provided for commencing the bombardment with an air strike lasting for a half hour; to be followed by gunfire for a period of approximately two hours ending at H minus five, at which time beaches were to be strafed until the troops were ashore.
3. The time for commencement of the air attack, twenty-five minutes before sunrise, was selected in order to provide light enough for the pilots to see their targets properly. This meant, of course, that the transports could also be seen from shore and exposed to gunfire from enemy batteries.
4. Anticipating this, all fire support groups were placed in position for counter-battery fire prior to daybreak, and when the shore batteries opened on the transports at 0510, orders were given to open fire.
5. The air attack scheduled for 0545 . . . was late, and did not actually arrive until 0620. . . . Had it arrived on scheduled time, however, the naval fire would have had to continue in order to neutralize the fire being directed into the transport area.
6. The proper balance between air and gunfire support during the preliminary bombardment is a difficult problem, but based upon the experience at TARAWA, and examination of beach defenses, the following conclusions have been reached:
   (a) Naval gunfire can effectively silence enemy coast defense and AA batteries, and will probably have to commence before there is sufficient light for air bombing.
   (b) Once gunfire has commenced, air bombardment against specific point targets such as guns, dugouts, bomb proofs, etc., will be impracticable, as the entire target area will be completely covered by a cloud of dust and smoke. Even area bombardment will be difficult.
   (c) Naval gunfire should not be ceased for air bombing attacks. This was demonstrated by numerous air strikes conducted in conjunction with gunfire, with safety to bombing planes.

(d) Strafing of beaches is ineffective against type of beach defenses found on [Betio] Island and should be considered only as a weapon of opportunity against exposed personnel to be used after gunfire in an area has ceased. The designation of a fixed hour and area for this type of attack should be discontinued.

(e) It is believed that gasoline bombs may prove very effective against enemy beach dugout personnel. Tests should be conducted as soon as possible.[108]

In his comments, Hill recognizes the problem presented by smoke and dust for both air and naval gunfire support. He does not offer any solutions for this particular issue, but he does make a suggestion concerning gunfire and air support coordination that is most interesting. According to Chapter 6 of *FTP 167,* the mission of supplying air support at the time that gunfire support lifts " . . . should not be previously laid out on an exact time schedule but should be left to the judgment of squadron commanders. Unless ships' gunfire ceases during the aircraft attacks, bombing and machine gun firing must be done at such altitudes as will avoid trajectories of gunfire from supporting vessels."[109] Chapter 5 also addresses this issue, stating that " . . . steps should be taken to insure that the naval gunfire does not endanger friendly planes arriving to dive bomb or strafe or smoke the beach just prior to the assault. All firing ships should be furnished with a copy of that portion of the order which prescribes low flying airplane attacks."[110] The writers of the doctrine were concerned that shells fired by naval gunfire support ships would shoot down friendly aircraft if both arms were scheduled to operate simultaneously. The solution was for aircraft to sacrifice accuracy of ordnance delivery by flying above the trajectories of incoming shells. Hill, in essence, calls for a change in this point of doctrine. He argues that experience at Betio proves that the two can operate together without the aircraft having to take any special precautions, thus increasing the overall accuracy of their delivery.

Hill also calls into question another point of doctrine. According to Chapter 6 of *FTP 167:* "A critical stage in the ship to shore movement occurs when ships' gunfire lifts; this may take place when the leading boats are 1,000 yards or more offshore. Commencing at this time, the advancing boats must receive intensive suport [*sic*] from the aviation units. Planes employing machine guns and bombs must neutralize beach defenses, anti-boat guns, artillery reserves, and possibly searchlights. It is highly important, when planning aircraft missions, to provide for a strong striking force for employment at this time, as aviation may be practically the only

---

[108] CTF 53 Operations Narrative, NGF Supplement, n.d., Coordination of Air and Gunfire Support, pp. 60–61.

[109] *FTP 167* with Change 1, Paragraph 624.b, p. 157.

[110] *FTP 167* with Change 3, Paragraph 526.b, p. 130.

supporting arm during this period."[111] The use of aircraft in this way proved completely ineffective at Betio. Hill recommends what, once again, was a change in the accepted doctrine: such a practice should be discontinued. He does not state as much, but discontinuing the use of aircraft for this purpose would also simplify coordination because time for such attacks would not have to be scheduled.

The attempt on the part of the planners to fool the Japanese as to where and when rounds would fall during the preliminary bombardment elicited an insightful response from Hill, which reads:

> [Phase ONE] prescribed seventy-five minutes of prearranged (scheduled) fire. The schedule was planned to accomplish a thorough and complete bombardment of the island with heaviness of concentration on target areas according to their defensive strength. The schedule called for a destructive bombardment rather than the neutralization bombardment generally required of naval gunfire support. . . . The old precept of keeping the enemy "guessing where to jump next" by placing the fire into areas in an unpredictable sequence was carefully written into the schedule. This resulted in difficulties of control, loss of effectiveness of fire, and a minor waste of ammunition. This precept is considered valuable for neutralization fire, but for destructive bombardment, the destruction depends on accurate control precluding sudden, large, and frequent shifts of target. A methodical and thorough coverage of an assigned area will be better accomplished in the future by laying the fire directly toward or away, and right or left from the established reference point, and precludes the necessity for applying a spot for each new target area. This phase should be conducted at a range which insures excellent control, full use of rangekeepers and sufficient angle of fall to ensure detonation of the projectiles.[112]

For destruction purposes, he argues, deliberate, unhurried precision is more important than anything else. This statement, in various forms, became one of the most frequently repeated "lessons of Tarawa." Hill's comment that neutralization was what naval gunfire support was generally meant to provide is based on the accepted doctrine of the time. Change 3 of *FTP 167* states in paragraph 505.a.1 that "[m]ost targets engaged by naval gunfire will be of the type for which neutralization is appropriate." Tarawa proved that fire for destruction was more necessary than heretofore had been realized.

Isely and Crowl point out that the amount of time allotted for the Phase I bombardment forced naval gunners to fire too rapidly. They attribute the problem,

---

[111] *FTP 167* with Change 1, Paragraph 624.a, pp. 156–57.

[112] CTF 53 Operations Narrative, NGF Supplement n.d., Naval Gunfire Support, Comment and Recommendation, p. 45.

ultimately, to confusion on the part of the Navy and Marine Corps planners as to the difference between neutralization and destruction. They cite the comments of a shore fire control party member as evidence of this fundamental terminological misunderstanding.[113] While it is true that Marines and sailors at the junior officer level obviously had trouble differentiating between the two terms, such was not the case for the doctrine itself and for those who were tasked with putting it into practice. Higher-level command officers did understand the difference. The problem was not one of terminology. It was, rather, one of perceived necessity. Historians, Isely and Crowl amongst them, have made much of the Galvanic planners' perceived need for speed in the assault.[114] It was this perception on the part of commanders and planners that created an environment that allowed any preconceived misconceptions on the part of lower-level officers and enlisted men to take root and flourish. The period allotted for Phase I bombardment was short because Spruance and others were concerned about Japanese counterattacks against the amphibious support group when it was most vulnerable to such retaliation.[115] Naval gunfire personnel knew that they had a short, preset time in which to deliver a prescribed amount of gunfire support. The time constraints compelled them to fire more rapidly than experience, in the end, would show to be prudent. The tempo of delivery did not allow dust to settle, thus compounding the target acquisition problem as the morning progressed and driving those attempting to acquire those targets for destruction purposes in the direction of area concentration fire. They gravitated toward area fire in an effort to make sure that dangerous enemy emplacements were destroyed even if they could not be seen well enough to be targeted individually.

Whether or not the naval gunfire bombardment had performed the job it was designed to execute was another question of great interest in the aftermath of the operation. It is with his comments concerning the third area, the expenditure of ammunition during the preliminary bombardment, that one begins to understand how Hill assessed this performance. Before giving his post-operational appraisal, it would be useful to document the planned ammunition expenditure for D-day, shown in Tables 3.1 and 3.2.

The rounds referred to in Table 3.1 were to be expended against enemy personnel and installations that doctrine recognized as the most dangerous to the troops coming ashore. The rounds referred to in Table 3.2 were to be fired upon enemy positions that did not threaten the invading force directly as it came ashore but, because of their ability to place fire on the landing beaches, were dangerous to the invading troops nonetheless.

---

[113] Isely and Crowl, *U.S. Marines and Amphibious War*, p. 232.

[114] Ibid., pp. 201–02.

[115] Ibid.

Table 3.1: Number of Rounds of Naval Gunfire Ammunition to be Expended Against Targets on Landing Beaches Only

W-hour to W+75

Projectile Size	No. of Projectiles to Be Fired	Weight of Metal per Single Projectile (in pounds)	Total Weight of Metal to be Placed on Targets (in pounds)	Total Weight of Metal to be Placed on Targets (in tons)
16″	20	1,746	34,920	17.46
14″	285	1,305	371,925	185.96
8″	15	239	3,585	1.79
6″	630	92	57,960	28.98
5″	720	46	33,120	16.56
		Grand Totals:	501,510	250.75

H-45 to H-hour

Projectile Size	No. of Projectiles to be Fired	Weight of Metal per Single Projectile (in pounds)	Total Weight of Metal to be Placed on Targets (in pounds)	Total Weight of Metal to be Placed on Targets (in tons)
16″	165	1,746	288,090	144.045
14″	60	1,305	78,300	39.15
8″	150	239	35,850	17.925
6″	870	92	78,200	39.1
5″	2800	46	128,800	64.4
		Grand Totals:	609,240	304.62

Total Ammunition Used (W-hour to H-hour)

Projectile Size	No. of Projectiles to be Fired	Weight of Metal per Single Projectile (in pounds)	Total Weight of Metal to be Placed on Targets (in pounds)	Total Weight of Metal to be Placed on Targets (in tons)
16″	185	1,746	323,010	161.505
14″	345	1,305	450,225	225.1125
8″	165	239	39,435	19.7175
6″	1500	92	138,000	69
5″	3520	46	161,920	80.96
		Grand Totals:	1,112,590	556.295

Sources: NARA, RG 127, USMC Geographic Files, Box 29, File A7-19, 2nd Marine Division, Report of Operations, GALVANIC, Tarawa, 2nd Marine Division, NGF Officer Report of NGF in TARAWA Operation, dated 20 December 1943, pp. 3–4. The weight of metal used for each size of projectile is an approximation based upon the following sources: *FTP 167* with Change 3, p. 119, for 5″, 6″, and 8″ shells; Department of the Navy, Bureau of Ordnance, *U.S. Explosive Ordnance*, OP 1664, 28 May 1947, pp. 59–64.

Table 3.2: Number of Rounds of Naval Gunfire Ammunition to be Expended Against Targets Other than Landing Beaches

W-hour to W+75

Projectile Size	No. of Projectiles To Be Fired	Weight of Metal per Single Projectile (in pounds)	Total Weight of Metal To Be Placed on Targets (in pounds)	Total Weight of Metal To Be Placed on Targets (in tons)
16″	380	1,746	663,480	331.74
14″	15	1,305	19,575	9.7875
8″	195	239	46,605	23.3025
6″	390	92	35,880	17.94
5″	2,840	46	130,640	65.32
		Grand Totals:	896,180	448.09

H-45 to H-hour

Projectile Size	No. of Projectiles To Be Fired	Weight of Metal per Single Projectile (in pounds)	Total Weight of Metal To Be Placed on Targets (in pounds)	Total Weight of Metal To Be Placed on Targets (in tons)
16″	20	1,746	34,920	17.46
14″	45	1,305	58,725	29.3625
8″	150	239	35,850	17.925
6″	60	92	5,520	2.76
5″	1,400	46	64,400	32.2
		Grand Totals:	199,415	99.7075

Total Ammunition Used (W-hour to H-hour)

Projectile Size	No. of Projectiles To Be Fired	Weight of Metal per Single Projectile (in pounds)	Total Weight of Metal To Be Placed on Targets (in pounds)	Total Weight of Metal To Be Placed on Targets (in tons)
16″	400	1,746	698,400	349.2
14″	60	1,305	78,300	39.15
8″	345	239	82,455	41.2275
6″	450	92	41,400	20.7
5″	4,240	46	195,040	97.52
		Grand Totals:	1,095,595	547.7975

Sources: NARA, RG 127, USMC Geographic Files, Box 29, File A7-19, 2nd Marine Division, Report of Operations, GALVANIC, Tarawa, 2nd Marine Division, NGF Officer Report of NGF in TARAWA Operation, dated 20 December 1943, pp. 1–3. The weight of metal used for each size of projectile is an approximation based upon the following sources: *FTP 167* with Change 3, p. 119, for 5″, 6″, and 8″ shells; Department of the Navy, Bureau of Ordnance, *U.S. Explosive Ordnance*, OP 1664, 28 May 1947, pp. 59–64.

Table 3.3: Actual Number of Rounds Fired on D-day

Projectile Size	No. of Projectiles Fired	Weight of Metal per Single Projectile (in pounds)	Total Weight of Metal Projectiles Actually Fired (in pounds)	Total Weight of Metal Projectiles Actually Fired (in tons)
16″	540	1,746	942,840	471.42
14″	450	1,305	587,250	293.625
8″	690	239	164,910	82.455
6″	1590	92	146,280	73.14
5″	10,905	46	501,630	250.815
		Grand Totals:	2,342,910	1171.455

Sources: CTF 53 Operations Narrative, p. 50. The weight of metal used for each size of projectile is an approximation based upon the following sources: *FTP 167* with Change 3, p. 119, for 5″, 6″, and 8″ shells; Department of the Navy, Bureau of Ordnance, *U.S. Explosive Ordnance*, OP 1664, 28 May 1947, pp. 59–64.

The tally referenced in Table 3.3 is based, Hill admits, on incomplete records. Apparently, the number of shells expended was determined by taking each ship's recorded allowance for each type of shell and subtracting the number of shells remaining on hand after Phases I and II and then after Phase III. How the tally for Phases I and II could be completed in the midst of the operation is not explained. Some guns were equipped with rounds-fired counters, but not all ships were so equipped.[116] Given the nature of this evidence, therefore, only a rough comparison can be made between the expected and the actual expenditure of ammunition, but an attempt at such a comparison is nonetheless useful. The number of sixteen-inch and six-inch shells actually fired is lower, 92% and 82% below projection respectively. The number of fourteen-inch, eight-inch, and five-inch, on the other hand, is higher than projected. The difference is modest for fourteen-inch ordnance, an 11% increase, but eight-inch firings are a significant 35% above projections. It is in the five-inch category, however, that the planners underestimated requirements to the greatest extent. The tally of actual firings is 41% above projections.

The most reasonable explanation for why the projections were off by so much is only tangentially related to any mistakes on the part of planners in assessing the overall strength of Japanese defenses on Betio. There was, indeed, a larger number of call fire missions against hardened positions than had been projected, but most

[116] In the USS *Ringgold* Action Report, the commanding officer reports that his ship did not have rounds-fired counters. He states that "[t]otal rounds fired and on hand were checked approximately after each firing period." CO USS Ringgold AR, p. 9.

of these occurred after the period of scheduled fire.[117] The dust and smoke kicked up by the bombardment itself during Phase I is the more likely culprit. Ships began area fire, as already explained, earlier than called for in the schedule. Large quantities of shells were expended in this effort, more than were allowed for in the projections. It would seem that the large quantity of ordnance fired at tiny Betio Island has unduly impressed even the most perceptive of analysts over the years, even to the point of influencing their analyses. Isely and Crowl, for instance, comment on page 230 that "About 3,000 tons of naval projectiles were hurled at Betio, the great bulk of it just before the landing on the morning of November 20. . . ." Hill's numbers do not support this contention, although the amounts reported are indeed high for such a small objective as Betio.

Hill then enters into his assessment of how effectively those rounds were used. His analysis is contained in a series of comments concerning issues related to that question:

> 8. In most respects, the fire support plan was effective. It quickly silenced the heavy batteries, AA batteries, and destroyed radar, searchlights, fire control instruments such as range keepers [*sic*] and range finders [*sic*]. Later inspection showed that the batteries were silenced in some instances by material damage, by killing the crews, or both. The gunfire wrecked everything above ground, or in open pits, such as bombs, trucks, torpedoes, etc. It started large fires on all parts of the island, and effectively destroyed all material stored above ground not in bombproof storage. Of special importance, it tore away all camouflage screens over dugouts and bombproofs, and completely paralyzed all the military communication network, which had been laid exposed on the ground. It made a shambles of [Betio], accounted for large numbers of Japanese personnel, and very largely eliminated the organized resistance of the island.
> 9. 5-inch air bursts proved to be wasted ammunition when fired during the general bombardment. There were undoubtedly a very few enemy troops in open fox holes during the bombardment. Air bursts are difficult to control except at ranges less than about 5000 yards and to be effective against personnel, must not occur higher than 50 feet above the ground. The cloud of smoke and dust that covered the island shortly after bombardment commenced, made judgment of this difficult, and in some cases prevented seeing bursts which did occur at proper height. Air bursts, like VF aircraft

[117] See CTF 53 Operations Narrative, p. 50, for approximated breakdown of ordnance expenditures "For other missions."

strafing, hereafter should be only delivered against personnel in the open; it should be considered a weapon of opportunity. To prevent the common error of ineffectiveness due to too high a burst, the fuzes should be cut to the advance range to provide approximately 50% graze bursts when anti-personnel fire is desired.

10. From best information at present available, a great portion of the beach defenses were temporarily knocked out. The assualt [*sic*] waves were opposed by only a few automatic weapons, the total on beaches Red TWO and THREE being only about five. That was five too many, however, and regardless of whether future landing plans provide for taking care of them by tanks or other weapons, it is considered necessary that future naval gunfire plans provide for the destruction of these strong points [*sic*] before the assault.
11. These heavily constructed defenses are immune to high capacity projectiles. In future bombardments of similar objectives, therefore, a large amount of A.P. projectiles must be used and time provided in the fire schedule to permit a deliberate fire at close range against beach defenses prior to the initial assault. Efforts should also be made to insure that any large bomb proof shelters and dugouts where beach defense personnel may be assembled pending cessation of gunfire, are definitely knocked out. Prior to this time, the general bombardment will have destroyed camouflage screens and the bulk of any anti-aircraft weapons, so that ships' aircraft will be able to accurately control this destruction fire.
12. A restudy of the TARAWA problem indicates that this additional bombardment could have been accomplished in about two hours, and that the timing of the fire support plan could have been rearranged so as to include this additional fire still permitting the use of the same H-hour, 0900. . . .[118]

These comments are rooted in the aforementioned neutralization versus destruction doctrinal debate. Hill recognizes the continued importance of neutralization, but he points out that its importance is greatest at a particular point in the movement ashore. Plans must be made and techniques developed and honed that allow for both destruction and neutralization fires, each type being delivered at appropriate times during the assault.

Hill then begins to discuss the question of ammunition allotment and expenditure. As far as allotment is concerned, he states:

[118] CTF 53 Operations Narrative, pp. 48–49.

15. The accomplishment of the above recommended method of conducting future bombardments of objectives similar to TARAWA will require an increase in expenditure allowances of ammunition for bombardment purposes. The easiest solution for this problem is the release from general fleet action requirements the battleships and heavy cruisers allocated for gunfire support. If all 16-inch service charges in the MARYLAND class battleships were replaced by reduced charges issued in 14-inch tanks, these ships could stow 150 rounds per main battery gun. If that is not feasible, that number of projectiles could be loaded prior to departure and arrangements made for the delivery of additional powder at sea in the target area. It is not considered practicable to transfer major caliber main battery projectiles while underway.
16. In addition to making A.P. projectiles of main batteries available for bombardment, 5″/38 batteries must be provided with a large percentage of common projectiles. Providing the 5″/25 battery with projectiles with longer delay fuzes should be also considered.[119]

These comments tie back into those made previously in number eleven. Setting aside less ammunition for possible fleet action than current doctrine called for was an innovative suggestion. To do so and then to prescribe such procedures in the future called for a modification, or change, in doctrine as it existed in late 1943.[120] He recognized the impossibility of transferring major caliber rounds at sea, but his suggestions nonetheless pointed toward the ultimate solution. Some method needed to be developed that would ensure an adequate bombardment ammunition supply.

In item numbers six and thirteen of his elaborated comments and recommendations, Hill addressed the issue that ties much of his analysis together: the timing of the bombardment during Phase II. Fearing that fire from the close-support vessels would come too near the troops as they went ashore, Hill ordered at approximately 09.00 that all support ships cease their fire. This action on his part was

---

[119] Ibid., pp. 49–50.

[120] Both *Tentative Landing Operations Manual, 1935,* Paragraph 17.a and *FTP 167* with Change 1, Paragraph 517.a stated: "Due to the limited magazine capacity aboard ship and the necessity of keeping combatant vessels and aircraft prepared for fleet engagements, the supply of the necessary ammunition for the support of a landing is a serious problem." *FTP 167* with Change 3, in Paragraph 507.d.2, goes further and supplies numbers: "The magazine capacity of a ship determines the probable duration of its employment. As a general guide it may be stated that 50 percent of the total magazine capacity of fire-support [*sic*] ships will be made available for shore-target ammunition." Although not explained in this paragraph, the other fifty percent magazine capacity was supposed to consist of ammunition suitable for fleet engagements.

mentioned in the narrative above. Calling this cease-fire at this time meant that there was no naval gunfire support during the all-important period when the Marines were making the transition from the sea to the land. Hill's summary recommendation number 10(e) was meant to make sure that such a situation never recurred in the future. He elaborated upon this suggestion by saying:

> 6(d) The scheduled fire of [Phase TWO] had the same somewhat rigid requirements described of Phase ONE, and . . . required accurate timing and coordination between fire support ships, landing teams, and supporting aircraft. At the best estimate of H minus five minutes, based on the time the boats crossed the line of departure and subsequent observations, gunfire was ceased, but due to reasons not known at this time, H minus five minutes turned out to be actually H minus twenty-two minutes, creating a bad situation and a breakdown of timing coordination. Heavy smoke and dust covered the landing beaches, the boats could not be seen from the ship controlling gunfire, and the situation was not certain. Fighters were already strafing the beaches at low altitudes, preventing a resumption of gunfire, and due to the inability to determine a more exact estimate of the actual H-hour and the safety of the boats if gunfire were resumed, the decision was made to rely on the fighter's ability to keep the beach defenses neutralized until the boats landed, rather than risk renewal of gunfire. *This was a mistake,* as from an examination of the type of beach defenses it is believed that the strafing by aircraft was ineffective at this time. . . .
>
> 13. During the last five or ten minutes before H minus five minutes, a general and heavy neutralization fire must be conducted, primarily by destroyers. These should be positioned relative to the beach in such a manner as to permit the continuation of their fire until the assault waves are close in to the beach. To prevent recurrence of the error made at TARAWA of ceasing this neutralization fire too early, these ships which can actually see the boat wave and accurately determine its distance from the beach at all times, must be authorized to continue this close-supporting fire after the general order to cease firing is given, until in the opinion of the Commanding Officer, further firing becomes dangerous to the landing personnel.[121]

In other words, the commander of an amphibious assault force would never again have to worry about a gap in naval artillery coverage, as Hill found himself doing off of Betio on the morning of 20 November 1943, if he allowed those who

[121] CTF 53 Operations Narrative, pp. 46 and 49, emphasis added.

provided that coverage to make decisions concerning naval gunfire based upon direct observation and not upon some prearranged schedule.

The question of whether or not naval gunfire was accurate enough to be used safely in lieu of close-support field artillery during the early stages of an amphibious assault had been on the minds of naval and Marine Corps officers since they had begun work on amphibious warfare doctrine during the 1920s and 1930s. Hill made several comments concerning the accuracy of naval guns at Tarawa:

> 20. Considering the small size and shape of the island, the necessity for enfilade fire to assure all shots of a pattern hitting land, the small size of target areas into which fire was to be delivered, the requirement erroneously made of sudden, large and unpredictable shifts of target area, smoke and dust interference, and many other difficulties, the delivery and control of the bombardment was considered excellent. Proof of the effectiveness of gunfire was evidenced by the small number of hits in the water, by the few hits on the landing strips, which was not in any target area although surrounded by them, and by the complete wreckage of all surface installations in the target areas.
>
> 21. The effectiveness of radar gunfire control for bombardment was well demonstrated. In order to obtain enfilade positions, most of the firing was from the westward, which also was the leeward side. Soon after the first salvos landed, the objective and reference points were completely hidden in a cloud of smoke and dust, and remained so throughout all periods of heavy firing.
>
> 22. Another point effectively demonstrated was the fact that naval gunfire can be safely placed closer to troops than heretofore realized. In certain instances at [Betio], when the line of fire was roughly parallel to the troop line, call fire from a destroyer was pulled in to within 50 yards of our troops, without casualty. This was with AA common; with 5″ common it would be safer still.
>
> 23. Ship's 40 MM batteries were not used to full advantage in the TARAWA operation, principally because ships did not close the island sufficiently to permit effective fire of these excellent guns. It is believed that close range use of 40 MM guns would have reduced the number of enemy automatic weapon positions still active after H-hour.
>
> One destroyer division commander stated that the outstanding destroyer gunnery weakness observed was the extremely poor 40 MM fire, unless controlled by 5-inch gun directors instead of 40 MM directors. He stated further that failure to use this fine weapon when range and conditions permit, is "nothing short of criminal."

24. Ricochets from destroyer batteries often occurred when fire was delivered at close range, the 5″/38 AA common projectile sometimes failing to detonate on impact with flat terrain at small angles of fall, which at 3000 yards is less than 2 degrees. However, destructive fire against specific targets *must be delivered at close range* and a certain amount of ricochets must be accepted if this fire is to be effective.
25. As concerns recommended ranges at which to deliver future bombardment against similar atoll islands, the following should be the guide: For bombardment of *areas,* such as required in the general bombardment, the range must be sufficient to insure detonation of the projectiles when striking flat terrain, and should be outside the lower range limit of the rangekeeper to permit maintaining continuous and accurate control. For destruction of *specific targets* which can be seen from the ship, such as the delivery of fire required in the phase following the general bombardment, fire should be delivered from as close a range as safely possible to permit pointer key fire, good view of the target, and higher hitting velocity.[122]

In the final analysis, Hill believed that naval gunfire had passed the test of accuracy with outstanding marks. The only question left in this regard was how could even more naval artillery be brought to bear in support of the assaulting troops.

The man who was ultimately responsible for providing the naval gunfire support for Hill at Betio was Rear Admiral H. F. Kingman, Commander of Battleship Division Two and overall commander of the Southern Gunfire Support Group (TG 53.4). Kingman had his own definite ideas about what needed to be done to improve gunfire support. In a report sent to Admiral Nimitz after the battle, he not only listed his recommendations, but he also vented his spleen about the deficiencies in the doctrine and techniques of naval gunfire as he perceived them. Selected entries from this list are as follows:

1. From an observer's viewpoint, after witnessing the aerial bombardment, the surface bombardment, and aerial strafing, it seemed almost impossible for any human being to be alive on BETIO Island. Ton after ton of explosives was rained upon an island less than 0.4 miles square, and yet, when bombardment was stopped, Japanese manned machine guns and literally annihilated the first two assault waves.

   Superficial examination of BETIO after its occupation revealed that military installations, bombproofs, and machine gun emplacements were, in most instances, practically intact. Our

[122] Ibid., pp. 51–52, emphasis in original.

HC [High Capacity] projectiles, with superquick fuzes, made a grand display, but accomplished little if any real destruction of installations or personnel. . . .

3. b. . . . Soon after Phase I bombardment started, BETIO Island was shrouded in a pall of dust and smoke which prevented observation from shipboard. All ships experienced great difficulty in spotting own fall of shot and therefore walked salvos around with arbitrary spots to cover thoroughly the assigned target area.

7. Lessons Learned and Recommendations:

(2) Gunfire Support:

a. Where practicable, deliver a slow, deliberate, penetrating bombardment with reduced charges from medium–long range (12,000–16,000 yards) on D-1 day. . . .

c. Repeat [a.] on D-Day before transports approach within range of shore batteries.

d. For Phase I and Phase II bombardment, arrange firing schedule so that ships are not firing simultaneously at adjacent or nearly adjacent targets in order that shipboard and aircraft spotters may observe fall of shot more readily. Suggest use of slow, aimed fire.

e. . . . do not have firing ships jump from target to target: arrange so that salvos can be walked around slowly.

f. Do not use HC projectiles with superquick fuzes against entrenchments. Reserve these for anti-personnel firing just prior to H-hour.

g. For Phase I and Phase II firing by major caliber guns, use slow, aimed fire for possible destruction. This will likewise accomplish neutralization. . . .

h. For latter part of Phase II and for fire on beach objectives, use destroyer 5″/38.

i. Destroyer range should be between 3,500 and 7,000 yards. . . .

j. Use destroyers for called fire. Fire airbursts for anti-personnel effect only.

k. Destroyers furnishing close supporting [*sic*] fires just prior to H-hour should not be bound by a firing schedule. Commanding Officers of these ships can see boat waves approaching beach and are in a good position to know when to cease fire in order not to endanger own troops. . . .[123]

[123] TG 53.4 AR, pp. 2, 5, and 16–17.

Kingman's descriptions and recommendations, for the most part, are reflected in Hill's report.

Finally, the Second Marine Division, Merritt Edson's own unit, made its own naval gunfire recommendations. Not surprisingly, they reflected the concerns of the men who had to face what was left after the Navy's "grand display" was finished. In a letter to Holland Smith dated 2 January 1944, Julian Smith wrote:

> 1. The purpose of naval gunfire is to make possible the landing of troops on the landing beaches with a minimum of casualties from enemy action.
>
> At Tarawa, on D-day, a great deal of ammunition was expended in neutralization of coastal turrets and batteries which were not on the landing beaches themselves, and in general bombardment of the island of Betio. If these enemy installations could have been destroyed prior to D-day, so that the [Naval Attack Force], on D-day, could have expended all ammunition on the landing beaches, except that ammunition reserved for close support of land operations, more destruction of beach installations might have resulted. It was found that only battleship's fire was effective on the steel reinforced concrete emplacements and that this fire should be as follows: (1) long range, high angle of fall, to penetrate the heavy emplacements; (2) close range, direct, slow fire, preferably one (1) gun firing, to destroy those known guns and emplacements above ground. This latter fire should be the equivalent of the artillery's precision adjustment. All battleship fire should be delay action with about 50% armor piercing and 50% high capacity shell. . . .
>
> The beach preparation should have been spread over a longer period of time, with slower fire, to allow ships to observe their targets and determine the effectiveness of this fire. The point of impact should be the beach itself. Depending upon the degree of enfilade fire obtainable, this would have wasted some ammunition as short in the water. However, the beach defenses would have been more thoroughly covered. During the final beach preparation, all guns that can bear on the target should fire at the maximum rate of fire.
>
> The flanks of a landing beach for a distance of at least six hundred (600) yards, and enemy strong points [*sic*] inland that can fire on the beach, should receive the same amount of fire that the landing beach itself receives.
>
> Fire should not be lifted from the beach until the last possible moment. At TARAWA, although acting on the best information

> available, the beach preparation was lifted too soon. It is recommended that the coordinating plane should carry a Marine Staff Officer to direct the time of lifting the preparation.[124]

The emphasis for the Marines is the amount of time that should be spent working over the landing beaches. This emphasis is also found in *FTP 167,* although there is no indication in that document as to the amount of time that should be spent softening up an objective prior to D-day. Paragraph 506.b of Change 3 specifies, in fact, that "[t]his chapter is primarily concerned with the requirements of D-day." The only direct allusion to preliminary bombardment is found in Paragraph 506.a, but there is no guidance as to duration: "The over-all requirement [for fire support of the infantry in an amphibious operation] may include fires executed in advance of D-day, such as bombardments for the destruction of enemy supplies and raids to confuse him as to the point of attack."[125] With this doctrinal shortcoming in mind, neither the Navy nor the Marine Corps saw themselves as arguing that the accepted naval gunfire doctrine was fundamentally flawed. Since doctrine did not directly address the length of pre-D-day bombardment, then doctrine was not what was at fault. Tarawa, rather than indicating where doctrine needed to be changed, instead showed where the Navy failed in its application of what was basically sound doctrine. In other words, what happened at Tarawa on 20–23 November 1943 was a failure to follow adequately the recognized standard. Guadalcanal had already taught the lesson that gunfire was ineffective unless emplacements took a direct hit.[126] Marines like Merritt Edson were well aware of what had happened in the Solomons and they, unlike their Navy counterparts, were not so sanguinely optimistic when contemplating what they might find when they got ashore on Betio. The Navy, according to the Action Reports filed after the completion of Galvanic, just needed to be reminded of that lesson.

This line of reasoning, one that both the Navy and Marine Corps continued to follow throughout the war and afterward, did not recognize that adding a component to the existing naval gunfire doctrine stipulating that an objective must be worked over for an extended period of time before D-day was, by definition, changing the existing doctrine. By this definition, then, the crucible of Tarawa incinerated a certain portion of the naval gunfire doctrine of pre-November 1943

---

[124] NARA, RG 127, USMC Geographic Files, Box 29, File A7–17, 2nd Marine Division Recommendations, Tarawa, CG 2nd Marine Division, Recommendations Based on Tarawa Operation, Number 5, Naval Gunfire, 2 January 1944, pp. 1–2.

[125] See *FTP 167* with Change 1, Paragraphs 501 and 503 as well as *FTP 167* with Change 3, Paragraphs 502, 503, and 506.

[126] NARA, RG 127, USMC Geographic Files, Box 39, File A7–2, 1st Marine Div. Phase II, Final Report, Guadalcanal, Division Commander's Final Report on Guadalcanal Operation, Phase II (from H-hour to Evening 9 August), n.d., p. 8.

and provided the impetus for rewriting it. If this epiphany is taken as the basis for argument, and this work does just that, then to what extent can it be said that the doctrine was rewritten? Was the old doctrine thrown out wholesale and a completely new one put in its place? No, that did not happen. The changes were incremental rather than revolutionary—but they were important just the same.

Probably the most important change as far as the Marine Corps was concerned was what it perceived to be the Navy's sudden willingness to accept the Marine argument that slow and deliberate bombardment over a longer period of time than just two to three hours before H-hour was necessary. Area bombardment for neutralization would not do. The Marines included instructions for this type of bombardment in their naval gunfire plan, but Spruance and Turner decided that surprise was of the essence.[127] Galvanic being the first Central Pacific Campaign operation, no one was certain how effectively the Japanese fleet would be able to react to the American invasion of the Gilberts. Nimitz told Spruance that he should "Get the hell in and get the hell out," and Spruance followed his boss' instructions to the letter.[128] The failure of the Japanese Combined Fleet to mount any kind of significant counterattack against the operation in the Gilberts caused the Navy to rethink this policy. As a result, naval planners were willing to allow for additional gunfire preparation time in the next operation. There would be many problems encountered in the Marshalls, but lack of adequate naval gunfire would not be one of them. The "lessons of Tarawa," at least those concerning the use of naval gunfire, would be learned well and applied decisively at Roi-Namur.

[127] VAC NGF Plan, p. 1.

[128] Joseph H. Alexander, *Storm Landings: Epic Amphibious Battles in the Central Pacific* (Annapolis: Naval Institute Press, 1997), p. 49.

Chapter 4

Operation Flintlock

The Amphibious Landings on Roi-Namur

Rear Admiral Richard L. Conolly's Northern Attack Force steamed through the pre-dawn darkness of 31 January 1944—the designated D-day for the American invasion of the Marshall Islands—on its way to take up positions to the northeast of Kwajalein Atoll. Conolly's main operational objective was Roi-Namur, two small islands joined together by nothing more than a spit of land and a man-made causeway. The job of eradicating the enemy presence on this objective fell to Major General Harry Schmidt's Fourth Marine Division, the Corps' newest division. The Fourth Division's goal for 31 January, in accordance with one of the many "lessons of Tarawa," was to secure several nearby islands for the installation of artillery. This artillery would then supply precision fire support for the D+1 landings on Roi and Namur. Schmidt created a special unit, the IVAN Landing Group, to carry out this mission and he put his Assistant Division Commander (ADC), Brigadier General James L. Underhill, in charge of it. Underhill's force was composed mostly of Colonel Samuel C. Cumming's 25th Marines, Reinforced. Cumming's objective consisted of five islets to the southwest and southeast of Roi-Namur. In keeping with the "lesson," he was to emplace units of the division's artillery regiment, the 14th Marines, on them. Possession of two of those islets, Mellu and Ennuebing, served an additional purpose as well. It gave Admiral Conolly control of a deep-water passage through the atoll's surrounding reef and, consequently, access to the huge lagoon within and to the protected beaches that bordered it. As a result, they would be his first targets.[1]

The transports carrying the IVAN Landing Group took position off Mellu shortly before daylight. Meanwhile, fire support units steamed to their designated areas east of Namur and west of Roi and waited for the first light of day to appear. At 06.51 these ships began pumping shells into their targets, only lifting for eight minutes, beginning at 07.15, to allow for a carrier-based air strike. This pummeling continued until just before the assault troops made landfall. The Marines

[1] Isely and Crowl, *U.S. Marines and Amphibious War,* pp. 266–67; Philip A. Crowl and Edmund G. Love, *Seizure of the Gilberts and Marshalls, United States Army in World War II, The War in the Pacific* (Washington, DC: U.S. Army Center of Military History, 1955; reprint, Harrisburg, PA: National Historical Society, 1995), pp. 180–81; Shaw et al., *Central Pacific Drive,* p. 144.

crawled down cargo nets draped over the sides of their transports under this umbrella of fire and steel, getting into LCVPs for the trip to a designated area where they climbed aboard amphibious tractors for the movement ashore. The tractor drivers, not having had adequate practice in performing this open-sea maneuver, struggled to perform their tasks in a timely manner. What was supposed to be a well-choreographed ballet degenerated for a short period into a gigantic amphibious traffic jam.[2]

Order was finally restored, however, and the LVTs formed into waves and made their way to the line of departure. This line, marked by the control officer aboard the destroyer USS *Phelps* (DD-360), was approximately 5,000 yards from Ennuebing and Mellu. The tractors waited there until a flag dropped from *Phelps*' yardarm, the signal to start for shore. When the flag dropped, off they went. Sporadic fire from a 127mm battery on the west coast of Roi splashed nearby while the LVTs made their way beachward, but fire support units quickly silenced it and the Marines continued on their way undisturbed. A nineteen-knot wind made the sea very choppy and the swells accompanying the wind made the already slow LVTs even slower. Traveling at approximately half-speed (2 mph), the amtracs took much longer to get to shore than allowed for in the schedule. The plan called for simultaneous landings on the ocean side of both Ennuebing and Mellu at 09.00, but it became obvious that this was not to be. Conolly delayed H-hour until 09.30 to adjust for the tardiness of the tractors, but doing so did not make them move any faster and even more time was lost as the LVTs continued to labor against wind and sea. Company B, 1st Battalion, 25th Marines (1/25), finally went ashore on Ennuebing at 09.52. Meanwhile, Company C, 1/25, and the division's scout unit, Company D, 4th Tank Battalion, struggled to make it ashore on Mellu. The combination of a rugged segment of reef, strong winds, and pounding surf thwarted every attempt to land on the ocean-side beaches of the islet. Cumming eventually expedited the landing by sending the scout unit around Mellu to the lagoon-side beaches where it went ashore at 09.55. A regimental staff officer then

---

[2] Shaw et al., *Central Pacific Drive,* pp. 144–45. In United States Navy, *Amphibious Operations: The Marshall Islands, January–February 1944* (hereinafter COMINCH P-002), p. 7-3, MCUA, Historical Amphibious Files (hereinafter HAF), Box 11B, Folders 250 and 250-B. Conolly is quoted as stating in his report on the Roi-Namur landings that "[p]revious use LVTs of the cargo carrying type, and the training of the drivers, to date, has been such that they have been generally deficient in seamanship and the necessary knowledge and ability required to properly handle LVTs in the open sea or even in the choppy water of a lagoon whipped by a normal trade wind of about 20 knots." He then recommended that LVTs that are to land in the assault be considered "boats" rather than "vehicles" and that their drivers be trained accordingly. Note: the pages in this document are denoted using a hyphenated system. For example, page 3 in chapter 8 is denoted as 8-3; page 24 in chapter 1 is denoted as 1-24.

got word through to Company C to do the same and that unit followed the scouts onto the southeastern beach at 10.15.[3]

The Marines reported Ennuebing secure at 10.35. Minesweepers then proceeded into the lagoon through North Pass next to the islet and began their initial sweeps of the areas that were to be used as boat lanes and anchorages for the landings to follow. Small boats and aircraft laid down a blanket of smoke to protect the sweepers from the sharp eyes of Japanese gun crews, but the obscuring smoke did not stop the enemy from firing blindly at the American ships in the lagoon. *Phelps* left her position at the Ennuebing-Mellu control line to knock out these persistent Japanese gun batteries, but she ran into a problem. She began to enter the lagoon through North Pass, but one of the minesweepers reported that the minimum depth through it was fifteen feet. The destroyer drew eighteen feet, so there was a further delay as she made her way to the pass west of Mellu. To add to all these troubles, she could not act as control vessel while providing gunfire support. Control had to pass, at that point, to *LCC 33*, a shallow-draft landing craft specially fitted out for just such an eventuality. A communications glitch, however, resulted in the commander of the alternate control craft failing to learn of the change in plans. Someone had to take the reigns, so responsibility for keeping tabs on the landing craft and forming them up for the next phase of the day's operations fell to personnel aboard the submarine chaser *SC 997*. The reason? This little boat embarked General Underhill and his staff and, since the ADC was in command of IVAN Landing Group, then default control fell to him. Underhill, however, did not have a copy of the control plan nor did *SC 997* have adequate communications capability to allow for the coordination of the forming waves, but he did what he could to maintain order until such time as the control officer aboard *Phelps* could once again take up his responsibilities.[4]

Boat waves began to form off of Ennuebing for landings on Ennumennet and Ennubirr as soon as Marines were ashore on their first two objectives. *Phelps,* once again able to act as control vessel, took up her position on the new line of departure. The boat waves began their journey from outside the lagoon, entering through North Pass and forming up on the line marked by the destroyer. A strong wind once again slowed the progress of the LVTs toward the line and inexperienced tractor drivers allowed their vehicles to drift downwind as they idled their engines while waiting for the assault waves to form. All of this caused further delays, but the additional time was not completely wasted. In the meanwhile, naval bombardment and air strikes continued on the next two objectives and, finally, at

[3] Isely and Crowl, *U.S. Marines and Amphibious War,* pp. 266–67; Crowl and Love, *Seizure of the Gilberts and Marshalls,* pp. 180–81; Shaw et al., *Central Pacific Drive,* pp. 144–45 and 147; COMINCH P-002, pp. 1-22 and 1-23.

[4] Shaw et al., *Central Pacific Drive,* pp. 148–49; Crowl and Love, *Seizure of the Gilberts and Marshalls,* p. 307; COMINCH P-002, p. 1-23.

14.35, the first wave started for Ennumennet and Ennubirr. The Marines landed at approximately 15.15 on both islets against light opposition and both were secured rapidly.[5]

Underhill did not waste any time emplacing artillery on the first two islands taken by IVAN Group. He sent 75mm guns ashore on Ennuebing and 105mm howitzers onto Mellu while the attacks on Ennumennet and Ennubirr were ongoing. Guns went in on these last two islets as soon as they were secure. The final D-day landing, a shore-to-shore assault from Ennumennet to Ennugarrett, took place at 18.20 after the latter had been softened up by an intense naval bombardment and air attack. Ennugarrett was in American hands by 20.00 and artillery was placed ashore immediately.[6] Conolly and Schmidt were now ready for the next day's landings.

Roi and Namur Islands were both subjected to very accurate air and naval gunfire bombardment throughout the day on 31 January while the five tiny islets off their shores were neutralized and captured. The destroyers USS *Porterfield* (DD-682), *Hopewell* (DD-681), and *Ellet* (DD-398) continued this bombardment intermittently through the night of 31 January–1 February in order to drive the Japanese defenders to distraction. The object was not to actually destroy any targets, an impossibly difficult task given the absence of daylight, but to keep the enemy from sleeping.[7] To that end, the destroyers fired on areas in which it was believed the defenders might concentrate personnel for the night. They also fired on the southern beaches of the islands in order to support the Underwater Demolition Teams (UDTs) in their efforts to clear the landing areas of obstacles.[8]

The LSTs embarking the units participating in the initial D+1 landings rode anchor in the lagoon during the night while waiting for the launching of the attack on 1 February. Other ships of the force put to sea, coming back to the attack area at daybreak. The original plan called for launching the LVTs from LSTs outside the lagoon on D+1. The LVTs were then to churn under their own power to the line of departure inside the lagoon, travel the final 5,000 yards to the beaches, and begin the assault. This plan was changed after the LVTs encountered the previously described problems on D-day. Nineteen-knot winds continued to concern Conolly as he considered what to do on 1 February. To mitigate the problem as much as possible, he ordered LSTs to disembark their LVTs inside the lagoon. This change was not an entirely new or unique idea, however. Conolly reported that it was part

[5] COMINCH P-002, p. 1-23.

[6] Ibid., p. 1-24.

[7] This is a longstanding point of doctrine. See the original *FTP 167,* United States Navy Department Library, Department of the Navy, *Fleet Training Publication 167, Landing Operations Doctrine, U.S. Navy, 1938,* Par. 507.a, p. 120, and compare it with *FTP 167* with Change 3, Par. 532.d, p. 133.

[8] COMINCH P-002, p. 1-24.

of an "Alternate Rough Weather Plan" that was already in place and with which everyone was familiar.[9]

Captain E. R. McLean, control officer aboard *Phelps,* had his hands full implementing this new plan because, regardless of the changes instituted by Conolly, problems continued to plague the operation. The 10th Amphibian Tractor Battalion (ATB), plus Company A, 11th ATB, were assigned to land the 24th Marines on Namur on D+1 after having carried out the landing of IVAN Group on 31 January. Amphibious tractor losses on D-day left the unit short of its full complement of LVTs. Time was lost on the morning of D+1 while replacements and alternate means of transport were found. The unit assigned to land the 23rd Marines on Roi, the 4th ATB, was in much better condition regarding its complement of tractors, but it had its own bedeviling problem with which to contend. Confusion reigned within the unit on the morning of 1 February as the commander of the 4th ATB and the drivers of the LVTs under his command struggled with drowned out radios, a problem encountered earlier at Tarawa, as they tried to communicate with one another. Conolly finally signaled at 08.53 that the original W-hour of 10.00 for Roi was to be reset for 11.00.[10]

In Roi's case, everything was ready to go as the new W-hour approached, but the line of departure off Namur stubbornly resisted all efforts to effect its establishment. Conolly, in consultation with Schmidt, decided that no more delays could be allowed—the attack had to go off immediately or not at all. So, to the surprise of the commander of the 24th Marines, Conolly signaled a "go" and the flag dropped at 11.12.[11] The 23rd Marines had little trouble in overcoming the Japanese defenses on Roi. Colonel Louis R. Jones, CO of the regiment, radioed General Schmidt at 13.11 with the exuberant message that "This is a pip. No opposition near the beach. . . . Landing teams moving in on O-1 line." At approximately 13.26, Jones followed up with the message, "O-1 ours. Give us the word and we will take the rest of the island." The only real difficulties the regiment encountered were of its own making and were the result of a breakdown in tactical discipline. Shortly after Jones made his excited radio reports to Schmidt, tanks from Company C, 4th Tank Battalion, grew impatient waiting around at the O-1 line for further orders and pushed on past it. Infantry followed the tanks in accordance with doctrine and a platoon of LVT(A)s joined in as well, working its way northward up Roi's west coast. The tanks, infantry, and LVT(A)s fired at any position that might harbor Japanese. The assault plan called for a halt at the O-1 line and then the launching

---

[9] Ibid., pp. 1-22 and 1-24.

[10] Samuel Eliot Morison, *Aleutians, Gilberts and Marshalls: June 1942–April 1944, History of United States Naval Operations in World War II,* Vol. 7 (Boston: Little Brown, 1951), p. 238; Robert D. Heinl, Jr. and John A. Crown, *The Marshalls: Increasing the Tempo* (Washington, DC: Historical Section, HQMC, 1954), pp. 66–67.

[11] COMINCH P-002, p. 1-25.

of a coordinated attack to capture the rest of the island. What Marines of the 23rd regiment were doing was unplanned and uncoordinated and, though it resulted in the deaths of many of the enemy, it thoroughly disrupted both regimental and division command and control on the island for approximately an hour. Jones finally reestablished order by 14.45 and he reorganized his men for the final push across the island. General Schmidt declared Roi secure at 18.05.[12]

The 24th Marines on Namur were not as fortunate. Elements of the regiment's 3rd and 2nd Battalions made it ashore on Beaches Green 1 and Green 2, respectively, at 11.55. Being not much more than an airstrip and the hangar facilities for the aircraft flying from it, Roi's terrain had allowed for the 23rd Marines rapid advance across their objective. Namur was different. Since it was not necessary to clear everything off of the island to make way for an airstrip, then the defenders could be more creative and thorough in setting up defensive works. Thick brush and trees covered Namur in places and there were many more buildings than on Roi. The rubble of these buildings and the island's vegetation provided the Japanese with numerous positions from which to fire on the advancing Marines.[13]

An accident also contributed to the slowing of the 24th Marines' advance, compounding the effects of all these terrain obstacles. At 13.05, a revetted building in Company F, 2nd Battalion's zone of action blew up, raining chunks of concrete and pieces of steel down on everyone within hundreds of yards of the explosion. Twenty Marines died and one hundred were wounded, approximately half of 2/24's casualties for the entire operation. The explosion resulted from the attempted demolition of what assaulting Marines thought was just another blockhouse. It turned out to be a storage facility for torpedo warheads. The immediate results of the accident were four-fold: all coordinated forward movement in 2/24's zone of action halted; the organization of units near the O-1 line was delayed; radio communications between assault companies and battalion headquarters were knocked out; and command and control was disrupted such that company commanders could not organize their men into proper unit order.[14]

The 3rd Battalion, 24th Marines, was dealing with its share of problems at the same time that its sister battalion was attempting to press home the assault. Third Battalion encountered more enemy fire initially than did 2/24 to their right. There was no organized enemy defense, however, because Namur's communications

---

[12] Shaw et al., *Central Pacific Drive,* pp. 161–65; quotation from page 163. The O-1 Line was the first inland objective for the assaulting force. Plans usually called for the attacking Marines or soldiers to reach this line by a certain time. The schedule would be modified based upon the attacking force's success in attaining this objective.

[13] Heinl and Crown, *The Marshalls: Increasing the Tempo,* p. 85; Shaw et al., *Central Pacific Drive,* pp. 169–70.

[14] Crowl and Love, *Seizure of the Gilberts and Marshalls,* pp. 325–27; Shaw et al., *Central Pacific Drive,* pp. 170–71.

center, the position from which the Japanese were to have coordinated the defense of Roi-Namur, had been destroyed by the American naval gunfire bombardment. Companies I and K made the O-1 line by 14.00, but they were ordered to hold their position while the regiment organized itself for a coordinated push across the rest of the island at 16.30.[15]

The coordinated attack kicked off at 16.30, but only 3rd Battalion was able to jump off the line on time. Second Battalion, still recovering from the torpedo warhead explosion, reorganized as quickly as possible and finally left the line at 17.30. The attack northward consisted of light tank penetration followed by infantry. Thirty-seven millimeter canister shot from tanks blasted away dense undergrowth and killed Japanese. Any defenders who attempted to jump aboard the lead tanks were eliminated by canister shot from the following tanks. This advance was tough going. Dense undergrowth, shell holes, and fallen trees presented an obstacle course that proved deadly for some of the Marine tankers, as illustrated by the story of Captain James L. Denig, the CO of Company B, 4th Tank Battalion. Denig became separated from his infantry support and the other elements of his company. After hitting a log and veering off into a clearing, he stopped to get his bearings before continuing on. A group of Japanese climbed aboard his tank as it sat there and one of their number dropped a grenade down a signal port that had been left open to allow engine fumes to vent. The explosion killed Denig and his driver and wounded the other two crewmen. At that point, a squad of infantry and another tank appeared and killed the Japanese attackers.[16]

The northward push eventually ran out of steam and at 19.30 Colonel Franklin A. Hart, the 24th Marines CO, ordered his regiment to halt, to set up a defensive perimeter, to hold the ground they had already captured, and to prepare to resume the attack the next morning.[17] The 3rd Battalion jumped off first on D+2 at 09.00. Medium tanks spearheaded their advance, firing armor-piercing rounds into pillboxes and other concrete structures to pierce their walls and then pumping HE rounds into their interiors. The 2nd Battalion joined the attack at 10.06. Both battalions met at Natalie Point, the most northern position on Namur, at 12.15. General Schmidt declared the island secure at 14.18.[18]

---

[15] Shaw et al., *Central Pacific Drive,* p. 170; Crowl and Love, *Seizure of the Gilberts and Marshalls,* pp. 323–24.

[16] Heinl and Crown, *The Marshalls: Increasing the Tempo,* pp. 93–94; Shaw et al., *Central Pacific Drive,* p. 172; Crowl and Love, *Seizure of the Gilberts and Marshalls,* pp. 327–28.

[17] Shaw et al., *Central Pacific Drive,* p. 173; Crowl and Love, *Seizure of the Gilberts and Marshalls,* p. 329.

[18] Shaw et al., *Central Pacific Drive,* p. 174; Heinl and Crown, *The Marshalls: Increasing the Tempo,* p. 97.

Strategic and Operational Objectives for Flintlock

The story of how American amphibious planning came to be focused on the Marshall Islands is an integral part of the story already related regarding the Gilberts. The two operations were intertwined with one another in their origins in such a way that the story of the genesis of one cannot be told without encountering significant overlap with the story of the genesis of the other. The following description of strategic thought concerning the Marshalls, as a result, covers territory already mapped out in greater detail in chapter three. The emphasis this time around, however, will be on providing background more specifically for Flintlock, the codename by which the Marshalls operation was known.

The Marshall Islands were part of Germany's North Pacific colonial empire prior to World War I. Japan, entering the war on the side of the Allies and claiming to be helping in Britain's search for a German cruiser squadron commanded by Admiral Graf Maximilian von Spee, raised the Imperial flag over the Marshalls and several other island groups of German Micronesia in the autumn of 1914. The Australian government became alarmed at this expansion of Japanese power and asked London for help. The British, reacting to Australia's concerns, requested that Japan go no farther than the equator in its penetration of the German colonies. To ensure that the Japanese paid attention to their request, they refused to help their ally take any of the colonies south of that line. Later, in February of 1917, Great Britain agreed to allow continued Japanese control of Micronesia in return for Japan's help in the naval war against Germany. The Japanese sent a flotilla of destroyers to the Atlantic in fulfillment of their part of the deal. The British were interested in more than just controlling the expansion of Japanese influence in the Pacific, however. Their ulterior motive for entering into this agreement with Japan was to control the expansion of American sea power. Aware of U.S. interests in the Central and Western Pacific and concerned about having to deal with an increasingly powerful ally during the war and a possible naval arms race with that ally afterward, Britain wanted to make sure that the former German colonies did not fall into American hands. The Japanese were only too happy to help them with their dilemma.[19]

The Treaty of Versailles translated the arrangement between Britain and Japan into an internationally recognized agreement, granting the Japanese a Class C Mandate over Micronesia under the auspices of the League of Nations. This League of Nations Mandate figured prominently in the various permutations of the American Orange plans of the interwar period. The Marshalls eventually became the first stop on the "Royal Road" to the Philippines, a concept that dominated U.S. Navy planning from 1934 through mid-1937. The goal of the thrust through the Marshalls was to provide bases for the eventual taking of Truk in the Carolines, a base from which the final push to the Philippines could be staged. The accepted

[19] Miller, *War Plan Orange*, pp. 110 and 112.

operational procedure for taking the Mandate atolls was basically the one prescribed by Major Earl H. "Pete" Ellis in his 1921 report "Advance Base Operations in Micronesia."[20] This was the historical and conceptual framework that was in place when United States planners began preparations for the Central Pacific Drive in mid-1943.

The first mention of the Marshalls as a possible objective along the road to the Japanese home islands was, as related earlier, in the campaign outline prepared by the Navy War Plans Division in mid-April 1942. The third stage of the projected advance against the Japanese described in the document consisted of the "seizure of the Caroline and Marshall Islands and the establishment there of Fleet and air advanced bases." The basic concept of using the Central Pacific as a highway to Japan remained intact, the Carolines and the great naval base at Truk continuing to hold the fascination of wartime Navy planners immediately after Pearl Harbor just as they had their prewar counterparts.[21]

The American Joint Chiefs of Staff arrived at the Casablanca Conference in January of 1943 with this idea as just one of several possible directions in which to go in the Pacific, but, not having worked out any particulars beforehand, they were at a loss when their British counterparts almost magically produced papers on practically every aspect of coalition strategy. The British Imperial Chiefs of Staff made it clear that they expected the Americans to adhere to the ABC-1 and Arcadia agreements that Germany was to be viewed as the primary enemy in the war. With that in mind, then, they wanted a decision to be made as to "what situation . . . we wish to establish in the Eastern Theater . . . in 1943, and what forces will be necessary to establish that situation."[22] The Joint Chiefs put their Joint Staff Planners to work on the problem and they came back with the study circulated under the title CCS 153. This was the study described in chapter three that included two enclosures, one (denoted "A") concerning the Pacific and the other (denoted "B") concerning Burma. Burma fell into the British area of strategic responsibility in the "Eastern Theater." The Americans, particularly the U.S. Navy, were most interested in their own area, the Pacific, and how to meet their own perceived responsibilities in it. Enclosure "A" contained their ideas in that regard. The ideas embodied in that enclosure were based upon the four basic assumptions delineated in the story of the Gilberts operation, the first of which was that "the ultimate objective of the basic global strategy is to bring the war to a successful conclusion at the earliest practicable date." The JPS recommended "that the Japanese be kept under continual pressure sufficient in power and extent to absorb the disposable Japanese military effort" so that the ultimate objective could be most efficiently met, and, with this idea in mind, they presented a plan calling for the undertaking

---

[20] Ibid., pp. 186–202.

[21] Hayes, *History of the JCS in WWII,* p. 139.

[22] Ibid., p. 283.

of four major operations in the Pacific in 1943. The third operation looked very similar to the third stage of the campaign that had been envisioned by Navy planners in April of 1942: "Seizure and occupation of Gilbert Islands, Marshall Islands, Caroline Islands, up to and including Truk. It is planned that these operations will be undertaken subsequent to Rabaul."[23]

Discussions with the British helped to clarify the plan further in the minds of both coalition partners. Talk turned to the subject of Pacific strategy on the next to last day of the conference, 23 January, and decisions were made, with great reluctance on the part of the British, as to the general direction to be followed. According to the JCS memo entitled "Conduct of the War in the Pacific Theater in 1943," one potential Japanese offensive action in the coming year was an attack on the Hawaii–Samoa–Fiji–New Caledonia line. Such an attack was considered dangerous because that line served as cover for the strategically necessary line of communications to Australia and New Zealand. Operations against the Japanese in the Solomons during 1942 and 1943 made an enemy offensive against the aforementioned line unprofitable except by way of the Gilbert and Ellice Islands toward Samoa. American offensive action with the highest probability of stopping such a move would be to reverse the route and advance on the Samoa–Jaluit line by way of those same groups of islands. To do so would make the all-important Australia–New Zealand line of communications secure and it would also draw Japanese forces away from Rabaul.[24] After the decision had been made to go to the Gilberts first and then to the Marshalls, the Joint Chiefs went back to the United States to begin implementing the overall strategy agreed to by the coalition partners.

The usual focus of the United States Navy's various prewar plans, as should be quite clear from the foregoing description of American strategic planning, was a thrust across the Central Pacific through two of the island groups of the Japanese Mandate: the Marshalls and the Carolines. It was not until mid-1941, when Franklin D. Roosevelt became interested in entering into a Lend-Lease arrangement with the British to use their Central and South Pacific islands as bases, that the possibility of going at the Marshalls from the Gilberts was seen as operationally feasible and strategically advantageous.[25] As it turned out, a Lend-Lease swap became a moot point when the Japanese tide of conquest washed over the Gilberts on 9–10 December 1941. When Navy planners began contemplating in April 1942 at least limited offensives in the Pacific, Admiral King requested and received the "blanket authority" described in chapter three.[26] The Americans used this authority within a few months.

---

[23] Ibid., pp. 283–85.

[24] Ibid., pp. 299–300.

[25] Miller, *War Plan Orange,* pp. 105 and 247.

[26] Hayes, *History of the JCS in WWII,* pp. 139 and 310. (See Chapter 3 herein.)

The end of fighting on Guadalcanal in early February 1943 presented King and Marshall with the question of what to do as a follow-up. King put the Navy War Plans Division to work on a plan that, in accordance with the decisions made at Casablanca, would send American forces into the Gilbert and Ellice Islands. The objective for these operations was the overall strategic advancement of U.S. forces and the diversion of Japanese forces from the Solomons. The ultimate goal of movement into these two island groups was the long-anticipated capture of the Caroline and Marshall Islands.[27] On 9 February, while meeting with Nimitz in Pearl Harbor, King asked his Pacific commander for his opinion as to the seizure of the Gilbert Islands in the near future. Nimitz, not averse to the bold stroke when he believed the results worth the risk, advised caution at this time. He did not believe that American forces were built up sufficiently in the Pacific as of early 1943 to allow for the undertaking of major operations such as those being proposed. King reluctantly agreed that the beginning of a Central Pacific offensive would have to be postponed until such time as the additional ships, materiel, and men could be amassed.[28] King and Nimitz eventually agreed that that point was reached by June 1943. From that time onward, the move against the Gilberts and Marshalls became two parts of a closely coordinated whole with the 20 July Joint Chiefs' directive ordering the taking of the Gilberts effectively differentiating one from the other.

Resources and Plans for Landings on Roi-Namur

Nimitz chose to use the same team he had employed for Galvanic to prosecute the new operation: Vice Admiral Raymond Spruance once again commanded the Fifth Fleet, Rear Admiral Richmond K. Turner commanded the V Amphibious Force, and Major General Holland M. Smith commanded V Amphibious Corps. As before, they would be responsible for creating the top-level command environment within which Nimitz's strategic and operational directives could be transformed into operational and tactical realities.

The Marshall Islands are composed of over 800 reef encircled atolls arrayed across an expanse of more than 400,000 square miles of ocean. These atolls lie in two roughly defined chains, the Ratak (or "sunrise") to the east and the Ralik (or "sunset") to the west.[29] The mid-1930s War Plan Orange emphasized beginning a campaign in the eastern chain, mainly because those islands were closer to Hawaii.[30] Influenced by Orange and in accordance with both the Navy War Plans

---

[27] Ibid., p. 310.

[28] Potter, *Nimitz,* p. 237.

[29] Crowl and Love, *Seizure of the Gilberts and Marshalls,* p. 166; Shaw et al., *Central Pacific Drive,* p. 117; Buell, *Quiet Warrior,* p. 229.

[30] Miller, *War Plan Orange,* p. 189.

Division's February conclusions and the directives issued by the Combined Chiefs of Staff at the Quadrant Conference in August, Nimitz proposed the following theater plan to the Joint Chiefs: "(a) Simultaneous seizure of key islands on the KWAJALEIN, WOTJE, and MALOELAP atolls, followed at once by the reduction of the remainder of the islands of those atolls; (b) Contain and neutralize JALUIT and MILLE; (c) Mount operation both from OAHU and South Pacific bases; (d) Use ELLICE and GILBERT positions as staging points; (e) Employ NAURU, GILBERT positions, and BAKER for photographic reconnaissance, search, and for repeated air strikes to soften up the MARSHALLS; (f) Target date 1 January 1944."[31]

The most difficult logistical problem presented by the plan was making sure that an adequate supply of shipping would be available when needed. The Joint Staff Planners of the Joint Chiefs of Staff began to work on this problem in earnest after the JCS returned from the Quadrant Conference. The JPS estimated, barring any additional losses, that there would be a shortage of nine attack transports and ten attack cargo ships in the Central Pacific on 1 January 1944. The planners believed that the deficit could be made up before the ships would be needed for the operation, but Army planners, worried that the projected Marshalls operation would interfere with MacArthur taking the final steps to isolate Rabaul (a far-flung operation codenamed Cartwheel), wanted to make Flintlock contingent "upon the availability of shipping." As preparations began for the operation, General Marshall became alarmed at the number of ships being requested by planners, more ships than Lieutenant General George S. Patton required when landing 34,000 troops on the coast of North Africa. Marshall recommended that the Joint Staff Planners study the affect that this one Central Pacific operation would have on the availability of shipping to other operations in the Pacific. The JCS approved the recommendation and the Joint Planners got to work. They determined that, except for a shortage of personnel shipping, Flintlock would not cause any problems. Converting some cargo vessels to troop transports would alleviate this shortage, however. The report satisfied Marshall and the other Chiefs that the operation would not interfere unduly with other Pacific actions, so they authorized it.[32]

The high number of casualties at Tarawa caused Spruance, Turner, and H. M. Smith to question the feasibility of assaulting three strongly-held atolls at the same time. Conferring with one another after returning to Hawaii from Galvanic, the three decided to voice their concerns to CinCPac. They suggested that the operation be divided into two phases: Wotje and Maloelap first and then Kwajalein using bombers based on those two previously secured atolls to provide air support. Nimitz took their concerns into account and decided to scale down the operation. He proposed an alternative plan that caught his chief operational subordinates by

[31] Hayes, *History of the JCS in WWII*, p. 476.

[32] Morison, *Aleutians, Gilberts and Marshalls*, p. 343; Hayes, *History of the JCS in WWII*, pp. 416 and 476–78; Shaw et al., *Central Pacific Drive*, p. 117.

surprise, however—he wanted to go straight for Kwajalein and completely bypass the eastern islands of the chain. Nimitz's Chief of Staff, Rear Admiral Charles H. "Soc" McMorris, and his chief planner, Rear Admiral Forrest P. Sherman, both believed that the plan would work. The JCS ordered Nimitz to send the Fifth Fleet's fast carriers to the South Pacific immediately upon capturing Kwajalein so that they could support Admiral Halsey's amphibious operations in that theater, but Sherman thought that the loss of the carriers would not matter. He reasoned that carrier air would be able to knock out Japanese airfields on the atolls to the east of Kwajalein before the assault took place and then land-based air operating from the two airfields the Americans would acquire by taking Kwajalein, along with bombers from the Gilberts, would maintain neutralization after the carriers left.[33]

Nimitz presented this plan on 7 December to the three men who would be responsible for implementing it, and all three of them argued that it should not be done. Spruance, in particular, was determined to change Nimitz's mind. He stated that, contrary to Sherman's assurances, he would not be able to maintain neutralization of the airfields on the bypassed islands once he lost the fast carriers to Halsey. Nimitz gave his Fifth Fleet team some time to ponder his proposal. Meanwhile, CinCPac began to receive intelligence that indicated the Japanese were strengthening their defenses in the eastern Marshall Islands at the expense of Kwajalein. Like Nimitz's subordinates, they expected the next American blow to fall there. At a meeting with all his Fifth Fleet flag and general officers on 14 December, Nimitz put his proposal to a vote. Every single one of them voted to take the eastern islands first. Nimitz, calmly, told them that the decision was made—the objective would be Kwajalein. Turner and Spruance stayed behind after the meeting to argue their point further. After they had exhausted their arguments, CinCPac put the matter to them bluntly: they would either carry out his orders or he would put someone in command who would. They chose to do as their boss directed.[34]

Allan Millett argues that Nimitz based his choice of Kwajalein over Wotje and Maloelap on his confidence in the ability of the Fifth Fleet to isolate amphibious objectives from Japanese air and naval intervention. He also postulates that the American ability to decode Japanese radio messages could have given Nimitz and Sherman knowledge of Tokyo's decision to defend a line running through the Marianas and the Carolines, leaving the Marshalls virtually undefended.[35] As it turned out, the Japanese military had decided to pull back the defensive perimeter

---

[33] Shaw et al., *Central Pacific Drive,* p. 121; Miller, *War Plan Orange,* pp. 186–202; Potter, *Nimitz,* pp. 264–65; Buell, *Quiet Warrior,* pp. 231–32; Crowl and Love, *Seizure of the Gilberts and Marshalls,* pp. 166–69; Millett, *Semper Fidelis,* p. 399.

[34] Miller, *War Plan Orange,* pp. 186–202; Potter, *Nimitz,* pp. 264–65; Buell, *Quiet Warrior,* pp. 231–32; Crowl and Love, *Seizure of the Gilberts and Marshalls,* pp. 166–69; Shaw et al., *Central Pacific Drive,* p. 121; Millett, *Semper Fidelis,* p. 399.

[35] Millett, *Semper Fidelis,* p. 399.

to the Marianas and the Carolines, but it had also decided that the most likely islands of the Marshalls to be attacked were those in the eastern chain. Consequently, most of what efforts the Japanese were prepared to make in an area that they had decided to de-emphasize were expended there.[36] Nimitz, Sherman, and McMorris, in other words, were correct in picking Kwajalein as the initial target in the Marshall Islands.

Admiral King was adamant that relentless pressure be applied to the Japanese. With this in mind, he insisted on a 1 January 1944 D-day for Flintlock. Nimitz argued for and eventually convinced King to accept 17 January as the earliest possible date, but events were to lead to a further postponement. Spruance was not happy at having to accept CinCPac's plan making the capture of Kwajalein the lynchpin for the Marshalls operation. His lack of confidence in his superior's choice of operational focus brought out a certain cautiousness that seemed to be integral to his personality. Consequently, he requested on 26 December that Majuro Atoll in the eastern Marshalls be added to the list of objectives. It was known to be lightly held and could serve as a valuable fleet base to support operations farther up the Marshalls chain. He also argued that his forces would not be able to undertake operations against Kwajalein and Majuro until 1 February. Nimitz agreed with Spruance's reasons for wanting to postpone the invasion until 1 February, but the best he could do with King was to reach a compromise setting D-day at 31 January. Spruance met this date by placing artillery on the relatively undefended islets surrounding Kwajalein Island and Roi-Namur, but he set the day for the main landings on his preferred date, 1 February.[37]

Another concern for Spruance was what to do about Eniwetok, an atoll 360 miles northwest of Kwajalein and the main conduit for Japanese aircraft being fed into the Marshalls from the Marianas and the Carolines. Turner reported that the capture of Eniwetok was discussed early in the planning stages of Flintlock. Even though it was believed that the atoll would be a complicating factor in keeping Japanese airpower in the Marshalls neutralized after securing Kwajalein, taking Eniwetok was not prescribed in the original directive for the operation. The reason for its exclusion had nothing to do with negligence on the part of the planners. It was simply that no one was certain of how great a percentage of available troops would be absorbed by the capture of the main objective. Plans for the capture of Eniwetok were drawn up, nonetheless, just in case they might be needed. Turner and his staff wanted to be prepared in case the Kwajalein operation progressed rapidly enough to justify extending the operation farther to the west.[38]

---

[36] Crowl and Love, *Seizure of the Gilberts and Marshalls,* pp. 212 and 218.

[37] Buell, *Quiet Warrior,* pp. 232–33; Shaw et al., *Central Pacific Drive,* p. 121; George C. Dyer, *The Amphibians Came to Conquer,* Vol. II, pp. 736–37; Crowl and Love, *Seizure of the Gilberts and Marshalls,* pp. 169–70.

[38] COMINCH P-002, p. 1-7; Buell, *Quiet Warrior,* p. 229.

Naval Gunfire at Roi-Namur: The "Lessons" Applied

Once the strategic and operational objectives and the command structure were set, it was time to begin the detailed planning process. How naval gunfire was to be used to reach operational and tactical objectives was a question to be answered by Turner, Conolly, and their various subordinates who were directly concerned with the planning and execution of the naval gunfire mission. According to doctrine and established practice, these men were to work together, and with their subordinates, produce an outline and then a comprehensive plan that provided guidance as to procedures and listed everything from general target areas to specific responsibilities of individual ships. The "Lessons of Tarawa" were heavy on the minds of all these men and the influence of that earlier bloodletting showed through in the naval gunfire annexes produced at every command level of the Fifth Amphibious Force. For Turner, as the chief architect of the amphibious plan used in the Gilberts, the motivation to erase the flaws inherent in that plan was particularly strong. In his post-operational report, he recognized this motivation when he pointed out the four advantages planning for Flintlock enjoyed over that for the earlier operation: "(a) More time than was available for GALVANIC; (b) Lessons learned from GALVANIC; (c) More appreciation by all hands of the problems involved gained by experience; (d) More equipment and material available."[39]

Turner also listed a single disadvantage, one that calls into question the extent to which the Navy's chief amphibious architect in the Pacific drew upon what was supposedly learned in the Gilberts: "Over-emphasis of certain problems which experience at TARAWA had exaggerated in the minds of those concerned. This caused general doubt regarding the effectiveness of our weapons and tactics, and much time and effort was expended on dubious and fruitless schemes."[40]

The "lessons," then, were a mixed blessing in his mind. This conclusion on Turner's part—that what happened at Tarawa should not necessarily call the effectiveness of American amphibious weapons and tactics into question—should be analyzed in conjunction with his already reported conclusion that the apparently brilliant performance of those weapons and tactics at Kwajalein proved their ultimate effectiveness. These two conclusions, in combination, affected the way Turner and his staff planned for future operations. It can be argued that refusing to recognize important differences between the two main objectives in these two related operations blinded Turner to the necessity of continuing the rigorous application of the "exaggerated" lessons learned at Tarawa, an argument that will be taken up

[39] NARA, RG 127, USMC Geographic Files, Box 207, File A6-1, TF 51 Report of Operations, Capture of Marshalls, 25 Febuary 44 AR—Encl. E, Commander Joint Expeditionary Force Report on Flintlock Operation, Enclosure (E), Naval and Air Bombardment and Beach Demolitions, p. 1.

[40] Ibid.

in greater detail later in this chapter. This confident frame of mind would eventually cost the Americans.

The preliminary air and naval bombardment of Marshall Island objectives began once the airfields obtained through the invasion of the Gilberts were activated. Rear Admiral John H. Hoover commanded all land-based air during Flintlock as he had for Galvanic. Pilots under his command increased the frequency of attacks on Marshalls targets and the tonnage of bombs dropped until they reached a peak on D-10. The attacks continued at this high rate until the end of D-day. Mille, Jaluit, Wotje, and Maloelap, the objectives Nimitz chose to bypass in going straight to Kwajalein, garnered most of Hoover's attention. Neutralization of the airfields on these islands was foremost in everyone's minds, naturally, but the attacks served the additional purpose of deceiving the Japanese as to ultimate American intentions. Surface bombardment began on 29 January when the new fast battleship USS *North Carolina* (BB-55) and the destroyers USS *Sterett* (DD-407) and *Lang* (DD-399) took up positions off of Roi, lobbing shells onto the island over the course of the late evening and night of both D-2 and D-1. The mission was "to keep the airfield inoperative, restrain aircraft from landing, prevent personnel from repairing the airfield, and for general nuisance value." At 11.00 on 30 January, these three ships were joined by the rest of Task Unit 58.2.2 (new battleships USS *South Dakota* (BB-57) and *Alabama* (BB-60) and the destroyers USS *Stack* (DD-406), *Hickox* (DD-673), and *Hunt* (DD-674)) to pump ordnance into Roi and Namur as well as islets to the southeast of Namur, stopping only to allow for periodic air attacks.[41]

Turner's rules for determining the proper range from which to fire on bombardment targets varied depending upon the type of target engaged. If it was a beach defense that stood upright, then direct hits from accurate, deliberate, pointer fire delivered from close range (deemed to be 2,000 yards or less) was the prescription. On the other hand, if the targets on the beach were low and flat or if the targets were not on the beach but somewhere in back of it, then plunging fire from moderately long range (usually in the neighborhood of 5,000–8,000 yards) was to be used. In this type of fire, shells fall upon a target at a sharp angle from above. Turner specifically states that both types of fire were incorporated into the gunfire plan.[42]

The choice of which projectiles and fuzes to use was also Turner's. He states that the policy he adopted was based upon the results of ongoing research and the advice of ordnance experts. His policy stipulated the use of:

[41] Ibid.; NARA, RG 127, USMC Geographic Files, Box 208, File A16–1, TU 58.2.2—Action Report of Bombardment, 30 January 44—Roi-Namur, Commander Task Unit 58.2.2, Action Report of Bombardment of Roi-Namur Islands by Task Unit 58.2.2, 30 January 1944, pp. 1 and 2.

[42] TF 51 Report of Operations, Enclosure (E), pp. 1–2.

(1) Armor-Piercing Projectiles—To be used only against exceptionally [thick] and strong structures, and then only when a reasonable percentage of direct hits is obtainable.

(2) Common—Same as for armor piercing.

(3) High-Capacity and A.A. Common—For all other purposes. Percentage of point-detonating fuzes to be 75% when covering an area, and 25% for all other purposes. Air bursts to be used only when requested by shore fire control parties or against enemy troops actually observed in the open [or] in open trenches. . . . [however,]

(5) Mark 32 Fuzes—*Not* to be used for shore bombardment. . . .[43]

Turner's job as Commander of the Joint Expeditionary Force (TF 51) granted him the authority to dictate the basic rules that everyone else, including Rear Admiral Conolly, had to take into account when making their own plans. The most pertinent sections of Turner's plan, and his reasons for adopting them, were as follows:

(d) *Timing of close support* [*sic*] *fires*—These fires should start at about H minus 30 and continue at the landing beach until the last possible moment. This is when the first wave is about 300–500 yards from the beach for 5″ and smaller calibers, and about 1000 yards from the beach for larger calibers. Ther [*sic*] should be no cessation of the fire even at H-Hour but it should be shifted to the flanks, or lifted to the back areas, for a period of time which varies with the speed of advance of the troops and the contour of the island. It was decided that close-in naval gunfire and artillery fire support would offer the best cover for the landing waves. Therefore the air strike in direct support of the landing was to be started and completed well before the first wave of boats reached the beach, the travel of boats from the line of departure to the beach being covered by ships gunfire and artillery fire. All conflicting gunfire was to be checked during the air strike (H-35 to H-20, W-50 to W-25).

(e) *Time of commencement of scheduled fires*—was scheduled at the first crack of dawn, using star-shells as necessary for spotting. This tends to protect the transports and other ships from coastal batteries. . . .

[43] Ibid., p. 2, emphasis in original.

(g) *LCI Gunboats*—Twelve of these were available (recently converted so as to enable to fire 40MM .50 caliber and 4." 5 [*sic*] barrage rockets as well as the 20MM originally installed) and were used to support every landing. The tactical plan for these gunboats was to slightly precede the first wave on each side of the boat lane firing rockets at 1100 and 800 yards, and machine guns when within range. To avoid blanking the fire of supporting destroyers, cruisers, and battleships it is necessary for the LCI's [*sic*] to remain close to the boat lanes at all times.

(h) *Night Activities*—At night it was considered necessary to: (1) Furnish intermittent fire all night to harass the enemy and reduce his activities; (2) Furnish illumination for the aid of advancing troops ashore; (3) Prevent movement of enemy from island to island across the reefs.

Task (1) can be accomplished by any type vessel which has the ammunition, preferably a battleship. A destroyer is the most suitable type for (2), while LCI's [*sic*] are quite suitable for (3)

(i) *Rolling Barrage*—just ahead of the troops is best accomplished by the artillery. Naval gunfire was scheduled to supplement this and call fires were continuously supplied in addition.

(j) *Areas of responsibility*—for each ship were established by assigning adjacent target areas to a ship for a long period of time. In GALVANIC ships exchanged areas frequently in order to ensure that all areas would be covered to some extent even if one or more firing ships dropped out for any reason. By *not* exchanging targets better accuracy of fire was achieved and definite areas of responsibility established for counter-battery and target of opportunity fires.

(k) *Permissable* [*sic*] *zones of fire*—In GALVANIC there were several instances after our troops had landed when ships observed excellent targets of opportunity, but were unable to obtain, from the troop commander, permission to fire in time to do so effectively. [Steps were taken in this operation to ensure that this situation would not present itself again.] . . .

(n) *Aerial spotting for shore fire control parties*—was provided for using observation aircraft. In GALVANIC shore fire control parties had usually been unable to find a suitable observation point due to flatness of the areas. The need for aerial observation had therefore been felt.

(o) *Shorts in the water*—are necessary when sho[o]ting perpendicular to the beach at the beach defenses in order to place the MPI [mean point of impact] of the salvo on the target. An effort was made to indoctrinate personnel in this principle because the general attitude is to avoid "wasting shots" by putting them in the water. . . .

(t) *Grid system*—To ensure that all hands used the same coordinates a standard grid system for the MARSHALL Islands was prescribed by JICPOA.

(u) *A combined sequence of events*—was issued showing how the air support, artillery and naval gunfire fitted together into one overall program.

(v) *Delay of H-Hour*—after firing schedule has begun will result in a period of silence unless some provision is made to avoid this. A simple solution was accepted, i.e. to repeat all fires for the otherwise silent period exactly as scheduled, but with a greatly curtailed allowance of ammunition. . . .[44]

These rules addressed all of the most important general flaws, as Turner perceived them, in the amphibious plan used in the Gilberts. Kelly Turner was not the only person to have learned lessons at Tarawa, however. Vice Admiral Spruance underwent a doctrinal conversion as a result of the high casualty rate on Betio, and his subordinates, Turner and Holland Smith, were totally on board with him. Spruance now believed that the proper way to execute an amphibious assault was to "use violent, overwhelming force, swiftly applied."[45] He elaborated on how his experience at Tarawa led him to formulate this philosophy in a speech he made after the war to an audience of Marines:

> On going into action for the first time, we found that our best thought-out plans required later modification in the light of actual combat experience, and that exceptional valor in the troops was called for in order to make good unforeseen deficiencies in our planning. As a matter of fact, even with the best of planning and of preliminary training, I always have had the feeling that the margin between success and failure in an amphibious operation conducted against strongly defended positions was a narrow one. I would never want to conduct such an operation with troops poorly trained, poorly led, or of poor quality. To do so would be to court defeat, and I do not think we can afford to risk defeat in an amphibious operation.[46]

---

[44] Ibid., pp. 2–5, emphasis in original.

[45] Buell, *Quiet Warrior*, p. 235.

[46] Quote from Buell, *Quiet Warrior*, p. 235. This statement is very interesting considering the inconsistent way Spruance allowed the "modification[s] in the light of actual combat experience" to be applied by his subordinates in later operations.

This new philosophy made its debut at Kwajalein. To make sure of its application at Roi-Namur, Turner provided Conolly with ships that could deliver a massive quantity of ordnance onto the Japanese defenses. Rear Admiral Jesse B. Oldendorf's Northern Support Group (TG 53.5), a combination of old battleships and cruisers, was the naval unit created to perform that task.[47]

Spruance's biographer, Thomas Buell, identifies a corollary "basic Spruance principle" to this one of rapidly applied violence—isolation of the objective area. The application of violence would not work, Spruance believed, if the objective area were not isolated from enemy surface and air interference. The difficulty of isolating Kwajalein Atoll from Japanese air interference, both before and after the invasion, was what argued most powerfully in his mind against Nimitiz's "bold stroke." A further complication, in Spruance's estimation, was the ability of the United States Navy to maintain secure lines of communication both during and after the invasion, the development of the captured bases being a primary concern in this regard.[48] During Operation Flintlock, the Americans successfully applied both of these most important principles of amphibious warfare to Spruance's satisfaction. As in the case of Kelly Turner, success in the Marshalls would influence Spruance's decisions in later operations, particularly concerning the use of naval gunfire. Unfortunately this influence was not always for the best.

Once all vessels had been assigned their general roles, it was up to Conolly to integrate the ships assigned to him into his plan for the Northern Attack Force and then to rehearse them so that the ships's crews could carry out their jobs effectively. Warships of the Fire Support Group designated to provide the necessary naval gunfire punch for Task Force 53, with the exception of *Indianapolis,* trained off San Clemente Island, California. The rehearsals were patterned as nearly as possible on the actual bombardment plans to be used at Roi-Namur.[49] Ship training commenced on 10 December 1943 with destroyers simulating gunfire missions into the Aliso Canyon (Camp Pendleton) area near San Diego. Two fire support units conducted firing exercises on San Clemente Island on 27 and 28 December and the complete fire support group, less *Indianapolis,* also fired on the island on 2 and 3 January 1944. The destroyers assigned to fire support units finished the rehearsals by firing on the island on 10 January, paying particular attention to practicing the

---

[47] Morison, *Aleutians, Gilberts and Marshalls,* p. 346; Paul H. Silverstone, *U.S. Warships of World War II* (Shepperton: Ian Allan, 1965), pp. 24, 67, 71, 94, 114, 126, 140, and 143; Stefan Terzibaschitsch, *Battleships of the U.S. Navy in World War II* (New York: Bonanza Books, 1977), pp. 188–89.

[48] Buell, *Quiet Warrior,* p. 239.

[49] NARA, RG 127, USMC Geographic Files, Box 207, File A7-1, TF 53—Report of Operations. Roi-Namur. Marshalls. Dated 23 Febuary 1944, Commander Task Force 53 Report on Flintlock Operation, Enclosure (B), Fire Support (hereinafter TF 53 Report of Operations, Enclosure (B)), p. 1.

delivery of destruction fire on beach targets at point-blank range.[50] Shore Fire Control Parties, members of the 1st Joint Assault Signal Company (JASCO), completed their training during the period from 10 December 1943 to 13 January 1944. Conolly states that the small size of the objectives in comparison to the large number of troops to be landed led him to believe that not many call-fire missions would be necessary during the upcoming operation, but the fire control parties were trained as though they would be needed continuously after the landing. He states that "[i]n a manner of speaking, the shore fire control parties were 'insurance' for the success of the operation, as regarded naval gunfire."[51]

Conolly's staff studied the landing force's attack plan in conjunction with all of the available intelligence on Roi-Namur and the surrounding islets. After developing a plan that they believed took all of this information adequately into account, they turned over the completed bombardment plan on 8 January 1944, and it was then coordinated with the air support and artillery plans. The decision to place artillery on adjacent islets presented a problem that was not encountered when planning for Galvanic. In order to fulfill the requirements for what was in essence a two-stage invasion of the primary objectives, the bombardment plan was divided into two parts, one for D-day and one for D+1. Each part contained all pertinent maps, time schedules, detailed procedures, and communications enclosures.[52]

Turner stressed in his overall operations plan that an adequate amount of bombardment ammunition be on hand aboard each class of vessel at the end of D-day and D+1 for use after the initial assault, so Conolly made sure that the ammunition allowances prescribed by the Commander Fifth Amphibious Force were used. Conolly reports that the firing schedules did not prescribe use of ammunition on a minute-by-minute basis, however. True, the schedules were time-sensitive, but he specified that bombardment time periods were to be determined based upon the actual time and place of the various landings. Rather than micromanaging the bombardment himself, Conolly gave the Fire Support Unit Commanders the freedom to use their own judgment as to what calibers to use, what rates of fire to prescribe, and what ranges to employ, as long as they stayed within limits set forth by Turner. He did order, however, that certain provisions be made for the time of the landings themselves, specifically that the rate of fire of all bombardment ships be increased when a landing was taking place, and he retained for himself the authority to check or lift naval gunfire relative to the position of the landing force.[53]

Both the needs of the landing force and the hydrography of the atoll dictated the composition of the various fire support units. Cruisers and battleships could

[50] Ibid., pp. 1–2.

[51] Ibid., p. 2.

[52] Ibid., p. 3.

[53] Ibid., pp. 3 and 4.

not enter the lagoon, so they had to deliver fire from the seaward side of the main objectives. Destroyers, on the other hand, could enter the lagoon and they consequently provided fire, in combination with LCI Gunboats, from the lagoon side of the main objectives on D+1. They were the principal fire support for the 25th Marines going into the surrounding islets on D-day because the small size of these objectives precluded the use of vessels carrying larger caliber guns. Finally, they provided the aforementioned harassing fire on Roi and Namur at night and they made sure that the Japanese could not reinforce adjacent islands while the attack was ongoing. The fire support areas within which the fire support units operated were clearly demarcated so that ships would not inadvertently fire into others of the bombardment group. The bombardment plan addressed the problem of overs and ricochets encountered at Tarawa by placing heavy ships in positions that would prevent their wayward shots from landing in fire support areas opposite them. Despite the care taken in this matter, however, shells from *Indianapolis,* the one fire support vessel that had not participated in the pre-operational rehearsals, narrowly missed the USS *Louisville* (CA-28). Fragments from one of these near misses caused damage to *Louisville's* stern plating and superficial injuries to several crewmen.[54]

Conolly stresses in his report that the Fire Support Commanders were given wide discretion in the execution of the fire support schedule, but there was one time when he exercised his prerogative as overall commander to change the decision of a subordinate. He describes the incident very nonchalantly in his report: "On one occasion . . . Commander Fire Support Unit TWO was directed by the Force Commander to send MARYLAND in very close to ROI ISLAND to destroy blockhouses and enemy installations." He received the respectful nickname "Close-in Conolly" from the Marines for his willingness, as in this instance, to send heavy ships "close in" to the point where their keels scraped coral, usually from 1,200–2,000 yards out, so that the cruisers and battleships could lay direct pointer fire on tough targets with their eight-, fourteen-, or sixteen-inch guns. The bombardment plan was structured so as to take maximum advantage during the landings of both the strengths and the weaknesses of naval gunfire, particularly its accuracy in deflection and its dispersion in range. Destroyers positioned inside the lagoon were instructed to place fire on the flanks of the landing force as it went ashore while cruisers and battleships from without were instructed to place enfilade fire across the front lines. Conolly states that this arrangement allowed for overs from the big guns of the heavy ships to hit profitable targets without endangering the landing force inordinately.[55]

All U.S. naval planners in the Central Pacific post-Tarawa realized that the destruction of reinforced concrete pillboxes, blockhouses, and other similar

[54] Ibid., pp. 3–4 and 5.

[55] Ibid., p. 4.

strongpoints required close-range accurate fire from large caliber naval guns. The delivery of highly destructive plunging fire requires moderate to long gun ranges, however, and is not accurate enough to produce a high percentage of hits on such relatively small targets. On buildings twenty-by-thirty feet, on the other hand, major caliber naval guns delivered approximately ninety percent hits from 2,000 yards. Based upon this data, Conolly recommended that the "best employment of available weapons" would be, first, to silence remaining shore batteries using air bombs and naval guns firing from medium range (6,000–8,000 yards) and then to close the range so that definite identification of targets can be made. Closing the range leads to a higher percentage of hits on hardened targets, especially by major caliber guns, because it allows cruisers and battleships to use more accurate pointer fire and direct spotting of targets. Penetration of these hardened targets by major caliber naval gunfire was expected to kill personnel within the structures and to destroy materiel and supplies stored therein. Air bombs, particularly 500-, 1000-, and 2,000-pounders, could be used as follow-up to naval gunfire bombardment, destroying already weakened structures by delivering the "plunging fire" *coup de grace.* The results of the bombardments by Fire Support Units 1 and 2 provide evidence that Conolly was correct in his conclusions. Unit 1 fired from the eastern side of Namur from a range of approximately 3,500 yards. The vessels of the unit hit targets and breached some of them, but their accuracy was not as high as that of Unit 2. Firing from 1,900 yards to the west of Roi, Unit 2 registered more direct hits than did Unit 1. Bombing, as Conolly saw it, did indeed provide the required plunging fire.[56]

Conolly and his staff gave a great deal of thought to the selection of targets. Re-emphasizing the process described earlier, he states in his report: "All available intelligence information, plus the tactical plan of the landing force, determined the targets on which fires would be delivered. Large and heavily constructed and steel reinforced enemy installations were assigned to battleships and cruisers. Beach installations and areas of a more vulnerable nature were assigned to 5 inch [*sic*] batteries. All ships were prepared to deliver point blank range fire on blockhouses and other heavy installations. Intelligence information received enroute was retransmitted to support units and additional targets assigned as required."[57]

The planners assigned direct fire support ships to each assault battalion and provision was made for the modification and augmentation of these assignments once the landings had begun. This is where the flexibility of the plan showed itself. Time periods specified in the firing schedules were to be subordinated to the observed progress of the ship-to-shore movement. Regardless of what the firing schedule directed, fire being delivered perpendicular to the beach was not to be lifted inland until the troops were 500 yards from the beach and enfilade fire was not to be redirected until they were 300 yards out. Conolly would send the

---

[56] Ibid., pp. 4 and 7.

[57] Ibid., p. 5.

command to lift fire over the naval gunfire common channel (2504 kcs) and the Talk Between Ships (TBS) channel, or just the TBS channel if the common channel was overloaded or otherwise not working. Conolly designated certain additional vessels as relief for the direct support ships. The commanders of these vessels were to listen to the naval gunfire common channel for the command to join the bombardment, at which time they were to switch to a specified frequency and listen for further orders. The designation of relief vessels provided insurance against unforeseen difficulties.[58]

Conolly believed that naval gunfire, at least in his part of Operation Flintlock, was quite effective. It achieved both neutralization and destruction on Roi-Namur, allowing the first four assault waves to land on the two main objectives without having to face any significant opposition. Post-operational investigation revealed that blockhouses, pillboxes, and gun emplacements all received direct hits by major caliber naval guns and that both HC and AP fourteen-inch and sixteen-inch penetrated as much as forty-four inches of heavily reinforced concrete. Coverage of both islands was so thorough and accuracy so high that only one blockhouse remained unbreached between the two. The number of enemy dead congregated in the penetrated blockhouses indicated that fragmentation upon penetration was more than adequate. Smaller caliber guns penetrated pillboxes with ease and five-inch gun emplacements, while not hit directly by naval gunfire, were rendered inoperable by shell fragments from near misses. Finally, naval gunfire destroyed troop shelters, ammunition dumps, and fuel storage areas.[59]

The recommendations Conolly makes in his report on naval gunfire are sprinkled throughout its sixteen pages, but he includes a 16-point summary near the end of it, which is reproduced here in full:

1. That the entire Fire Support Group be assembled and participate in the final training periods and rehearsals conducted by the landing force.
2. That all Fire Support Units be briefed in detail before proceeding to the combat zone. (*This is particularly important*) [emphasis added]
3. That Fire Support Unit Commanders and fire support ship commanding officers be given as much leeway as possible in determining the details of their scheduled fires. This includes calibre [*sic*], rate of fire, and range to use.
4. That destruction fire be the primary objective of all naval gunfire against atoll targets, with neutralization fire as an important objective immediately preceding a landing.

---

[58] Ibid., pp. 5–6.

[59] Ibid., pp. 9–10.

5. That against reinforced concrete structures heavy Fire Support Units be used at very short ranges (about 2000 yards) when hydrography permits, in order to obtain a high percentage of hits on definitely identified targets.
6. That every effort be made to outline fire support areas in such manner as to prevent ships or units from firing into each other.
7. That destroyers be sent inside lagoons to provide support in operations where atolls are to be seized.
8. That naval gunfire lines of fire be considered so that the known dispersion in range of naval gunfire may be capitalized upon in enfilading enemy targets. Also the excellent deflection performance of naval guns must be considered, and it must be realized that naval gunfire can be placed very close to own front lines when the line of fire is parallel to the front line of the troops.
9. That LCI's [*sic*] (converted to gunboats) be used in all landings to precede and protect the assault boat waves. The use of rockets is particularly recommended since their psychological effect alone is tremendous. Their destructive effect has been well demonstrated.
10. That all fire support ships be cautioned to base their close support not on the rigid time schedule (furnished as a guide only) but on the position of the leading assault boat waves. Fire should continue on the landing beaches until leading assault waves are 500 or 300 yards from the beach, depending upon whether the line of fire of supporting ships is respectively perpendicular to the beaches or parallel to them (in enfilade).
11. That air observers and close support [*sic*] destroyers report the position of assault waves so that supporting fires can be checked or lifted by the Task Force Commander in order to avoid firing into own boats, but at the same time to provide safe and effective support up to the last possible moment before troops land.
12. That regimental naval gunfire liaison officers, with their radio personnel and equipment, be assigned each regimental commander by the Attack Force Commander. These officers should assist in the training and equipping of the three shore fire control parties assigned to each of their regiments working in close cooperation with the landing force naval gunfire officer and with the Attack Force Commander's gunnery officer.
13. That destroyer gunfire be employed to keep the enemy awake and harassed during all the nights of the assault phase (most of the captured Japanese on ROI and NAMUR ISLANDS were in a state of near collapse from the steady incessant attention that was paid

them, day and night during the entire assault). Star-shells should be fired to silhouette enemy movements and to confuse him, but should not be placed where they will interfere with own units, for example, demolition parties destroying beach mines and defenses.

14. That the Army type SCR-694 radio be substituted for the TBX and the SCR-284. This light, paratroop design SCR-694 radio is ideal for amphibious operations. Using the SCR-694, both the naval gunfire liaison officer and the forward observer would have the same radio equipment. A casualty to one would not interrupt the scheme of things. The other could immediately take over the functions of the casualty. They are trained to do just that.
15. That, if the SCR-694 radio be adopted, arrangements be made with Commander Central Pacific Force [Spruance] to assign a higher frequency to insure ability of SCR-694 radio to come up on it. (In KWAJALEIN operation, 2504 kcs was assigned Northern Attack Force as naval gunfire support common. The SCR-694 radio cannot guard this low frequency).
16. That all radios used by shore fire control parties be completely waterproofed.[60]

These recommendations can be seen as the ultimate validation of the naval gunfire "lessons" taught at Tarawa. The problem was that only one man seemed to truly understand that that was the case, and it was not Richmond Kelly Turner. That man was Richard Conolly, who would demonstrate—not just state—that he understood these concepts by once again turning in a stellar performance as attack force commander at Guam later in the year.

Ernest King's headquarters, in its summary of the lessons learned from Operation Flintlock, stated that the "salient features of the employment of naval gunfire during the Marshalls campaign" were:

A—It was delivered on a larger scale than in any previous amphibious operation.

B—A continuous bombardment over a period of several days was fired on several objectives.

C—Gunfire support ships moved in to short ranges for deliberate destructive fires and in one case a battleship at anchor inside the lagoon supported the landing at a range of 800 yards.

D—There was extensive use of LCI(L) Gunboats also equipped with rockets for close support.

---

[60] Ibid., pp. 12–14.

E—A high degree of flexibility in the application of naval gunfire was attained.

F—Naval gunfire was continued on the landing beaches until leading assault waves were 300 to 500 yards from the beach before it was lifted to the flanks and inland.[61]

It will be noted that this list incorporates several of Conolly's points. These elements featured prominently in the general planning and execution of the Marshalls campaign because officers involved in that planning and execution were beginning to understand their importance. The troop commanders tasked with taking the various objectives insisted on them for a number of reasons, none more important than the fact that they saved lives.

Thus Flintlock was believed to contribute to the ongoing process of fine tuning the sea services' naval gunfire bombardment doctrine and its application. Participants in the Central Pacific Campaign went so far as to remark on numerous occasions that Galvanic and Flintlock proved that the Navy-Marine Corps doctrine for amphibious warfare worked. Kelly Turner was most pleased with the effectiveness of naval gunfire at Roi-Namur and Kwajalein Island as opposed to its ineffectiveness at Tarawa. Flintlock, in his mind, proved that carefully aimed, massive quantities of ordnance made a significant difference in the outcome of amphibious assaults. There is one problem with this conclusion in the case of the invasion of Kwajalein Atoll: a comparison of Kwajalein to Tarawa was essentially an apples-to-oranges analogy.[62]

---

[61] COMINCH P-002, p. 3-32.

[62] Isely and Crowl, *U.S. Marines and Amphibious War*, p. 302. Conolly, in his Fire Support report, states the following concerning the tonnage of shells fired on Roi-Namur:

IX. General Information

1. Approximate combined area of Roi and Namur Islands: 1,520,000 square yards.
2. Number of projectiles fired by Task Force 53:

Caliber	Number of Rounds
5″ (Incl. WP & Ill.)	18,559
6″	3,337
14″ HC	783
16″ HC	862
16″ AP	20
Total rounds fired, all calibers	25,004

3. Weight of projectiles fired: 4,502,275 lbs.; Weight of projectiles fired (in tons): 2,251.14 tons; Ratio of projectile weight to island area: 3 lbs. per sq. yd.

TF 53 Report of Operations, Enclosure (B), pp. 14–15.

There were some similarities, of course, the most obvious being the topography of the two atolls. Betio Island and both of the principal objectives in Kwajalein Atoll are tiny specks of land that rise no higher than twenty feet above sea level. In the case of Betio, the entire island was rightly considered an invasion beach. Even taking smoke and dust into account, it was relatively easy to thoroughly bombard every meaningful square inch of these targets. The main variable in being able to do a good job was time—how much time was the United States Navy willing to spend to saturate the objectives with precisely placed shells. At Tarawa, the plan only called for a three-hour bombardment before the assault and the Marines paid the price. At Roi-Namur, Conolly took the extra time given him, relative to the assault on Betio, to work over all of the targets within his area of responsibility with care and deliberation.

The principal dissimilarity, the one that makes a comparison between Tarawa and Kwajalein problematic, is the difference in the level of Japanese defensive preparation in each case. Spruance, Turner, and their subordinates were so intent on improving upon their performance in Galvanic that they failed to make accurate comparisons between the two operations both during the planning for and the euphoric aftermath of Flintlock. Samuel Eliot Morison provides us with documentation of this error in the volume of his history covering the Marshalls operation: "Kelly Turner was right when he predicted that Roi-Namur would be a tougher nut to crack than Betio. Of even smaller extent, it was more heavily defended with fixed emplacements and had a bigger garrison in proportion. The comparative ease of the assault was due almost entirely to the length and strength of the preliminary bombardment, and to the application of the other lessons learned at Tarawa."[63] The error was in believing, based more on supposition than hard intelligence, that the Japanese must have built up the Marshalls more than they had hardened the Gilberts because they had been in control of the former for a much longer time than the latter.

The basis of the supposition was true enough—the Japanese had been in control of the Marshalls for many years longer than they had been in control of the Gilberts—but that was not the determining factor in the equation. As pointed out earlier in this chapter, two important bits of information were unknown to the Americans at the time: the Japanese had decided to make their stand in the Mariana Islands and not the Marshalls, and they had not foreseen the Americans bypassing the eastern chain of the Marshalls to strike at Kwajalein.[64] Add to these factors two additional facts. First, the American submarine campaign against Japanese merchant shipping was already taking a significant toll on the Imperial Navy's ability to supply far flung Japanese garrisons in the Pacific. Second, the American campaign in the Solomons, in combination with the wide-ranging use of U.S. Navy fast carrier

---

[63] Morison, *Aleutians, Gilberts and Marshalls*, p. 240.

[64] Crowl and Love, *Seizure of the Gilberts and Marshalls*, pp. 210 and 212.

task forces against the air pipeline from the Home Islands, was quickly destroying Japanese air power. With all of these facts taken into account, it becomes quite clear that Kwajalein was not the hardened target American planners at first believed it to be.[65] Considering Morison's firmly expressed opinion as to the strength of Kwajalein's defenses, it is interesting that Philip A. Crowl and Edmund G. Love, in a work published just four years after Morison's volume, included a more accurate assessment in their description of the U.S. Army's part in Operation Flintlock:

> Kwajalein Atoll had been the hub of Japanese military activity in the Marshalls since August 1941. . . . Reinforcements coming into the Marshalls almost invariably passed through Kwajalein, to be parceled out from there. Supplies were usually distributed from this atoll, which was the closest major base to Truk and to the supply lines from the homeland. . . . Kwajalein was the center of communications not only for all other bases in the Marshalls, but for the Gilberts, Nauru, and Ocean as well. The air base on Roi commanded all Japanese air forces in the Marshalls and Gilberts. All this gave Kwajalein some of the characteristics of a rear area, with more red tape than bullets, far from the front-line outposts on the periphery of the Marshalls. . . . The three most heavily defended islands of the atoll were Roi-Namur, Kwajalein, and Ebeye . . . , in that order of strength. Roi-Namur was somewhat better fortified than Kwajalein Island, but neither approached Tarawa as to the size and number of weapons or the construction and concentration of positions.[66]

Why the wide discrepancy? All that can be offered here is conjecture, but there is evidence upon which to base an opinion. Morison reports that he and his assistants collected materials and wrote a draft of their description of both the Gilberts and Marshalls operations before the war ended. Morison himself undertook a revision of both of these descriptions over the years 1950 and 1951.[67] It would appear that he incorporated Turner's early opinion as to the extent of Kwajalein's defenses into the first version of his narrative and did not update that description when undertaking the 1950–51 rewrite. Philip Crowl came to the Army's official history project after Edmund Love had completed a draft of the Gilberts and Marshalls volume. Crowl undertook a major rewrite of Love's draft, incorporating into his work a later, post-operational determination of the actual strength of Japanese

---

[65] Ibid.; E. B. Potter and Chester W. Nimitz, eds., *Sea Power: A Naval History* (Englewood Cliffs, NJ: Prentice-Hall, 1960), p. 808; George Baer, *One Hundred Years of Sea Power: The U.S. Navy, 1890–1990* (Stanford: Stanford University Press, 1993), pp. 236–37.

[66] Crowl and Love, *Seizure of the Gilberts and Marshalls,* pp. 212 and 213.

[67] Morison, *Aleutians, Gilberts and Marshalls,* pp. viii–ix.

defenses in the Marshalls.[68] This later determination, based upon close inspection of the destroyed defenses, was more accurate than Turner's early speculations.

Taking the greater strength of Betio's defenses as a given, therefore, what can we conclude? If Kwajalein had been a more heavily defended target than Betio Island and the Navy-Marine Corps team had been victorious over its defenses after having adjusted their doctrine and technique according to their experience in the Gilberts, then it would be correct to proclaim that the modified doctrine of gunfire preparation was without serious flaw. That was not the case here, however. Application of the doctrine easily overcame Japanese defenses at Roi-Namur and Kwajalein Island because those defenses were relatively easy to overcome. It can be argued that the Japanese on Roi and Namur could have been defeated with acceptable losses, though higher in number than what was actually suffered, even if Turner and Conolly had not lavished three days of careful bombardment on them. Expecting a Verdun, so to speak, the Americans encountered a Fort Necessity instead. This is not to say that the three days allowed should not have been taken to do the job right. The argument here is simply that the results obtained by naval gunfire in the Marshalls could not be indicative of improved effectiveness of the newly modified doctrine because the targets were not sufficiently hardened so as to act as an adequate test of that doctrine. The next major operation, in the Marianas, revealed continuing doctrinal and technical inadequacies. It also revealed that some of those who were tasked with applying the newly refurbished naval gunfire doctrine and techniques were willing to neglect some of the lessons they said they had learned, despite their loud assertions to the contrary.

---

[68] Crowl and Love, *Seizure of the Gilberts and Marshalls,* p. ix. For a comparison of the Japanese defenses at Tarawa and at Kwajalein Atoll, see Shaw et al., *Central Pacific Drive,* pp. 50–51 and 140–41.

USS *Indianapolis* (CA-35) off the Mare Island Navy Yard, California, 2 May 1943, after her second wartime overhaul. Photograph from the Bureau of Ships Collection in the U.S. National Archives.

USS *Maryland* (BB-46) off the Puget Sound Navy Yard, Washington, 25 April 1944. Photograph from the Bureau of Ships Collection in the U.S. National Archives.

USS *Maryland* (BB-46) firing her after 16″/45 guns, during the pre-invasion bombardment of Tarawa, 20 November 1943. Rear Admiral Harry W. Hill, Commander, Task Force 53, and members of his staff are observing the bombardment from *Maryland's* port bridge. Official U.S. Navy photograph, now in the collections of the U.S. National Archives.

Invasion of Saipan. LVTs moving toward the beach, past bombarding cruisers, on D-day, 15 June 1944. Cruiser firing in the background is USS *Indianapolis* (CA-35). Official U.S. Navy photograph, now in the collections of the U.S. National Archives.

USS *Montpelier* (CL-57) en route to Saipan from the Marshalls, 11 June 1944, to take part in the Saipan Invasion. From the U.S. National Archives.

USS *Iowa* (BB-61) fires a salvo from number 2 16″/50 turret during the bombardment of Tinian, 14–15 June 1944. From the U.S. National Archives.

Saipan Operation, June 1944. Ships of Task Force 52 prepare to depart Roi for Saipan, 12 June 1944. Seen from USS *New Mexico* (BB-40). These ships are (left to right): USS *McNair* (DD-679); USS *Montpelier* (CL-57); USS *Honolulu* (CL-48); USS *Tennessee* (BB-43). From the U.S. National Archives.

USS *Alabama* (BB-60) underway in the Pacific with Task Force 58.2, circa 1943–44. Official U.S. Navy photograph, now in the collections of the U.S. National Archives.

Iwo Jima Operation, 1945. Pre-invasion bombardment of Iwo Jima, photographed from a USS *Makin Island* (CVE-93) plane on 17 February 1945. A battleship, a heavy cruiser, and several minesweepers are in the foreground. The cruiser at left appears to be USS *Tuscaloosa* (CA-37). The view looks northeastward, showing the entire island in the upper right with Mount Suribachi nearest to the camera. Official U.S. Navy photograph, now in the collections of the U.S. National Archives.

USS *North Carolina* (BB-55) underway at sea during Operation Galvanic, circa November 1943. Official U.S. Navy photograph, now in the collections of the U.S. National Archives.

Invasion of Saipan, June 1944. View taken aboard a *New Mexico*-class battleship, firing her guns in support of the landings. A sister-ship appears astern; USS *Pennsylvania* (BB-38) appears in the far background. From the U.S. National Archives.

USS *New Mexico* (BB-40) firing her after 14″/50 guns during the pre-invasion bombardment of Guam, circa 14–20 July 1944. Official U.S. Navy photograph, now in the collections of the U.S. National Archives.

USS *Salt Lake City* (CA-25) firing her forward 8″/55 guns while bombarding Iwo Jima, 23 January 1945. Naval History and Heritage Command photograph.

USS *Indianapolis* (CA-35) under fire from Japanese shore batteries during the invasion of Saipan, June 1944. Naval History and Heritage Command photograph.

USS *Pennsylvania* (BB-38) firing her 14″/45 and 5″/38 guns while bombarding Guam, south of the Orote Peninsula, on the first day of the landings, 21 July 1944. Official U.S. Navy photograph, from the collections of the Naval History and Heritage Command.

USS *Laffey* (DD-459) in harbor, probably at Espiritu Santo, New Hebrides. Official U.S. Navy photograph, from the collections of the Naval History and Heritage Command.

Chapter 5

Operation Forager

The Amphibious Assault of Saipan

At 05.20 on the morning of 15 June 1944, transports and LSTs carrying the Second and Fourth Marine Divisions took position off of Saipan in the Mariana Islands. Richmond Kelly Turner, newly promoted to Vice Admiral and in command of a naval attack force for another major American amphibious operation, waited for daybreak to issue the order to "land the landing force." The order went out at 05.42 and Turner set H-hour for 08.30. The American invasion of the Mariana Islands, codenamed Operation Forager, had begun.[1] Delays in getting the LVTs into the water from their parent LSTs caused him to postpone H-hour to 08.40, but, aside from this slight delay, it appeared as though the landing would progress according to plan. LVTs circled almost lazily in the ocean, waiting to form up for the movement toward the line of departure.[2] Reaching this line would be the point at which Turner and all the men under his command would be committed to the landing, for better or worse.

---

[1] Operation Forager consisted of three related amphibious landings. This chapter describes and analyzes the naval gunfire component of two of these, the landings on Saipan and on Guam. The third, the landing on Tinian, is not included in this analysis. There are three main reasons for why it was decided not to include it. First, the naval gunfire preparatory phase was integrally related to and carried out concurrently with the preparatory phase for Saipan, with the emphasis being on the latter. Second, the postponement of the invasion of Guam allowed additional bombardment vessels to take part in the continued support of the difficult Saipan operation as well as the softening up of Tinian. Third, and most importantly, a major component of the pre-landing bombardment preparation for Tinian was provided by 155mm artillery pieces located on Saipan. These artillery pieces fired on the northern landing beaches for a prolonged period, long enough to change the naval gunfire support dynamic that is the focus of this study.

[2] Carl W. Hoffman, *Saipan: The Beginning of the End* (Washington, DC: Historical Division, HQMC, 1950), pp. 45–46; Shaw et al., *Central Pacific Drive,* p. 263; Isely and Crowl, *U.S. Marines and Amphibious War,* p. 319. Both Saipan and Guam were substantially larger than the two previous objectives in the Central Pacific Campaign—Saipan encompassing seventy-two square miles and Guam, the largest island north of the equator between Hawaii and the Philippines, covering 225 square miles—and the Americans knew that they would present different challenges than had the atolls. Shaw et al., *Central Pacific Drive,* pp. 238 and 439.

Naval gunfire preparation began at dawn and continued as the landing craft maneuvered into their assault waves and began to move toward the shore. Cruisers and battleships providing this support lifted the fire of their main batteries when the tractors were 1,000 yards from the beach as a precaution against raining death down on their own. To ensure that the Marines would have artillery support on the beaches as long as possible, the majority of the gunfire support ships waited until the landing craft were only 300 yards from shore before lifting the fire of their five-inch secondary batteries. The USS *Birmingham* (CL-62) and *Indianapolis* continued to pump six- and eight-inch shells, respectively, into Afetna Point until the last possible second. This projection of shoreline was located between the landing areas of the two Marine divisions and, consequently, Japanese weapons located thereon needed to be neutralized, if not destroyed.[3]

A few rounds of enemy artillery fell among the LVTs of the first assault wave as it left the line of departure at 08.12, but the number of rounds coming their way did not overly concern the Marines at first. This turned out to be a rather false impression of the situation they were facing, however. According to captured documents, the Japanese had planned a reception for the Americans that was anything but cordial. Enemy artillery units on Saipan intended to hit the approaching landing craft with fifteen percent of their ammunition and then savage the landing beaches with another fifteen percent. The defenders began to implement this plan as the LVTs crawled over the reef, which was located 300–500 yards off the beaches assigned to the Fourth Marine Division and 700 yards to 1½ miles off those assigned to the Second Division. Automatic weapon, anti-boat, field artillery, and mortar fire ripped into the landing craft in earnest as the first amphibious tractors waddled across the reef and plopped into the water on the other side, the fusillade growing more and more intense and accurate as each succeeding wave approached the shore.[4]

Navy carrier-based aircraft attacked the beaches ahead of the assault waves with five-inch rockets, 100-pound bombs, and .50-caliber machine guns from the moment the tractors reached a line 800 yards from shore. The pilots began to advance their strafing inland when the tractors came within 100 yards of the beach and they maintained a 100-yard safety interval from that point on.[5] Armored amphibious tractors (LVT/As) of the 2nd Armored Amphibian Battalion (USMC) and the 708th Amphibian Tank Battalion (USA) made up the first wave ashore. They commenced firing 300 yards from the beach and continued to blast away as

[3] Hoffman, *Saipan,* p. 48; Shaw et al., *Central Pacific Drive,* p. 263.

[4] Hoffman, *Saipan,* pp. 48–49; Shaw et al., *Central Pacific Drive,* pp. 264 and 267. The distance between the reef and the shoreline is an approximation based upon the scaled maps found in *U.S. Army in World War II Atlas: The War in the Pacific* (Harrisburg, PA: National Historical Society, 1993), p. 48.

[5] Hoffman, *Saipan,* pp. 48–49; Shaw et al., *Central Pacific Drive,* p. 267.

they emerged from the surf at anything that looked like a target.[6] The first troops in all sectors hit the beach at approximately 08.43 and 700 LVTs carrying 8,000 troops stormed ashore within the next twenty minutes.[7]

The Second Division, commanded by Major General Thomas E. Watson, landed north of Charan Kanoa while the Fourth Division, commanded by Major General Harry Schmidt, landed adjacent to and to the south of the town. Within the landing zone of the Second Division, the 2nd and 3rd Battalion Landing Teams (BLTs) of the 6th Marines (2/6 and 3/6) were supposed to go ashore over Beaches Red 2 and Red 3, respectively, while the 3rd and 2nd BLTs of the 8th Marines (3/8 and 2/8) were supposed to land over Beaches Green 1 and Green 2. The 3rd and 2nd BLTs of the 23rd Marines (3/23 and 2/23) and the 2nd and 1st BLTs of the 25th Marines (2/25 ad 1/25) were to simultaneously assault Beaches Blue 1 and Blue 2 and Beaches Yellow 1 and Yellow 2, respectively, in the Fourth Division landing zone. The 2nd Marines and the 24th Marines were to make a diversionary landing movement toward the town of Garapan, located to the north of Charan Kanoa, just before the main landings were to begin and then to go into reserve for their parent divisions. Meanwhile, the Army's 27th Infantry Division (ID) served as floating reserve in case Japanese resistance stretched the operation beyond the time-frame allotted by the schedule.[8]

The Second Marine Division ran into trouble from the start. To put it bluntly, the ship-to-shore movement for the division was a failure and at times it bordered on chaos. LVTs carrying 2/8 veered north and ended up jamming Marines onto Green 1 in the midst of 3/8. At the same time, the 6th Marines also jogged to the left and ended up going ashore across Red 1 and 2 instead of Red 2 and 3 as planned. There are a number of theories as to why this happened. One holds that the tractors were veering away as a result of heavy fire coming from Afetna Point, fire that continued despite the pounding being meted out to the Japanese positions located thereon by *Birmingham* and *Indianapolis.* Another attributes the course change to compass error on the part of the Navy guide boat assigned to the Second

---

[6] Hoffman, *Saipan,* p. 50. The Marine unit was equipped with the newer LVT/A-4 which mounted a snub-nosed 75mm howitzer mounted in a turret and a .50-caliber machine gun. The Army unit was equipped with a few of the LVT/A-4s, but most of their tractors were the older LVT/A-1s that mounted a 37mm gun and three .30-caliber machine guns. The LVT/As were proceeded by LCI Gunboats that were equipped to fire rockets. The LCIs stopped at the reef and the LVT/As continued on toward the shore (Shaw et al., *Central Pacific Drive,* p. 248).

[7] Hoffman, *Saipan,* p. 50.

[8] Hoffman, *Saipan,* pp. 50–51; Shaw et al., *Central Pacific Drive,* pp. 266–68; Isely and Crowl, *U.S. Marines and Amphibious War,* pp. 316–17. Watson replaced Julian Smith as commander 2nd Marine Division on 11 April 1944 according to Gordon Rottman, *U.S. Marine Corps World War II Order of Battle* (Westport, CT: Greenwood Press, 2002), p. 134.

Division's landing craft. A third blames the foul-up on a strong northerly current running between the reef and the beach that the Underwater Demolition Team (UDT) had not detected during its survey of the beaches and the reef on 14 June. Whatever the reason, 2/8's veer to the left opened up a much wider gap between the Second and Fourth Marine Divisions than was intended. It took three days of hard fighting to establish firm contact between the two divisions as a result. And as if this were not enough, the Second Division faced another not insignificant problem as well. Some of the LVT(A)s were overtaken by faster LVTs carrying the assault troops as the waves of tractors made their way toward the beach after crossing the reef. The LVT(A)s were forced into column formation as the nimbler troop carriers shouldered passed them, breaking down the echeloned organization of the ship-to-shore movement. To complicate matters even more, some of the LVTs masked the fire of the LVT(A)s as they passed in front of the latter, decreasing the effectiveness of gunfire support at the most crucial time, that being the point at which tractors emerged from the water and began to deposit troops ashore.[9]

Starting off on the wrong beaches was just the first incident of a most difficult day for the Second Marine Division. Troops of both the 6th and 8th Regiments encountered heavy, organized resistance as they made the transition from sea to land. Defenders maintained good discipline as the Marines came out of the water, not wasting themselves in useless "banzai" charges like Japanese troops had done so many times on other islands. Instead, enemy observers located along the ridges that formed the O-1 Line directed artillery and mortar fire down on the heads of the Americans. Machine gun bullets mingled with the artillery's explosions and resulting shrapnel to inflict heavy casualties on the invasion force. The 6th Marines on Red 1 and 2 were hit so hard that they could force only a shallow 75–100 yard deep beachhead extending across the coastal road just inland from the shoreline.[10]

All four commanders of the Second Division's assault battalions were casualties within the first few hours of the battle for Red and Green Beaches. Congestion and confusion reigned as artillery and mortars landed in and around each battalion's command post. Death delivered from a distance was not the only danger on the beach that day, however. At a little after 10.00, as Colonel James P. Riseley established the regimental CP for the 6th Marines practically at the water's edge on Red 2, between fifteen and twenty-five Japanese attacked southward along the shoreline. Marines in the vicinity promptly cut down the attackers, but it was unnerving to meet such opposition right there on the beach as the assaulting

[9] Philip A. Crowl, *U.S. Army in World War II, The War in the Pacific, Campaign in the Marianas* (Washington, DC: U.S. Army Center of Military History, 1960; reprint, Harrisburg, PA: National Historical Society, 1994), pp. 83 and 85 (page citations are to the reprint edition); Hoffman, *Saipan,* p. 50.

[10] Hoffman, *Saipan,* pp. 51–52; Shaw et al., *Central Pacific Drive,* p. 269.

troops were trying to organize themselves for the push inland. Naval gunfire was supposed to take care of such opposition, was it not?[11]

Riseley was in a tough position. Casualties robbed him of momentum, something he desperately needed if he wanted to get out from under the firestorm breaking over the landing beaches. It was too early to be calling in his regimental reserve, but he needed help. At 10.40 this reserve, the 1/6, began landing. By 11.05, however, he had only advanced his front line another 300 yards with the additional forces. Twenty minutes later he had to pass 1/6 through 3/6 because the third battalion's casualties were so heavy that it could not maintain necessary offensive pressure against the Japanese. First battalion was to revert to regimental reserve after gaining the O-1 Line, allowing 3/6 to take up the offensive once again, but the plan fell through because Japanese opposition prevented 1/6 from reaching its objective. As it turned out, it did not really matter. Heavy casualties forced Riseley to put all three of his infantry battalions in the line just so that he could maintain a front that could expand as the 6th Marines advanced.[12] Compounding the regimental commander's problems was a growing gap between his Marines and the 8th Regiment to his right. The 6th Marines landing 400 yards north of their assigned beaches originally caused this gap, but it was growing as the two regiments advanced in diverging directions. Riseley ordered Companies K and L, 3/6, to close it, but they were only partially successful. A 300-yard-wide hole still remained even after K and L expended the best effort they could muster, and all Riseley could do was cover the space by fire and continue with his advance.[13]

The Japanese launched two tank-based counterattacks against the 6th Marines as Riseley struggled to maintain his regiment's momentum. The first, at 12.00, began as two enemy tanks left their camouflaged positions in front of 2/6 and began to travel south along the coastal road. They stopped to get their bearings and, as a crewman opened the turret of one of them, Company F, 2/6, used bazookas and anti-tank grenades to destroy them both. The second counterattack began at 13.00 as three Japanese tanks attempted to penetrate the American line between 1/6 and 2/6. Marines destroyed two of these tanks short of the line, but one made it to within seventy-five yards of Colonel Riseley's CP before it was dispatched. The 6th Marines were catching it hard with approximately thirty-five percent of Riseley's men having been killed or wounded by 13.00.[14]

---

[11] Hoffman, *Saipan*, pp. 50–51; Crowl, *Campaign in the Marianas*, p. 87; Shaw et al., *Central Pacific Drive*, p. 269.

[12] Crowl, *Campaign in the Marianas*, pp. 87–88; Shaw et al., *Central Pacific Drive*, p. 270; Hoffman, *Saipan*, p. 53.

[13] Crowl, *Campaign in the Marianas*, p. 88; Hoffman, *Saipan*, p. 53.

[14] Shaw et al., *Central Pacific Drive*, p. 269; Hoffman, *Saipan*, p. 65.

Meanwhile, on the Green Beaches, 8th Marines had its own problems with the Japanese. Third Battalion, in what was an unusual occurrence for the Second Division on 15 June, pushed inland from Green 1 and met its first objective on time. Second Battalion, however, had landed 700–1,000 yards north of its assigned beach and, as a consequence, it spent most of D-day fighting to secure the beach over which it should have come ashore. To do this, Company G attacked south along the beach toward Afetna Point. The Marines needed to capture this geographical feature because the weapons the Japanese had emplaced there were in a position to enfilade Beaches Green 2 and 3. It came as a bonus that possession of it gave the Americans control of the only channel through the reef in the immediate area. Tank-carrying landing craft could be sent through this channel so that armored vehicles could be landed as early as possible. Companies E and F, meanwhile, attacked to the southeast, fanning out as they went. This scheme of maneuver caused the three companies to diverge from one another, complicating their coordination and destroying their ability to support one another. As E and F advanced inland, they approached a swamp just to the north of Lake Susupe. Elements from Company F crossed the swamp but did not stay there for long. Realizing how isolated they were, they decided to pull back and establish a line along firm ground to the west of the swamp.[15]

Company G met strong Japanese resistance as it pushed through the sand dunes on the beach to begin its advance. The company's objective was a series of nine mutually supporting pillboxes located on Afetna Point that contained 37mm and 47mm guns. Riflemen in trenches protected the pillboxes, a fact made quite clear to the Marines when they began to approach the enemy positions from below. As Company G advanced, Japanese emerged from their defensive positions to attack the Marines with bayonet and sword. Fire from enemy weapons was not the only danger facing these Marines on that day, however. Since an assault on Afetna Point meant that 2/8 would be firing rifles in a direction almost perpendicular to the advance of the 23rd Marines over Beaches Blue 1 and 2, the 8th Marines carried ashore a lethal but shorter-ranged weapon—the shotgun. Company G was issued the 8th Regiment's entire supply of shotguns, enough for one weapon for every two men, because their position in the line put them on point for an attack in the direction of their brother Marines. The men of Company G blasted away at the Japanese coming at them with buckshot and stopped them in their tracks. When enemy riflemen fired on the company's left flank from the east side of the Charan Kanoa airstrip, the unit's organic 60mm mortars and machine guns took them out.[16] The pillboxes the Japanese were trying so hard to defend were positioned so that the guns inside them could fire seaward at oncoming landing craft.

[15] Hoffman, *Saipan*, pp. 54–55; Crowl, *Campaign in the Marianas*, p. 89; Shaw et al., *Central Pacific Drive*, p. 271.

[16] Hoffman, *Saipan*, p. 54; Shaw et al., *Central Pacific Drive*, p. 270.

The enemy soldiers manning the guns were totally dedicated to their job of killing the Americans as they congregated on the beach; so dedicated, in fact, that they did not turn their weapons on the Americans who were making their way toward the defenders' positions. Consequently, the approaching Marines simply went around the pillboxes and attacked them from the rear, the attached combat engineers using bazookas, demolitions, and flamethrowers to take them out one by one. By nightfall, Company G had overrun seven of the nine and the Americans controlled all of Green 2.[17]

Colonel Clarence R. Wallace, CO of the 8th Marines, landed between Beaches Green 1 and 2 at 09.45 and took stock of the situation ashore. He ordered his reserve battalion, the 1/8, to land at 09.50 and proceeded to use it to strengthen his line. He then attached Company B to 2/8, using it to cover Company G's left flank as the latter advanced against the pillboxes on Afetna Point. He also committed Companies A and C between 2/8 and 3/8, ordering them to attack east into the swamp just north of Lake Susupe. Darkness, however, forced a withdrawal to the line occupied by Companies E and F on the west side of the swamp. Withdrawing to this position allowed the Marines to establish a defensible perimeter.[18] Needing more reinforcements, General Watson committed his division reserve, 1st Battalion, 29th Marines, during the early afternoon and attached it to the 8th Regiment. Colonel Wallace ordered Company B, 1/29, to fill a gap between Companies E and G in 2/8's zone of action, but, ignorant of the terrain and neglecting to employ guides, the reserve battalion ended up 600 yards north of the position where it was needed. Company A, 1/29, set out at 17.30 to fill the same gap, but the rapidly encroaching darkness contributed to this unit losing its way as well. The Japanese took advantage of Company A's predicament, raining artillery rounds on them as the lost Marines groped around in the gathering twilight. Meanwhile, Company B finally found the position to which it had been sent in the beginning. Since Company B was filling its allotted slot at last, Company A's continued efforts became unnecessary and the order went out for that unit to settle in for the night where it was. It would act, along with the other uncommitted units of 1/29, as a general reserve for the next day's attack.[19]

At 18.00, 3rd Battalion, 2nd Marines came ashore over Beach Red 2 and attached to the 6th Regiment, taking up a position on the Second Division's left flank. An hour later, Company F and the Headquarters echelon of 2/2 came ashore over Red 2 and moved to a point north of the Charan Kanoa airstrip. This would be the last ship-to-shore activity for Watson's command on D-day. At 19.00 word came down that all LCVP-LVT transfers at the reef were to be suspended immediately and that there would be no more landings on that day. Deteriorating sea

---

[17] Shaw et al., *Central Pacific Drive*, pp. 270–71; Hoffman, *Saipan*, p. 54.

[18] Hoffman, *Saipan*, p. 55.

[19] Ibid.; Shaw et al., *Central Pacific Drive*, p. 271; Crowl, *Campaign in the Marianas*, p. 89.

conditions as the evening wore on contributed to this decision. The fact that an LVT carrying part of the Second Division's Headquarters almost swamped as early as 17.30 did not bode well, and when huge waves began to crash over the reef, General Watson decided that it would be best to wait for the morning to finish bringing his Marines ashore.[20]

The Fourth Marine Division faced a similar set of problems on 15 June, but there were plenty of twists to make its experience unique. Generally speaking, the 23rd Marines, landing over Beaches Blue 1 and 2, was not able to make a coordinated drive toward the O-1 Line once it made landfall. Eight LVTs and three LVT(A)s carrying elements of the 3rd Battalion penetrated all the way to O-1 from Blue 1, but, like elements of 1/8 attacking across the swamp at Lake Susupe to their north, they had to fall back to battalion lines for the night because of lack of support.[21] The 2nd Battalion, on 3/23's right flank, did not fare as well. Its Marines debarked from their LVTs at different distances inland causing its line to be staggered and discontinuous. As a result, a battalion-level attack could not be coordinated and fighting degenerated into a series of small-unit actions. The battalion commander, Lieutenant Colonel Edward J. Dillon, did not gain effective tactical command and control until mid-afternoon. Meanwhile, three LVTs and five LVT(A)s carrying elements of the 2nd Battalion penetrated to the O-1 Line, but they, like the tractors from 3/23, had to be recalled at nightfall. There were several reasons for the 23rd Marines' lack of progress beyond the beach. The first was the hailstorm of enemy artillery and mortar fire slamming into the Marines at the waterline. The second and third reasons, however, had nothing to do with the Japanese: to the north there was a swamp and a lake and to the south there was a vertical rise of between four and five feet. Both of these obstacles, the second of which was not detected in aerial photographs, effectively stopped the advance of any LVTs that made it through the hell of the landing. Colonel Louis R. Jones, wanting to gain control of the situation and drive his regiment inland as quickly as possible, came ashore shortly after noon and temporarily set up his CP in a slight depression between Beaches Blue 1 and 2. Once on the beach, however, Japanese artillery and mortars pounded Jones and his staff mercilessly for the rest of the day.[22]

Farther to the south on Beaches Yellow 1 and 2, the 25th Marines were in an even tougher bind. Lieutenant Colonel Hollis U. Mustain's 1st Battalion on Yellow 2 took the brunt of the punishment, penetrating only twelve yards beyond the shoreline by 09.43. The main source of Mustain's woes was Japanese pillboxes and mortars firing from Agingan Point, located to his south, but that was not the only

[20] Hoffman, *Saipan,* p. 67.

[21] Shaw et al., *Central Pacific Drive,* pp. 271 and 273; Hoffman, *Saipan,* pp. 58–59.

[22] Crowl, *Campaign in the Marianas,* p. 91; Shaw et al., *Central Pacific Drive,* p. 273; Hoffman, *Saipan,* pp. 59–60.

source. There were also four or five 75mm direct fire artillery pieces located on the high ground 800 yards to the battalion's front that poured ordnance onto the beach. This heavy shelling pressured the LVT drivers of the Army's 773rd Amphibian Tractor Battalion to spend as little time ashore as possible. They unloaded troops, but that was about all they could do. Communications gear, crew-served weapons, and ammunition were left onboard and, as a result, 1/25 was short of these items for the next three days, particularly communications equipment.[23] At 09.30, 1/25's situation became even more dire. The Japanese counterattacked from the ridge at the O-1 Line and simultaneously from Agingan Point. Lieutenant Colonel Mustain called in air strikes and naval gunfire against the attacking Japanese and requested that tank support and an additional rifle company from reserves be sent as soon as possible. Regimental command sent Mustain his requested reinforcements once the reserve battalion, Lieutenant Colonel Justice M. Chambers' 3/25, landed. First Battalion, newly recharged, then attacked Agingan Point. Progress was slow, however, because the Japanese had covered part of the point with camouflaged spider holes in which defenders remained concealed until a Marine fire team passed by. The Japanese then emerged to shoot the Marines in the back. Difficulties encountered in clearing out these spider holes ensured that the threat to the 1/25's right flank could not be completely eliminated in a timely manner and nightfall found the situation ongoing.[24]

North of Mustain's 1/25, Lieutenant Colonel Lewis C. Hudson, Jr.'s 2nd Battalion on Yellow 1 fared better. LVTs deposited about half of the battalion's assault Marines 500–700 yards inland despite heavy mortar, artillery, and small arms fire. This position placed them under the cover of a railroad embankment. Japanese rifle and machine gun rounds peppered the battalion from just beyond this embankment until the LVTs defiladed themselves behind it, but enemy mortar and artillery fire from the same location continued to hit the Marines for some time afterward. Fire also came from the direction of Nafutan Point and from two Japanese mortars 500 yards to the rear of 2/25's advance elements. Air support took out the two mortars before anyone sent a request to do so, but the other fire continued to cause problems for the battalion as it pushed forward towards its objectives. Despite the continuous plastering by Japanese artillery, mortar, and machine gun fire, however, the 25th Marines as a whole penetrated farther inland on D-day than did any other unit of the Second or Fourth Marine Divisions—over 2,000 yards. Colonel Merton J. Batchelder, CO of the 25th Regiment, came ashore by mid-afternoon and established his CP against the west side of the railroad

---

[23] Crowl, *Campaign in the Marianas,* p. 91; Shaw et al., *Central Pacific Drive,* p. 274; Hoffman, *Saipan,* pp. 55–56.

[24] Crowl, *Campaign in the Marianas,* p. 91; Shaw et al., *Central Pacific Drive,* p. 274; Hoffman, *Saipan,* pp. 56–57.

embankment where, unlike Colonel Jones of the 23rd Marines, he and his staff were protected from much of the Japanese defensive fire.[25]

Major General Watson established the Second Marine Division's CP ashore on Beach Red 2 at 17.30.[26] Major General Schmidt came ashore on Yellow 2 at 19.30 and did the same for the Fourth Division. At first, Schmidt's CP was nothing more than a group of foxholes approximately fifty yards from the beach. Enemy light artillery, firing from the high ground 1,500 yards inland, made the job of coordinating the actions of his division difficult. Schmidt later recalled, "Needless to say the command post during that time did not function very well. It was the hottest spot I was in during the war, not even excepting Iwo Jima." Despite the problems getting ashore, the Marines were on Saipan to stay once both Watson and Schmidt were settled in for the night, but it would take them until 9 July to secure the rest of the island.[27]

The Amphibious Assault of Guam

Dawn, 21 July 1944—more than a month after American forces had first stormed ashore in the Marianas—the United States was poised to violently take back from the Japanese what had been taken from them at the beginning of the war. Guam, the largest of the Mariana Islands, had been an American possession prior to 7 December 1941. Losing it to the enemy at the very outbreak of hostilities left a sour taste in the mouth of many a Navy man and Marine. Captain Geary R. Bundschu, commander of Company A, 3rd Marines, considered what lay ahead for himself and his men as he looked out at the first rays of light streaking across the darkness from the eastern horizon. Pre-combat fear and nervousness was a given for every man in the outfit, and Bundschu was no exception, but he had to put such thoughts aside while he dealt with the myriad tasks of preparing his command for the mission at hand. The plan called for the 3rd Marines to storm ashore over the left-hand beaches of the Third Marine Division's zone of attack, to secure Adelup Point on its left, and to secure Chonito Cliff and the high ground to its southeast.[28] Company A was assigned the neutralization of a 400-foot high, 200-yard square ridge that planners had unceremoniously named after the officer commanding the men tasked with carrying out the mission. Bundschu did not spend much time thinking about the possibly dubious honor, however. There were numerous Japanese troops manning mortars and machine guns among the rocky

---

[25] Hoffman, *Saipan,* pp. 56–57; Shaw et al., *Central Pacific Drive,* pp. 274–75.

[26] Hoffman, *Saipan,* p. 66; Crowl, *Campaign in the Marianas,* p. 90.

[27] Crowl, *Campaign in the Marianas,* p. 90 (including quote); Shaw et al., *Central Pacific Drive,* p. 345.

[28] Crowl, *Campaign in the Marianas,* p. 344.

crags and crevices of that terrain feature and he knew that they would exact a high price from his Marines in return for their lives.[29]

The assault on the island of Guam was to be Phase II of Operation Forager, and it was to have begun on 18 June 1944, three days after the beginning of the invasion of Saipan to the north. Difficulties encountered in taking that island forced Admiral Raymond Spruance to push back W-day, as the first day of the assault on Guam was termed, to 21 July. The invasion would prove to be different from the Saipan operation in a number of respects, and one of the most obvious was apparent from the beginning: it would consist of two totally separate military operations that were meant to use their initial momentum to join together inland from the landing beaches. The combined force would then terminate the Japanese presence on the island. This meant that there would be two sets of landing beaches, one set just west of the town of Agana and the other just south of the town of Agat with several miles and much difficult terrain separating them.[30]

The first set, referred to as the "northern" beaches, was the objective of Major General Allen H. Turnage's Third Marine Division. His plan called for landing all three of his infantry regiments abreast of one another across 2,500 yards of beach. This width of sand was subdivided into codenamed beaches designated, from east to west, Red 1, Red 2, Green, and Blue. The 3rd Marines would land its 3rd and 1st Battalions (3/3 and 1/3) across Beaches Red 1 and Red 2, respectively, in line abreast while the 9th Marines would land across Beach Blue on the right and the 21st Marines would land across Beach Green in the center, both in column. At either end of the landing beaches were terrain features that the Marines dubbed "the devil's horns"—Adelup Point to the east and Asan Point to the west.[31]

The 1st Provisional Marine Brigade, commanded by Brigadier General Lemuel C. Shepherd, Jr., would take on the second set of beaches, usually referred to as the "southern" beaches to differentiate them from the Third Marine Division's landing area. The brigade consisted of two battle-tested regiments, the 4th and the 22nd. The addition of the 77th Infantry Division's 305th Regiment brought Shepherd's command up to division strength. The plan called for the 22nd Marines to land on the left, just south of the town of Agat, over Beaches Yellow 1 and Yellow 2. The 4th Marines, meanwhile, were to land on the right, just north of Bangi Point, over Beaches White 1 and White 2. The 305th Infantry, after acting as reserve for the landing, would come ashore, pass through the 4th Marines, and take up a position on the right of the beachhead, securing it for the 1st Provisional Marine Brigade's drive inland.[32]

---

[29] Ibid., p. 466.

[30] Shaw et al., *Central Pacific Drive,* pp. 462–63.

[31] Shaw et al., *Central Pacific Drive,* p. 463; Crowl, *Campaign in the Marianas,* pp. 343–44.

[32] Shaw et al., *Central Pacific Drive,* pp. 451–52; Crowl, *Campaign in the Marianas,* pp. 344–45.

The first of the Third Marine Division's LVTs headed for shore at 07.40. Naval gunfire support reached a fever pitch by 08.22 and continued at that level until the tractors were 1,200 yards from shore. Large caliber guns then lifted their fire inland while five-inch guns continued shelling the beaches until the leading LVT(A)s crossed the reef. These armored amphibians emerged from the surf on the northern beaches at 08.29 and by 08.32, only two minutes past the H-hour set by the naval attack force commander Rear Admiral Richard L. Conolly, troops were going ashore in both the northern and southern landing zones. It was at this point that the Japanese began to open up on the Americans.[33]

Enemy fire was very accurate as Bundschu's Company A made the transition from sea to land. Mortars and artillery claimed some Marines while they were still on the water and several more died once they came onto the beach. The company commander assessed the situation for a few minutes and then reorganized his remaining men. He sent two platoons in assault across the dry rice paddies that lay between the shore and the inland ridge and kept one platoon in reserve. At 09.20, Japanese mortar and machine gun fire had his lead platoons pinned down in a gully to the west of the ridge, unable to move. In order to try and get things going again, he had to commit his reserve platoon to the east side of the attempted advance. The additional men allowed Bundschu to push to within 100 yards of the top of the ridge, but his company paid a heavy price for the ground they had gained. At about 14.00 he requested permission from his battalion CO, Major Henry Aplington, II, to disengage, but Company A was too heavily involved at the time to be allowed to drop back. Colonel W. Carvel Hall, commander of the 3rd Marines, ordered another attack on the ridge and Bundschu, though doubtful of the results, once again reorganized what was left of his men and prepared to try to take the last 100 yards. Toward nightfall the attack commenced. His Marines tried to advance toward the ridge, but the same withering machine gun fire that had stopped the initial advance came at them out of the gathering darkness. As men in the vanguard were felled, they tumbled down to the flat ground at the foot of the steep slope. Geary Bundschu was among the fallen. Support from the 40mm guns of Battery I, 14th Defense Battalion, eventually allowed a "thin line" of men from Company A to reach the crest of the ridge, but the position proved to be untenable and they had to fall back. At the end of the day, the Japanese still held the position and the ridge bearing Captain Bundschu's name had become his memorial.[34]

The experience of Company A, 3rd Marines, was not unusual among the units fighting in the battle for the northern beaches on W-day. Colonel Hall anticipated stubborn Japanese resistance to his regiment's advance and accordingly drew his first objective line (O-a) along the first high ground inland. He expected to use his

[33] Orlan R. Lodge, *The Recapture of Guam* (Washington, DC: Historical Branch, G-3 Division, Headquarters, USMC, 1954), p. 37.

[34] Shaw et al., *Central Pacific Drive,* pp. 466–67.

reserve, the 2nd Battalion, either at the center of the objective line if the assault battalions reached it or, if they did not, he would pass it through the left-hand company of 3rd Battalion so that it could take Adelup Point on the far left of the Third Division's zone of action. Japanese opposition to the landing did not disappoint Hall for the 3rd Marines faced the most determined enemy resistance on W-day. In fact, over the next four days Hall's regiment essentially disintegrated, requiring help from the adjoining 9th Marines to continue the fight. Chonito Cliff, northeast of Red 1, was covered with caves. It was in theses caves that the Japanese set up a system of defenses from which Hall's men had to extract them. Doing so contributed to the 3rd Marines' high casualty rate. It was readily apparent why the Japanese had decided to use Chonito Cliff in this way because from these caves the defenders could pour fire mercilessly upon the Marines as they came ashore.[35]

Companies I and K of 3rd Battalion were supposed to rush across the beach and, carried along by their momentum, they were expected to overwhelm the Japanese on Chonito Cliff before the defenders could recover from the effects of the bombardment. To the chagrin of the Marines, however, the Japanese appeared to have recovered by the time of the assault. Company I, attacking to the right, attempted to move up a draw just to the south of the same objective. Company K, meanwhile, attacked to the left, crossed the beach, and pivoted in an attempt to flank the cliff. Heavy enemy fire halted both attempts. Sergeant Cyril O'Brien later recalled the scene that day:

> Nearly half my old company lies dead on the barren slopes of Chonito Cliff. Four times they tried to reach the top. Four times they were thrown back. They had to break out of a twenty-yard beachhead to make way for later landing waves. They attacked up a 60-degree slope, protected only by sword grass, and were met by a storm of grenades and heavy rifle, machine gun and mortar fire.
>
> The physical act of forward motion required the use of both hands. As a consequence they were unable to return the enemy fire effectively. Most of the casualties were at the bottom of the slope. They had been hit as they left cover.[36]

Lieutenant Colonel Ralph L. Houser, 3rd Battalion CO, used flamethrowers and tanks from Company C, 3rd Tank Battalion, to break this impasse and followed it up by committing his reserve, Company L, creating a breech in the Japanese defenses at that point. Momentum carried them all the way to the flat land to

---

[35] Crowl, *Campaign in the Marianas,* p. 344; Lodge, *Recapture of Guam,* pp. 42–43; Millett, *Semper Fidelis,* p. 418.

[36] Quote contained in Harry Gailey, *The Liberation of Guam: 21 July–10 August 1944* (Novato, CA: Presidio Press, 1988), pp. 95–96.

the north of the obstructing precipice and, by noon, Chonito Cliff was cleared of enemy resistance. The tanks then turned their guns on Adelup Point. Destroyers and LCI Gunboats had been working this enemy strongpoint over since early morning, but their bombardment had failed to knock out all of the enemy guns that were firing on the Third Division's left flank. These guns were finally silenced later in the afternoon when Marines from 3/3 attacked Adelup Point supported by tanks and LVT(A)s. Even with all of this progress, however, the 3rd Marines had not made contact with the 21st Marines to its right by the end of W-day.[37]

The assault waves of the 21st Marines, by contrast, encountered relatively little resistance coming ashore across Beach Green. The Japanese had abandoned their organized shoreline defenses in the regiment's zone of action, saving their strength for when the Marines moved inland. Colonel Arthur H. Butler, having to send his men in over a single beach, landed his battalions in column in reverse sequential order with Lieutenant Colonel Wendell H. Duplantis' 3rd (3/21) in assault followed quickly by Lieutenant Colonel Eustace R. Smoak's 2nd (2/21). Lieutenant Colonel Ronald R. Van Stockum's 1st Battalion (1/21), upon coming ashore, would mop up behind the other two and then go into division reserve. The 21st did not disappoint its commander. Third Battalion quickly secured the high ground immediately inland of the beach and then used it as an assembly area where it could reorganize before attacking the cliffs farther inland. Enemy mortar fire from those cliffs began to land amongst the Marines as they prepared for the drive into the interior of the island, increasing in intensity until the shells were falling every few seconds. By the time regimental headquarters landed in the eleventh wave, fire on the beach area was so heavy that Colonel Butler, seeking protection from the rain of fire and steel, had to set up his CP temporarily in a ditch near the shoreline.[38]

Part of the plan for the 21st Marines called for it to secure the line of cliffs inland from the landing beaches and then to defend its position until the division was ready to expand the beachhead. Third Battalion prepared to execute that part of the regiment's mission when, by mid-morning, it reached the high ground in back of Asan Village. Second Battalion then passed through 3/21's Company K at 12.50 so that it could begin the assault on the cliff area beyond. The battle for the cliffs went on for days. Remembered as "The Battle for Banzai Ridge," it was actually a series of battles involving several different cliffs "where every ridge gained by the 21st Marines disclosed another pocket of the enemy behind it."[39] Approximately one

[37] Lodge, *Recapture of Guam,* pp. 43 and 46; Shaw et al., *Central Pacific Drive,* pp. 463, 465, and 467; Crowl, *Campaign in the Marianas,* p. 344.

[38] Shaw et al., *Central Pacific Drive,* pp. 467–68; Lodge, *Recapture of Guam,* pp. 40–41.

[39] Shaw et al., *Central Pacific Drive,* pp. 468–69; quote is from MCUA, Box 24, Folder 5, Third Marine Division Special Action Report, FORAGER Operation, dated 19 August 1944, Narrative Section, p. 3 (hereinafter 3rd MarDiv SAR).

mile from the beach, 2/21 encountered a steep 100-foot cliff as it moved up a narrow passage in the terrain. The cliff cut diagonally across the battalion's axis of attack leaving Lieutenant Colonel Smoak no option but to take it on and, since there was no room for maneuver, a frontal assault would be necessary to do so. Company F led the attack with Company E echeloned to the right rear. Company G served as reserve, waiting below the cliff until needed. The Japanese decimated Company F's rifle platoons as the Marines pushed the assault up three indentations in the face of the cliff. Company E, following behind, suffered heavy casualties as well. Some Marines, showing the effects of long shipboard confinement before landing, could not make the climb. At the top, those Marines who could pull themselves up the cliff's face were immobilized by heavy machine gun fire originating from enemy positions on a ridge only about fifty yards away. Smoak prepared his defenses for the night as the first units to the top held the position under increasingly heavy artillery and mortar fire. Company G protected his left flank while Company E secured his right. Company F, battered but still functioning, defended the center while continuing to absorb punishment from the Japanese on the ridge in front of them.[40]

As the 2nd Battalion dug in for the night, Lieutenant Colonel Duplantis attempted to tie in his 3rd Battalion to Smoak's right flank. Dense jungle vegetation made contact difficult, so the best that could be accomplished was a connection through outposts. Meanwhile, as the 2nd and 3rd Battalions slugged it out on the front lines, 1st Battalion performed mopping up duties in the rear. Not having encountered many of the enemy in the process, it went into division reserve as planned. A deep ravine, choked with jungle vegetation, separated the 21st Marines from the 3rd Marines to its left. The gap was 150 yards wide and, despite efforts by patrols from both regiments to make contact, it could not be closed by nightfall. The 3rd MarDiv Special Action Report states that the gap was "well neutralized," however, because "[e]nemy mortar fire kept [it] open; our own kept out the enemy."[41]

Terrain was not as much of a problem for Colonel Edward A. Craig's 9th Marines as it was for Third Division's other two regiments and, even though it encountered stiff enemy resistance, it made the most progress of the three on W-day. Like the 21st Marines, Craig's regiment had to come ashore over a single beach, codenamed Blue, so he also landed his battalions in column: Lieutenant Colonel Walter Asmuth, Jr.'s 3rd in assault; Lieutenant Colonel Robert E. Cushman, Jr.'s 2nd in support; and Lieutenant Colonel Carey A. Randall's 1st in reserve. Third Battalion was to capture the high ground immediately inland from the beach, including Asan Point, and then hold its position. First Battalion and 2nd Battalion were then to pass through 3/9 to attack the regiment's O-1 objective, a

---

[40] Shaw et al., *Central Pacific Drive,* p. 469.

[41] Shaw et al., *Central Pacific Drive,* p. 469; quote is from 3rd MarDiv SAR, p. 3.

line 1,000 yards inland from the beach and just short of the Tatgua River, while the 3rd Battalion went into regimental reserve.[42]

Company I stormed ashore on the 3rd Battalion's right. Enemy fire from both the high ground directly in front of Asan Point as well as from the Point itself, located on the company's right flank, poured down on the Marines' heads as the they tried to move inland. Momentum from the ship-to-shore movement could not be maintained against this increasingly destructive barrage coming from the Japanese guns. The attack stalled out and Lieutenant Colonel Asmuth committed his reserve, Company L, to try to get it started again, but to no avail. The battalion commander requested tank support, the Shermans having landed at 09.40 as scheduled, and Companies I and L began to advance slowly as the tanks fired their 75mm guns at the enemy over the heads of the assaulting Marines.[43]

Company K, 3/9's left-hand assault unit, was moving inland rapidly in the meantime. It crossed the dry rice paddies just beyond the first high ground above the beach and took its first objective, a ridge fronting its line of attack. This was a most important movement for the Third Marine Division because the capture of this rice paddy area near the mouth of the Asan River allowed the division artillery regiment, the 12th Marines, to set up and begin delivering fire in support of the infantry assault across the northern beaches. By 13.50 all of 3rd Battalion was at its first objective line and the time had come for the next phase of the attack to begin. That phase kicked off at 14.15 when the 1st and 2nd Battalions, after passing through the 3rd, attacked toward the Tatgua River. The advance, though resisted by the Japanese, ended within only 400 yards of the river at 16.00. Colonel Craig, having reached his regiment's objective for the day, ordered his Marines to dig in for the night. By 18.30 the regiment had tied in to the 21st Marines on their right.[44]

Major General Roy S. Geiger, commander of the III Amphibious Corps, was generally pleased with the performance of the Third Marine Division on 21 July. Though not perfect, things went as well as could be expected. The division bled (105 KIA, 536 WIA, and 56 MIA), but the losses never seriously impeded its ability to carry the fight to the Japanese. By the time Major General Allen H. Turnage came ashore and assumed command at 17.15, the Third Division was firmly established ashore on the northern beaches and was well on its way to consolidating its portion of the III Amphibious Corps' mission.[45]

While terrain, with the exception of the 3rd Marines, proved to be the greatest obstacle for the Marines to the north, such was not the case in the south. The 1st Provisional Marine Brigade found plenty of enemy in its zone of action and had to

---

[42] Shaw et al., *Central Pacific Drive,* pp. 469–70; Lodge, *Recapture of Guam,* pp. 38–39.

[43] Lodge, *Recapture of Guam,* p. 39.

[44] Shaw et al., *Central Pacific Drive,* pp. 470–71; Lodge, *Recapture of Guam,* p. 39.

[45] Shaw et al., *Central Pacific Drive,* pp. 471 and 472.

slug its way through them to the interior. Colonel Merlin F. Schneider's 22nd Marines came in over the northernmost beaches, 1st Battalion (1/22) over Yellow 1 and 2nd Battalion (2/22) over Yellow 2. Both of these assault units suffered considerable losses while landing and their reorganization on the beach was difficult as a result. Enfilading fire from one 75mm and one 37mm gun on Gaan Point on the right front of Beach Yellow 2 complicated the reorganization even further. Pulling surviving men and equipment together as quickly as possible under the barrage raining down on the beaches, the 22nd's units began to move fitfully toward their first objectives. Progress became easier once the first assault Marines had moved about 200 yards inland, a distance that put them out of range of the Japanese guns that were flailing their comrades as they came ashore. Their efforts earned them what proved to be only a momentary respite, however.[46]

Enemy artillery began to register hits on Lieutenant Colonel Donn C. Hart's 2nd Battalion at approximately 12.00 after it had advanced 1,000 yards inland to the high ground above the beach. Weathering the pounding for fifty minutes, Hart started his Marines off toward their segment of the brigade's first-day objective hoping that the shelling would let up. He had no such luck. Progress slowed to a crawl as the fire increased and it stopped completely when a Japanese dual-purpose anti-aircraft gun opened up on Company E. Hart requested an air strike to take out the enemy position, but the pilots ended up doing about as much damage to his Marines as they did to the Japanese. Bullets from strafing airplanes ripped into 2/22's front lines and bombs slammed into Company F. This friendly fire incident prevented 2nd Battalion from resuming its attack by the time the order came down to dig in for the night.[47]

Lieutenant Colonel Walfried H. Fromhold's 1st Battalion turned left after coming ashore and began battling toward the town of Agat. Company B advanced up the beach on the left and met stiff opposition as it approached the perimeter of the village. Naval and air bombardment had destroyed the buildings, but the resulting rubble provided the Japanese defenders with excellent cover from which to snipe at the advancing Marines. Company A, meanwhile, moved rapidly to the right across the inland rice paddies, encountering little opposition as it went. Fromhold committed his battalion reserve, Company C, to his seaward flank as a precaution. First battalion was in control of most of Agat by 10.20 and at 10.30 the commander ordered the rest of the village captured. At 12.45, after completing this task, 1/22 jumped off on its drive toward the O-1 Line. Colonel Schneider attempted to send his reserve battalion, the 3rd, ashore at 09.30 so that it could help with the push toward O-1, but a communications failure meant that its commander, Lieutenant Colonel Clair W. Shisler, did not receive orders to land until 12.36. Such a late start

[46] Ibid., pp. 472–73; Lodge, *Recapture of Guam*, pp. 48–49; Gailey, *Liberation of Guam*, p. 100.

[47] Shaw et al., *Central Pacific Drive*, p. 473; Lodge, *Recapture of Guam*, pp. 49 and 50–51.

prevented the majority of 3/22 from participating in the action on W-day, but Schneider went ahead with the advance toward O-1 despite the lack of reserves.[48]

Captain Charles F. Widdecke's Company C, 1/22's reserve, ran into some tough going as it covered Fromhold's left flank during the advance toward O-1. The company was making good time until heavy machine gun fire from a rather innocent looking hill just to the east of Agat brought its progress to a halt. Widdecke attempted a flanking movement around the hill at about 15.00, but enemy fire stopped it as well. The machine gun on the hill kept Company C pinned down for over an hour, even after a reserve rifle platoon from Company I, 3/22, was sent up to join in the attack. The day's action took a heavy toll on Widdecke's command. At 17.05 he reported that he had only 100 men left, including the men from the reserve platoon, and he requested more help. Fromhold sent him another reserve platoon, but the attack still went nowhere. Finally, the battalion commander ordered Widdecke to fall back fifty yards and to tie in with Company B. By 20.00 all units of the 22nd Marines had dug in for the night.[49]

Action on the White beaches to the south proved to be no less dynamic. Lieutenant Colonel Alan Shapley, CO of the 4th Marines, landed his 2nd Battalion (2/4) over Beach White 1 and his 1st Battalion (1/4) over Beach White 2. Major Bernard W. Green's 1/4 landed with Companies A and B in assault. A machine gun opened up on Company B while its LVTs were still about thirty yards from the beach, killing two Marines. The pillbox responsible was destroyed and its five defenders were killed. Company A was more fortunate coming ashore, but one of its platoon leaders died as he crossed a rice paddy that lay behind the landing beach. Green's reserve unit, Company C, landed when both A and B had reached approximately 700 yards inland. It wheeled to the right after coming ashore and attacked Hill 40 and Bangi Point. The point had been devastated by naval gunfire and was easily overrun. The Japanese, however, still heavily defended Hill 40. Fire from machine guns located on the hill brought Company C's attack to a halt. These weapons also fired on Company A. Neither unit could take out the Japanese positions without suffering heavy casualties. Green requested armor and two tanks came forward to provide additional strength for a second assault on the hill. The Marines were successful in taking the position with the help of this armored support.[50]

Major John S. Messer's 2nd Battalion encountered a rise ten to twenty feet in height only 100 yards in from the shoreline, a terrain feature that did not appear on any maps. Japanese defenders, lying in defilade behind the rise, pounded Messer's men with ordnance. Progress was slow, but Lieutenant Colonel Shapley reported at 09.47 that elements of 2/4 had penetrated 700 yards inland. By noon,

[48] Shaw et al., *Central Pacific Drive,* p. 473; Lodge, *Recapture of Guam,* pp. 49 and 50.

[49] Shaw et al., *Central Pacific Drive,* p. 473–74; Lodge, *Recapture of Guam,* pp. 49 and 50.

[50] Shaw et al., *Central Pacific Drive,* pp. 475–76.

the pocket of resistance was reduced completely and both 2/4 and 1/4 were ready to advance to their O-1 objectives. On brigade order, the 4th Marines resumed the attack toward O-1. One of the regiment's goals was the capture of Mount Alifan's peak. The Marines reached the foot of the mountain by 17.00 after brushing aside scattered enemy resistance. The regiment then dug in for the night. There were many gaps in the 1,600-yard-long line held by the 4th Marines, but strongpoints were established in order that these gaps could be covered by fire. Also, Lieutenant Colonel Shapley tied in his Reconnaissance Platoon and an engineer detachment to the left of Company A and he kept Company C in reserve near the regimental CP just in case it was needed.[51] And so the Marines and soldiers of III Amphibious Corps spent their first night on Guam, holding on to the ground that they had won from the Japanese at the cost of so many of their comrades and waiting for the next day in order to continue their offensive against the enemy.

Strategic and Operational Objectives for Forager

The Marianas are located along an approximately north–south line stretching from 20° 32' N, 144° 54' E to 13° 15' N, 144° 43' E. Ferdinand Magellan discovered the group of fifteen volcanic islands in 1521 while on his circumnavigation of the globe. Spain controlled the islands until the late 19th century, a period of time during which Spanish power in the world waned significantly. Proof of Spain's irrelevance in global affairs by the 1890s can be seen in the ease with which the island group was taken from them: Germany forced the Spaniards to give up ownership of most of the islands in 1899 while the United States took Guam, the largest and most southern island of the group, as part of the spoils of the Spanish American War. The Germans did not maintain control of the islands they had taken from Spain, however. Another change in ownership occurred at the end of World War I when Japan received the islands north of Guam, including the other three large southern islands—Saipan, Tinian, and Rota—as part of a League of Nations Mandate. The establishment of Japanese interests in the Marianas created a worrisome strategic situation for the United States. There would be no problems as long as the U.S. and Japan remained on good terms with one another. But relations between the two nations had already begun to sour by 1919, and they really began to deteriorate after the Japanese were relegated to a *de facto* secondary naval power status by the Washington Treaties of 1921 and 1922. Whether or not to maintain Guam in the event of a war with Japan was a question pondered by the planners who worked on the various permutations of War Plan Orange during the interwar period.[52]

---

[51] Ibid., pp. 476 and 477; Lodge, *Recapture of Guam,* pp. 51 and 53.

[52] Crowl, *Campaign in the Marianas,* pp. 21–22 and 24.

Up until February of 1944, the United States' Central Pacific Drive followed the basic route prescribed in the majority of the U.S. Navy's versions of these plans. It is at the point of deciding where to go after the Marshalls that a significant divergence occurs. According to the two most popular Orange Plan scenarios of the 1920s, either the U.S. would plow right across the Pacific and relieve Manila in the Philippines, or the Navy would attack through the Marshalls toward the Carolines. Eniwetok in the Marshalls and Truk in the Carolines, according to this second scenario, would be developed into major service and staging bases for attacks farther into the western Pacific. The exact direction of those attacks would have been determined later based upon the situation that existed after Truk had been conquered.[53]

Neither of the plans did any more than flirt with the idea of taking the largest of the Japanese-held southern Mariana Islands. The harbors of Saipan, Tinian, and Rota were considered to be too small and too exposed to the ferocity of Pacific weather for them to be worth the blood and sweat that would be expended to secure them from the Japanese. Airfields could be constructed on them, but they were too far off of the main line of attack across the Pacific for the short-ranged aircraft of the 1920s to be of any use in furthering the war effort. Guam's harbors were not much better than those of the other southern islands and it suffered from the same disadvantages as far as potential airfields were concerned. Some admirals strenuously argued from time to time that a major base ought to be built on Guam, but, in the end, Congress decided that nothing more than a tiny garrison of Marines should occupy the island. The theory to which the lawmakers adhered was that the Marines would be defeated and captured by the Japanese early in a Blue-Orange war, a fate that was expected to befall all major American bases west of Hawaii before the U.S. could mobilize to protect them from Japanese attack. It was decided that it did not make sense to lose any more men and naval assets to the Japanese at the beginning of a war than was absolutely necessary. Isolationist congressmen during the 1930s doggedly refused to even consider spending money for a base on Guam, a base the building of which the Japanese would most certainly view as a threat.[54]

The Navy, then, was not all that excited during the interwar period about the prospect of seizing the Japanese Marianas, viewing them to be of no strategic value. The Army, however, saw things differently. According to a work-sharing agreement between the two services, the Army's responsibilities included studying the Marianas with an eye toward possible operations therein. Colonel Walter Krueger, the head of the Army War Plans Division in the mid-1930s, was particularly interested in the potential use of the Marianas in an overall plan for war against Japan and he embodied his ideas in the Army Strategic Plan of 1936. He

[53] Miller, *War Plan Orange*, pp. 100–31.

[54] Ibid., pp. 208 and 209–10.

expected strong resistance on the part of the Japanese, but overcoming that resistance would be worthwhile for a number of reasons. First, taking the Marianas would allow the Navy to establish bases for a trade war against Japan. Second, American forces in the Marianas could interdict Japanese traffic with the Philippines. Third, taking the Marianas would clinch the conquest of the Palaus. Fourth and most importantly, taking the Marianas would, in Krueger's estimation, lead directly to the defeat of Japan because attacking the Marianas would draw out the Imperial Japanese Fleet. The United States Navy could engage it and then destroy it. With its destruction the Japanese could no longer effectively project power beyond the Home Islands nor could they effectively defend themselves against further American attacks.[55]

For Krueger the key to the Japanese "Main Line of Resistance," or the place at which the Japanese would have to make a stand, was Saipan. Losing Saipan would, according to Krueger, "force the Orange fleet to give battle soon to avoid collapse at home." Going against years of Army planning, he argued that attacking Japan at what was essentially the fulcrum of its defenses would bring on a climactic battle far sooner than would an attack on the Philippines. To round out this clairvoyant *tour de force,* Krueger also saw the Marianas as being an important staging point for long-range aircraft, though he did not foresee a decisive, strategic role for them given the range of the bombers of the mid-1930s. The Army's interest in a war against Japan was short-lived, however. After Japan invaded China in mid-1937, the Army decided not to support a Central Pacific offensive, preferring to concentrate on defending the homeland through adopting a defensive posture in the Pacific.[56]

The Joint Board of the Army and Navy decided in November of 1938, given the state of the world at the time, to address the possibility that the United States might find itself at war with Germany, Italy, or Japan, either separately or in combination. As far as a war against Japan was concerned, the Joint Board planners decided that the Philippines and Guam would not be able to hold out and that the U.S. would have to fight its way back to the western Pacific. The proposed lines of attack were the same as had been studied since the early years of the century: (a) by way of the Aleutians; (b) directly to Luzon by way of Pearl Harbor and Midway Island; (c) in stages from Hawaii by way of the Marshalls, the Carolines, and possibly the Marianas, Yap, and the Palaus; or (d) to the southern Philippines by way of Samoa and New Guinea. It is out of this concern for imminent war that the various Rainbow Plans were developed, Rainbow Five being the one the United States implemented at the beginning of hostilities.[57]

---

[55] Ibid., pp. 184 and 209.

[56] Ibid., pp. 208–09 and 214–15.

[57] Hayes, *History of the JCS in WWII,* pp. 7–8.

The Pacific war unfolded in both foreseen and unforeseen directions in late 1941 and early 1942. As expected, the Philippines and Guam fell within a short period of time. The destruction of the Pacific Fleet's effective offensive capabilities at Pearl Harbor on 7 December 1941, however, made impossible the implementation of any form of the Orange plans, at least for the time being. The Marianas were hardly on the minds of those who had to try to stop the Japanese as they marched relentlessly across the western Pacific. By early 1943, however, Admiral King was ready to start planning for the downfall of Japan, and the sooner he could begin to take the fight to the Japanese the better. At an afternoon meeting of the Combined Chiefs of Staff at the Casablanca Conference on 14 January 1943, King laid out what he believed should be the direction of operations against Japan once the Rabaul campaign was finished. King said that Allied forces should attack the Marshall Islands as soon as possible and should follow that attack by assaulting Truk in the Carolines. American forces should then invade the Marianas, the ultimate goal being the recapturing of the Philippine Islands. This was the first of many times that King would stress the importance of the Marianas in his vision of how to defeat Japan. He explained his reasoning by saying that the Marianas were "the key of the situation because of their location on the Japanese line of communications." Without control of them, Allied forces could not hope to maintain momentum against the enemy.[58]

King once again presented his ideas concerning Pacific strategy to the Combined Chiefs four months later at the Trident Conference in Washington. While commenting on CCS 239, a revision of the Joint Chief's document JCS 304, "Operations in the Pacific and Far East in 1943–44," King essentially restated the position he had taken earlier at Casablanca, elaborating somewhat in the process. The objectives, as he saw them, should be the severing of Japanese lines of communication and the recapture of the Philippines. The best route for attaining these two objectives lay through Truk and the Marianas in the Central Pacific. An important point for King, one that he emphasized again and again, was that unremitting pressure had to be maintained against the Japanese. Allied forces must never let up. New offensives needed to begin as old ones were completed. According to King, the Joint Chiefs had chosen objectives in the Pacific for 1943 and 1944 with two criteria in mind: "(a) Would [an operation] further threaten or cut Japanese lines of communication? (b) Would [an operation] contribute to the attainment of positions of readiness from which a full-scale offensive could be launched against Japan?"[59]

After modifications based upon comments by the American and British Chiefs were incorporated into the final draft, the objectives for 1943 and 1944, as stated in CCS 239, were as follows: "(1) Conduct of [*sic*] air operations in and from CHINA;

---

[58] Ibid., pp. 280–81; quote is from p. 280.

[59] Ibid., p. 403.

(2) Operations in BURMA to augment supplies to CHINA; (3) Ejection of the Japanese from the ALEUTIANS; (4) Seizure of the MARSHALL and CAROLINE ISLANDS; (5) Seizure of the SOLOMONS, the BISMARCK ARCHIPELAGO, and Japanese held NEW GUINEA; (6) Intensification of operations against enemy lines of communication."[60] The Marianas were not specifically mentioned as objectives, but King was able to get a mention of operations against Japanese lines of communications included. He would build on this tiny foundation.

The American Chief of Naval Operations had not mentioned the Southwest Pacific in his discussion of Pacific strategy at Trident. General MacArthur feared that King and others in Washington wanted to change the direction of strategy in the war against Japan, a change that he believed would take the emphasis off of his theater and shift it to an area over which the Navy could exert more direct control. On 28 June 1943, the Joint Strategic Survey Committee (JSSC) issued a study to the Joint Chiefs that threatened to do just that. The JSSC argued that the only reason the South and Southwest Pacific had received so much attention during the first part of the war was because it was necessary to meet and stop the Japanese offensive that was plowing its way through those areas. Political as well as military considerations seemed to dictate a strategy of moving against the enemy northward from Australia, essentially reversing the Japanese offensive and following the same path they had taken against the Allies. The committee contended, however, that to do so was not wise. The Japanese would be in a better strategical position than the Allies at all times, making progress against their defenses very difficult. Rather than follow this course, they reasoned, why not take advantage of increasing Allied naval strength in the Pacific and shift the emphasis from the South and Southwest Pacific to the Central Pacific through the Marshalls and Carolines? Admiral King agreed wholeheartedly with the JSSC proposals, but he was alone. The other members of the JCS were not ready to accord full priority for a Central Pacific Campaign over the Southwest Pacific. The paper, as a result, was sent to the Joint Staff Planners for further consideration and the Chiefs went on to other matters.[61]

On 6 August 1943, in preparation for the upcoming Quadrant Conference, the Joint Chiefs began discussing a report submitted to them by the Rainbow Team of the Joint War Plans Committee. Entitled JCS 446, the report outlined 1943–44 operations in the Pacific. The five projected for the Central Pacific Campaign were as follows: (1) 15 November 1943—Gilbert Islands (Nauru, Tarawa, Makin); (2) 1 January 1944—Marshall Islands (Kwajalein, Wake, Kusaie); (3) 1 June 1944—Ponape (in the Carolines); (4) 1 September 1944—Truk (in the Carolines); (5) 31 December 1944—Palau Islands. The planners emphasized that momentum be maintained against the Japanese by transferring forces and equipment between areas of the Pacific, never allowing any Allied assets to remain idle for long. If

[60] Ibid., pp. 402–03.

[61] Ibid., p. 423.

conflicts over men and materiel arose, JCS 446 stated that "due weight should be given to the fact that operations in the Central PACIFIC promise more rapid advance." Admiral King was the only member of the Joint Chiefs to offer any objections to the contents of the report. Although he was pleased that the report recognized the primacy of the Central Pacific campaign, he was not happy that mention of the Marianas had been left out. He reminded his fellow Chiefs that occupation of the Marianas would be considered a serious threat by the Japanese while the Palaus were nothing more than a staging area on the way to the Philippines. At his recommendation, then, the following was added to the report: ". . . It may be found desirable or necessary to seize Guam and the Japanese MARIANAS, possibly the BONINS, in conjunction with the seizure of the western CAROLINES, and in particular with the attack on the PALAUS. The MARIANA-BONIN attack would have profound effects on the Japanese because of its serious threat to the homeland. . . ." This statement left open the possibility of heading in the direction of the Marianas once the conquest of the Carolines was completed.[62]

The Joint Chiefs presented the revised JCS 446 at the Quadrant Conference as the combined paper CCS 301. The British Chiefs asked three major questions of their American counterparts during discussions of the paper, only one concerning the Central Pacific: Would it not be a better idea to limit operations in the Japanese Mandates in order to release resources for use in the upcoming European Theater Operation Overlord? The American Chiefs argued that the requisite forces for operations in both the Central and Southwest Pacific were already in theater and could not be used effectively in Europe. Therefore, it made better sense to use the men and materiel where they were and to treat Overlord as something entirely separate. Admiral King defended the American strategy of attacking along two paths in the Pacific by arguing that each route was complementary to the other and that both were essential for ultimate victory. Their existence provided Allied forces with options: either the two routes could converge on the Philippines or the Central Pacific forces could turn north from Truk to attack the Marianas. The Americans further assured the British that the planned operations for the Pacific would not interfere with the invasion of Nazi-held Europe. The British appeared to be satisfied with the American responses to their questions and gave CCS 301, with a paragraph concerning China added, their tacit approval. The Quadrant Conference, upon its closing on 24 August 1943, signaled the end of the idea that the Allies should hold the line against the Japanese until such time as Germany was defeated. The American offensive was on in the Pacific.[63]

---

[62] Ibid., pp. 427–31; quote is from p. 431.

[63] Ibid., pp. 431–33. The British appeared to be suggesting that the majority of the "savings" in the Pacific be at MacArthur's expense. King defended American actions in the Southwest Pacific because of his belief in unremitting pressure on the Japanese and because he did not want to give back any gains in the European Theater vs. Pacific Theater logistical contest.

United States planners were rather optimistic about the possibilities 1944 held for the war against Japan by the time the next Allied conference was held in November of 1943. The supply of men, materiel, and shipping was growing, and it began to make sense that the increase justified a reexamination of plans for the coming year. Accordingly, the Joint War Plans Committee drafted a new report on recommended operations against Japan for 1944 that were aimed at "obtaining positions and reducing Japan's military strength to such an extent as will permit the eventual invasion of Honshu not later than the spring of 1946, in order to force her unconditional surrender at the earliest practicable date." The report listed the following operations for the Central Pacific: (1) 1–31 January 1944—Marshall Islands (including Eniwetok and Kusaie); (2) 1 May 1944—Ponape (in the Carolines); (3) 20 July 1944—Eastern Carolines (Truk area); (4) 1 October 1944—Guam and the Japanese Marianas; (5) 31 December 1944—Palau Islands. The Joint Chiefs looked at this report as they crossed the Atlantic to attend the Sextant Conference at Cairo, recorded a few remarks, and sent the paper to the Joint Staff Planners for revision.[64]

The Chiefs made more detailed comments when the revised paper came back to them. General Marshall questioned whether or not the JCS could say with certainty that they wanted to go into Ponape and Truk. Admiral Cooke, one of the Joint Staff Planners, explained that this was a tentative list and that objectives could be changed depending upon how the war unfolded. Admiral King requested the removal of the Palaus from the list of objectives, but General Marshall wondered whether that island group ought not be an objective for both the Central and Southwest Pacific Areas. Since there was time to consider whether or not the Palaus should be taken, they were dropped from the list for the time being. General Arnold then brought up the question of how the new very-long-range B-29 was to be used in the Pacific war. The plan so far was that the bombers would fly against Japan from bases in China. Arnold and his advisors, however, had reservations about this decision. Security of the Chinese bases was proving to be a problem and, as the Japanese pushed farther and farther into China in the direction of the airfields, the bombers had to fly farther and farther distances to get to their targets in the Home Islands, thus necessitating a decrease in bomb tonnage so that fuel efficiency could be increased. The Marianas offered a solution to these problems. Their distance from Japan was well within the range of the new bomber and, once taken, it would be much easier to defend them against Japanese counterattacks. At Arnold's suggestion, then, the Joint Chiefs set 31 December 1944 as the date by which B-29 operations would begin from the Marianas.[65]

The Combined Chiefs of Staff approved the American Joint Chief's program for Central Pacific operations in 1944 at the Sextant Conference on 6 December

---

[64] Ibid., pp. 488–90; quote is from p. 489.

[65] Ibid., p. 491.

1943. The approved plan embodied a significant acceleration over the previous Quadrant chronology. Rather than ending the year 1944 in the Carolines and Palaus heading toward the Philippines, the new plan placed Allied forces in the Marianas by October on a heading for the Home Islands and had very-long-range bombers operating against the Japanese by the end of the year. This acceleration is especially impressive, however, when one compares the Sextant plans with the timetable of action prepared by the Combined Planning Staff during their meetings in Washington over 31 July–8 August 1943. That timetable sketched out a campaign against Japan that would have lasted into 1947 and possibly even 1948. As it turned out, the acceleration in actual execution would be even greater than the one on paper.[66]

The general outline of what the United States would do in the Pacific during 1944 was in place, but now those plans had to be translated into something the theater commanders could use. Once American forces were in control of the Marshalls, a firm decision would have to be made as to the next target for the Fifth Fleet juggernaut, but there was no agreement as to exactly what that target should be as the new year dawned. Admiral King flew to San Francisco on 2 January for one of his periodic meetings to discuss Pacific strategy with Admiral Nimitz. Nimitz presented King with a plan, entitled Granite, that the CinCPOA staff had developed based upon the program set forth at Sextant. This plan called for, among other operations, the taking of Truk in the Carolines on or shortly after 1 August and the simultaneous seizure, if possible, of Saipan, Tinian, and Guam around 1 November. Granite allowed for bypassing Truk and either taking the Palaus and the Marianas in sequence or simultaneously, but it provided no target dates for any of these possibilities. King did not seem to have a problem with what the theater planners had in mind, but he made a point of reminding them that the key to the Pacific was the Marianas because of their position relative to Japanese lines of communication and because of their potential use as bases from which American forces could strike the Home Islands. Capturing the Marshalls, an operation that was already in process, would bring the Marianas much closer and make the success of an invasion more likely. Rear Admiral Forrest P. Sherman, Nimitz's chief planner, suggested that Saipan, Tinian, and Guam could be attacked next if Truk could indeed be bypassed. King left San Francisco on 5 January believing that Nimitz and his staff agreed with him about the importance of the Marianas in overall Pacific strategy and that they would begin work to carry it out.[67]

---

[66] Ibid., pp. 492 and 459–61.

[67] Hayes, *History of the JCS in WWII*, pp. 543–46; Ernest J. King and Walter Muir Whitehill, *Fleet Admiral King: A Naval Record* (New York: W.W. Norton, 1952; reprint, New York: Da Capo Press, 1976), pp. 533–34. King and Whitehill differ with Hayes as to the location of the meeting between King and Nimitz. Since King was one of the participants, it is most likely that the meeting occurred in San Francisco and not Hawaii.

King was mistaken. At a conference of Pacific Ocean Areas and Southwestern Pacific theater representatives held at Pearl Harbor on 27–28 January, CinCPOA backpedaled away from his boss' concept of the war, going so far as to offer no effective rebuttal to General MacArthur's Chief of Staff, General Sutherland, when he recommended that all forces in the Pacific be concentrated on one axis of attack, from the Southwest Pacific. Nimitz and his staff, in fact, evidenced opposition to the general idea of going into the Marianas, King's pet project, and especially the idea of using the islands as a base for B-29s. These men, who King thought to be his advocates, never even mentioned Cominch's main arguments for operations against the Marianas—the endangerment of Japanese lines of communication, the neutralization of the Carolines, and the protection of American lines of communication to the Philippines.[68]

The men meeting in Hawaii could not make overall strategic decisions for how the war in the Pacific would be fought, and King knew this, but when he read the minutes of the Pearl Harbor conference he was furious. He shot a message to Nimitz on 8 February that laid out his thoughts in no uncertain terms:

> Apparently, neither those who advocated the concentration of effort in the Southwest Pacific, nor those who admitted the possibility of such a procedure, gave thought nor undertook to state when and if the Japanese occupation and use of the Marianas and Carolines was to be terminated. I assume that even the Southwest Pacific advocates will admit that sometime or other this thorn in the side of our communications to the western Pacific must be removed. In other words, at some time or other we must take out time and forces to carry out this job. . . .
>
> A number of conferees, particularly [Deputy CinCPac CinCPOA John H.] Towers, stated, and his statements were allowed to go unrefuted, that the object of taking the Marianas was to provide for B-29 bombing attacks against the Japanese Empire. Of course, that was never the object. That was merely one of the results that would ensue from this operation, which was to be taken to dry up the Carolines, facilitating the capture or neutralization of the Carolines, and to speed up the clearing of the line of communications to the northern Philippine area. . . .
>
> The idea [espoused by General MacArthur] of rolling up the Japanese along the New Guinea coast, throughout Halmahera and Mindanao, and up through the Philippines to Luzon, as our major strategic concept, to the exclusion of clearing our Central Pacific line of communications to the Philippines, is to me absurd. Further, it is not in accordance with the decisions of the Joint Chiefs of Staff. . . .[69]

---

[68] Hayes, *History of the JCS in WWII*, pp. 546–47.

[69] Quote from message found in Potter, *Nimitz*, p. 283.

In order to drive his point home with Nimitz, King presented his own strategic plans for the defeat of Japan:

(1) Japan will ultimately be forced to her "inner ring" of defense—Japan, Korea, Manchuria, Shantung, etc.
(2) Everything that we do must be related to [point] (1).
(3) [Point] (1) requires use of China as a base—and of Chinese manpower to secure and maintain the base.
(4) [Point] (3) requires availability of ports in China—none of which are accessible north of Formosa.
(5) LUZON is the key point for opening up sea routes to ports in China.
(6) Central Pacific general objective is LUZON.
(7) [Point] (6) requires clearing Japs out of Carolines, Marianas, Pelews [Paluas]—and holding them.
(8) [Point] (7) cuts Jap lines of communications to Netherlands East Indies east of Philippine Islands—also protects flank of advance from S.W. Pacific to Mindanao.
(9) [Point] (7) has priority over advance from S.W. Pacific to Mindanao.
(10) Occupation and use of Mindanao will not open communications with ports in China—Mindoro Strait is controlled from Luzon [and] Balabac Strait is too far to southward.
(11) Occupation and use of Mindanao is primarily to effect reoccupation of Philippine Islands which will roll-up against tremendous difficulties.
(12) [Points] (10) and (11) emphasize [points] (5), (6), (7), (8).

King also sent a message to General Marshall on 8 February in which he let the Army Chief of Staff know how much he disagreed with MacArthur's ideas. He also recommended that Marshall require MacArthur to submit a plan for implementing the operations already designated for his theater by the Combined Chiefs of Staff.[70]

On the same day King wrote these messages to Nimitz and Marshall, Admiral Sherman and General Sutherland attended a meeting of the Joint Chiefs to discuss their respective commander's plans. Sherman presented an accelerated Granite plan, arguing that an invasion of either the Carolines or the Marianas could be undertaken in June if Eniwetok could be taken in February instead of April and if

[70] Hayes, *History of the JCS in WWII,* pp. 549–50.

the Japanese Navy could be neutralized. Sutherland recommended that U.S. forces be concentrated along the New Guinea–Mindanao axis of attack with the object of taking Mindanao by 1 December. An important objective of both plans was the taking of the Philippines, though they differed as to how that would be brought about. Since the successful completion of both required the assignment of South Pacific Area forces to their respective theaters, General Marshall suggested and Admiral King agreed that the JSSC give advice as to which line of attack was best.[71]

The JSSC, as it had so many times before, recommended in its 16 February report that the principal route to Japan should be the one across the Central Pacific. Operations in other areas, such as the Southwest Pacific, should support this main effort. They argued, in terms reminiscent of King's argument to Nimitz, that the principal objective of the war against Japan was reaching and attacking what they referred to as "the Japanese citadel"—Japan, Korea, Manchuria, and Shantung—and that the attack should be staged from the China coast. The line from Luzon to Formosa to the China coast, therefore, should be the principal path along which the Americans should attack the "citadel." General Marshall did not disagree with this conclusion. He questioned whether or not the JSSC had taken into account such important questions as how amphibious craft, that most precious of commodities, should be allocated and how airpower should best be employed in the suggested campaign. For Marshall, one of the most important considerations was that plans in the Pacific be kept as flexible as possible. He feared that, since the JSSC had neglected to suggest a time schedule, the theater commanders would find it difficult if not impossible to coordinate with one another. Admiral King reminded Marshall that the Central Pacific Campaign was in an excellent position to be accelerated as a result of the swift and early completion of the Marshalls operation. The way was open either to seize Truk or, if Truk were to be bypassed, to attack either the Marianas or the Palaus or both. King did not mention a target date for any of these possible operations, but Nimitz had already assigned a tentative date of 15 June for an operation against Truk or an alternative objective. After further discussion, General Marshall recommended that the JCS hold off on sending any directives to the Pacific theater commanders until the Chiefs heard from Admiral Nimitz, who was due to arrive in Washington shortly for consultation.[72]

Nimitz, accompanied by Admiral Sherman, attended the JCS meeting on 7 March and he presented his opinions as to the state of the war in the Pacific. The Joint Chiefs listened to what Nimitz had to say and, after several days of discussions and deliberations that involved the various JCS planning agencies, they issued a directive to the two theater commanders on 12 March informing them of

[71] Ibid., pp. 550–51.

[72] Ibid., pp. 551–54.

the strategy the Chiefs had adopted. The directive, as it affected Nimitz's plans for the Marianas, stated:

> . . . the Joint Chiefs of Staff have further decided that the most feasible approach to the Formosa-Luzon-China area is by way of Marianas-Carolines-Palau-Mindanao area, and that the control of the Marianas-Carolines-Palau area is essential to the projection of our forces into the former area, and their subsequent effective employment therefrom. Examination leads us to the decision that effective lodgment in the former area will be attained by the following main courses of action:
>
> d. Establish control of Marianas-Carolines-Palau area by POA forces
>
> (1) By neutralization of Truk.
> (2) By occupation of the southern Marianas, target date June 15. The objective is to secure control of sea communications through the Central Pacific by isolating and neutralizing the Carolines and by the establishment of sea and air bases for operations against the Japanese home land.

Nimitz now knew what he was to do next: Truk was to be bypassed and he was to attack the Mariana Islands.[73]

Resources and Plans for Forager

Nimitz once again designated three men, Spruance, Turner, and Holland Smith, to head the team that would carry out a forceful eviction of the Japanese, this time from the Marianas. According to his 23 April 1944 Operation Plan 3–44, Spruance was once again to command the Fifth Fleet. Turner, Spruance's immediate subordinate, was to act as the commander of amphibious operations. He would do so directly at Saipan and indirectly through his two immediate subordinates, Admiral Hill and Admiral Conolly, at Tinian and Guam, respectively. General Smith, while exercising command over all of the operations' landing troops as Commanding General, Expeditionary Troops, was to act directly as landing force commander on Saipan while General Schmidt was to perform the same function on Tinian and General Geiger on Guam. Nimitz, knowing that the operation would be much bigger and more complicated than the previous two undertaken in the Central Pacific, assigned three Marine divisions, one Marine brigade, and two infantry divisions with various reinforcing elements to Forager for a total of 105,859 assault troops—66,779 for Saipan and 39,080 for Guam. The landing on Saipan was assigned to the Fifth Amphibious Corps—the Second and Fourth Marine Divisions, designated Northern Troops and Landing Force (NTLF)—while the 3rd Amphibious Corps—the Third Marine Division and the 1st Provisional Marine

[73] Ibid., pp. 555–60; quote is from pp. 559–60.

Brigade, designated Southern Troops and Landing Force (STLF) and under the command of Marine Major General Roy Geiger—were to take Guam. The Army's 27th Infantry Division was to serve as Expeditionary Troops reserve and the brand new 77th Infantry Division remained in Hawaii as a strategic reserve, waiting to be brought to the Marianas on D+20.[74]

Holland Smith and Roy Geiger submitted their Operation Plans on 1 and 11 May, respectively. For the NTLF, Smith had in mind a two-division attack across an 8,000-yard front along the southwestern coast of Saipan. The Marines would have to cross an extensive barrier reef to get to the beach and Smith made sure that his forces had plenty of LVTs to get the job done. Believing himself to be taking into account the lessons learned thus far in the war, he allowed for what he considered to be sufficient preliminary and pre-landing bombardment and he decided to try an innovation in the use of the amphibious tractors. Rather than stopping at the water's edge to debark troops, Smith wanted the LVTs to go inland a distance before disgorging their human cargo. His objective was to establish as quickly as possible a beachhead of a sufficient breadth and depth to allow for efficient and rapid penetration inland. The Fourth Marine Division followed this plan and suffered for it, whereas General Watson, the Second Division's commander, requested and received permission to deviate from the plan in this respect. He did not have Smith's faith that LVTs could stand up to the rigors of such tactical usage and the experience of the Fourth Division on Saipan proved him correct. Geiger's plan for the STLF at Guam, as already described, had the Third Marine Division and the 1st Provisional Marine Brigade landing across a fringing reef on beaches that were approximately five miles apart, separated from one another by the Orote Peninsula. The two units would then penetrate inland, pinch off the peninsula, destroy Japanese resistance thereon, and unite with one another for a drive across the island.[75]

The 12 March JCS directive had set D-day for the recapture of the Marianas at 15 June. Spruance determined that Saipan was to be the first island taken, and he assigned 18 June as the date for the invasion of Guam. The timing for the second invasion changed, as already described, as a result of two developments. First, the well-laid plans for the conquest of Saipan began to break down almost immediately upon the approach of the troops to the shore. Holland Smith found that he had to commit his Expeditionary Troops reserve, the 27th Infantry Division,

[74] Shaw et al., *Central Pacific Drive,* pp. 239 and 433; Crowl, *Campaign in the Marianas,* pp. 33–37 and 310–11; Hoffman, *Saipan,* pp. 22–23 and 27; Lodge, *Recapture of Guam,* p. 18.

[75] Shaw et al., *Central Pacific Drive,* pp. 246–48 and 450–52; Crowl, *Campaign in the Marianas,* pp. 39–40 and 312; Isely and Crowl, *U.S. Marines and Amphibious War,* pp. 316–18 and 371–72; Hoffman, *Saipan,* pp. 27–30; Lodge, *Recapture of Guam,* p. 20; Joseph H. Alexander, *Storm Landings: Epic Amphibious Battles in the Central Pacific* (Annapolis: Naval Institute Press, 1997), p. 75.

earlier and more completely to the battle than he had estimated. Needing a replacement, he designated Geiger's III Amphibious Corps as floating reserve, effectively postponing the Guam invasion. Second, the Imperial Japanese Navy reacted to the invasion of the Marianas by sending a major portion of its fleet to attack and destroy Spruance's forces. The consequent Battle of the Philippine Sea (19–20 June) forced Spruance to divert his attention from prosecuting the Marianas amphibious landings to the defense of Turner's amphibious forces against the threat posed by the Imperial Japanese Navy. As a precaution, Spruance ordered III Amphibious Corps out of floating reserve and back to Eniwetok to await the results of the sea battle. The Guam operation was not given a new date at the time. In early July, Spruance, in conference with his subordinate commanders, decided to reschedule for 25 July. Admiral Nimitz wanted an earlier date, 15 July, but Spruance explained that the fighting on Saipan clearly indicated that commitment to an invasion without adequate reserves in place was not wise. The complete 77th Infantry Division could not reach the Marianas from Hawaii by 15 July, so, he reasoned, the 25th was the better date. Nimitz deferred to Spruance's facts and logic and set the invasion of Guam for 25 July, but an earlier arrival in Eniwetok of the 77th Division than had been anticipated caused Spruance to up the date by four days to 21 July and there it stayed.[76]

Naval Gunfire at Saipan—The "Lessons" Modified

Richmond Kelly Turner, in much the same fashion as in Operations Galvanic and Flintlock, was given two hats to wear in the Marianas. His first hat was as commander of Task Force 51, the Joint Expeditionary Force. In this position, he was Fifth Fleet boss Raymond Spruance's top amphibious commander. His second hat was as commander of Task Force 52, the Northern Attack Force. This billet put him in the position of implementing the plans for Saipan and Tinian that he issued as commander of TF 51. Turner promulgated on 6 May 1944 his Operation Plan A10–44 for Forager. Annex (D) of this plan, entitled "Instructions for Bombardment by Ship's Gunfire," laid out the basic naval gunfire plan for the operation. He stated at the very beginning that this annex, along with other referenced documents, was to be used as a guide for scheduling and executing naval gunfire against shore targets, but he also stated that the instructions that followed should not be viewed as restrictive. He ends his "General Directive" by stating that "[i]t may become necessary for responsible Commanders to depart from certain of these instructions as the circumstances warrant, particularly in regard to ammunition

[76] Crowl, *Campaign in the Marianas,* pp. 314–15; Samuel Eliot Morison, *History of United States Naval Operations in World War II,* Vol. 8, *New Guinea and the Marianas: March 1944–August 1944* (Boston: Little Brown, 1953), pp. 257–304; Isely and Crowl, *U.S. Marines and Amphibious War,* p. 373.

expenditure, but this should not be done without good reason."[77] This exhibition of tolerance for the independent thought of subordinates on the part of a man not known generally for such graces raises the question of just what Turner would consider to be a "good reason."

Many aspects of the plan set forth by Turner on 6 May would hold for both the Saipan and Guam assaults, so they will be laid out at length here and referred to later on when discussing naval gunfire at Guam. The invasion of the Mariana Islands was to begin with a bombardment of gun positions on both Saipan and Tinian on D-2 by the fast battleships and aircraft of Vice Admiral Marc Mitscher's Task Force 58. Turner wanted Mitscher to pay particular attention to the following:

> (a) Destruction of enemy aircraft and disabling of airfields.
>
> (b) Destruction of enemy guns and emplacements; location of enemy field artillery installations, and promulgation of this information.
>
> (c) Covering fire during the minesweeping of the shelf to the westward of SAIPAN.
>
> (d) Destruction of enemy fuel and ammunition dumps.
>
> (e) Firing of all unburned cane fields lying south of the general line MUTCHO POINT—CHATCHA Village.
>
> (f) Bombardment of enemy reserves and possible reserve areas.
>
> (g) Harrassing [*sic*] fire by Destroyers from time of departure of heavy ships until arrival TF 52 Bombardment Group.
>
> (h) Destroyers and DMS [Destroyer-Minesweepers] will be stationed so as to interdict movement of troops between islands.[78]

On D-1 the destroyers, cruisers, and old battleships of the bombardment group would take over. Their principal objectives would be:

> (a) Bombardment of gun positions on SAIPAN and TINIAN, and the beach defenses on SAIPAN by vessels of TF 52 and TF 53. All detailed objectives listed above for [D-2] should again be covered, where necessary. In addition thereto, enemy gun positions in MAGICIENNE BAY (particularly in the North portion thereof) must be destroyed on [D-1] to prevent obstruction to the landing

[77] MCUA, Box 53, Folder 888, Naval War College, Naval Gunfire Support Planning Data, Enclosure B, Commander Task Force 51 Operation Plan A10–44, dated 6 May 1944, Annex D, "Instructions for Bombardment by Ship's Gunfire," FORAGER Operation (hereinafter CTF 51 Op. Plan A10–44), p. 1B.

[78] Ibid.

in that area. [Early in the planning stages of the assault on Saipan the landing of 1st Battalion 2nd Marines on the east coast of the island on the night of 14–15 June was considered. The objective of 1/2 was to be the crest of Mount Tapotchau, the highest point on Saipan. This part of the plan was eventually abandoned.] Beach defenses and installations in the neighborhood of CHARAN-KANOA and TAMAPAG [*sic*] HARBOR, and gun positions which can bear on the landing beaches, boat lanes and transport areas must be destroyed to the greatest possible extent. Particular attention should be given to positions which would enable the enemy to deliver flanking fire at beach areas. Mobile artillery positions and mortar positions bearing on the landing beaches should be taken under fire after aerial reconnaissance to verify the actual presence of enemy weapons. Spotting planes must be available from OBB's, CA's, and CVE's [*sic*].

(b) Covering close range [*sic*] fire for continuation of minesweeping tasks and for Underwater Demolition Team personnel engaged in beach reconnaissance and clearing obstacles. This coverage should be maintained throughout [D-1] day, when necessary, and continued during the following night, until Underwater Demolition Team activities terminate.[79]

[79] Ibid., p. 2B. The bombardment groups, according to MCUA, Box 53, Folder 888, Naval War College, Naval Gunfire Support Planning Data, Enclosure C, Commander Task Force 52 Attack Order A11–44, dated 20 May 1944, Annex C, Ship's Gunfire Support Plan (Revised), FORAGER Operation (hereinafter CTF 52, Attack Order A11–44), pp. 1C–2C, are as follows (underlining in original; italics added):

<u>Fire Support Group ONE (52.17)</u>—Rear Admiral OLDENDORF

(a) <u>Fire Support Unit ONE (52.17.1)</u>—Rear Admiral KINGMAN

OBB 43 *Tennessee* (Unit Flag), OBB 44 *California,* CA 35 *Indianapolis* (Fleet Flag), CL 62 *Birmingham,* DD 688 *Remey* (Flag ComDesRon 4), DD 689 *Wadleigh,* DD 690 *Norman Scott,* DD 691 *Mertz*

(b) <u>Fire Support Unit TWO (52.17.2)</u>—Commander FITZGERALD (not available on Dog minus ONE)

DD 562 *Robinson* (Flag ComDesDiv 112), DD 492 *Bailey,* DD 649 *A. W. Grant*

(c) <u>Fire Support Unit THREE (52.17.3)</u>—Captain JARRETT (not available on Dog minus ONE)

DD 686 *Halsey Powell* (Flag ComDesRon 53), DD 606 *Coghlan,* DD 798 *Monssen*

(d) <u>Fire Support Unit FOUR (52.17.4)</u>—Rear Admiral OLDENDORF

CA 28 *Louisville* (Group and Unit Flag), OBB 46 *Maryland* (Flag CBD 4), OBB 45 *Colorado,* DD 677 *McDermut* (Flag ComDesDiv 108), DD 680 *Melvin,* DD 679 *McNair*

(e) <u>Fire Support Unit FIVE (52.17.5)</u>—Rear Admiral HAYLER

CL 57 *Montpelier* (Unit Flag), CL 55 *Cleveland,* DD 541 *Yarnell* (Flag ComDesDiv 106), DD 540 *Twining* (Fighter Director), DD 683 *Stockham*

D-day received most of Turner's attention. His plan stated that all cruisers and battleships that were not needed for screening duties provide support for the landings on Saipan and the work of the Underwater Demolition Teams. He then listed, in general order of priority, the objectives for naval gunfire on the day the troops stormed ashore. Those dealing with the preparation of the beaches for invasion were as follows:

> (1) Counter battery [*sic*] fire, commencing near dawn, and covering known and suspected positions of enemy coast defense guns, anti-aircraft, dual purpose and field artillery batteries on SAIPAN and TINIAN, and at probable observation and command post sites. Full utilization should be made of last minute intelligence information, and very careful observation, in order that this bombardment coverage may be as complete as is possible.
>
> (2) Destruction of beach defense[s]. Those defenses in and near landing areas, and possible flanking positions should be bombarded by close range [*sic*] fire, commencing at low waterline and extending 400 yards inland. This fire should generally progress from the south end of the beach northward toward GARAPAN in order that evacuation of laborers and natives may be forced toward the north, thereby interfering with any southward movement of enemy reserves. This firing must be planned to furnish the maximum possible support to Underwater Demolition Teams.
>
> (3) Supporting fire in the TANAPAG HARBOR Area covering the ships and landing craft which make the demonstration landing.
>
> (4) Area bombardment of secondary defenses, particularly of supply installations, barracks and bivouac areas, and possible reserve assembly areas. The use of roads should be denied the enemy in order that reserves may not be moved toward landing areas. Consequently, interdiction fire should be placed at critical points

---

Fire Support Group TWO (52.10) (From TF 53)—Rear Admiral AINSWORTH
(a) Fire Support Unit SIX (52.10.6) (From TF 53)—Rear Admiral AINSWORTH
CL 48 *Honolulu* (Unit Flag), OBB 38 *Pennsylvania,* OBB 41 [*sic*] *Idaho,* DD 515 *Anthony* (Flag ComDesDiv 90), DD 516 *Wadsworth* (Fighter Director), DD 475 *Hudson,* APD 9 *Dent,* DMS 6 *Hogan*
(b) Fire Support Unit SEVEN (52.10.7) (From TF 53)—Rear Admiral WEYLER
OBB 40 *New Mexico* (Unit Flag), CA 36 *Minneapolis,* CA 38 *San Francisco,* DD 480 *Halford* (Flag ComDesRon 45), DD 513 *Terry,* DD 630 *Braine,* APD 7 *Talbot,* DMS 8 *Stansbury*
(c) Fire Support Unit EIGHT (52.10.8) (From TF 53)—Rear Admiral JOY
CA 45 *Wichita* (Unit Flag), CA 32 *New Orleans,* CL 49 *St. Louis,* DD 472 *Guest,* DD 473 *Bennett* (Fighter Director), DD 474 *Fullam*

on the road net leading west from the ASLITO Airfield Area, the coastal road near AGINGAN POINT and CAPE OBIAM, and the coastal road to the south of GARAPAN Town.

(5) Counter-battery bombardment of installations on TINIAN which present possible interference to landing operations on SAIPAN. This will be accomplished partly by vessels of TF 53, but these vessels particularly will exercise economy in ammunition expenditure. Total expenditures by those ships on [D-1] and [D-day] will approximate 20% of their bombardment ammunition.

(6) Close supporting [*sic*] fire commencing shortly before [H-hour] and delivered at both the CHARAN-KANOA beach area and the TANAPAG HARBOR area, the latter being in support of the demonstration landing and on a smaller scale than for the main landing. Close supporting [*sic*] fire should include close range [*sic*] fire by battleships, cruisers, destroyers and LCI(G)'s [*sic*]. Air bursts should be used when firing with AA batteries at open trench systems. When the leading wave arrives approximately 1200 yards from the beach, battleship and cruiser main batteries will lift fire to Phase Line O-1. 5 inch [*sic*] batteries will similarly lift fire to Phase Line O-1 when the leading wave arrives 300 yards from beach. Fire will be maintained at Phase Line O-1 until the order is given by the Division Commanders to lift the fire, at which time fire will be lifted 1000 yards beyond Phase Line O-1 and shifted to the flanks. . . .

(10) Commencing at approximately [H-5] and continuing until otherwise directed, intermittent fire should be delivered at the north flank of the landing beach area. This fire should be placed 300 yards north of the line of friendly troops and should extend from the beach to a point approximately 1000 yards inland.[80]

The instructions for D-1 and D-day follow the basic doctrine promulgated in *FTP-167* with Change 3 fairly closely. Where there are differences, they are the result of Turner's faithful adaptation of the doctrine to specific circumstances presented by the assault of Saipan. It will be noted that under (a) for D-1, Turner attempted to address the problem of enemy inland artillery and mortar positions from which the Japanese could rain fire down on the landing beaches. Lifting fire in front of the advancing troops on D-day was supposed to destroy any of these positions that survived the D-1 bombardment. It was also supposed to keep those not destroyed neutralized until such time as naval guns, advancing troops, or

[80] CTF 51 Op. Plan A10–44, pp. 2B–4B.

land-based artillery could take them out. How successful the plan was in getting this job done is one of the most important stories of D-day on Saipan.

On 20 May 1944, Turner issued a revised version of Attack Order A11–44 as Commander Task Force 52. This was the plan that would implement his CTF 51 Operation Plan A10–44 for Saipan. In his naval gunfire plan (Annex C, revised), he divided up his bombardment group into eight Fire Support Units and assigned each unit responsibilities that attained various of the prioritized objectives specified in A10–44. One of the "lessons of Tarawa" that apparently stuck in his mind and in the minds of his staff, at least during the planning stages of Operation Forager, can be seen in three of his instructions concerning the delivery of scheduled fires:

> (d) Ships will use every opportunity to close the range and employ direct fire for destruction of guns, pillboxes, dugouts, concrete shelters, and blockhouses.
>
> (e) Individual ships while scheduled to fire at assigned target areas will be responsible for prompt counter-battery fire and suitable engagement of targets of opportunity within those areas, particularly when shore fire is against transports, LST's [*sic*] or troops embarked in boats and LVT's [*sic*]. Observation aircraft must be alert to discover enemy batteries and designate them to firing ships. Commanders of Fire Support Units will be responsible for the engagement of targets of opportunity within their Fire Support Sector but outside of individual ship target areas.
>
> (f) Assigned targets must be covered by fire, even though interruptions necessitate a reduction in volume.[81]

His various subordinate commanders over the next weeks prepared their own gunfire support plans, following the guidelines provided by Turner, and, as these plans were completed, they were promulgated to all those involved in the planning process for Forager. By 15 June, Turner and the Joint Expeditionary Force had in place a naval gunfire plan that they believed would carry U.S. forces ashore on Saipan with an acceptable level of casualties.

The first bombardment of the Marianas immediately preceding the invasion occurred on 11 June when planes from Mitscher's Task Force 58 attacked enemy positions on Saipan, Tinian, Rota, and Guam. Preliminary naval gunfire bombardment began on the morning of D-2, 13 June, with the arrival off Saipan of seven fast battleships from TF 58 along with a contingent of destroyers. The battleships fired 2,432 HC sixteen-inch shells over the course of the day and the combination of battlewagons and destroyers lobbed 12,544 five-inch shells at the island for good measure. The results were less than stellar. The big ships were not allowed

[81] CTF 52, Attack Order A11–44, p. 8C.

any closer to Saipan than 10,000 yards because they were considered too valuable to be sent into possible shoal waters near the island. Keeping them at such a distance from their targets was not a good idea given that they were not, first and foremost, bombardment vessels. Since the fast battleships spent their time steaming over the Pacific providing anti-aircraft protection for the fast carriers of TF 58, they never got a chance to practice shore bombardment at the Kahoolawe gun range and their lack of proficiency in the proper techniques of shore bombardment was very much on display. Many shots were wide of their mark and most of the damage actually inflicted was on large targets that were of no military value, such as farmhouses and the sugar mill at Charan Kanoa. Samuel Eliot Morison reports one enlisted sailor's take on the day's activities. He said that the bombardment was "a Navy-sponsored farm project that simultaneously plows the fields, prunes the trees, harvests the crops, and adds iron to the soil."[82]

The results of the D-2 bombardment were, unfortunately for the Marines who were tasked with making the landing, a harbinger of things to come. On 14 June, Turner's TF 52 bombardment group, under the command of Rear Admiral Jesse Oldendorf, pummeled Saipan with tons of ordnance in preparation for the next day's landings. At dawn on 15 June, Oldendorf's ships closed to within 2,500 yards of the shore and fired on the beach and its immediate flanks to begin the pre-landing bombardment. At 07.00, fire lifted to allow an air strike that ran parallel to the beach. Battleships and cruisers resumed fire when the air attack was completed and continued to fire on the beach until the LVTs were approximately 1,200 yards from shore. They then either shifted their fire to the flanks or lifted it inland. Destroyers continued to fire five-inch shells onto the beach until the troops were 300 yards from the shore at which time they too lifted fire inland. At the same time that the fire lifted, LCI(G)s ran in close to shore and let loose on the landing beaches with 20mm and 40mm machine cannons and fired their 4.5-inch rockets in order to keep the Japanese neutralized as long as possible.[83]

What was the outcome of these two days of naval gunfire on the beaches of Saipan? The report prepared by the Expeditionary Troops Naval Gunfire Officer, Lieutenant Colonel E. G. Van Orman, regarding the D-2 bombardment, states:

> a. This bombardment was delivered by the fast battleships and destroyers of Task Force 58, firing with plane spot. Special attention

---

[82] Morison, *New Guinea and the Marianas*, pp. 179–80. The seven battleships were: BB 55 *North Carolina*, BB 56 *Washington*, BB 57 *South Dakota*, BB 58 *Indiana*, BB 60 *Alabama*, BB 61 *Iowa*, BB 62 *New Jersey*. List of battleships from MCUA, Box 11, Folder 2, Fifth Amphibious Corps, NTLF OpPlan 3–44, Annex C, Naval Gunfire Support, p. 1.

[83] Isely and Crowl, *U.S. Marines and Amphibious War*, p. 330; MCUA, Box 11, Folder 1, Headquarters Northern Troops and Landing Force, Report of Marianas Operation, Phase I (Saipan), dated 12 August 1944 (hereinafter NTLF Op Rpt), p. 25.

was given to heavy enemy installations, especially in the CHARAN KANOA, GARAPAN, and ARINGAN [*sic*] POINT areas, the vicinity of ASLITO AIRFIELD, and the points of land commanding the landing beaches. Heavy gun installations, power plants, barracks, the buildings of the town, and installations at and near the airfield received a particularly heavy shelling.

b. The effectiveness of the bombardment was somewhat limited, however, by a number of factors, including the following:

   (1) Lack of training and experience on the part of the fast battleships, as a group, as compared with many older ships of the same type, in shore bombardment. This type of firing, involving slow, patient adjustments on specific targets is fundamentally different from the firing necessary to succeed in an engagement at sea, and the effectiveness of a shore bombardment has considerable limitations where the ships have not had specific training for this mission.

   (2) Lack of training on the part of the air spotters in recognizing important targets ashore. A study of intercepted radio transmissions shows that, in general, spotters concentrated on buildings of any type at all, rather than on the many camouflaged and semi-concealed positions of definite military significance, especially gun positions.

   (3) Lack of coordination between air spotter and ship. In several cases, when the spotter transmitted his spot to the ship, the ship shifted fire to a new target without ever applying the spot, even though some of these targets were important.

   (4) The fact that it was felt necessary to direct these ships to deliver all fires from beyond the range of enemy shore batteries. This order resulted in the delivery of the entire bombardment at ranges in excess of 10,000 yards, with a consequent reduction in its effectiveness.

   (5) Some battleships fired 5"/.38 [*sic*] caliber at ranges in excess of 16,000 yards. Firing on point targets such as coast defense guns and AA batteries at such ranges is considered to be ineffective.

c. Destroyers of Task Force 58 maintained fire throughout D minus 2 night in order to harass the enemy.[84]

---

[84] MCUA, Box 7, Folder 1, Part 1, Headquarters Expeditionary Troops, Task Force 56, Report on Marianas Operation, n.d., Enclosure G, Reports by Special Staff Officers, Naval Gunfire Support Report, p. 10.

Van Orman is not only critical of the use of fast battleships in the role of naval gunfire support vessels, but he offers explanations as to why they are not adequate in that role.

Concerning the D-1 bombardment, Van Orman was more complimentary:

> a. This bombardment was executed by ships of Task Group 52.17 [Oldendorf's command], nearly all of which had had considerable experience in shore bombardment. Their fire, delivered with both air and ship spot, was very effective, including direct hits on many important installations.
>
> b. Some of the factors that limited the effectiveness of this bombardment were:
>
> (1) Shortage of time with respect to the very large number of targets, all of which required slow, painstaking adjustments of time. The result was, in several cases, area coverage rather than specific destruction of important installations.
>
> (2) Lack of training on the part of air spotters in distinguishing important targets ashore.[85]

He was much more critical of the results of the D-day bombardment:

> a. This firing was executed by ships of Task Group 52.17. It destroyed or neutralized a great many important targets and neutralized the beaches sufficiently that the assault troops were able to effect a landing.
>
> b. Important targets did, however, escape this bombardment, of which the most important were enemy mortars and artillery which continued to fire on the beaches, and light gun and troop positions in the low ground immediately behind the beaches. The size of the island, the large number of defense installations, the enemy's excellent use of camouflage, and the mobility of many of his weapons contributed to prevent complete neutralization or destruction of all targets. Other important factors were:
>
> (1) Lack of sufficient time to allow sufficient fire on all targets.
>
> (2) Requirement that, prior to H hour, all targets over 1000 yards inland be left to air support.
>
> (3) Difficulty of getting accurate information to the ships regarding the locations of active enemy weapons.

[85] Ibid., pp. 10–11.

(4) Necessity that ships of Task Force 53 conserve ammunition for the bombardment of GUAM, expected to take place within a few days.

c. As a result of Naval Gunfire and air bombardment, many coast defense guns were destroyed and the enemy was, according to POW statements, forced to evacuate his prepared beach defenses except for a small delaying force. Foward [*sic*] slopes facing seaward were rendered only temporarily tenable to the enemy, and his supply, transport, and communication facilities and organizations were reduced to a state of chaos. The town of CHARAN KANOA was heavily damaged, although many buildings were left standing. The CHARAN KANOA sugar mill, as well as many vital installations at TANAPAG, GARAPAN, and AGINGAN POINT, were demolished. *Mortar and artillery positions immediately behind the beaches, however, were not detected or fired on, so that the enemy was able to inflict many casualties on our troops.*[86]

Van Orman and others looking at the results of three days of preliminary and assault-day bombardment could see that Turner had not met a number of his objectives, most particularly the destruction of mobile artillery and mortars within range of the beach.

A Marine who seemingly could not make up his mind as to what he thought about the naval gunfire preparation at Saipan was Expeditionary Troops commander Holland Smith. At one point in his report on Forager, Smith states that naval gunfire "was a decisive factor in the conduct of operations . . . ," but at another he states that "it was obvious that the three day preparatory bombardment was inadequate. . . ."[87] His opinion appears to have shifted completely in the latter direction by the time he published his controversial post-war autobiography, *Coral and Brass*. In that work he states the following concerning naval gunfire preparation at Saipan:

> The Japanese never before had displayed the type of mobile defense they employed at Saipan. Lessons learned previously were of no value against the improvised defenses they had installed here. . . . Naval and air bombardment, aided by very good air reconnaissance, had knocked out most of the big coastal guns, pillboxes and permanent installations but enemy resistance was not effectively diminished. . . .

[86] Ibid., pp. 11–12, emphasis added.

[87] MCUA, Box 3, Folder 2, Part 1, Headquarters Expeditionary Troops, Task Force 56: Report on Marianas Operation, dated 2 October 1944, pp. 7 and 104.

> We faced the heaviest and most diversified assembly of weapons and the best developed system of terrain defenses we had encountered. . . . The initial mistake we made at Saipan was this: we did not soften up the enemy sufficiently before we landed.
>
> For Saipan we could use no preliminary artillery bombardment from neighboring islands, as we had done at Kwajalein. There was no continuous naval and air preparation, a fault we remedied later at Guam and Tinian. Three and a half days of surface and air bombardment were not enough to neutralize an enemy of the strength we found on Saipan.
>
> A more significant reason for the partially ineffective Saipan bombardment is one which I have never seen in the operation reports, and that is the fact that most of the pre-landing shelling was delivered by the new battleships and cruisers of Task Force 58, the mighty carrier task force which was always on the march in the Western Pacific. . . .
>
> Through no fault of their own . . . the Task Force 58 ships, which were almost always at sea, covering the carrier sweeps and bringing the war to Hirohito's front door, had little if any opportunity to go through our Kahoolawe bombardment mission, they were far less experienced than the Marine-trained older ships in finding, hitting, and evaluating the critical and less obvious targets.[88]

Viewed through the lens of his post-war criticism, one is tempted to interpret Smith's more positive post-operational comment quoted above to mean that the execution of the naval gunfire mission by Turner and his subordinate naval commanders was a decisive factor in ensuring excessive casualties after the Marines hit the beach on 15 June. Given that the casualty count stood at approximately 4,000 by the end of D+1, one could argue that Smith was more accurate upon reflection than he was in the immediate aftermath of Operation Forager.[89]

The comments and recommendations from the Marine units in assault are always educational. Harry Schmidt took command of the Northern Troops and Landing Force on 12 July 1944, after the infamous "Smith vs. Smith" controversy resulted in Holland Smith's removal from that position. Schmidt stated in the NTLF Operations Report on the Saipan operation that: "(1) The fire support ships

[88] Holland M. Smith and Percy Finch, *Coral and Brass* (New York: Scribner's, 1948; reprint, New York: Bantam Books, 1987), pp. 150–52 (page citations in the present volume are to the reprint addition). Smith's comment that he had never seen any mention of the ineffectiveness of the D-2 bombardment by the new battleships of TF 58 is very surprising given that his own naval gunfire officer, Lieutenant Colonel Van Ormand, had critiqued that very aspect of the naval gunfire bombardment in his report, a report which Smith should have read.

[89] Casualty figure found in Isely and Crowl, *U.S. Marines and Amphibious War*, p. 330.

were aggressive, enthusiastic and cooperative in the support of the troops on SAIPAN . . . ; (2) Preliminary bombardment commencing on [D-2] by fast heavy battleships was continued by other fire support ships until the time of landing. Undoubtedly naval gunfire destruction played a large part in the success of the landing on and capture of SAIPAN. . . ."[90]

His first statement is rather general. The question, however, was not how enthusiastically, nor aggressively for that matter, the sailors provided fire support, but how skillfully. The second statement is more specific but no less meaningless. Yes, naval gunfire "played a large part in the success of the landing," but, once again, this is not the real question. Could its part, however large, have been played more effectively? More to the point, could improved planning, more in line with stated doctrine and self-proclaimed "lessons," produce better results? Schmidt comments on the gunfire doctrine itself by saying: "(3) . . . The doctrine established is basically sound and effective support improves with every operation and continued training. . . ."[91] Then he nonchalantly tosses in one final comment pertaining to that doctrine: "Provision should, however, be made to ensure continuous fire on areas inland from beaches from which light artillery and mortars can harass troops after landing."[92] Using the word "harass" to describe the wholesale slaughter of men under one's command is interesting in itself, but what is much more important is that Schmidt is only hinting at a concern that Action Reports from lower command echelons address more directly.

One of those lower echelons was the Fourth Marine Division, the division Schmidt himself commanded on D-day. In the naval gunfire section of the Operations annex of its Operational Report, the Fourth Division stated:

> a. Pre-[D-day] fires were, in general, designed to destroy aircraft, aircraft installations, coast defense, and anti-aircraft batteries. It is essential that fires be scheduled during this period against located or suspected artillery and mortar positions which can cover the landing beaches. Because of the excellence of the camouflage to be expected from more seasoned enemy troops to be met in future operations, it will be impossible to locate all such positions from aerial photographs but, from a study of the probable defensive plan, fires must be scheduled on logistical locations of mortars and artillery batteries in order to neutralize and destroy as many of these installations as possible prior to [D-day].

[90] NTLF Op Rpt, p. 25.

[91] Ibid.

[92] Ibid.

b. Information from enemy documents captured on SAIPAN reveals that the enemy took advantage of the failure to engage these inland artillery positions stating "those away from the water's edge were able to last four days."[93]

An additional criticism stands front and center in the Special Comments section of Annex E of the same report. According to this comment, it was not so much a question of a complete lack of naval gunfire coverage beyond the beaches, but the thinning of that coverage. This dilution of coverage explains, in part, why the inland Japanese artillery positions could last as long as they did. The solution to this problem, at least as far as the Marines were concerned, was straightforward. In the words of the report: "During close support phase, scheduled fires must lift inland to predetermined areas with same intensity as used in beach preparation to cover the landing from enemy artillery and mortar fire."[94]

What was the reason for this dilution of coverage and why were enemy weapons, arms of known lethality and capabilities, overlooked? Isely and Crowl place the blame on the failure of naval planners to apply properly the lessons already learned in the Central Pacific campaign.[95] While they are right to assign responsibility to the planners, that group's level of failure was much more fundamental than the two scholars were willing to allow. First, the dilution of coverage beyond the landing beaches was an easily foreseeable problem that pragmatic and proper planning could have addressed. Second, and much more fundamentally, U.S. Navy doctrine going back at least to August of 1943 addressed this very problem. *FTP 167* with Change 3 states:

> . . . In the absence of definite information to the contrary, it must always be assumed that the assault will be met by an organized defense, and a suitable fire plan must be executed based on this assumption with probable targets located by a study of the terrain. . . .
>
> . . . Any active defense of an area suitable for landing operations will normally be supported by both field artillery and coast artillery batteries. . . .
>
> . . . Field artillery is mobile and can move rapidly from place to place in the accomplishment of its mission to place fire on attacking troops. The location of field artillery batteries will rarely be known prior to the attack, but from a study of the terrain, positions suitable for batteries can

---

[93] NARA, RG 38, Box 328, File A14–1, 4th MarDiv-Op Report SAIPAN 15 June–19 July 1944, 4th Marine Division Operations Report, Saipan, n.d., Annex C, pp. 18–19.

[94] NARA, RG 38, Box 329, File A14–1, 4th MarDiv Operations Report—Saipan, 4th Marine Division Operations Report, Saipan, n.d., Annex E, p. 22.

[95] Isely and Crowl, *U.S. Marines and Amphibious War*, p. 330.

> be determined and fires should be planned for these areas. Naval gunfire must be prepared to place fire immediately on field artillery batteries discovered in position whether or not they are actually firing.[96]

The Forager planners, in other words, chose to modify a very basic doctrinal point. Their failure, therefore, had less to do with learning lessons from recent operations as it had to do with an insufficient understanding of standing doctrine.

The question remains, however, of why the planners chose to address the problems of providing naval gunfire support at Saipan in the way that they did. Rear Admiral Harry Hill, commander of the Western Landing Group (TF 52.2) and the man who controlled naval gunfire support at Saipan during the landing phase, offered some explanations in his report on the operation.[97] Concerning the problem of providing close-fire support for a landing over a broad front, Hill writes:

> Heretofore, amphibious landings in the Pacific had to be made on a relatively narrow front, on one or more well separated beaches whose width rarely exceeded 800 yards. It had been a simple matter to provide excellent close supporting [*sic*] fire from the flanks of these beaches and to continue supporting fire until the assault waves were 300 yards from shore. At SAIPAN, with a simultaneous landing of two divisions abreast (eight battalions), the provision for sufficient and continued close supporting fire on the 6000 yard beach presented a new problem and one which is not believed satisfactorily solved. Due to the configuration of the land, enfilade fire on the landing beaches of SAIPAN was not possible from the north flank. From the southern flank, enfilade fire could not be observed by supporting ships. Maximum fire on the beaches could only be accomplished by stationing ships on each flank of the 6000 yard boat lane area and by positioning additional ships between division and regimental boat lanes. Close supporting ships were approximately half way [*sic*] between the line of departure and the beach, and from their final supporting positions could deliver excellent supporting fire until the boat waves reached positions inshore of the supporting ships. Upon passing the line of close supporting ships, safety to the boat waves required that ships' lines of fire be moved toward the flanks in the case of the flanking

[96] *FTP 167* with Change 3, par. 502(a) and 502(g). The original 1938 version of *FTP 167* placed the emphasis on the weapons on the beach, but the doctrine had been modified by August of 1943, before Tarawa, to what is quoted in the text.

[97] MCUA, Box 8, Folder 12, CO PhibPac, TF 52.2, Report of Saipan Op, Gunfire Support, 31 August 1944, Commander Group Two, Amphibious Forces, U.S. Pacific Fleet (CTG 52.2), Report of Saipan Operation, dated 23 August 1944 (hereinafter CTG 52.2 Saipan Report), p. 86.

> ships, or in a direction parallel to the boat lanes and directly down the narrow gap between them, in the case of ships stationed in interior positions. This, of course, resulted in a cessation of fire on the beach areas directly ahead of the boat waves during the most critical time of their approach to the beach. Ships on the flanks which were farthest from the lanes were able to maintain supporting fire the longest but could not adequately cover the entire beach. A better solution for positioning close supporting ships for similar future situations is not apparent, and the advantages gained by a landing on a wide front must be weighed against the inherent reduction in the density and duration of supporting fire.[98]

Hill, at least after the fact, recognized that the general effort had been inadequate. He blames the transition from narrow to broader front assaults and the lessons that had been learned in successfully completing assaults against much smaller objectives, lessons that no longer held for larger islands such as Saipan, for the planning mistakes that facilitated the bloodletting on the beaches on 15 June. Regarding the problem of not providing for effective counter-battery fire once the assault got underway, Hill states:

> In the close support [*sic*] fire plan for the SAIPAN landing, provision was made for assigning ships on each flank to the primary mission of observing for and delivering counter-battery fire on enemy guns located on the flanks and areas behind the beach, which opened fire. A ship delivering scheduled close supporting fire on the beach must not divert its attention or fire to emergency targets, since in so doing, scheduled support becomes lost and the landing support becomes a target-of-opportunity program. If there are insufficient ships to provide for definitely designated counter-battery ships, the secondary batteries of heavy ships must be made available for this specific duty. In previous assaults, the stationing of ships for counter-battery was not necessary, but large land masses now make this a necessary precaution.[99]

Once again, the larger size of the islands assaulted lay at the heart of the naval gunfire support effectiveness problem. He elaborates further:

> At SAIPAN, deep supporting [*sic*] fires commenced at HOW Hour when a light neutralizing fire was placed on road junctions just beyond the first objective line, and continued for thirty minutes. The value of this fire as delivered is questionable. The large area which must be neutralized to

[98] Ibid., p. 104.

[99] Ibid., pp. 104–05.

prevent enemy mortar and artillery fire from camouflaged and defiladed positions, requires a prohibitive expenditure of ammunition, a large percentage of which is wasted by falling in areas where no results are produced. For two days after the landing on SAIPAN, the main resistance to the landing came from the high ground behind the beaches where the enemy had prepared his artillery and mortar positions for use against a landing. These had to be silenced by counter-battery and direct supporting fires after the landing. To destroy or neutralize these weapons during the critical landing period is the problem now confronting amphibious assault commanders. At SAIPAN, the deep supporting fire scheduled was neither intense enough or prolonged sufficiently to accomplish the desired neutralization. Its delivery prevented aircraft from searching out and methodically destroying the sources of enemy fire. The value of naval gunfire deep supporting fires to cover the large areas to be encountered in the future, [*sic*] is doubtful.[100]

Admiral Hill obviously understood that the naval gunfire support at Saipan, both before and after H-hour, was not adequate to the task. The extent to which he was at a loss as to a solution to the problem of Japanese mortar and artillery fire on the landing beaches is displayed in the note of resignation in the following comment: "With larger land masses now being encountered in amphibious landings, naval gunfire will not be able to destroy as much of the enemy resistence [*sic*] as was possible on atoll landings. In future operations, as in the SAIPAN attack, a reasonable amount of mobile artillery and mortar fire must be accepted. Naval bombardment, even over a long period of time and by large expenditures of ammunition, cannot be expected to destroy each of these small, portable, yet dangerous weapons concealed over a large land area."[101]

Like Schmidt, Hill's choice of language leaves much to be desired. What is a "reasonable" amount of mobile artillery and mortar fire? It is a certainty that Marines would disagree with the admirals as to a calculated quantity. Despite his resignation in the face of the problem, Hill does offer three recommendations:

(1) Prowler aircraft [should] orbit over the entire area to deliver strafing, bombing and rocket attacks on any indication of enemy activity or fire. This avoids the necessity of accurately locating a target for counter-battery fire for naval gunfire, since the pilot attacks what he sees without reference to target maps.

(2) Counter-battery fire from designated ships, as previously recommended, to search thoroughly and continuously for enemy

[100] Ibid., p. 106.

[101] Ibid., p. 105.

gun flashes. Naval gunfire by these ships would necessarily have to be coordinated with the deep support of aircraft . . . and should be fired from ranges to insure a maximum ordinate which would not interfere with aircraft strikes.

(3) Earliest priority to landing of artillery, and employment of 4.2″ rifled mortars landed simultaneously with assault troops.[102]

The problems are not considered unsolvable. Hill just does not have an adequate solution as of yet. It is interesting that his report shows no evidence that he is familiar with Conolly's solution to the coordination of aircraft and naval gunfire support, a solution that will be described later. Isely and Crowl state that much of the carnage wreaked upon the Marines as they came ashore on Saipan could have been avoided if the planners had provided for more fire on the flanks of the assault troops and, more specifically, if the ships had laid down a box barrage as the Marines moved ashore and inland.[103] Hill's description of the naval gunfire mission at Saipan indicates that he and other naval commanders believed that there were insufficient naval assets assigned to the Saipan operation to allow for such a methodical destruction of enemy positions given the time with which the ships' gunnery officers had to work.

So, the emphasis had to be on the obvious beach defenses because, in part, destruction of mobile and well-camouflaged artillery and mortars was deemed a problem for which there was no feasible solution. The fact that the destruction of Japanese beach defenses received the most attention on the part of the planners does not mean, however, that the men tasked with performing that job did so in an effective manner. The Second Marine Division's Operations Report includes these words concerning naval gunfire: "It is believed that there will be no radical changes necessary for naval gunfire in future operations. . . . It is further recommended that in effecting landings in future operations, where resistance is thought to be heavy, a more concentrated beach preparation be delivered. The visible effects of the beach preparation on SAIPAN in this Division's zone of action were not considered adequate. Assault wave units reported several instances of Japs in relatively open emplacements still active and untouched at the time the first waves hit the beach."[104]

Here is an indication of a modification made at Saipan, and this is most definitely a modification of the "lessons" supposedly learned at Tarawa and subsequently proven at Roi-Namur. Tarawa reputedly taught that long, slow preparation

---

[102] Ibid., p. 106.

[103] Isely and Crowl, *U.S. Marines and Amphibious War,* p. 331.

[104] NARA, RG 38, Box 323, File A11–1, 2nd MarDiv Op Report Phase I 11 September 1944 Saipan, 2nd Marine Division Operations Report, Saipan, 11 September 1944, p. 21.

was necessary and Roi-Namur apparently showed how effective such preparation could be. At Saipan, an island larger than both of the first two objectives of the Central Pacific Campaign combined, two days were allotted to the bombardment, and one of those was by the inexperienced gunners aboard TF 58's fast battleships. Research has not revealed a satisfactory answer as to why Spruance and Turner decided to use TF 58 in this capacity other than the fact that the fast battleships had performed a similar function to Spruance's satisfaction in the Marshalls. Not allowing the battleships closer than 10,000 yards guaranteed that they would not do an adequate job, and all authorities agree on this point, yet Spruance decided to use them anyway even with the necessary restrictions. As a result, one whole day of gunfire preparation was wasted. The Second Marine Division report's comment lends support for the conclusion that the old battleships, with only one day and the morning before H-hour to bombard objectives, had too many targets with which to deal in such a short time. In sum, Saipan could stand as a "lesson" in itself: do not significantly modify on a whim the painful lessons one claims to have learned. As was usually the case, it was the Marines who paid the price for such inconsistent applications of lessons and doctrine.

Naval Gunfire at Guam—The "Lessons" Reconfirmed

As stated earlier, CTF 51's plans for Operation Forager held for the assault of both Saipan and Guam. In other words, the same overall guidelines applied in both cases. The Guam operation was originally set to begin on 18 June, three days after the beginning of the invasion of Saipan, but greater than anticipated enemy resistance on that island and a major engagement with the Japanese Fleet led Spruance eventually to postpone the Guam invasion until 21 July. Task Force 53 actually began its preliminary bombardment of Guam on 16 June in keeping with the original date for W-day, but this action was terminated and rescheduled for later. The postponement allowed for two important developments: the Bombardment Group assigned to Admiral Conolly for the Guam operation (TG 53.5, Rear Admiral W. L. Ainsworth commanding) could contribute to the naval gunfire support of the Saipan invasion and, beginning on 8 July, Ainsworth's naval gunfire support ships could indulge in a truly long, slow, and deliberate working over of Guam's defenses.[105]

On the morning of 8 July, the heavy cruisers USS *Wichita* (CA-45), *Minneapolis* (CA-36), *New Orleans* (CA-32), and *San Francisco* (CA-38)—and their screening destroyers—opened up with eight-inch and five-inch guns on various selected

[105] MCUA, Box 23, Folder 1, III PhibCorps, Report on Guam, Vol I, Naval Gunfire, 3rd Amphibious Corps Report on Guam Operation Naval Gunfire (hereinafter 3rd Amphibious Corps Report on NGF), pp. 1–2. See footnote 79 for a list of the vessels under Ainsworth's command. These ships are designated TG 53.15 when providing naval gunfire support at Guam and TG 52.10 when providing naval gunfire support at Saipan and Tinian.

shore targets. These vessels poured fire onto enemy positions until 11 July. On the morning of 12 July, the battleships USS *New Mexico* (BB-40), *Idaho* (BB-42), and *Pennsylvania* (BB-38) arrived and began pounding the Japanese with their fourteen-inch guns. Admiral Conolly arrived off Guam on 14 July to take command of the bombardment.[106] Samuel Eliot Morison relates the story of how Conolly came to exercise this authority on top of his responsibilities as CTF 53. Conolly and Major General Roy Geiger, 3rd Amphibious Corps commander, wanted the bombardment to begin as many days ahead of W-day as possible, but Admiral Spruance did not want the native Chamorros, a people who viewed the Americans as friends and protectors, to suffer the hell of a naval bombardment any longer than was absolutely necessary. Spruance finally relented, but on one condition: someone had to be found who could plan and conduct a systematic bombardment of Japanese guns and strongpoints. Conolly and Geiger were attending a meeting aboard Turner's flagship concerning the rescheduling of W-day when the latter got the message from Spruance. Turner told Conolly that he had to find someone who would oversee the longer bombardment personally or it would not be allowed. Conolly climbed down the ladder from Turner's sea cabin and then bounded right back up. He said as he reentered, "I have the fellow, Kelly; his name is Conolly!"[107]

Having volunteered for the job, he then fell to work. The system he devised for keeping tabs on what was destroyed during the bombardment displayed his engineer's knack for meticulous planning and design. First, he set up a board of officers drawn from the Gunnery, Air, and Intelligence sections along with a representative from General Geiger's headquarters. This "target board" was responsible for

---

[106] MCUA, Box 24, Folder 6, Commander TF 53, Report on Capture of Guam, 1944, Commander Task Force 53 Report of Amphibious Operations for the Capture of Guam, July–August 1944, dated 10 August 1944, Enclosure A (hereinafter CTF 53 Guam Rpt), pp. 16A–17A. Combined Arms Research Library Digital Library, World War II Operational Documents Collection, Commander Task Force 53 Operation Plan A162–44, p. 6, lists the ships assigned to Rear Admiral C. Turner Joy's Task Unit 53.18.1 and Rear Admiral Felix B. Stump's TU 53.18.2 as follows:

TU 53.18.1
CruDiv 6
CA 45 *Wichita* (F), CA 36 *Minneapolis,* CA 38 *San Francisco,* CA 32 *New Orleans*
DesRon 45 (less *Braine*)
DD 474 *Fullam* (F), DD 472 *Guest,* DD 473 *Bennett,* DD 480 *Halford,* DD 475 *Hudson,* DD 515 *Anthony,* DD 516 *Wadsworth,* DD 513 *Terry*
TU 53.18.2
CarDiv 24 (less two CVEs)
CVE 58 *Corregidor* (F), CVE 57 *Coral Sea*
DesDiv 96 (less *Black,* plus *Abbot*)
DD 660 *Bullard* (F), DD 661 *Kidd,* DD 667 *Chauncey,* DD 629, *Abbot*

[107] Morison, *New Guinea and the Marianas,* pp. 1–2.

gathering targeting data. Second, he directed that a list of shore targets be compiled and that, as each target was engaged, the board enter a note on the list as to any damage inflicted. Additional targets were added to the list, after being vetted by the board, as direct observation and photographic analysis uncovered them.[108] Major W. M. Gilliam, 3rd Amphibious Corps Naval Gunfire Officer, described the result in this way: "The extended period for bombardment plus a system for keeping target damage reports accounted for practically every known Japanese gun that could seriously endanger our landings. When the morning of W-day arrived it was known that the assault troops would meet little immediate resistance."[109]

Admiral Conolly, in the naval gunfire enclosure appended to his report on the Guam operation, elaborates further:

> The assault troops of both the Third Division and the First Brigade landed with very little interference or opposition from enemy troops and with sporadic mortar fire as the only enemy gunfire to hinder them. This feat was due in large part to the intense naval gunfire placed upon the landing

---

[108] CTF 53 Guam Rpt, p. 6: "A 'target' board composed of officers from the Gunnery, Air, and Intelligence sections and a representative of the ComGenSoLanFor, was engaged in evaluating all reports of bombardments and air strikes together with information from frequent photo interpretation. This board made up a daily list of profitable targets together with their priorities for assignment to Bombardment and Support Units."

MCUA, Box 24, Folder 7, Enclosure B-I of CTF 53, Report on Capture of Guam, 1944, Commander Task Force 53 Report of Amphibious Operations for the Capture of Guam, July–August 1944, dated 10 August 1944, Enclosure C, Air Support (hereinafter CTF 53 Guam Rpt, Encl. C), p. 12C: "A target list prepared by the Force Air, Gunnery, and Intelligence Officers was used by the Attack Force Commander [Conolly] in carrying out a systematic plan of destroying the enemy defenses. This list was kept constantly up to date by intelligence material gathered from the following sources:

(1) Photographic Interpretation.

(2) Air Observers and Roving Patrols.

(3) Captured enemy documents.

(4) Prisoners of War and Natives.

(5) Observation from ship and ground.

(6) Reports of pilots on results of attacks.

As targets were destroyed, they were checked off, but occasionally re-examined. New targets were discovered every day and added until they too in their turn were destroyed. Daily conferences between the Gunnery Officer, the Intelligence Officer, and CSA [Commander, Support Aircraft] kept the target check-off list up to date and furnished data for daily Naval gunfire and Air Bombardment targets."

[109] 3rd Amphibious Corps Report on NGF, p. 3; quote is from the same source.

> beaches and adjacent areas just before the Marines first set foot on the beach. Coastal defense guns, heavy and light AA guns, dual purpose guns and all types of defensive installations were rendered impotent prior to the landing of troops. Most of the houses and other structures on the west coast of the island were completely razed by deliberate destructive fire, which prevented their use by enemy troops.
>
> It is believed that not one fixed gun was left in commission on the west coast that was of greater size than a machine gun.[110]

How was Conolly able to produce this result? The amount of time allowed him prior to W-day, thirteen days in all, definitely had something to do with it—but the time element does not tell the whole story. True, if the Third Marine Division and the 1st Provisional Marine Brigade had had to rely on only two days of preliminary naval gunfire bombardment, the initial assault casualties of both would have been much higher—photographs and enemy POW testimony indicate that the original bombardment did little if any real damage to Japanese defenses.[111] Time, however, was not the only, nor necessarily the most important, variable here. Conolly and his staff had devised a flexible naval gunfire and air support plan for the 18 June invasion date and it was this plan, refined and expanded, that he would use to great effect beginning on 8 July.

Naval gunfire support for the Guam operation was divided up differently than at Saipan because of the unique landing plan employed by 3rd Amphibious Corps. Having two sets of landing beaches separated by five miles distance and divided by a rather substantial peninsula dictated the division of the Southern Attack Force into two Attack Groups: the Northern Attack Group for the Third Marine Division's beaches at Agana and the Southern Attack Group for the 1st Provisional Marine Brigade beaches at Agat. Conolly assigned two battleships, *New Mexico* and *Idaho,* to the northern group for close support of the landing waves and to the southern group he attached *Pennsylvania,* which he described in his report as "the best fire support battleship," for the same purpose. Each of these landing zones was treated as a separate area for the purposes of providing naval gunfire and air support, the two arms alternating with one another between the two zones over the thirteen-day preliminary bombardment period so as to keep interference to a minimum. To maximize the destruction of all possible sources of small arms fire against the assault waves, Conolly ordered all heavy ships to close the range and fire on houses and other structures in the towns of Agana, Piti, Tepugan, Asan,

---

[110] MCUA, Box 24, Folder 7, Enclosure B-I of CTF 53, Report on Capture of Guam, 1944 Commander Task Force 53 Report of Amphibious Operations for the Capture of Guam, July–August 1944, dated 10 August 1944, Enclosure B, Naval Gunfire Support (hereinafter CTF 53 Guam Rpt, Encl. B), p. 11B.

[111] Gailey, *Liberation of Guam*, p. 81.

and Agat. All ships used pointer fire and direct spot to ensure as high a percentage of hits as possible. Known enemy guns received first priority and were fired upon repeatedly and bombed from the air to make doubly sure that they were taken out.[112]

Naval rifles began firing in support of the assaults in both the northern and southern landing zones on W-day at first light and continued, as per TF 51's guidelines, right up to the point of men storming ashore. To give the assaulting troops the maximum amount of gunfire and air support as possible, Conolly implemented a system, denoted "Plan Victor," whereby air attacks could take place at the same time that naval gunfire was being delivered. Ships' gunners adjusted the trajectories of the projectiles they fired such that they reached a maximum of 1,200 feet. Pilots were instructed to pull out of their runs no lower than 1,500 feet. This system, which ensured that the Japanese were bombarded and bombed almost continuously, solved a difficult problem that had plagued American amphibious assaults during the first two operations in the Central Pacific.[113]

Admiral Conolly made thirteen recommendations for the improvement of naval gunfire support in his report. All were relatively minor in scope. Five dealt with pre-W-day and W-day matters:

---

[112] CTF 53 Guam Rpt, Encl. B, pp. 3B–5B; CTF 53 Guam Rpt, Encl. C, p. 12C.

[113] CTF 53 Guam Rpt, Encl. C, pp. 5C–6C. Conolly's comments concerning Plan Victor are as follows (emphasis in original):

IV. *Simultaneous Naval Gunfire and Air Bombardment*

A. As a result of study, it became evident that Naval gunfire and air bombardment could both operate in the same coastal area simultaneously with an attendant increase in overall bombardment volume and efficiency provided the maximum ordinates of gunfire trajectories were restricted to 1200 feet above sea level for aircraft protection. The plan adopting these restrictions was known as Plan Victor and was put into effect during periods of simultaneous Naval gunfire and air bombardment. While Plan Victor was in effect, pilots were instructed to remain above 1500 feet in the maximum ordinate areas.

B. During the briefing, the pilots expressed great interest in Plan Victor and the chart included in the Air Plan showing the areas in which these maximum ordinates would take place. . . .

C. The simultaneous employment of Naval gunfire and air bombing which Plan Victor permitted not only increased the material and psychological damage to the enemy, but decreased the intensity and accuracy of enemy anti-aircraft fire in their aim against our aircraft.

Conclusions—With careful planning and with adequate safety precautions simultaneous Naval gunfire and air bombardment is practical and of great value.

Recommendation—Simultaneous Naval gunfire and air bombardment should be regularly used in amphibious operations wherever practicable. Careful study should be made considering the possibilities of a similar plan affecting the union and cooperation of artillery and air bombardment.

(1) That all fire support units be briefed in detail before proceeding to the combat zone (This is particularly important).

(2) That fire support unit commanders and fire support ship commanding officers be given as much leeway as possible in determining the details of their scheduled fires. This includes caliber, rate of fire, and range to use. . . .

(4) That all fire support ships be cautioned to base their close support not on the rigid time schedule (furnished as a guide only) but on the position of the leading assault boat waves. Fire should continue on the landing beaches until leading assault waves are 500 or 300 yards from the beach, depending upon whether the line of fire of supporting ships is respectively perpendicular to the beaches or parallel to them.

(5) That air observers and close support [*sic*] destroyers report the position of assault waves so that supporting fires can be checked or lifted by the Task Force Commander in order to avoid firing into own boats, but at the same time to provide safe and effective support up to the last possible moment before troops land. . . .

(10) That commanding officers of ships be prepared to fight duels with shore batteries. The old adage that ships cannot engage shore batteries must be discarded once and for all. Ships must move in to extremely close ranges and must be prepared to lie to for hours in fire support areas (In order to do these things, the shore batteries should have been softened up and an adequate anti-submarine screen must be provided and organized).[114]

His recommendations look very much like a restatement of some of the most important "lessons of Tarawa," but the list is not a simple restatement of the ideas of others. He had applied these concepts at Roi-Namur and he proved the depth of his understanding of them through his masterful application of them at Guam. When the war in the Pacific ended in August of 1945, it was evident that Conolly understood better than most other naval commanders, including Richmond Kelly Turner, what those "lessons" really were and what they really meant. While at Roi-Namur he did not face a hardened objective like the ones others faced at Tarawa, Peleliu, and Iwo Jima, he demonstrated that he knew, almost intuitively, what his priorities should be given the nature of his objectives and the amount of time he was allotted to destroy them. His performance at Guam proved that his intuition had indeed evolved into a practiced understanding.

[114] CTF 53 Guam Rpt, Encl. B, p. 14B.

Operation Forager Summary

The Marianas Operation presented the men who had just completed that part of the campaign against Japan that most resembled certain aspects of the old War Plan Orange with a new set of challenges. As Holland Smith and others emphasized at the time, the American drive to push the Japanese out of the islands of the Central Pacific and back to their native archipelago had left the atolls and was entering a new phase. The United States amphibious forces now had to adapt the modified Tarawa-derived doctrine to much larger land masses. These land masses were not only greater in size than the relatively tiny specks of flotsam with which the American planners were familiar, but they exhibited a more varied topography—everything from mountains to lakes to large towns to dismal swamps. Rear Admiral Harry Hill, fully realizing the significance of his experiences at Saipan, pointedly stated in his report that "With larger land masses now being encountered in amphibious landings in the Central Pacific, our procedures and methods of naval gunfire are requiring modification to meet the new problems imposed."[115]

Operation Forager, then, can be said to have performed a similar function in the evolution of naval gunfire support doctrine to that performed earlier by Operation Galvanic. As in the case of Galvanic, important lessons were learned that were then incorporated into the doctrine and the related Navy and Marine Corps training regimens. The ultimate purpose for the gathering together of data and the application of theory and practice based upon experience was the improvement of the effectiveness of subsequent naval gunfire support missions. Naval gunfire support training for the Marianas operation was based upon the modification in Chapter V of *FTP 167* with Change 3 found in PacFlt Conf. Ltr. 13CL-44 (dated 1 May 1944). The modifications of the earlier doctrine that were embodied in this document were based upon the lessons learned in the Gilberts and the Marshalls. The lessons learned in the Marianas, as well as those learned in the Palaus and at Iwo Jima, would eventually be incorporated into the doctrine with the issuance of PacFlt Conf. Ltr. 38CL-45 (dated 22 July 1945). Chester Nimitz, under whose name the confidential letters from his command were issued, recognized that the letters pertaining to naval gunfire support were issued specifically for the purpose of modifying the existing doctrine. At the very beginning of 38CL-45 he states: "The doctrine for naval gunfire support of landing operations as set forth in Chapter V of FTP 167 was modified by [PacFlt Conf. Ltr. 13CL-44]. Combat experience has indicated a further modification necessary. It will be further modified from time to time as additional combat experience dictates."[116]

---

[115] CTG 52.2 Saipan Report, p. 104.

[116] NARA, RG 313, Box 39, Folder FF 12–1, Pacific Fleet Letters Commander in Chief, U.S. Pacific Fleet and Pacific Ocean Areas, Pacific Fleet Confidential Letter 38CL-45 (PacFlt Conf. Ltr. 38CL-45), dated 22 July 1945, p. 1.

Table 5.1

Saipan		**Guam**	
Total Rounds		Total Rounds	
5″	117,248	5″	81,405
6″	12,228	6″	7,760
8″	3,821	8″	10,089
14″	1,966	14″	6,397
16″	3,128	16″	459
Total:	138,391	Total:	106,110
Total lbs.:	17,082,292	Total lbs.:	16,859,143
Total tons:	8,541.15	Total tons:	8,429.6

Apparently, Nimitz understood two things that Turner was never able to admit: doctrine was modified during the war and modification equaled a change in the doctrine. Nimitz further shows that he understood the difference between modifying the doctrine and changing techniques when he goes on to state that "Type and Force Commanders may issue supplementary instructions covering details of procedure and technique of gunfire support applicable to their own forces."[117] The doctrine was never carved in stone. It had to be modified during the war, and it was.

Regarding Operation Forager itself, naval gunfire preparation for Saipan and for Guam stand in contrast to one another. Both planning and execution at Saipan proved inadequate, even when the explanations of participants and an allowance for variables such as time are figured into the analysis. The total tonnage and number of rounds delivered on targets was greater for Saipan than for Guam, but much of the ordnance in the case of the former was delivered after the pre-landing and landing phases and were of no help to the Marines going ashore in assault. There are a number of summaries extant of the amount of ordnance expended in the Marianas, all of them incomplete to one extent or another. For the purposes of comparison, numbers generated for a summary report by Holland Smith's command approximately four months after the end of hostilities will be used. Smith admits that some of the figures were based upon estimates, a necessary expedient because he did not have complete reports from all the participating vessels even at the late date of preparation of his own report. With this caveat in mind, then, Table 5.1 shows the number of rounds and the weight of ordnance expended at Saipan and Guam, as reported by Smith. The difference in numbers of eight-inch, fourteen-inch, and sixteen-inch rounds can be explained, in part, by the mix of capital ships assigned to each assault, the larger number of sixteen-inch shells used at Saipan, in particular, being the result of the D-2 bombardment by the fast battleships of TF 58. The large difference in

[117] Ibid.

five-inch rounds, 35,843, is especially interesting given the additional time allowed for the working over of Guam. Why were there so many fewer rounds used at Guam?

These numbers emphasize a fact that goes a long way toward explaining that difference: time, and not quantity of ordnance, was the most important variable in the naval gunfire support equation.[118] This was a "lesson" that supposedly had been taught at Tarawa and had been drilled into the heads of all naval and Marine Corps personnel involved in the planning of Central Pacific operations since preparations for the Marshalls invasion had begun. Time and again, however, other considerations took precedence over the application of this "lesson," the most commonly encountered one being Admiral King's insistence that unremitting pressure be kept on the Japanese. Achieving this level of pressure required that the tempo of operations remain as fast-paced as possible. Such a rapid tempo precluded long, leisurely bombardments over several days. The length of time afforded the Guam bombardment allowed for a more leisurely and precise targeting of Japanese defensive positions. A slower pace resulted in fewer rounds used, but it also resulted in a tremendous increase in effectiveness. Naval authorities were willing to accept the higher level of assault-phase casualties that would result from a policy of speed over deliberation, believing that the total number of American casualties would be fewer in the long run. The final two operations included in this study would test that theory to its breaking point.

---

[118] MCUA, Box 1, Folder 12, Naval Gunfire Support in the Marianas Operation, December 1944, Commanding General, Headquarters Fleet Marine Force, Pacific, Appendix A to Part 2, Enclosure G, Expeditionary Troops, Marianas Report, Naval Gunfire Support, pp. 3 and 6.

For comparison purposes, and for the sake of being complete, the numbers given in the same report for Tinian (p. 5) are as follows:

Total Rounds
5″ 61,927
6″ 9,792
8″ 2,244
14″ 1,693
16″ 876
Total 76,532
Total lbs. 8,629,640
Total tons 4,314.82
Grand Totals for the operations (p. 6) were as follows:
Grand Total Rounds 321,033
Grand Total Pounds 42,571,145
Grand Total Tons 21,285.5

Chapter 6

Operation Stalemate II

The Amphibious Assault of Peleliu

Dawn of 15 September 1944 brought calm winds and clear skies, perfect weather for an amphibious landing. Transports and LSTs containing the assault units of the 1st Marine Division took their position offshore of Peleliu Island and started preparing to send their charges out into the diminishing darkness toward the beaches. The general preliminary bombardment by naval vessels began at 05.30 as the first LVTs lined up for the trip ashore and continued while the assault Marines prayed that the firestorm ashore would translate into as many dead Japanese and destroyed defensive works as possible. From 07.50 to 08.05, fifty carrier planes attacked the beaches while, just like at Guam, the gunfire support ships kept right on firing.[1]

While this attack was proceeding, at about 08.00, the flags dropped on the control vessels and the LCI Gunboats and LVT(A)s in the first waves began to make their way toward the reef. At the same time, destroyers offshore fired white phosphorus shells at the Umurbrogol ridges to the north of the invasion beaches in order to blind Japanese observation of the ship-to-shore movement while battleships and cruisers in the fire support task units focused their attention on the beaches themselves. At about 08.22, the LCI Gunboats reached a point approximately 1,000 yards offshore, just short of the reef, and began firing their 4.5″ rockets at the beach. They allowed the first three waves of LVTs to pass through them before moving to the flanks in order to deliver on-call fire for the assault forces. LVT(A)s, following close on the heels of the LCIs, climbed over the reef and made first contact with the beach at 08.32, only two minutes past the planned H-hour. Marines were ashore on all beaches within four minutes of this time.[2]

Heavy fire from the naval gunfire support units destroyed most of the Japanese defensive works on the beaches and killed most of the Japanese defenders in the immediate vicinity of those defenses. Consequently, the attacking Marines in the first waves encountered less direct resistance than anticipated as they emerged

[1] George W. Garand and Truman R. Strobridge, *History of U.S. Marine Corps Operations in World War II*, Vol. IV, *Western Pacific Operations* (Washington, DC: Historical Branch, HQMC, 1971; reprint, Nashville: The Battery Press, 1994), pp. 106 and 108 (page citations in the present volume are to the reprint edition).

[2] Garand and Strobridge, *Western Pacific Operations*, p. 108; Harry Gailey, *Peleliu, 1944* (Annapolis: Nautical and Aviation Publishing Company of America, 1983), p. 69.

from the surf. However, the enemy spewed out murderous fire onto the LVTs as they came across the reef and headed for shore. Tom Lea, an illustrator and writer for *Life* magazine, rode in on a tractor in one of the later waves. His description of the experience is typical:

> At 0830 we wallowed aft the control boat on the transfer line, the reef a hundred yards ahead, and beyond the edge of the reef 700 yards of green shallow water thick with black [coral heads]. The first Jap mortar burst hit just inside the reef as our coxswain worked us up alongside an LVT for transfer. While the two craft bobbed and smashed at each other, we numbly piled ourselves and our gear into the LVT. The coxswain of the LCVP waved, backed his craft clear, and headed seaward. . . . Standing on a field radio case forward, I managed to poke my head up so I could see the first wave of LVTs go in. As I watched, . . . on the lip of the beach we saw many pink flashes—the Japs, coming out from under our shelling, were opening up with mortar and artillery fire on the first wave. Dead ahead there was a brighter flash. Looking through his binoculars, [Captain] Farrell told us, "They hit an LVT." . . .
>
> Mortar bursts began to plume up all over the reef and walk along the edge of the beach. Farrell, who could have waited another hour to take our Free Boat (not belonging to a specific assault wave) into the beach, [decided now was the time].
>
> The clatter of our treads rose to the pitch of a rock crusher and our hell ride began. In that clanking hearse it was impossible to stand without holding on to something, impossible to sit on the deck without the risk of fracturing our tailbones. So we grabbed and lurched and swore. Suddenly there was a cracking rattle of shrapnel on the bulkhead and dousing water on our necks.
>
> "Get down! Squat!" yelled Farrell, and we bent down on our hunkers, grasping at each other's shoulders, at the bulkheads, at anything. That was the first mortar that came close. There were two more, and then the ping and whine of small arms in the air over us. . . .
>
> We ground to a stop, after a thousand years, on the coarse coral. The ramp aft, seaward, cranked down fast and we tightened our holds on our gear. The air cracked and roared, filled our ears and guts with its sound while Farrell bellowed, "OK! Pile out! Scatter! But follow me to the right! The right, goddammit, remember!" And we ran down the ramp and came around the end of the LVT, splashing ankle-deep up the surf to the white beach.[3]

[3]S. E. Smith, ed., *The United States Marine Corps in World War II* (New York: Random House, 1969), pp. 634–35.

Lea's description of his own experience is evidence of the Japanese emphasis at Peleliu during the first phase of the American invasion: destroying the Marines while they were at their most vulnerable—in the LVTs and DUKWs on their way to the beaches. Every Marine Corps report of what happened on 15 September shows how successful the new Japanese defensive tactics were. The ship-to-shore movement at Peleliu from the reef to the beach was sheer hell.[4]

The landing scheme for the day called for the 1st Marines to land on the left with two battalions in assault over Beaches White 1 and 2; the 5th Marines, also with two battalions in assault, to land in the center over Beaches Orange 1 and 2; and the 7th Marines to land on the right over Beach Orange 3 in column.[5] Of the three, the 5th Marines suffered, relatively, the least both from anti-boat fire while going ashore and from Japanese defenses once on the beach and moving inland. Most of the battalion's losses were the result of enemy artillery and mortar fire as the LVTs crossed the reef.[6] Of its two assault battalions, the First encountered fewer problems while establishing its beachhead and beginning its advance. Landing over Beach Orange 1, it pushed eastward to the O-1 Line, located just west of an enemy airfield, by 09.00 and tied in with 1st Marines, 2nd Battalion on its left. The Divisional O-2 Line lay just to the other side of the airfield, but both 1/5 and 2/1 waited for an order to advance. When that order did not come, 1/5 set up a strong defensive line. Pre-invasion aerial photographs showed possible tank tracks in 1/5's zone of action, indicating that the Japanese operated tanks in the area and that they might launch a tank-supported counterattack from north of the airfield. To counter this possible threat, most of the 5th Marines' anti-tank weapons and support tanks had been given over to 1/5 for the invasion. Lieutenant Colonel Robert W. Boyd, 1/5's CO, placed Marines armed with rifles and automatic weapons in positions along the front and backed them with others armed with grenade launchers and bazookas in order to provide a defense in depth. In addition, he positioned four 37mm anti-tank guns defiladed in various shell craters and backed everything up with machine guns in case a Japanese counterattack broke through. Finally, Boyd placed three tanks from Company B, 1st Tank Battalion, in hull defilade among the all too numerous shell craters.[7]

The story was different for Lieutenant Colonel Austin C. Shofner's 3rd Battalion, landing over Orange 2. Difficulties cropped up early as much of the battalion's communications equipment was destroyed when the LVT carrying it ashore went

---

[4] Gailey, *Peleliu,* p. 69.

[5] Garand and Strobridge, *Western Pacific Operations,* pp. 110, 115, and 119.

[6] Frank O. Hough, *The Assault on Peleliu* (Washington, DC: Historical Section, HQMC, 1950), p. 41. Since World War II-era artillery and mortar fire lacked pinpoint precision against moving targets, the amount of Japanese fire to achieve this result was incredible.

[7] Garand and Strobridge, *Western Pacific Operations,* pp. 115–16.

up in a geyser of flame and debris before it ever reached the beach. The loss did not stop the assault, however. Company I, landing on battalion left, cleared the beach quickly and attacked directly east. It was able to tie in at the O-1 Line with elements of 1/5 by 09.30. Captain Andrew A. Haldane's Company K was not so fortunate. For about fifteen minutes it held the right flank of the landing beaches essentially by itself because of a problem encountered by 3rd Battalion, 7th Marines, coming ashore just to Company K's right over Beach Orange 3. The LVTs carrying 3/7 encountered underwater obstacles on the way in and were hit hard by enfilading and direct fire from an unnamed island and a promontory, both located to the south of the assault beaches. The LVTs veered to the left in an attempt to get around the obstacles and to get away from the heavy enemy fire, but doing so caused some of them to land on Orange 2 instead of Orange 3. Company K, 3/5, had to spend precious minutes on the assault beach trying to sort things out before it could begin its drive inland.[8]

Shortly after Haldane straightened out the 3/5-3/7 mix-up but before his company could move very far off the beach, the southern part of Beach Orange 2 was slammed with an extremely heavy enemy mortar barrage. The rain of 81mm and 90mm mortar shells trapped Haldane's men out in the open with no real cover to protect them. Eugene B. Sledge, a 60mm mortarman with Company K, 3/5, described the experience in harrowing detail:

> The heavy mortar barrage went on without slackening. I thought it would never stop. I was terrified by the big shells arching down all around us. One was bound to fall directly into my hole, I thought.
>
> If any orders were passed along, or if anyone yelled for a corpsman, I never heard it in all the noise. It was as though I was out there on the battlefield all by myself, utterly forlorn and helpless in a tempest of violent explosions. All any man could do was sweat it out and pray for survival. It would have been sure suicide to stand up in that fire storm.
>
> Under my first barrage since the fast-moving events of hitting the beach, I learned a new sensation: utter and absolute helplessness. The shelling lifted in about half an hour, although it seemed to me to have crashed on for hours. Time had no meaning to me. (This was particularly true when under a heavy shelling. I never could judge how long it lasted.) Orders then came to move out and I got up, covered by a layer of coral dust. I felt like jelly and couldn't believe any of us had survived that barrage.

Haldane and his men advanced toward the O-1 Line as elements of 3rd Battalion, 7th Marines, took position on their right flank, but increasing enemy resistance

---

[8] Ibid., pp. 116 and 117; Hough, *Assault on Peleliu*, p. 46.

slowed their progress as they approached the airfield just inland from the beach. The Japanese had constructed several mutually supporting concrete and log pillboxes for defense of the airfield and Company K had to reduce these before being able to make contact with Company I, 3/5, to its left. Finally, at about 10.00, Haldane was able to tie in with Company I just short of the airfield at the O-1 Line.[9]

Third Battalion, 5th Marines, resumed the attack to the east at about 10.30. Companies I and K lost contact with one another as the battalion front advanced because Company I had to stay in contact with stationary 1/5 to its left. While it lost communication with Company I on the left, Company K maintained contact with 3/7 to its right as it moved forward. Thick undergrowth and enemy sniper fire, however, made it very difficult for Haldane to coordinate the advance of his two assault rifle platoons. Lieutenant Colonel Shofner, concerned about the growing gap between his two assault companies, inserted his reserve, Company L, between I and K. Company L's zone of action was less brush-covered than those of the other two companies, so the going was much easier for it. While the 3rd Battalion made these adjustments, Companies I and K ran into another series of mutually supporting enemy pillboxes and trenches. Fire from these positions brought a halt to the Marines' uncoordinated advance and a platoon of tanks was brought up to reduce the enemy strongpoint so that progress could be resumed. Company K lost contact with 3rd Battalion, 7th Marines, to its right while it was waiting for the tanks to reduce these enemy defenses.[10]

At 10.15, 2nd Battalion, 5th Marines' regimental reserve, completed landing over Beach Orange 2. Colonel Harold D. Harris, 5th Marines regimental commander, decided to commit his reserve so that the 5th Regiment could resume its inland advance. Second Battalion, consequently, relieved Company I, 3/5, on the left. Company I, then, moved to a position between Companies L and K, 3/5, thus shortening Company K's frontage and reducing pressure on Haldane to maintain his position with his diminishing assets. After affecting the relief of Company I, the 2nd Battalion launched an attack eastward and, later in the afternoon, turned the attack to the north, all the while remaining in contact with 1/5's stationary defensive line on the left. After completing this turning movement, elements of 2/5 took position along the southern edge of the enemy airfield.[11]

Company L, 3/5, stayed in contact with the right flank of 2/5 while the latter settled into place on the perimeter of the airfield. At the same time, it took part in the resumption of the attack that had stalled earlier in the day at the enemy strong-

[9] Garand and Strobridge, *Western Pacific Operations,* p. 116; Eugene B. Sledge, *With the Old Breed at Peleliu and Okinawa* (Novato, CA: Presidio Press, 1981; reprint with new introduction by Paul Fussell, New York: Oxford University Press, 1990), pp. 62–63 (page citations in the present volume are to the reprint edition); quotation from Sledge, p. 63.

[10] Garand and Strobridge, *Western Pacific Operations,* pp. 116–17.

[11] Ibid., p. 117.

point just short of the airfield. Several factors made this advance very difficult. First was the thick underbrush that helped conceal the Japanese defensive positions. Second, the maps supplied to Haldane and the other company commanders were incomplete, portraying the inland terrain features in 3rd Battalion's zone of action only vaguely and, many times, inaccurately. Finally, the loss of much of the battalion's communications equipment during the ship-to-shore movement wreaked havoc with regimental- and battalion-level command and control.[12]

The extent to which these factors contributed to the confusion that prevailed within the ranks of 3/5 on D-day is best exemplified by Lieutenant Colonel Shofner's attempts to regain contact with 3/7 to his right. The 3/5's commander received a radio message from 3/7's CP shortly after resuming his battalion's attack to the east. He was informed in that message that 3/7's left flank elements were positioned on a north–south trail approximately 200 yards ahead of 3/5's right flank elements. Shofner ordered his companies I and K to advance as quickly as possible to close the gap while 3/7's units remained in place, waiting for contact. Companies I and K, 3/5, carried out their orders, but they did not come upon any units from 3/7. Some time after 15.00, Shofner received another message from 3/7's CP stating that the information in the earlier message was incorrect: 3/7's units were actually behind companies I and K, 3/5, not in front of them. This explained why 3/5's advance did not result in contact with 3/7, but this knowledge did not relieve Shofner's concerns in the least. What this meant was that, rather than decreasing the gap, his movement of companies I and K had actually widened it. Something needed to be done immediately before the situation worsened, so Shofner ordered Company K, 3/5, to bend its right flank back to make contact with 3/7, committing HQ personnel to lengthen the line as much as possible. Try as they might, though, Haldane and his men had not sighted 3/7 by nightfall.[13]

The last straw for 3/5 came at approximately 17.00. Shofner had battled the Japanese and his own communications problems all day and had become extremely frustrated by his inability to effectively coordinate his rifle companies. It was then that an enemy mortar hit Shofner's CP, injuring him badly enough to require his evacuation. Lieutenant Colonel Lewis W. Walt, 5th Marines executive officer, assumed command and immediately set out on a personal reconnaissance to find 3/5's scattered units. He was not able to locate all three rifle companies until after 21.00, at which time he adjusted their positions as best he could. The battalion line was not continuous during the night, however, because Company I could not find its assigned position in the darkness. Fortunately, no Japanese counterattack of any consequence hit 3/5's positions that night.[14]

---

[12] Ibid.

[13] Ibid., pp. 117–18.

[14] Ibid., pp. 118–19.

Interference in the landing of and problems maintaining contact with the 5th Marines to his left were hardly the only problems encountered by Colonel Herman H. Hanneken, CO of the 7th Marines. His regiment, unlike the 1st and 5th, was allotted only one beach for the assault. This meant that he had to send his battalions ashore in column, one at a time, with the 3rd in the lead immediately followed by the 1st. His 2nd Battalion remained afloat as the division reserve. Hanneken devised an unusual scheme of organization that was meant to minimize confusion during the first minutes on the beach. He exchanged Company A, 1/7, for 3/7's reserve, Company L. Command of each of these companies would revert to its proper battalion upon completion of the landing. Company A, following 3/7's assault elements ashore, was supposed to advance off the beach to what would be the left side of 1/7's zone of action once that battalion landed. It would provide flank protection for 3/7 as the latter began its advance eastward. Also, Company A being in position from the beginning of the assault meant that 1/7 would not have to move through another battalion's units to get into position for the advance inland. The scheme of maneuver for the 7th Marines called for 3/7 to push across the island to the eastern shore in conjunction with 3/5. Meanwhile, 1/7 would wheel to the right and begin a drive against the Japanese who were being isolated in the southern pocket created by 3/5's and 3/7's attack. Once across the island, 3/7 would then wheel to the right, fall into line with 1/7, and contribute to the assault southward.[15]

Like Company K, 3/5, Major E. Hunter Hurst's 3/7 sorted itself out and reunited quickly after coming ashore. Very few Japanese were encountered on the beach. The assault troops eliminated them and advanced to contact with the first inland Japanese defenses, Company I on the left and Company K on the right. The obstacles that made up the defenses generally slowed 3/7's progress, but one of them actually helped the Marines—a large anti-tank trench that ran approximately parallel to the assault beach. Its location had been radioed to Major Hurst and his staff just before the landings. The fact that it ran approximately parallel to the assault beach simplified and accelerated the job of reuniting and reorganizing his command tremendously. Once in the trench, his men were protected from enemy fire coming from their front. Thus protected, they could move rapidly down the trench to the right or left, positioning themselves for the continuation of the assault. By 09.25, 3rd Battalion reported that it had seized its beachhead and that it was beginning the advance inland.[16]

Progress was rapid in the beginning. By 10.45, Company K, 3/7, had pushed approximately 500 yards beyond the shoreline and had captured a Japanese radio direction finder in the process. Company I, 3/7, meanwhile, had difficulty

---

[15] Ibid., p. 119; Hough, *Assault on Peleliu,* p. 45.

[16] Garand and Strobridge, *Western Pacific Operations,* pp. 119–20; Hough, *Assault on Peleliu,* p. 47.

maintaining contact with Company K's left flank. At approximately 13.00, Company I ran into a Japanese defensive position consisting of a large blockhouse, the ruins of a concrete barracks, several pillboxes and concrete gun emplacements, as well as a series of mutually supported gun positions. Company I's commander radioed for tank support and waited for it to arrive. These defenses were not a surprise; they had been pinpointed on aerial photographs before the landing and the tankers had been briefed on their position beforehand. It is at this time that the questionable wisdom of landing two 3rd Battalions from two different regiments in assault right beside one another became all too apparent. Moving forward to support Company I, 3/7, the tanks had to travel along the southern edge of the airfield in order to avoid the aforementioned anti-tank trap. Coming upon a group of Marines, the tank commander stopped to ask where he could find "Company I." The Marines told him that they were from "Company I," and the tankers began operations in support of these Marines. After some time, the tank commander began to realize that these Marines were not from 3rd Battalion, 7th Marines, but from 3rd Battalion, 5th Marines. All during this time, Company I, 3/7 was immobile, waiting for tank support that was not coming. Third Battalion, 7th Marines could not advance as a unit until its Company I could move, so, consequently, it did not meet its objective—reaching the eastern beach—for D-day. Waiting for tank support to arrive had another adverse effect: it completely severed Company I, 3/7's connection to Company K, 3/5 on its left flank. Major Hurst sent out patrols trying to reestablish contact and these patrols emerged from the jungle on the fringes of the airfield, approximately 200 yards behind Company K, 3/5. It was at this time that the cat and mouse game between 3/5 and 3/7 described above began.[17]

At 10.30, while the saga of 3/7 was just beginning, 1st Battalion, 7th Marines came ashore over Beaches Orange 2 and 3, having suffered from the same problems coming in as had 3/7 before it. Since Company A was already ashore and established on the battalion left, having landed with 3/7 in the assault, 1/7's CO, Lieutenant Colonel John J. Gormley, advanced his Company C to the south on the battalion right and kept Company B as his reserve. Enemy resistance was relatively light until approximately 12.00 with the exception of some intermittently heavy mortar fire. The situation changed, however, when the battalion wheeled to the right to begin its advance against the Japanese who had been isolated in the southern extreme of the island. Enemy defensive fire increased noticeably and even the terrain worked against the Marines. A large mangrove swamp that did not appear on operational maps blocked movement through the majority of the battalion's right zone of action. The only trail around it skirted its western fringe, but it was strongly defended by enemy pillboxes and bunkers. Company A, 1/7, attempted to

[17] Garand and Strobridge, *Western Pacific Operations*, pp. 120–21; Hough, *Assault on Peleliu*, pp. 47–48.

work its way around the swamp to the east, but in doing so it found itself approximately 250 yards inside 3/7's zone and out of touch with Company C.[18]

Lieutenant Colonel Gormley brought his reserve, Company B, forward in order to tie together the flanks of his other two rifle companies. The heavy fighting that had begun at about noon continued into the evening. Major General William H. Rupertus, commanding general of the 1st Marine Division, became worried about the 7th Marines' lack of progress as he watched the action in the southern sector unfold. In order to reinforce the effort that was underway, he committed the Division Reconnaissance Company to the fight shortly before noon and made plans to do the same with the Division Reserve (2/7). At 17.15, the 7th Marines received the order to dig in for the night. As the Americans began to tie in their lines, the Japanese began to move against the 7th Marines' front with light machine gun teams. The Marines organized defensive positions as best they could, but movement along the lines was difficult in the dark.[19]

Colonel Lewis B. Puller's 1st Marines faced the most ferocious enemy resistance on D-day. Things did not get off to a good start—the five LVTs carrying Puller's headquarters were destroyed coming ashore. As a result, the 1st Marines was out of communication with the rest of the 1st Marine Division for much of 15 September.[20] The experience of Puller's 2nd Battalion, commanded by Lieutenant Colonel Russell E. Honsowetz, did not seem to portend anything disastrous as it landed. Aside from the pounding it took crossing the reef and making its way to the beach, resistance was only moderate once it came ashore over Beach White 2. It then pushed inland fairly quickly and reached the O-1 Line, about 350 yards from the shoreline, by 09.30, tying in with the 5th Marines to its right and awaiting orders to proceed to the O-2 Line. Despite its promising start, however, 2/1 remained stalled at the O-1 Line until the next morning while 3/1's situation played out to the north.[21]

Unlike 2/1, Lieutenant Colonel Stephen V. Sabol's 3rd Battalion, 1st Marines received no favors on D-day. Hit hard by Japanese fire from the time it crossed the reef, the pounding did not let up even when the battalion came ashore. Progress toward the O-1 Line, consequently, was difficult from the start. Captain George Hunt's Company K came ashore in assault on the left. Its first objective was a coral outcrop that the Marines dubbed "The Point." Hunt, in his book *Coral Comes High,* provided an excellent description of just how formidable an objective he

---

[18] Garand and Strobridge, *Western Pacific Operations,* p. 121; Hough, *Assault on Peleliu,* pp. 48–49.

[19] Garand and Strobridge, *Western Pacific Operations,* p. 121; Hough, *Assault on Peleliu,* p. 49.

[20] Garand and Strobridge, *Western Pacific Operations,* p. 130.

[21] Ibid., pp. 114–15; Hough, *Assault on Peleliu,* pp. 38–39; MCUA, O. P. Smith Collection, Box 22A, Folder 2, Major General Oliver P. Smith, Personal Narrative, Peleliu (hereinafter Smith, Personal Narrative), Part III, p. 24.

faced: "The Point, rising thirty feet above the water's edge, was of solid, jagged coral, a rocky mass of sharp pinnacles, deep crevasses, tremendous boulders. Pillboxes, reinforced with steel and concrete, had been dug or blasted in the base of the perpendicular drop to the beach. Others, with coral and concrete piled six feet on top were constructed above, and spider holes were blasted around them for protecting infantry. It surpassed by far anything we had conceived of when we studied the aerial photographs." The Marines decided that such a powerful defensive position made a frontal assault from the beach suicidal, so the plan called for Company K to fight inland and then pivot to the north so that it could come up behind the Japanese positions. Hunt pushed inland as planned and made his left turn. He then began his attack with two rifle platoons in assault, the 3rd on the left and the 2nd on the right.[22]

The 3rd Platoon advanced against The Point, keeping its left flank close to the shore. It approached to within fifty yards of the coral outcropping before its attack stalled. The 2nd Platoon advanced approximately seventy-five yards toward the objective, stumbled into a tank trap, and was pinned down by extremely heavy fire coming from the northern end of a long coral ridge thirty to forty feet from the platoon's right front. The Marines were taken totally by surprise when this fire slammed into their faces. The ridge did not show up on any photographs or maps and it was literally crawling with Japanese defenders hidden in caves and dugout positions. The battle to take The Point devastated Hunt's two assault platoons, reducing the effective strength of each from forty-six men to no more than thirteen. On top of everything else, contact between the two platoons was severed.[23]

Hunt continued to press the attack against his objective. Ignoring the gap between his two assault platoons, he sent his reserve platoon (the 1st) forward where its leader, Second Lieutenant William A. Willis, joined what was left of 3rd Platoon to his own and then pushed ahead into a hail of enemy fire. He and his men fought their way up to the crest of The Point from the rear, taking out Japanese defensive positions as they went. Once there, they found that a 47mm gun that had been devastating the landing beaches all morning from the safety of the coral outcropping was still operational. Willis had to take it out. He and his men made their way down to the gun where he tossed a smoke grenade in front of the gun portal to blind the crew while another Marine fired a rifle grenade into the reinforced concrete casemate. White-hot flames erupted from the emplacement as the grenade set off the stored ammunition within. Survivors of the explosion, some with their clothes afire and the ammunition in their cartridge belts cooking off, emerged to a warm welcome from pre-positioned Marine riflemen.[24]

---

[22] Garand and Strobridge, *Western Pacific Operations*, p. 110; Hough, *Assault on Peleliu*, p. 40; quote from George P. Hunt, *Coral Comes High* (New York: Harper and Brothers, 1946), p. 58.

[23] Garand and Strobridge, *Western Pacific Operations*, pp. 110–12.

[24] Ibid., pp. 112–13; Hough, *Assault on Peleliu*, pp. 40–41.

Lieutenant Willis completed the assault on The Point by 10.15. After it was over, Captain Hunt could only find thirty-two survivors of the original fifty-nine men who began the attack. His 2nd Platoon was still pinned down in the tank trap, so he had no other choice but to establish a perimeter defense using what was left of the other two platoons. The shot-up remnant of Company K found itself isolated on the extreme left flank of the division, beating off periodic Japanese counterattacks with a captured enemy machine gun. Hunt got down to only eighteen men on that first night, but he and his Marines were able to hold out for the next thirty hours with only minimal support getting through.[25]

Third Battalion was rapidly becoming ineffective as a fighting unit. It could not expand its beachhead because unit cohesiveness was breaking down at several levels: Hunt's problems maintaining contact with the elements of his company have been described, but company-to-company communication suffered as well. Company I attacked through swampy terrain on the battalion right and, while doing so, lost its tenuous connection to Company K. Lieutenant Colonel Sabol committed two platoons from his reserve (Company L) to plug the resulting gap, but they were forced to halt before completing their mission when extremely heavy fire hit them, seemingly from nowhere. The source of the fire was the southern end of the same coral ridge that was keeping 2nd Platoon, Company K, pinned down in the tank trap. Repeated attempts to overrun or flank the ridge failed and the losses incurred in trying to make contact with Hunt and his men were unsustainable. Finally, Sabol sent in his last reserve platoon to set up a secondary defensive line that, hopefully, would protect the division's flank, consigning Company K to its fate.[26]

Brigadier General Oliver P. Smith, the 1st Marine Division's Assistant Division Commander, provides us with a summary of D-day on Peleliu in his journal:

> What General Rupertus had hoped to accomplish on D Day [*sic*] was to seize Objectives 01 and 02. 01 was a coordinating objective which included 300 yards of beachhead behind White 1, White 2, Orange 1 and Orange 2, and, in addition, that part of the island south of the airfield. Objective 02 included Objective 01 plus all of the airfield. What we actually captured the first day was approximately Objective 01 north of Orange 3 and a wedge across the island east of Orange 3. Until several days later, when we got complete casualty reports from the transports, we did not fully realize what this shallow beachhead had cost. Then we found that the toll of the first day was 92 killed in action, 1148 wounded in action, and 58 missing in action. [These were the numbers known to Smith at the time. The final tally, not counting combat fatigue and heat

[25] Garand and Strobridge, *Western Pacific Operations*, p. 113; Hough, *Assault on Peleliu*, p. 41.

[26] Garand and Strobridge, *Western Pacific Operations*, p. 113; Hough, *Assault on Peleliu*, p. 41.

prostration cases, was 1,111 casualties.] These were very heavy losses and could not have been sustained for very many days in succession without destroying the combat efficiency of the division.[27]

Strategic and Operational Objectives for Stalemate II

The Palaus are a complex archipelago of 343 islands and islets located at the far western-most reaches of the Carolines between 2° and 8° N latitude and 131° and 135° E longitude. This places their 189 square miles of land area approximately 500 nautical miles from the Philippines to the west and Papua New Guinea to the south, 722 nautical miles from Guam to the northeast, and approximately 1,800 nautical miles from Japan to the north. Surrounded, with the exception of the southernmost major island of Angaur, by a wide reef, the physical characteristics of the constituent islands vary widely. Flat atolls similar to what United States forces had encountered early in the Central Pacific Campaign intermingle with islands that are more like the rugged interiors of Saipan and Guam.[28]

Babelthuap, the second largest island in all of Micronesia after Guam, dominates the group with a greater land area than all the rest of the Palaus combined. Peleliu, just north of Angaur, lies astride latitude 7° N just inside the southwest tip of the Palau reef. It is composed of two elongated strips of coral and limestone stretching to the northeast from a relatively flat common base, giving the impression of a large lobster claw. A rugged ridge, the Umurbrogol, which rises to a height of 550 feet, dominates the longer, northern strip of land. It is perfectly suited for use in a defensive struggle because of its numerous natural caves and sharp, craggy peaks. The southern strip is separated from the northern one by swamps and shoal coral and is itself almost cut in two by a large mangrove swamp. Peleliu's climate is tropical with average monthly temperatures of between 80° and 82° Fahrenheit and an average rainfall of ten inches per month. The result is a sauna-like relative humidity of 82%. The heavy rainfall was a godsend, however, because there are no rivers or streams on the island. The small native population had to catch rainwater in cisterns in order to have drinking water. Overall, Peleliu's topography and climate guaranteed that the 1st Marine Division would once again have to endure the type of hell they had experienced on Guadalcanal in 1942.[29]

The Palau Islands were sighted by Spanish explorer Ruy Lopez de Villalobos in 1543, but their secluded location ensured that no Europeans, Spanish or otherwise, would go out of their way to visit them until some Spanish missionaries did so in

---

[27] Smith, Personal Narrative, Part III, p. 34; final tally information from Garand and Strobridge, *Western Pacific Operations,* p. 131.

[28] Miller, *War Plan Orange,* p. 106; Garand and Strobridge, *Western Pacific Operations,* p. 55.

[29] Garand and Strobridge, *Western Pacific Operations,* pp. 55–58; Hough, *Assault on Peleliu,* pp. 4–6 and 9.

1712. Spain did nothing to develop the Western Carolines over the years and Imperial Germany, seeking to carve out an overseas empire for herself, attempted to take advantage of this apparent Spanish disinterest. In 1885, the Germans landed naval forces on the island of Yap and claimed control of several islands in the Western Carolines. A neutral arbitrator disallowed this challenge to Spain's sovereignty, but the Spaniards eventually sold the Marshalls, Marianas, and Carolines to the Germans in 1899 after their humiliating loss to the United States in the Spanish-American War. The Palaus came under Japanese control after World War I, along with the rest of the League of Nations Mandate, and they established their administrative headquarters for all of the mandated territory on the Palauan island of Koror. Even more so than was the case in the other island groups of the Mandate, the Japanese kept a tight reign on foreign visitors to the Palaus. As a result, there were few tourist or seafarer accounts to reference and there were no Allied coast watchers to provide vital intelligence, as had been the case in the Solomons and Gilberts, when Navy and Marine Corps planners began to prepare for the invasion of Peleliu. This dearth of information would prove troublesome, to say the least, when it came time to plan for naval gunfire support.[30]

The Palaus did not figure importantly into the U.S. interwar Orange plans. Their proximity to the many possible harbors available in the Philippines undercut their strategic value. The only Navy planner to see them as important in any way was Captain Samuel W. Bryant, the Chief of the Navy War Plans Division under CNOs William V. Pratt and William H. Standley. Bryant believed that the logical first step on the way to the southern Philippines after taking Truk was the Palau Islands. Another planner, Commander Cary W. Magruder, disagreed. Magruder argued that the Palaus could be bypassed and the Japanese forces thereon suppressed and neutralized by air from the Philippine island of Mindanao. It was there that the argument over whether or not to include the Palaus in U.S. plans for a war with Japan rested when the U.S. Navy decided in mid-1935 that it was not a good idea to prepare detailed plans for action against Japan beyond the capture and development of the first Advanced Base, that being Truk in the central Carolines. It was considered best to wait for the "fog of war" to clear before committing to anything beyond that point. Colonel Walter Krueger mentioned the Palaus in his 1936 Army Strategical Plan Orange as a possible objective, but he determined that the Marianas were more tactically and strategically important to Japan's defense and, therefore, an attack on that island group was more strategically important to the United States in defeating those defenses. Given these conclusions on the part of U.S. planners, the question of whether or not to take the archipelago in a war with Japan did not rank high on the list of strategic considerations contemplated by the prewar U.S. naval and military authorities.[31]

---

[30] Hough, *Assault on Peleliu,* p. 7; Garand and Strobridge, *Western Pacific Operations,* pp. 54–55.

[31] Miller, *War Plan Orange,* pp. 203–07.

In 1938, when the Joint Planning Committee began to consider what the U.S. should do in case it should find itself at war with Germany, Italy, and Japan all at the same time, they were already familiar with the various Army and Navy versions of the interwar Orange plans for a war against Japan alone. Assuming that Guam and the Philippines would be lost, they predicted that the best route across the Pacific to the Home Islands would most probably be a combination of the old direct route from Pearl Harbor and Midway to Luzon and the step-by-step route from Hawaii to the Marshalls and Carolines, possibly including the Marianas, Yap, and the Palaus. These ideas concerning a Pacific war were incorporated into the various Rainbow plans. As it turned out, Rainbow 5, the plan for a war against Germany and Japan with the emphasis being on Germany, eventually provided the basis for U.S. planning and action at the beginning of World War II.[32] As a result, the possibility of the United States being interested in the Palaus remained in the backs of the planners' minds as they began to consider what to do after 7 December 1941. It took the clearing of the "fog of war," as the interwar Navy planners had predicted, and the conflict between the Pacific Ocean Areas and Southwest Pacific commands to bring the old argument up once again.

The fog had begun to clear by 6 August 1943 when the JWPC submitted JCS 446 to the Chiefs for their consideration. The importance of this document in the planning for the Marianas operation has already been discussed.[33] It was also important regarding the Palau Islands, however. For the first time since the mid-1930s, United States planners considered invading the archipelago, scheduling an invasion for 31 December 1944. The planners expected heavy Japanese resistance to this invasion because, as they put it, the enemy understood that American success "would facilitate operations of any nature, in any direction, against some of the enemy's most vital holdings and lines of communication." The plan for an invasion envisioned at the time consisted of the capture of Yap and various other supporting positions first, to be followed by the seizure or neutralization of all eight major islands in the Palau archipelago. Control of the Palaus would then allow the United States to attack the Philippines.[34] Admiral King's objections to the report, noted in Chapter 5, brought attention to the strategic importance of the Marianas as opposed to the relative unimportance of the Palaus. His suggestions for revision, while not excluding the latter from the list of objectives, definitely reoriented priorities for the Central Pacific Campaign.[35]

This reorientation was apparent in the report given to the Joint Chiefs just prior to the Sextant Conference in November 1943. An invasion of the Marianas

---

[32] Hayes, *History of the JCS in WWII,* pp. 7–8.

[33] See chapter 5 in the present volume.

[34] Hayes, *History of the JCS in WWII,* pp. 428 and 430; quote from p. 428.

[35] Ibid., p. 431.

had been inserted for 1 October 1944, but the Palau operation was still set for 31 December. During the discussions after Sextant, the JCS entertained one set of dates after another, listening to the arguments of representatives from the Pacific Ocean Areas and the Southwest Pacific commands and making changes as they saw fit. The date for the Palau operation was moved from 31 December to 15 July, then to 1 September, and finally to 15 September. Their final word as to the date for the operation was expressed in the 12 March 1944 directive sent to both Nimitz and MacArthur. Concerning the Palaus, it stated: "d. Establish control of Marianas-Carolines-Palau area by POA forces. . . . (3) Occupation of the Palaus by FOA [*sic*] forces, target date September 15. The objective is to extend the control of the eastern approaches to the Phillippines [*sic*] and Formosa, and to establish a fleet and air base and forward staging area for the support of operations against Mindanao, Formosa and China."[36]

An argument would erupt in the future as to whether or not Peleliu should have been taken, given the high price paid in casualties and the fact that MacArthur changed his plans concerning the capture of the Philippines. As far as MacArthur's original plans were concerned, they were based upon instructions from the JCS. Immediately following the above instructions in the 12 March directive, another set was aimed at MacArthur: "e. Occupation of Mindanao by SOWESPAC forces, supported by the Pacific fleet, target date November 15. The objective is establishment of air forces to reduce and contain Japanese forces in the Philippines preparatory to a further advance to Formosa either directly or via Luzon, and to conduct air strikes against enemy installations in the N.E.I. [Netherlands East Indies]."[37]

As evidenced here, the original justification for taking the Palaus was that controlling them would allow POA forces to support SWPA forces in taking Mindanao and, ultimately, to provide support for the invasion of Formosa and the China coast. These plans, both at the strategic and theater levels, would change radically, but the Palau operation would still go off. Admiral Nimitz, in a 1949 letter to historian Philip A. Crowl, echoed these instructions when he stated that there were two main reasons for wrenching control of the Palaus from the Japanese: "first, to remove from MacArthur's right flank, in his progress to the Southern Philippines, a definite threat of attack; second, to secure for our forces a base from which to support MacArthur's operations into the Southern Philippines."[38] General O. P. Smith, in his personal journal, expands beyond the instructions from the Chiefs to explain the importance of the Palaus:

---

[36] Ibid., pp. 555–60; quote from p. 560.

[37] Quote from Hayes, *History of the JCS in WWII,* p. 560.

[38] Quote from Isely and Crowl, *U.S. Marines and Amphibious War,* p. 392.

The question may arise "why capture the Palaus?" At the time the concept was drawn up there appeared to be several good reasons:

(a) There was a good airfield on Peleliu and an uncompleted airstrip on Babelthaup [*sic*]. Angaur was suitable for the construction of an airfield. Planes based in the Palaus could support General MacArthur's invasion of the Philippines. Mindanao was only 550 miles from Peleliu.

(b) Possession of the Palaus, together with the Marianas which were being attacked first, would effectively cut off the by-passed Japanese bases in the Central Pacific.

(c) Possession of the Palaus would give us a fair anchorage, Kossal Passage, at the north end of Babelthaup [*sic*] and a more limited anchorage at Koror.[39]

Disagreement over the ultimate value of Stalemate II would be just one of the many controversies that continues to tarnish the memory of this operation to this very day.

Resources and Plans for Stalemate II

The 12 March directive gave Nimitz the guidance he needed to start serious planning for post-Marshalls operations. His staff had been busy preparing contingency plans since late 1943 and had produced the first Granite plan by early January 1944. General O. P. Smith found the planning section of the CinCPOA staff working on an invasion plan for Babelthuap when he came through Hawaii that same month. He remarked in his journal that Colonel R. R. Robinson, a CinCPOA planner, was intending to use the same beaches that Smith and other Marines had used in a landing operations problem at the Marine Corps Schools during the late 1930s.[40] Preliminary planning was far enough along by 10 May for Nimitz to launch Operation Stalemate formally. He issued on that date CinCPOA's "Joint Staff Study, Revised" for the Palau operation. In it, he designated Commander Third Fleet as overall commander for the invasion; Commander III Amphibious Force as Joint Expeditionary Commander; and the Commanding General of III Amphibious Corps as Commanding General Joint Expeditionary Troops. Following the 12 March JCS directive, he tentatively set the invasion date for 15 September.[41]

---

[39] Quote from Smith, Personal Narrative, Part I, p. 62.

[40] Smith, Personal Narrative, Part I, p. 62.

[41] Garand and Strobridge, *Western Pacific Operations,* p. 60; Hough, *Assault on Peleliu,* p. 10; Isely and Crowl, *U.S. Marines and Amphibious War,* p. 392.

Thus far in the Central Pacific Campaign, Nimitz used the descendant of the Central Pacific Force, the Fifth Fleet, in all the planned amphibious operations. Along the way, Spruance's command became practiced in the art of the amphibious assault and CinCPOA came to rely on their expertise. Forager was the first operation in which Fifth Fleet needed outside units to meet the manpower and shipping demands of an operation, so III Amphibious Force and III Amphibious Corps from the South Pacific were added for the invasion of Guam. Stalemate II went further, however. It was the first full-scale amphibious assault operation in the Pacific Ocean Areas that was not planned and executed under Spruance's direct command.

A reorganization of the Pacific Fleet that allowed this change to occur began to take shape while the Fifth Fleet was on its way to the Marianas. It all began innocently enough: Nimitz needed to find a place for Admiral William F. Halsey. Halsey had been the commander of the South Pacific Area since 18 October 1942. He had worked with both Nimitz and MacArthur from that time until the end of 1943 to tame the enemy in the Solomons and the Admiralties, among other places, and U.S. naval forces under his command had become the scourge of the Japanese in the waters immediately east of New Guinea. By 1944, he had done his job so well that the enemy was under control in the South Pacific and his command was about to be transformed into a rear area. Keeping a fighting admiral like Halsey ashore to oversee supply and recreation issues was a waste, and Nimitz knew it. Halsey had to be used somewhere else and quickly. This apparent conundrum turned out to be fortuitous for CinCPOA, however, because it offered him a neat solution for a growing problem. Both Nimitz and King, and Halsey as well, wanted to accelerate the Pacific war as much as possible. The problem was that the constant planning and training that such an acceleration required, on top of the actual execution of the necessary operations, was exhausting the Fifth Fleet Staff. The solution Halsey's dilemma provided was that it would allow Nimitz to change out fleet commanders and their staffs, alternating between Halsey and Spruance, in order for each man to have the time to recharge and plan while the other was busy at sea executing an operation. The beauty of the system that evolved was that no additional ships were necessary, the name of the fleet simply changed depending on who was in command: Third Fleet for Halsey, Fifth Fleet for Spruance.[42]

Since Fifth Fleet was busy planning and executing Forager in May and June of 1944, Nimitz gave Third Fleet the task of preparing for Stalemate. The various command echelons for the operation and the men who headed them were as follows: Third Fleet, Admiral William F. Halsey; III Amphibious Force, Vice Admiral Theodore S. Wilkinson; III Amphibious Corps, Major General Roy S. Geiger. Wilkinson, as specified in Nimitz's study, was named Joint Expeditionary Commander for the Western Carolines campaign and Geiger the Commanding General of the Joint

[42] Morison, *New Guinea and the Marianas*, p. 161.

Expeditionary Troops. All three echelons immediately began preliminary studies of the Palaus upon receiving Nimitz's 10 May study. Wilkinson, Geiger, and their staffs were involved with the upcoming Guam operation at the time, so planning for both Forager and Stalemate had to run concurrently. On 29 May, CincCPOA issued a Warning Order to Third Fleet concerning the invasion of the Palaus and followed it on 3 June with a new plan, Granite II, which set the date of the invasion at 8 September, a week earlier than the JCS had directed. Granite II called for an undertaking almost as big as the Saipan and Guam operations combined: four assault divisions divided into two corps invading all of the major islands of the archipelago. The 1st Marine Division and the 81st Infantry Division, comprising the III Amphibious Corps, would attack the southern islands of Peleliu and Angaur while, at the same time, the 7th and 77th Infantry Divisions, comprising the XXIV Corps, U.S. Army, would assault Babelthuap. The 27th Infantry Division would serve as operational reserve.[43]

Being involved in both operations complicated planning for Geiger and his staff. Stalemate planning needed to continue while III AC executed its part of Operation Forager, so Geiger detached a provisional planning staff and sent it to Hawaii where it became operational on 12 June. This staff was eventually renamed X-Ray Provisional Amphibious Corps and command was given to Major General Julian C. Smith, Commanding General of the 2nd Marine Division at Tarawa and presently Deputy Commander of the V Amphibious Corps. Problems developed very early. The 8 September date was dependent upon the use of several of the units involved in Forager. When the invasion of Saipan lasted longer than anticipated, causing the reserve 27th Infantry Division to go in earlier than planned and the invasion of Guam to be put off until July, the plans for the Palaus had to be rethought. In addition, Julian Smith's planners began to have second thoughts about trying to take Babelthuap. First, they became concerned that the allocated forces were not enough to overcome a growing Japanese garrison on an island larger and more rugged than Saipan. It was quite sobering to consider that it took three divisions twenty-five days to secure that objective. Smith was expected to take Babelthuap with only two divisions. Second, Babelthuap was too rugged to allow for much airfield development and its harbor facilities were not the best to be had in the region—the island of Yap and Ulithi Atoll, both near the Palaus, had better harbors and the Japanese already had built and were operating a fine airfield on Peleliu. On 7 July, another Warning Order went out to all subordinate commands involved in Stalemate. The operation, renamed Stalemate II, would now be carried off in two phases. The first phase would involve the capture of Peleliu and Angaur and the neutralization of Babelthuap and Koror while the second phase would consist of the capture of Yap and Ulithi. The date for Phase I was

[43] Isely and Crowl, *U.S. Marines and Amphibious War,* p. 393; Garand and Strobridge, *Western Pacific Operations,* pp. 60–61; Hough, *Assault on Peleliu,* pp. 10–11.

pushed back to the original JCS date of 15 September. It would then coincide with MacArthur's assault on the island of Morotai. Phase II, meanwhile, was scheduled tentatively for 5 October.[44]

Admiral Halsey never agreed that the Palaus needed to be taken. He believed that the cost of invading them far outweighed the usefulness of the harbors and airfields they contained. Instead, he argued that the U.S. should go directly into the Philippines. He based this argument upon a belief that Japanese resistance would swiftly collapse at a certain point in time and that the United States needed to be in a position to apply even more pressure on the enemy in order to complete his destruction when this collapse occurred. Halsey encountered evidence of weakening Japanese resistance while directing pre-invasion carrier strikes in the Philippines immediately prior to the beginning of Phase I of Stalemate II and he saw this as an indication that the enemy's anticipated collapse was imminent. MacArthur, following the 12 March JCS directive, was preparing to invade Mindanao on 15 November after securing Morotai. Halsey determined that there were virtually no Japanese on Mindanao, so he radioed to Nimitz on 13 September three recommendations: (1) cancel Stalemate II; (2) immediately turn over the ground troops mounted for that operation to MacArthur; and (3) tell MacArthur to revise his plans in order to allow for an immediate invasion of the central Philippines. Nimitz replied that Phase I had to go on as planned because the operation had progressed too far to call it off, but Phase II would be reviewed with Halsey's advice in mind.[45]

Nimitz's biographer, E. B. Potter, states that there was another reason why CinCPac did not want to cancel Phase I: the admiral believed that Peleliu's airfield and the anchorage to the north of Babelthuap in the Kossol Passage would prove useful in staging MacArthur's invasion of Leyte. Nimitz sent a message to MacArthur with Halsey's recommendations attached requesting a decision. On 15 September, as the 1st Marine Division hit the beaches on Peleliu, CinCPOA received a dispatch that was written in MacArthur's name. The message said that MacArthur was willing to make the recommended changes in his schedule if XXIV Corps could be transferred to his command. A message describing all of these changes was then sent to the Joint Chiefs for approval. The Chiefs and President Roosevelt were attending the Quebec Octagon Conference at this time. The thought of Nimitz and MacArthur working together so impressed them that approval of the plan was radioed back within ninety minutes. Upon receipt of this message, Phase II of Stalemate II was canceled and the 7th and 77th Infantry Divisions were sent to the Southwest Pacific.[46]

---

[44] Garand and Strobridge, *Western Pacific Operations*, pp. 60–61; Hough, *Assault on Peleliu*, pp. 10–11.

[45] Hough, *Assault on Peleliu*, pp. 190–91.

[46] Potter, *Nimitz*, p. 323; Hough, *Assault on Peleliu*, pp. 190–91.

These changes affected Julian Smith more than anyone else. General Geiger and the III Amphibious Corps staff returned from the Marianas on 15 August and Geiger relieved Smith of command of the Western Landing Forces. X-Ray Provisional Amphibious Corps was at that point deactivated. Smith retained his title of Commanding General Expeditionary Troops, having under his command two corps—III AC and XXIV Corps. This made him, in essence, an army commander. The transfer of XXIV Corps to MacArthur's command left Smith without an army to command. He retained his position and title but he became superfluous to the operation since General Geiger was, in essence, the overall ground commander for Stalemate II. Admiral Wilkinson was also affected, however. As Commander Joint Expeditionary Force, he was in overall command of the amphibious aspects of Operation Stalemate II. Like Kelly Turner, he had to wear two hats. He chose for his second hat that of commander of the Eastern Attack Force (TF 33), the unit scheduled to take Yap and Ulithi. He delegated command of the Western Attack Force (TF 32), the group given the task of covering the Peleliu and Angaur landings, to Rear Admiral George H. Fort. When Phase II was canceled, this took away one of Wilkinson's hats, letting him concentrate on overall support of the operation.[47]

Division- and Force-level planning and coordination took place over August 1944, with staff members from the various units traveling across the Pacific for conferences and meetings. First Marine Division training began in June and was capped off with Division landing rehearsals in the Cape Esperance area of Guadalcanal on 27 and 29 August. General O. P. Smith describes these rehearsals in his journal:

> The first rehearsal was made without firing by Naval gunfire ships. This was a pre-dress rehearsal for the purpost [*sic*] of testing communications. The part of the exercise which involved the landing of LVT waves and the later transfer operations went off with reasonable smoothness. The communications were not very good. A good many of the radios had been received just before embarkation and there had been no opportunity to calibrate them. I set up the advance CP in the proper location ashore and eventually got communication with the regiments by telephone, but not by radio. The radios were calibrated by the time of the dress rehearsal....
>
> General Geiger visited me at the CP during the first rehearsal. He had not realized that General Rupertus was unable to make the trip ashore and was somewhat concerned about him going on the operation. I assured General Geiger that in the two weeks remaining before the landing I felt General Rupertus' ankle would mend sufficiently to permit him

---

[47] Garand and Strobridge, *Western Pacific Operations,* pp. 63–64; Isely and Crowl, *U.S. Marines and Amphibious War,* p. 394.

> to carry on. (At Peleliu, General Rupertus managed to get around pretty well with the aid of a cane.)[48]

General Smith continued:

> On the dress rehearsal of August 29th, Naval gunfire ships and planes bombed the beaches prior to the landing. This resulted in quite a few rocket duds which were a hazard to the amphibian tractors when they were barging around back of the beaches. The dress rehearsal went off very smoothly, including communications. The next landing would be on the beaches at Peleliu.
>
> On August 30th, there was a critique at Corps Headquarters. It was attended by all the "brass" of the fleet and the ground forces. As I remember the Generals and Admirals included Admirals Oldendorf, Fort, Ainsworth, Sample and Durgin; and Generals Geiger, Rupertus, Mueller (Eighty-first Division), Marcus Bell (Eighty-first Division), Omar Peiffer (an observer from the Navy Department), Silverthorn and myself. There was nothing particularly constructive about the critique. Everyone was pleased with everyone else. The critique did, however, give all hands an opportunity to get acquainted.[49]

Everyone, therefore, appeared satisfied with the preparations they had made prior to the beginning of Operation Stalemate II. General Rupertus was so sure of the 1st Marine Division's readiness that he made the following comment during the 30 August critique: "We're going to have some casualties, but let me assure you this is going to be a short one, a quickie. Rough but fast. We'll be through in three days. It might take only two."[50] The coming battle would show just how unrealistically optimistic he and the other commanders were.

Naval Gunfire at Peleliu—The "Lessons" Ignored

Optimism prevailed among the planners because they and the entire Central Pacific command were not paying close enough attention to the changes in Japanese defensive tactics that were already evident by the time Geiger and his staff began crafting the Stalemate II operational plan. The first real evidence of these changes began to come to light in May of 1944 at Biak in the Schouten Islands. This

[48] According to Garand and Strobridge, *Western Pacific Operations,* p. 94, Rupertus had broken his ankle during one of the Regimental-level landing exercises prior to the 27 August Division-level exercise.

[49] Smith, Personal Narrative, Part I, p. 83.

[50] Quote from Isely and Crowl, *U.S. Marines and Amphibious War,* p. 396.

invasion was part of General MacArthur's mopping up at the end of the New Guinea campaign. The 41st Infantry Division met little resistance on the beach, but resistance grew to the point where the 162nd Regimental Combat Team was almost forced back on its initial landing site. The American forces found that they were dealing with a defense in depth that used the caves and other terrain features of the island to the greatest advantage of the defenders. In addition, the Japanese commander, Colonel Naoyuki Kuzume, had instructed his troops to not waste themselves in useless banzai attacks against the American invaders. These tactics caused the battle for Biak to last until August, much longer than MacArthur had anticipated. Kuzume's goal was to overwhelm the Americans once they had established themselves ashore rather than to try to destroy them on the beach. The Japanese Imperial General Headquarters, noting the resilience of the Biak defenses and the troubles encountered by the Americans on Saipan, decided to issue a change in defensive doctrine in July 1944. This doctrine emphasized the preparation of a main line of defense far enough inland to escape the brunt of the American pre-landing bombardment, the organization of a defense in depth with the objective of wearing down the invaders, and the retention of sufficient reserves to allow Japanese defenders the option of mounting effective counterattacks at the optimal time. The Japanese planned to open fire at close to maximum effective range, when the enemy was crossing the reef, attriting the Americans unrelentingly as they advanced. Given the relative disparity in combat power, this doctrinal change made more effective use of Japanese resources. The 1st Marine Division faced these tactics at Peleliu.[51]

The purpose of naval gunfire support, prior to Tarawa, was to soften up the enemy's defenses so that men could be put ashore. The doctrine, after Tarawa, emphasized deliberate destruction of targets both on and near the beach that endangered assaulting troops. The new Japanese tactics attempted to neutralize the overwhelming firepower advantage that the United States Navy could bring to bear on any objective it chose. Biak and Saipan showed that these tactics were effective. The Americans encountered well-developed defenses on Guam, but their prolonged bombardment of that island showed that even defenses in depth could be substantially weakened if naval gunfire were applied with deliberation over a long period of time and if Japanese fighting positions were located with precision by means of air reconnaissance. The assault of Peleliu would show that the Americans were not paying as close attention to either the Japanese or to their own successes as they believed at the time.

---

[51] Robert Ross Smith, *United States Army in World War II, The War in the Pacific, The Approach to the Philippines* (Washington, DC: Center of Military History, 1953), pp. 280–303 and 390; Garand and Strobridge, *Western Pacific Operations,* p. 71; Samuel Eliot Morison, *Leyte, June 1944–January 1945, History of United States Naval Operations in World War II,* Vol. 12 (Boston: Little Brown, 1958), p. 35.

To Rear Admiral George H. Fort, commander of the Western Attack Force, fell the responsibility of taking Peleliu from the Japanese. He chose to keep tactical control of the assault on that objective for himself, giving control of task groups assigned to take Angaur and to sweep the Kossol Passage north of Peleliu for mines to subordinates. The man responsible for providing Fort with preliminary naval gunfire support was a veteran of several operations prior to Stalemate II: Rear Admiral Jesse B. Oldendorf. Oldendorf had served with distinction at Saipan and he would become famous in October of 1944 as the commander of the U.S. battle-line in the Battle of Surigao Strait in which several American battleships that survived Pearl Harbor were able to wreak their revenge on the Japanese. Operation Stalemate II would not be his finest hour.[52]

Most of the fire support ships that would take part in the invasion of Peleliu assembled in the Solomon Islands area after the completion of Operation Forager. Things got off to a rough start when the bombardment force lost the services of one of its old battleships to an accident on 23 August. The various ships were enroute to their staging areas when *Tennessee* lost steering and collided with USS *California* (BB-44). Navy repair crews got *Tennessee* in shape in time to participate in the bombardment of Angaur, but *California,* more severely damaged, could not make it to the staging area in time and consequently had to be left behind. Once the force was assembled, it underwent replenishment and then engaged in rehearsals in the Cape Esperance Area of Guadalcanal on 27–29 August.[53] Rear Admiral Fort described the last day of these rehearsals in his Action Report: "An Official rehearsal on August 29, 1944 [*sic*] was carried out which closely followed the DOG Day Schedule. A pre-HOW Bombardment (reduced ammunition allowance) was carried out and HOW Hour strafing runs were made on the beach area. Communications was [*sic*] established between the [3rd Battalion, 1st Marines; 2nd Battalion, 1st Marines; 1st Battalion, 5th Marines; 3rd Battalion, 5th Marines] and the ships assigned to them for the operation."[54] Following post-rehearsal replenishment, the Palau bombardment force set out to begin preliminary gunfire preparation of the operation's objectives.[55]

---

[52] Morison, *Leyte,* pp. 33–34; Isely and Crowl, *U.S. Marines and Amphibious War,* p. 393; NARA, RG 38, Box 578, Commander Cruiser Division Four (CTG 32.5, CTU 32.5.1, CTU 32.5.3), Action Report, Bombardment and Capture of Peleliu Island, Palau Group, 12 September to 24 September 1944, dated 26 September 1944 (hereinafter Oldendorf), p. 1; Shaw et al., *Central Pacific Drive,* pp. 280–81; Morison, *Leyte,* pp. 198–241.

[53] NARA, RG 38, Box 578, Commander Third Amphibious Force (CTF 31), Action Report, Stalemate 2 Operation, dated 11 November 1944, Enclosure E (hereinafter Wilkinson AR), p. 1.

[54] NARA, RG 127, Box 297, Commander Task Force 32, Action Report, Peleliu, dated 16 October 1944, Enclosure E (hereinafter Fort), p. 1.

[55] Wilkinson AR, p. 1.

The question of just how closely American naval commanders and planners outside of the Fifth Fleet were paying attention to the "lessons of Tarawa" and the changes in Japanese tactics must be raised concerning the earliest steps of preparation for Operation Stalemate II. Vice Admiral Wilkinson stated that CinCPac and 5th Amphibious Force documents concerning naval gunfire support of landing operations were referenced in preparing his basic plan and that subordinate commands were to use these same documents in preparing their plans, but he also gave them an out. He stated, "Responsible Attack Force Commanders may modify these instructions as circumstances warrant to conform to requirements for their specific objective."[56] Modifications could thus be made whether or not the modifying commander was aware of the latest information concerning Japanese tactics. Compounding this ignorance of Japanese tactics was ignorance of what the Japanese were doing on Peleliu. As Samuel Eliot Morison put it:

> Since there were no tourists' photographs of Palau beaches for planners to study, as in France—no Australian coastwatchers or trading-schooner skippers to consult, as in the Solomons; no information gathered before the war, as in the Marianas and the Philippines—Jicpoa (Joint Intelligence Center Pacific Ocean Areas) had to rely on aerial photographs and submarine reconnaissance. One purpose of . . . fast carrier force raids on the Palaus at the end of March 1944 was to photograph the islands. Special photographic missions were flown in July and August. But the 1:20,000-scale maps compiled from those aerial photos were defective, owing to cloud cover, heavy jungle growth and clever Japanese camouflage which concealed the important features of Peleliu and gave the general impression that this rugged island was low and flat.[57]

Later reconnaissance by Underwater Demolition Teams prior to the operation did nothing to correct this false impression because the "frogmen" were only interested in reconnoitering the landing beaches.[58]

Wilkinson's basic instructions for how the preliminary bombardment of Peleliu should be carried out went as follows:

> Preparatory Naval gunfire bombardment should be coordinated with Air bombardment to produce the maximum softening up and harassing effect. This should include a steady naval or air bombardment from D-2 . . . until troops are well established on the beach.

---

[56] Ibid.

[57] Quote from Morison, *Leyte*, pp. 32–33.

[58] Ibid., p. 33.

> The D-2 . . . and D-1 Naval bombardment should be scheduled with the following definite purposes:
>
> (a) Destruction of enemy aircraft and rendering airfields unserviceable.
>
> (b) Destruction of enemy guns and emplacements in the objective area.
>
> (c) Destruction of enemy ammunition dumps, fuel dumps, and buildings.
>
> (d) Destruction of enemy shipping, including barges and small craft.
>
> (e) Destruction of beach defenses and strong points [*sic*] in landing areas.
>
> (f) Bombardment of enemy reserves and personnel concentrations.
>
> (g) Close fire support of Underwater Demolition Teams during reconnaissance and clearing obstacles on the landing beaches.
>
> (h) Night harassing fire to prevent reconstruction of fortifications and movement of enemy reserves.[59]

Wilkinson then stated that "[a]11 fires on these two days should be slow and deliberate in order to produce the maximum destruction of defenses."[60] The first indication that Wilkinson did not really understand the "lessons" that had been learned thus far in the Central Pacific Campaign is evident in these instructions: he was allowing for only two days of preliminary bombardment. General Geiger recognized the implications of this decision immediately. His experience at Guam proved to him that the effective use of naval gunfire made a real difference in the success of a beach assault. He deemed two days to be an extremely ineffective use of the firepower at the disposal of the Peleliu Attack Force and he requested that the bombardment period be increased to four days. Wilkinson eventually allowed for an additional day and Geiger was glad to get it, but the III Amphibious Corps commander was not truly satisfied with this compromise. In the end, the amount of ordnance was not increased. Instead, the modified plan called for the use of the same amount of ammunition over the longer time frame, allowing for greater deliberation and, hopefully, greater effectiveness.[61]

---

[59] NARA, RG 38, Box 578, Commander Third Amphibious Force (CTF 31), Operation Plan A302–44, Stalemate II, dated 4 August 1944, Annex H (hereinafter Wilkinson OpPlan), p. 1.

[60] Wilkinson OpPlan, p. 2.

[61] NARA, RG 127, Box 298, File A4–8, III MAC Operation Report, Enclosure G, Naval Gunfire, Third Amphibious Corps Naval Gunfire Officer Report, Palaus Operation, dated 14 October 1944 (hereinafter IIIAC NGF Rpt), p. 2; Garand and Strobridge, *Western Pacific Operations*, p. 104.

Additional evidence of a lack of understanding of the fundamentals of proper naval gunfire integration in the assault of a hostile beach on the part of the Stalemate II team can be found in the planning of the 1st Marine Division. This veteran unit had spearheaded the first attempt to stop the Japanese expansion on land at Guadalcanal, and had followed up that experience with action in the northern Solomons through 1943 and early 1944 in support of General MacArthur's isolation of Rabaul.[62] In all of these operations, however, the 1st Marine Division had never made a true amphibious assault landing. Consequently, the staff of the division was not thoroughly schooled in the latest lessons from the Central Pacific Campaign. One of those lessons taught that a division-level naval gunfire officer was a necessary part of the staff when planning for an amphibious assault. The First Division's SAR described their predicament in this way:

> This Division did not have a Marine Naval Gunfire Officer. No officer in the Division had been trained in any way for such an assignment. A naval officer (Lt. jg) of III Phib Corps who had previously worked with the Division was requested for purposes of planning. This officer assisted during this phase. Later, Lt. Marvin P. Morton, U.S.N., reported from V Phib Corps. Although late for the planning, this officer applied himself with vigor and intelligence. With little time to work, he did everything possible to properly indoctrinate and instruct the various [Naval Gunfire Liaison Officers and Shore Fire Control Parties]. In this his success was limited only by time. Lt. Morton had had no previous combat experience although his training was excellent.
>
> The present [Table of Organization] authorized a Major as Artillery and Naval Gunfire Coordinator. This member of the staff in an amphibious operation can be invaluable. However, that officer must have had training in both artillery and naval gunfire. As previously mentioned, this Division had no officer with those qualifications.[63]

Having no staff officer trained in both these specialties handicapped the division planners when it came time to coordinate the training and use of the Marines and naval personnel who would ultimately control naval gunfire in support of troops once the assault was underway. The lack of this most important staff officer also led to problems communicating division requests for naval gunfire support to the higher naval authorities responsible for supplying that support.

Once each command echelon had distributed its plans upward to higher authority and downward to its subordinate commands, and after the rehearsals of

[62] MCUA, Peleliu Project, Box 46, Folder 3, First Marine Division Special Action Report, Palau Operation (hereinafter 1st MarDiv SAR), Phase II, Operational Phase, p. 1.

[63] 1st MarDiv SAR, Annex K, p. 7.

27–29 August that were based upon those plans had taken place, Rear Admiral Oldendorf set out with his task group to take up position off Peleliu so that he could begin the preliminary bombardment. The fast carriers of Task Force 38 attacked the Palaus beginning on D-9 while Oldendorf was at sea and the fast battleships and cruisers accompanying the carriers shelled the islands from long range to help soften up Japanese defenses prior to his arrival at dawn on D-3, 12 September 1944. When his ships were in position, he got right to work, hammering Japanese emplacements beginning at 05.30. He reported that "[t]he entire island was systematically bombed and bombarded. The Commander of the Fire Support Group [that is, Oldendorf] accomplished this by assigning the most profitable targets observed and obtained by photographic interpretation." Over the three days preceding D-day, Oldendorf oversaw UDT preparations and his ships carried out the bombardment of Peleliu according to plan with only one variation: poor visibility kept one of the fire support units from being able to deliver its scheduled fire during the period 05.30–06.30 on D-2.[64] The Peleliu Fire Support Unit threw 2,255 tons of ordnance against the Japanese defenders during the three days of preliminary bombardment.[65] Describing his treatment of the landing beaches, Oldendorf stated: "The designated, White and Orange, landing beaches received heavy and sustained punishment as did the high land that overlooked the beaches. This high land was covered with thick tropical growth when the Fire Support Group arrived on Dog Minus THREE Day, but by Dog Day, when the Attack Force arrived, this growth had been systematically destroyed and only charred tree stumps and scarred rocks remained. Numerous caves were then visible on the slopes of the high land."[66]

Rear Admiral Fort arrived off Peleliu at dawn on D-day, 15 September, and, according to plan, took command of the fire support ships, minesweepers, and UDTs.[67] The naval gunfire support ships then poured 1,373 more tons of ordnance onto Peleliu over the course of D-day as the 1st Marine Division struggled to establish itself ashore.[68]

The preliminary bombardment of Peleliu has been subjected to withering criticism since the end of the war. Jeter Isely and Philip Crowl were among the first to scrutinize the operation, and they raised some very interesting points. First, they mention a radio transmission from Admiral Oldendorf to Admiral Fort in which the former told the latter that the fire support units had silenced all known targets

[64] Oldendorf, pp. 1–15 and 35; 1st MarDiv SAR, Phase II, p. 2; Isely and Crowl, *U.S. Marines and Amphibious War,* p. 402; quote from Oldendorf, p. 1.

[65] IIIAC NGF Rpt, Enclosure A.

[66] Oldendorf, pp. 1–2.

[67] Ibid., p. 16.

[68] IIIAC NGF Rpt, Enclosure A.

and that he could find no more to attack.[69] In announcing this to Fort, Oldendorf essentially brought the preliminary bombardment to a halt before he had used his allotment of approximately 1,406 tons of ammunition.[70] Second, they compare the three days allowed for the preliminary bombardment at Peleliu unfavorably with the thirteen days of pre-invasion punishment delivered by Conolly at Guam, stating: " . . . the conclusion cannot be avoided that preliminary naval gunfire on Peleliu was inadequate, and that the lessons learned at Guam were overlooked. Guam had demonstrated without shadow of doubt that slow, prolonged, and deliberate naval bombardment could accomplish amazing results even against a strong, well-equipped, and determined force. Peleliu, like Tarawa and to a lesser extent Saipan, demonstrated that the only substitute for such prolonged bombardment was costly expenditure of the lives of the assault troops."[71]

Rear Admiral Fort, who, as Oldendorf's immediate superior, was ultimately responsible for his subordinate's performance, took great exception to their critique. In two letters written to Crowl and Kenneth W. Condit in 1950, Fort stated:

> I cannot accept . . . [the] statement that thirteen days shore bombardment are necessarily a lot better than three. If three days are sufficient, the remaining ten days are an absolute waste of expensive and scarce ammunition. . . . If Admiral Oldendorf broke off fire before he had used up his allowed ammunition on the grounds that there were no more targets, he was entirely correct. The idea that some people seem to have of just firing at an island is an inexcusable waste of ammunition. . . . [As far as the time constraints were concerned, even if there were plenty of visible targets] some of the fire support ships reported so late that it was impossible for them to arrive at the objective until D-3. The D date was set to coordinate with MacArthur's simultaneous landing in S.W. Pacific and could not be delayed. Hence three days bombardment was all that was possible.[72]

Any questions as to the timing of Stalemate II relative to MacArthur's actions in the Southwest Pacific must be closely tied to the greater question of whether or not the Palaus needed to be captured once MacArthur modified his plans for the invasion of the Philippines. Since Nimitz chose to continue with Phase I of Stalemate II, any argument against the timing of the operation is moot because that

---

[69] Morison states that this transmission was sent on the evening of D-1, 14 September. Morison, *Leyte,* p. 35.

[70] Allotment figure from IIIAC NGF Rpt, p. 2. 1st MarDiv SAR, Annex K, p. 8, states that fewer projectiles were fired than originally allotted.

[71] Isely and Crowl, *U.S. Marines and Amphibious War,* p. 403.

[72] Quote found in ibid., p. 403.

decision set the timetable in stone, as Fort points out. Concerning Fort's comments regarding the number of days that one ought to allow for the destruction of a given target, however, much can be said in rebuttal. His statement that "If three days are sufficient, the remaining ten days are an absolute waste of expensive and scarce ammunition" is a truism if, indeed, three days are enough to reduce the defenses of an objective. The problem with his using such a truism as the basis for his critique of Isely and Crowl's analysis of the Peleliu preliminary bombardment is that there is good reason to question whether three days were, indeed, sufficient to reduce Japanese defenses on this particular objective. His argument that "just firing at an island is an inexcusable waste of ammunition" is also open to criticism. While firing at an island blindly without any thought as to where one's rounds might fall is a mistake that should be avoided, refusing to fire when one simply runs out of visible targets is a mistake as well. The doctrine embodied in *FTP 167* stressed that: " . . . it must be clearly understood that definite information on targets will be meager prior to the attack, that enemy tactics and doctrine will vary. In the absence of specific information the principle must be followed of placing fire at the proper times in all areas from which, should he be there, the enemy could defeat the attack."[73]

While the naval gunfire chapter of *FTP 167* specifically dealt with the requirements of D-day, the basic concepts presented in the manual held for the entire time, however long that might be, during which naval gunfire could be used profitably in support of operations ashore. Curiously, considering the argument Admiral Fort uses in his letters to vindicate his subordinate's actions, Oldendorf takes a position very much like the doctrine expressed in *FTP 167* in a letter he wrote to the Director of Marine Corps History in 1950. In it, he stated that, in a situation like the one he encountered at Peleliu, the "best that can be done is to blast away at suspected positions and hope for the best."[74] The bottom line here is this: ammunition may be expensive, but human lives are infinitely more valuable. If intelligently expending his entire allotment of ammunition prior to H-hour on D-day could have destroyed additional known or suspected enemy weapons, then Oldendorf should have used every last projectile at his disposal. If he suspected that there were more enemy weapons to be found, then he should have made a greater effort to obtain the intelligence he needed to locate those weapons and target them. Failing that, he at least should have used his ammunition in the way specified by doctrine.

Proof of the inadequacy of the preliminary bombardment came as the Marines went ashore. The assault troops were hit by small arms, mortar, and light artillery fire as they emerged from their landing craft onto the beaches. General Geiger's

[73] *FTP 167* with Change 3, p. 113.

[74] Letter referenced and quote found in Garand and Strobridge, *Western Pacific Operations,* p. 104.

naval gunfire officer states that the short time frame given over for the preliminary bombardment ensured that only the more obvious targets could be taken out and that "[m]any of these enemy installations [that were left] were of such a nature that it is doubtful if they could have been discovered except by a person on the ground."[75] It was from installations such as these, many of them caves that proved extremely difficult to reduce, that much of the fire that descended upon the assaulting Marines originated—but not all of it. The 1st Battalion, 1st Marines referenced Oldendorf's comment concerning a lack of targets in their report:

> [17 Sept. D+2] From patrol information of the day before it had been ascertained that a large concrete structure 60 feet by 60 feet and about 20 feet high with 4 feet reinforced concrete walls lay directly in the center of the Battalion's advance to the south of the road which begins in 133S. Contrary to previous reports from the task force Commander that not a target was standing, this blockhouse—almost, it could be called a fortress because of the pill boxes [*sic*] surrounding it—had not been touched by Naval gunfire nor bombing. The Battalion C.O. ordered the JASCO [Joint Assault Signal Company] Platoon which was attached to us to obtain gunfire support. The USS Idaho obliginly [*sic*] fired a mission and punctured the fortress with 2 direct hits from her 14 inch [*sic*] guns. The surrounding pill boxes were pasted with 14 inch and 6 inch fire by the JASCO, and the tanks placed direct fire in them.[76]

This incident occurred two days after the landings when personnel trained to call in accurate naval gunfire had come ashore. This emplacement was prominent enough to have been detected by photo interpreters and should have been included on maps given to units of the 1st Marine Division. Consequently, it should have been targeted by the preliminary bombardment and destroyed before the 1st Battalion, 1st Marines ever came near the structure. It was not. Why?

Admiral Oldendorf addressed this question in the letter he wrote to the director of Marine Corps History in 1950. He stated in the letter that the blockhouse in question was not indicated on the maps he had been given. In addition, his entire staff was ill from the time of the preliminary bombardment until several days after the landing. Isely and Crowl stated that Oldendorf's staff was small to begin with—the Bureau of Naval Personnel allowed him only a cruiser division staff of four officers even though he carried the responsibilities of a much larger command during the balance of the operation in the Palaus. With inadequate maps and

---

[75] IIIAC NGF Rpt, p. 2. The Japanese were known to be experts at camouflage and concealment. Given this expertise, such a statement is most likely accurate.

[76] MCUA, Peleliu Project, Box 1, Folder 1, First Battalion, First Marines, Historical Report, p. 14.

usually only a flag lieutenant to help him, the job of coordinating gunfire over the three days prior to the landings was just short of overwhelming.[77] The lack of adequate staff and the illness among what staff he had was beyond his control. The lack of accurate maps, however, is a different story. Under normal circumstances, great pains were taken to make sure that the maps used by the commanders of fire support units and the maps given to the assaulting troops were accurate. Doctrine as far back as *FTP 167* emphasized the importance of accurate maps and the distribution of those maps to everyone involved in supplying gunfire support: "A map of suitable size and scale is prepared from the best available data (air photos, hydrographic charts, reconnaissance reports, etc.) and is furnished [to] firing ships, shore fire control parties, air observers, liaison officers, and any others directly concerned with naval gunfire. The standard grid system prescribed for the operation is superimposed on this map, in order that locations of targets from other sources such as infantry front line commanders may be readily plotted on the fire-control map."[78]

That Oldendorf's maps did not correlate accurately to the maps supplied to the 1st Marine Division is an indication that communication between these two echelons of command did not function adequately. Here is where the lack of a Marine Naval Gunfire Officer at the division level probably affected the operation most directly. Without this additional staff officer in the chain of command whose job would have included coordination between the division and the fire support units, such a mistake was more likely to go undetected until it was too late to rectify. The division acquired the services of two naval officers to fill in for the missing Marine, but it is obvious that the system failed both Oldendorf and the 1st Marine Division at some level.

The naval participants in the Palaus operation have spent a lot of time and ink explaining away the deficiencies of the preliminary naval gunfire bombardment delivered at Peleliu. When one considers what the record shows and what the apologists have said in their own defense, however, it is difficult to come away from an analysis of this operation disagreeing with Isely and Crowl's conclusion that the effort was inadequate. The ultimate reason for this inadequacy was blissful ignorance. This ignorance operated on two different levels. First, the planners of Operation Stalemate II chose to ignore the lessons that Spruance, Turner, and H. M. Smith had learned thus far in the war, choosing instead to trust more in the massive application of firepower than in its intelligent application. General Geiger, fresh from his schooling in the lessons of the Central Pacific Campaign at Guam, attempted to affect a change in the gunfire schedule when he and his staff returned

---

[77] Oldendorf letter referenced and quoted in Garand and Strobridge, *Western Pacific Operations,* p. 104; Isely and Crowl's comments concerning Oldendorf's staff found in Isely and Crowl, *U.S. Marines and Amphibious War,* p. 402.

[78] *FTP 167* with Change 3, p. 125.

from the Marianas. He was only able to get one additional day and then had to make the best of it. Even his naval gunfire officer, however, showed the American penchant for equating tonnage of ordnance with effective use of gunfire support when he commented in his report that "[d]espite [the] tremendous weight of explosives" used on D-day, the assaulting Marines were hit with a large volume of enemy fire as they came ashore.[79]

The second level of American ignorance was even more deadly to the Marines going ashore at Peleliu, however—ignorance of changing Japanese tactics. Faulty reconnaissance was a problem for the Americans, true, but Japanese tactics made the situation much worse for the Marines than it otherwise would have been. The skillful use of camouflage and the decision to build a defense in depth using the natural caves of the island as an integral part of their system demonstrates that the Japanese had taken their defensive doctrine and tactics to the next level. The U.S. Navy and Marine Corps, on the other hand, had allowed their operational planning and execution skills to degrade, almost to the level demonstrated at Tarawa. The result was a tragic slaughter that was unnecessary and avoidable.

[79] IIIAC NGF Rpt, p. 2.

Chapter 7
Operation Detachment

The Amphibious Assault of Iwo Jima

At 06.40 on 19 February 1945, naval gunfire support vessels began the pre-H-hour bombardment for what would prove to be the bloodiest operation in the history of the United States Marine Corps—the invasion of Iwo Jima. At 08.05, the gunnery vessels lifted their fire so that seventy-two fighters and bombers from Task Force 58 could attack the eastern and northern slopes of Mount Suribachi, the landing areas, and the high ground on the north flank of the assault beaches with rockets, napalm, and general-purpose bombs. Forty-eight additional fighters immediately followed up this attack by dropping napalm on, firing rockets at, and strafing the same areas.[1] The men waiting aboard ship to go ashore witnessed this pounding. To their eyes, there was no way that such power could not be effective. A couple of examples of their thoughts are instructive in this regard. One Marine was dismissive in his assessment: "We were sitting there [aboard ship] watching [the H-hour bombardment]. Big battlewagons were sitting back there [firing], and aircraft were coming in. The whole island looked like a big dust bowl. They told us that the thing was bombed for seventy-two days, around the clock. I thought to myself, 'Oh, a couple of days, and we'll be out of here. Nothing to it!'"[2]

Another Marine was more morbidly philosophical:

> We got out of our bunks that morning and had breakfast. We were anchored off of Iwo Jima. I remember coming out of the ship and walking along the rail. I looked out, and we weren't too far off of the island. It was my first view of it, and it was everything that the map said—but not quite. I thought maybe it was a place with palm trees, something like Saipan, Tinian, and the Marshalls. When I first saw it, the only thing I could see was death. . . . It was dead. I've often described it as something that nobody wanted, and they burned it up. All that was left was ashes. It was gray, and there was smoke coming up from different places where they

[1] Whitman S. Bartley, *Iwo Jima: Amphibious Epic* (Washington, DC: Historical Division, HQMC, 1954), pp. 49–51; Garand and Strobridge, *Western Pacific Operations,* pp. 502–03.

[2] Charles W. Lindberg, interview by Ronald E. Marcello and John Chalkley, 19 February 1998, University of North Texas Oral History Program, interview OH 1224, transcript, p. 27.

had bombed. There couldn't be any life on it. It was a picture that one would call Hell.[3]

Only time and circumstance could prove the accuracy of these individual observations, and the time for that proof had come.

The first wave of LVTs crossed the line of departure at 08.30. Armed with a 75mm howitzer, these LVT(A)(4)s were to provide the following assault waves with much needed artillery support as the latter crossed the beach and headed inland. Each wave was allotted thirty minutes to travel the 4,000 yards between the line of departure and the shore while maintaining 250–300 yards between each wave. The second wave, LVT(2)s carrying 1,360 Marines, crossed the line of departure at 08.32, followed five minutes later by the third wave carrying 1,200 more. Altogether, there were ten assault waves, each of the last eight waves following the second at five-minute intervals. At 08.57, with the first wave of LVTs approximately 400 yards from the shore, naval gunfire lifted inland and to the flanks. From this point, gunfire support vessels began laying down a "rolling barrage" 400–500 yards in front of the advancing troops. Fighters simultaneously began to strafe the landing beaches and they continued this strafing until the first wave came ashore, at which time the focus of the strafing attacks shifted inland approximately 500 yards.[4]

Amphibian tractors first crawled onto the beach at approximately 09.02, only two minutes behind the targeted H-hour. The Marines made two unwelcome discoveries as they emerged from the surf. First, an eight to fifteen foot high terrace existed directly behind the landing beaches. This terrace blocked the LVT(A)(4)s' field of fire inland. Second, the beach turned out to be covered with a coarse, grainy, primarily black volcanic sand that lacked the cohesiveness necessary to hold up an individual Marine much less a wheeled vehicle. Even tracked vehicles like the LVTs and M-4 medium tanks found the going difficult at best. Some of the LVT(A)(4)s advanced 50–75 yards inland, beyond the first terrace, by hitting the beach at full speed and letting their momentum carry them up the incline. Those that could not make it across the first terrace positioned themselves offshore so they could support the landing by firing their 75mm howitzers inland. The second assault wave came ashore under cover of this barrage at 09.04, the third at 09.07, and the fourth, carrying 1,600 Marines, at 09.12.[5]

---

[3] Donald Boots, interview by Ronald E. Marcello, 17 May 2001, University of North Texas Oral History Program, interview OH 1405, transcript, p. 156.

[4] Garand and Strobridge, *Western Pacific Operations*, pp. 506–07.

[5] Isely and Crowl, *U.S. Marines and Amphibious War*, p. 478; Garand and Strobridge, *Western Pacific Operations*, pp. 506–08. Underwater Demolition Teams took samples of beach sand on D-2. According to the Operation Plan for the UDTs, among the types of information that they were to obtain was "[the w]idth, gradient, and material of beach proper, with

Organized enemy resistance was not apparent during the landing of the first four or five assault waves. Holding to their commander's orders, the Japanese did not fire on the initial waves as they churned across the 4,000 yards from the line of departure to the beach, nor did they fire anti-boat guns at the tractors during their final approach. Isolated enemy artillery and mortar rounds began to land in the surf as the later waves reached the shore, however. The first Marines to feel the effects of determined Japanese resistance were the men of Major Robert Davidson's 2nd Battalion, 23rd Marines (2/23) on Yellow 2. At approximately 09.04, his unit reported that they were under moderate mortar attack, and by 09.20, Fourth Division Marines on both Yellow and Blue beaches were reporting heavy enemy fire. The men of the Fifth Division were spared at first, but by 09.35, the Green and Red beaches were under an intense mortar barrage as well. Japanese resistance grew rapidly more intense after this slow start until, at its peak, the ferocity of the

---

special attention to the following: (a) gradient and condition of beach at high water mark; (b) contour of beach as to feasibility for attack forces to exit quickly with vehicles from high water mark; (c) material of beach and an estimate as to what type of vehicle it will support." Isely and Crowl report that, with a few exceptions, the UDTs "optimistically" deemed the beaches suitable for landings. One of those exceptions was Sergeant Frank E. Schnell. Sergeant Schnell was an observer with UDT #14. He filed a report of his observations after the operation. Included in this report was the following: "[After UDT operations on 17 February were finished,] [w]e then headed back toward SAIPAN to meet the landing force. On the morning of 18 February 1945, I left the APD (USS WATERS), and went aboard the AGC #10 (USS AUBURN) to report to Admiral Hill. The following questions were ask [*sic*] by him: If the condition of the beaches would permit an LVT to climb over the terraces and I answered, 'in most places they would.' If rubber tired vehicles could climb them, and I said, 'that I didn't think they could make it.' Whether or not the beach was hard surfaced? I said no, they were soft sandy beaches." Hill decided to go with the majority opinion. At the point when he received this information from Sergeant Schnell, there was not much else that he could do. It could be argued that an assessment of beach conditions should have been made earlier than two days before the landings were to occur, but putting men ashore on Iwo before the U.S. was prepared to launch an assault could have compromised the security of the operation. An accurate understanding of what the assault forces would be facing might have made a difference on D-day, but two days is precious little time to make any significant changes in the landing plan. MCUA, Iwo Jima Project, Commander Underwater Demolition Teams, Amphibious Forces, U.S. Pacific Fleet, Operations Plan, Commander UDTs Amphibious Forces Pacific Operation Plan No. A1–45, 23 January 1944, Annex (A)—Daylight Reconnaissance Procedure, Appendix (I), p. (A)(I)-1; Isely and Crowl, *U.S. Marines and Amphibious War,* p. 469; MCUA, Iwo Jima Project, Fifth Amphibious Corps Landing Force, Volume V, CG V Amphibious Corps, VAC Report, Iwo Jima Campaign, 13 May 1945, Annex CHARLIE, Appendix 13 (Headquarters Commandant Report), Enclosure B, p. 1; MCUA, Iwo Jima Project, Fifth Amphibious Corps Landing Force, Volume V, CG V Amphibious Corps, VAC Report, Annex CHARLIE, Appendix 10 (Shore Party Report), pp. 14–15, contains a description of the beach conditions.

artillery and mortar barrage that poured down on the beaches of Iwo Jima was greater than any yet encountered in the Pacific. The landing beaches were covered with smashed and swamped landing craft, the scattered paraphernalia of combat, and dead, wounded, and crawling Marines within an hour and a half of the first tractors clattering ashore.[6]

Colonel Harry B. Liversedge's 28th Marines, landing across Green 1, was one of those Fifth Division units that encountered light opposition as it came ashore. The 1st Battalion (1/28) advanced approximately 150 yards by 09.30, and at 09.35, the 2nd Battalion (2/28) began to land behind it over the same beach. By 09.40, however, 1/28's pace slowed considerably as it came under increasingly heavy fire. By the time it had covered 300 yards it was being blanketed with mortar and artillery rounds fired from the vicinity of Suribachi and the high ground north of the landing beaches. Battalion Landing Team 2/28, meanwhile, found it extremely difficult going as it attempted to organize its companies on the beach under an increasingly lethal enemy barrage. Battalion Landing Team 1/28 was supposed to move across the 700 yards of the island's narrow neck just to the northeast of Suribachi, thereby isolating it from the rest of the Japanese positions, while 2/28 was supposed to take up positions facing the mountain for the purpose of protecting the left flank of the entire landing force. Completing that mission was beginning to appear problematic.[7]

Coordinated movement by the Marines became impossible and momentum was lost as increasingly intense and accurate small arms fire took its toll. Advance beyond the first terrace was proving to be very difficult. Anyone attempting to leave its protection was immediately fired upon by numerous rifles and machine guns emplaced in well-concealed pillboxes, blockhouses, and caves. Besides battling the Japanese, the men of the 1/28 also fought with the volcanic sand as they clawed their way off the beach. The knowledge each Marine possessed of the proper way to dig a foxhole was a useless bit of trivia there on the shores of Iwo Jima. The volcanic sand that caused so many problems for vehicles was so slippery that it filled in any hole as fast as a man could shovel. Filling sandbags with the stuff seemed to be the answer, so urgent calls began to go out over the radio net for as many bags as could be found and brought ashore.[8]

Having spared the first assault waves until they were on land, the Japanese changed their tactics as the later waves came in. They began to target LVTs and landing craft, creating a maze of wreckage through which the Navy coxswains had to navigate in order to get to the shore. Landing craft broached as their bows were pinned to the beach by wheeled vehicles that sank into the soft volcanic sand as they attempted to exit. Men and supplies kept piling up—and the system kept

---

[6] Garand and Strobridge, *Western Pacific Operations*, p. 508.

[7] Ibid.

[8] Ibid.

shuttling more and more of both ashore. All eight assault battalions had hit the beach within one and a half hours of the time when the first Marines set foot on the island.[9]

Enemy positions that had been bypassed in 1/28's area of responsibility continued to fire on Marines. The heavy casualties sustained by 1st Battalion prompted Colonel Liversedge to request that 5th Marine Division commander Major General Keller E. Rockey release 3/28, in division reserve, to his control. Rockey agreed to do this and preparations were begun to land the battalion. The first boats containing elements of 3rd Battalion crossed the line of departure at 12.20. Heavy fire from Suribachi and the high ground to the north of the landing beaches splashed among the landing craft as they approached the shore, tearing into the boats as they attempted to discharge their troops onto the beach. Battalion Landing Team 3/28 suffered many more casualties than did 1/28 and 2/28 during their earlier ship-to-shore movement. All elements of the 3rd were ashore by shortly after 13.00, but they were not able to insert themselves into the line of combat until late in the afternoon.[10] The 2nd and 3rd Battalions were slated to attack south toward Suribachi at 15.45. The attack was to be preceded by preparatory naval gunfire and it was to be accompanied by what was described as "adequate" air support. Battalion Landing Team 2/28 finally launched its attack just before 17.00 supported by tanks from Company C of the 5th Tank Battalion. It advanced 150 yards by 17.30 at the cost of many casualties, but this ground had to be given up when orders were received to fall back and tie in with 3/28 for the night.[11]

The 27th Marines, in the meantime, was fighting its own battle for survival. Landing across beaches Red 1 and 2, the 2nd and 1st Battalions, like the 28th Marines to their south, encountered only scattered resistance at first. Also like the 28th, however, casualties mounted from enemy mortar and artillery fire as the Regimental Combat Team (RCT) advanced beyond the immediate landing areas. Battalion Landing Team 1/27 entered the south end of Motoyama Airfield No. 1 at 11.30. Company C crossed the field and took up a position along a 250-yard line extending from its southwestern portion to the northwest. Unable to make its planned turn to the north, the battalion began consolidating along the western edge of the airfield. Company A of the 5th Tank Battalion supported 1/27 in its attacks against strong Japanese defenses around the airfield, but, even with tank support, the BLT was not able to make a significant advance for the rest of D-day. The 2nd Battalion encountered its first pillbox approximately fifty yards inland off the beach. Having been ordered to cross the island as quickly as possible, the advancing assault companies took on only those installations that were in their immediate path. The positions that were bypassed were left for regimental reserve

[9] Ibid., pp. 508–09.

[10] Ibid., p. 512.

[11] Ibid., pp. 512–13.

3/27 to deal with after it had landed at 11.30. The technique used to take out a pillbox was brutal and effective. Assault teams equipped with flamethrowers and riflemen throwing hand grenades killed all or most of the Japanese within a targeted installation and engineers then blew it up. Battalion Landing Team 2/27 was able to push all the way to the cliffs overlooking the island's west coast by approximately 15.00 using these tactics. Battalion Landing Team 1/26 completed its landing over Red 1 by this time and was attached to the 27th Marines. It was then ordered to take up defensive positions behind 2/27.[12]

The situation on Iwo's southern beaches deteriorated so rapidly on the morning of D-day that General Schmidt found he needed to release his Landing Force reserve, the 26th Marines, back to its parent Fifth Division within one hour after beginning operations. At 09.55, Schmidt released the 26th, less the 1st Battalion, and reconstituted his corps reserve by designating the newly-arrived 21st Marines of the 3rd Division to take their place. 26th Marines (1st Battalion) started for the line of departure at 11.06, but crowded conditions on the beach and limited space inland for an advance delayed its landing until 17.32 that afternoon. Going in over Red 1, it advanced to an assembly area at the southern tip of Motoyama Airfield No. 1 and took up defensive positions there. The situation ashore also complicated the landing of the division's organic artillery support regiment, the 13th Marines. It finally started going across the beach at 14.00, but was not able to have batteries emplaced and ready to provide support to the embattled infantry regiments until 04.40 on D+1.[13]

It may be difficult to believe, given the foregoing description of events transpiring in the Fifth Division's zone of operations, but accounts of the day's action generally agree that the beaches within the Fourth Division's zone were even more deadly. Landings on the northern beaches began at the same time as did those on the southern ones—the 1st Battalion, 23rd Marines (1/23) landing over Yellow 1 and the 2nd Battalion (2/23) over Yellow 2 at 09.00, precisely at H-hour. Like its counterparts in the south, the RCT encountered little trouble going ashore and the advance to the first terrace was without significant incident. Then the situation changed—drastically. Heavy and accurate fire began to tear into the men of both battalions from the front and flanks as they approached the second terrace. At 09.30, 1/23 reported having advanced 250 yards inland and 2/23 reported a similar advance at 09.40, but the enemy's defensive fire was beginning to take its toll. The Japanese were firing at the Marines from the remains of two blockhouses and fifty pillboxes that had not been destroyed by the preliminary naval gunfire and air bombardment. This stiff opposition was proof that armor support was needed and, at 10.05 sixteen tanks of Company C, 4th Tank Battalion began landing over the

---

[12] Ibid., pp. 513–15; Bartley, *Amphibious Epic,* pp. 57–58.

[13] Garand and Strobridge, *Western Pacific Operations,* pp. 515–16; Bartley, *Amphibious Epic,* p. 58.

Yellow beaches. The volcanic sand and land mines combined to slow Company C's advance to the front lines, but the tanks that survived were able to provide enough support for 1/23 to allow the battalion to advance an additional 500 yards by noon, just 200 yards short of the airfield. Battalion Landing Team 2/23 was not so fortunate. Tanks were unable to find a way to get into position to provide support and, consequently, the battalion's advance was only half that of 1/23's by noon.[14]

The left flank of 1/23 finally reached the boundary of Airfield No. 1 at 14.05. The tank support that had helped 1/23 to advance so much farther than 2/23 was temporarily taken out of the fight at this point, however. The tanks began to draw intense anti-tank fire and had to pull back to the revetted edge of the airfield, leaving the infantrymen to push the attack without their immediate support. The slow advance of 2/23, in the meantime, began to greatly concern the 23rd Marines' regimental commander, Colonel Walter W. Wensinger. At 13.00, he called for the landing of his regimental reserve, 3/23, the plan being for the 3rd Battalion to move inland approximately 200 yards and then to provide 81mm mortar support to the beleaguered 2nd Battalion. That landing, like the landings of the assault battalions, went off without significant incident. The situation 3/23 encountered ashore was also, unfortunately, similar to the one experienced earlier by the assault battalions. The Japanese laid down an extremely heavy barrage on the beach and casualties mounted as 3/23 tried to push its way through the wreckage and bodies strewn across the narrow strip of sand that was their barely adequate refuge from the pounding surf of the Pacific. Colonel Wensinger ordered the battalion to pass through 1/23 in order to exit the congested beach. Casualties and congestion took their toll, but 3/23 finally reached the airfield boundary by 17.00 and, despite the confusion of battle and a lack of tank support, Company F, 2/23, reached the apron of Airfield No. 1 by 17.30 and took a defensive position there for the night.[15]

Major General Clifton B. Cates, commander of the Fourth Marine Division, was as concerned as Colonel Wensinger about the slow progress of 2/23. He was also worried about the terrible beating the battalion was taking. At 14.05, he ordered two battalions of his divisional reserve ashore, 1/24 and 2/24. Battalion Landing Team 1/24 was to provide support for the 25th Marines, but 2/24 was earmarked to relieve 2/23. The 2nd Battalion went ashore at 16.50 over Yellow 2 and proceeded to advance 700 yards inland to the front line. It then carried out the relief of 2/23 at 18.00 and tied in for the night between 3/23 on the left and 1/25 on the right.[16]

---

[14] Garand and Strobridge, *Western Pacific Operations,* pp. 517–18; Bartley, *Amphibious Epic,* pp. 60–61.

[15] Garand and Strobridge, *Western Pacific Operations,* pp. 518–19; Bartley, *Amphibious Epic,* p. 61.

[16] Garand and Strobridge, *Western Pacific Operations,* p. 519; Bartley, *Amphibious Epic,* p. 61; MCUA, Iwo Jima Project, 4th Marine Division Operations Report, 18 May 1945, Annex GEORGE, Headquarters 24th Marines Final Report, pp. 171–72.

The northernmost invasion beach, Blue 2, was located directly below a cliff from which the Japanese could rake the incoming assault forces almost with impunity. The 25th Marines' regimental commander, Colonel John R. Lanigan, attempted to overcome this problem by having his two assault battalions, the 1st and 3rd, land abreast over Blue 1 and the southern edge of Blue 2. Similar to the experience of the other assault forces on D-day, Lanigan's Marines encountered only light enemy fire going into the beach at a little past 09.00. When they had gotten only twenty-five yards out onto the beach from their LVTs, however, the Japanese unleashed upon them a hailstorm of mortar, artillery, rocket, and heavy machine gun fire. Battalion Landing Team 1/25 reported at 09.35 that it had advanced 300 yards, and at 10.05, 3/25 reported that elements of the battalion had moved 350 yards northeastward along the beach and that its left flank had penetrated inland 400 yards making contact with 1/25.[17] Marine casualties were mounting steadily while relatively little damage was being done to the Japanese in return.

At 12.00, BLTs 1/25 and 3/25 found that a 100-yard gap had opened between them. This gap obviously had to be plugged, but it could serve a useful purpose while it existed. The source of the murderous volume of fire that the Japanese were bringing down upon the assault battalions was the high ground to the northeast of Beach Blue 1. Colonel Lanigan decided to use his regimental reserve, 2/25, to advance in columns of companies through the gap between the 1st and 3rd Battalions and then to assault the Japanese positions on the high ground. With this plan in mind, BLT 2/25 landed over Beach Blue 1 at 12.50 and moved inland 300 yards to an assembly area. Company E prepared to take up a position between 1/25 and 3/25. The now complete RCT 25 then began a coordinated regimental attack against the high ground above Blue 2 at 14.00. Intense enemy resistance made the going hard and slow. By 17.30, 3/25 was so debilitated by casualties and disorganization that Colonel Lanigan had to request permission from Division to reinforce the battalion with a company from 1/24. Permission was given for this move and the battle raged on. Battalion Landing Team 2/25 reported at 17.45 that it had reached the high ground around the quarry and, at 18.30, Company L, 3/25, reported the same. At 19.00, contact between 2/25 and 3/25 was reestablished. At about the same time, Lieutenant Colonel Justice M. Chambers, commanding officer of 3/25, reported that the combat strength of his battalion was down to 150 men. Relief of the 3rd Battalion, 25th Marines by elements of the 24th Marines, Division Reserve, took place during the night beginning at 18.45 and ending at 23.30.[18]

While RCT 25's desperate battle for the high ground above Blue 2 was being played out, the two direct support battalions of the Fourth Division's artillery

[17] Garand and Strobridge, *Western Pacific Operations,* p. 519; Bartley, *Amphibious Epic,* p. 61.

[18] Garand and Strobridge, *Western Pacific Operations,* pp. 520–21; Bartley, *Amphibious Epic,* pp. 62–63.

regiment, the 14th Marines, were ordered ashore. The 1st Battalion, armed with 75mm Pack Howitzers, struggled to make it onto the island over Beach Blue 1. Its guns were in place and registered by 17.45, ready to provide a much needed artillery punch to RCT 25's attack. The 2nd Battalion, slated to supply direct support for RCT 23, encountered even greater difficulties than did 1/14. The DUKWs carrying its 105mm howitzers could only land on Beach Yellow one at a time because of a combination of surf and beach conditions, but it was finally in place and ready to fire shortly before dusk. The 3rd and 4th Battalions did not make it ashore on D-day.[19]

Strategic and Operational Objectives for Detachment

Thus ended the first day of what was to be the Marine Corps' most difficult battle in its history. An operation that some thought would take only a couple of weeks at the most lasted for thirty-six days and cost the Americans more casualties than they inflicted on the enemy. Such an outcome can be expected from time to time and can be chalked up to "the fortunes of war," but Iwo would be the third time in nine months that the United States failed to properly divine Japanese defensive plans and, as at Biak and Peleliu, the assaulting soldiers and Marines paid the price. As far as Iwo Jima was concerned, what was so important about this small, inconsequential hunk of volcanic rock and sand that it attracted the interest of American planners in the first place? To answer that question, one first needs to understand both the physical characteristics of the objective and how interservice rivalry influenced the decision making process within the Joint Chiefs of Staff.

Iwo Jima ("Sulfur Island") is located in a chain of islands, the Nanpo Shoto, stretching from just beyond the entrance of Tokyo Bay to within 300 miles of the Mariana Islands. There are three island groups making up the chain. The northernmost group, known as Izut Shichito, is composed of six main islands and a number of smaller ones. The center group, named the Ogasawara Gunto but more commonly referred to by Americans during World War II as the Bonin Islands, consists of four islands: Muko Jima, Nishino Shima, Chichi Jima, and Haha Jima. Iwo Jima is found in the center of the third group, the Kazan Retto ("Volcano Archipelago" or "Islands"). American planners tended to lump the Volcano Islands together with the Bonins and use the latter name for all of them, but, technically, the Volcanoes and the Bonins were not the same.[20] As far as Pacific Ocean distances are concerned, this location (24°44' N 141°22' E) placed Iwo in close proximity to several

---

[19] Garand and Strobridge, *Western Pacific Operations,* pp. 521–22; Bartley, *Amphibious Epic,* pp. 64–65.

[20] It can be assumed that when the documents mention the "Bonins," the planners were usually referring to the Bonin and Volcano Islands groups together.

important American objectives: 670 miles south of Tokyo, 625 miles north of Saipan, and 700 miles north of Guam.[21]

Iwo's appearance from the air has been described variously over the years. To this writer's eyes, however, the most accurate comparison is to a pork chop. Covering a total of seven and one-half square miles, the island stretches four and two-thirds miles to the northeast from Tobiishi Point (just southwest of Mount Suribachi) to Kitano Point, and it expands from a width of 700 yards at the landward base of Suribachi to two and one-half miles across the widest part of the northeastern portion. The profile of the island from seaward has been described as looking like a partially submerged whale with Suribachi, an extinct volcano rising 546 feet above sea level, providing the tail and the northeast plateau gently rising above the surface giving the appearance of a whale's head and back.[22]

The presence of Suribachi provides the observer with the most obvious clue as to the origin of the island: Iwo Jima is a young volcanic island, geologically speaking, with sparse vegetation and a moon-like landscape. There is no fringing reef like American forces had encountered so often before in the Pacific and the surrounding waters are free of rock outcroppings. The island affords no natural harbors or protected anchorages of any kind. This is the main reason that Sulfur Island was rarely ever mentioned in the prewar Orange plans. The seabed rises to the beaches very steeply so that within just a few feet of the shoreline, the water is ten to twelve feet deep. Without the protection of a reef or harbor, ships attempting to offload their cargo onto Iwo are pounded by unrelenting open ocean surf that makes a mockery of their efforts. American forces would find just how difficult these conditions could be to overcome on 19 February 1945 when it was too late to do anything but stay the course and hope to God that they could persevere.[23]

To understand how Iwo Jima rose from a strategic irrelevancy to the level of necessary objective one must look into the inner workings of the Joint Chiefs. Robert S. Burrell argues in *The Ghosts of Iwo Jima* that their decision to take this obscure piece of volcanic flotsam was influenced more by interservice rivalry than by realistic strategic considerations.[24] An argument can be made for such a case, and Burrell does a workmanlike job of putting that case forward, but the process was more intricate and open to various and extraneous influences than his explanation implies. One of those influences was Admiral King's insistence that the Marianas be seized and another was his interest in the eventual capture of Formosa. The first

---

[21] Gordon L. Rottman, *World War II Pacific Island Guide: A Geo-Military Study* (Westport, CT: Greenwood, 2002), pp. 417–21; Bartley, *Amphibious Epic*, pp. 4–5; Garand and Strobridge, *Western Pacific Operations*, p. 447.

[22] Rottman, *World War II Pacific Island Guide*, pp. 421–22.

[23] Ibid., p. 422; Miller, *War Plan Orange*, p. 101.

[24] Robert S. Burrell, *The Ghosts of Iwo Jima* (College Station: Texas A&M University Press, 2006), pp. 123–26.

mention of islands in the Nanpo Shoto in the records of the JCS occurs in August of 1943 during the debate over JCS 446. As described in Chapter 5, King wanted to insert a statement into that document that would allow for an eventual movement toward the Marianas. He included the Bonin Islands in this statement along with the Marianas because the inclusion of the former strengthened his argument for an invasion of the latter. Shortly after King won his argument for including this broadening statement in JCS 446, air planners in Washington recommended to the JWPC that the timetable for seizing the Marianas be accelerated and that, by the way, it would be a good idea to establish fighter bases in the Bonin Islands to protect the bombers that would be flying missions over Japan from the Marianas.[25]

Another factor influencing American interest in the Bonins was preparation for the Octagon Conference (12–16 September 1944) and the need to push the British to support an invasion of Japan. The most the British would promise at Sextant was support for an invasion if one should be necessary. The American planners by mid-1944 believed that the preponderance of air, sea, and land power built up by the U.S. in the Pacific argued for the mounting of an invasion as early as was practicable. They presented this argument to the Joint Chiefs on 30 June 1944 in a Joint Staff Planner's report (JCS 924). This paper defined the objective of the war with Japan as the "invasion of the industrial heart of Japan and the seizure of objectives therein, in order to force the unconditional surrender of Japan." What should be the intermediate objectives on the way to the Home Islands? The paper lists them as: "a. Concurrent advances through the Ryukyus, Bonins, and Southeast China coast for the purpose of intensifying the blockade and air bombardment of Japan and creating a situation favorable for: b. An amphibious assault on Kyushu for the purpose of further reducing Japanese capabilities by engaging and fixing major enemy forces and establishing a tactical condition favorable to: c. A decisive stroke against the industrial heart of Japan by means of an amphibious attack through the Tokyo plain assisted by continued pressure from Kyushu."[26] In addition, the JWPC recommended dates from about 1 April to 30 June 1945 for air attacks on the Home Islands and the invasion of the Bonins and the Ryukyus.[27]

The JWPC ventured even further in its recommendations. The members believed that invasion and unconditional surrender needed to be made the basis for future Pacific war planning, but they understood that could be the case only if the British agreed. With persuasion of the British Chiefs at the next conference in mind, then, the American planners suggested that the Combined Chiefs undertake a restatement of the overall objective for the Pacific. They recommended the following wording: "[The overall objective of the war in the Pacific will be t]o force

---

[25] Hayes, *History of the JCS in WWII,* pp. 431 and 496.

[26] Quote found in Hayes, *History of the JCS in WWII,* p. 627.

[27] Hayes, *History of the JCS in WWII,* pp. 627–28.

the unconditional surrender of Japan by: 1. Lowering Japanese ability and will to resist by establishing sea and air blockades, conducting intensive air bombardments, and destroying Japanese air and naval strength. 2. Invading and seizing objectives in the industrial heart of Japan."[28] The British Chiefs, upon receiving a copy of the recommended change, voiced concerns that such a change in the overall objective in the Pacific might jeopardize the already agreed-to priority of "Germany first." The JWPC recommended that the JCS send a reply to the British assuring them that it was not the intent of the United States to jeopardize the war in Europe by undertaking an expansion of the war effort in the Pacific. The JCS sent this reply to the British Chiefs on 4 August, but there was no answer. Finally, during the Octagon Conference, the British gave their approval of the restated objective. It is from this point, then, that the invasion of Japan became the stated ultimate goal of the Pacific war.[29]

The importance of the Army Air Forces' support for King's Marianas operations has already been discussed. What needs to be detailed here is how that same support influenced Operation Detachment. A year after the debate over JCS 446, the idea of capturing an island in the Bonins caught the fancy of more than just the Army Air Forces' planners, but for different reasons. Raymond Spruance, upon returning to Pearl Harbor from the Marianas in early September, met with Nimitz to discuss future operations for the Fifth Fleet. Nimitz told Spruance that the next operation would be Formosa and Amoy, a port on the Chinese coast. Spruance had been studying the question of where U.S. forces should go next whenever a lull in the fighting off the Marianas allowed him the time to do so, and he had come to a different conclusion. He immediately told his boss that he did not like Formosa as an objective. When Nimitz asked him his preference, Spruance said he would prefer seizing Iwo Jima and Okinawa. He knew that the invasion of Formosa was an important component of King's strategy for bringing about the defeat of Japan through the use of a blockade as opposed to an invasion of the Home Islands. Although King had convinced the other members of the JCS at least to consider his Formosa/blockade strategy, however, Spruance knew that there were others beside himself who had doubts about it. One of those people was Chester Nimitz.[30]

Admirals King and Nimitz held another of their periodic conferences in San Francisco from 29 September through 1 October 1944, and, as usual, they discussed the results of recently completed operations as well as issues relating to future operations in the war against Japan. It was during their conversations about the future that Nimitz and his staff put before King their arguments against invading Formosa.

---

[28] Quote found in Hayes, *History of the JCS in WWII*, p. 628.

[29] Hayes, *History of the JCS in WWII*, pp. 628–29.

[30] Buell, *Quiet Warrior*, pp. 331–32; Garand and Strobridge, *Western Pacific Operations*, p. 465.

Instead of Formosa, Nimitz argued in favor of General MacArthur's plan to invade Luzon in the Philippines on 20 December 1944 to be followed by the POA invasion of Iwo Jima on 20 January 1945 and of Okinawa on 1 March 1945. Spruance, who was in attendance, was quiet through most of Nimitz's presentation of the argument for the substitution of Iwo and Okinawa for King's cherished objective off the coast of China. He remained quiet even when Nimitz and some members of his staff mentioned the Army Air Forces' arguments in support of an invasion of Iwo, arguments that Spruance had not relied upon to justify his preference to Nimitz and others prior to the conference. According to Spruance's biographer, his early reasoning was based upon the classic strategic concept of interior versus exterior lines of communication. Since interior lines can be more easily protected than exterior lines, it behooves the strategist to strive to establish the former. Spruance saw Iwo Jima as the focus of an arc running through Tokyo, Kyushu, and the Ryukyus, its capture allowing the U.S. to establish an airbase that would augment American carriers in protecting the fleet from the thousands of airplanes the Japanese had hoarded in the Home Islands. In other words, the capture of Iwo Jima would allow the U.S. to operate along interior lines of communication as it tightened its grip on Japan. Faced with determined and logical opposition to his treasured Formosa strategy from the men he had trusted to fight the Pacific war, King finally relented and agreed to recommend the invasions of Iwo Jima and Okinawa to the Joint Chiefs.[31]

On 2 October, King circulated among the Chiefs the draft of a directive to Nimitz and MacArthur that essentially embodied all that he had discussed with Nimitz and his staff in San Francisco. On 3 October, the JCS sent a directive to MacArthur telling him to prepare to take Luzon on 20 December and they sent another to Nimitz telling him to provide cover and support for MacArthur's operation. Additionally, Nimitz was to begin planning operations against one or more positions in the Bonins and the Ryukyus. With the successful completion of all of these operations, a lodgment on Formosa or the China coast would be unnecessary for the prosecution of a naval and air blockade of Japan. King, Nimitz, and Spruance hoped that it also would mean that there would be no reason for an invasion of the Home Islands. It was now up to Spruance and his Fifth Fleet to carry out the first of the newly-scheduled POA operations—the seizure of Iwo Jima.[32]

---

[31] Potter, *Nimitz,* pp. 326–27; Buell, *Quiet Warrior,* pp. 330–35; Burrell, *Ghosts of Iwo Jima,* p. 35; Hayes, *History of the JCS in WWII,* p. 623.

[32] Hayes, *History of the JCS in WWII,* pp. 623–24; Maurice Matloff, *United States Army in World War II, The War Department, Strategic Planning for Coalition Warfare, 1943–1944* (Washington, DC: Office of the Chief of Military History, Department of the Army, 1959), pp. 530–31.

Resources and Plans for the Assault of Iwo Jima

Tying Operation Detachment so closely to the invasions of Luzon and Okinawa would prove costly in the end. The adverse effect of Luzon and MacArthur's other Philippine operations became evident very early. Nimitz recognized by mid-November that the planned one-month interval between the Luzon and Iwo assaults was too short a period to allow for the transference of shared amphibious and support shipping between commands. In the first of two delays, he recommended that Iwo be put off until 3 February and Okinawa until 15 March to compensate. As MacArthur's forces became bogged down on Leyte, the Japanese fighting tenaciously to hold on to every square inch of the island as long as possible and nature conspiring with the enemy to slow U.S. troop progress and airfield construction to a standstill, the Southwest Pacific commander decided that the Luzon operation would have to be postponed to 9 January. Once again, Nimitz was forced to change the dates of his operations to coordinate with ComSWPac. In early December, Nimitz sent a message to the JCS requesting that the Iwo operation be postponed until 19 February and Okinawa until 1 April. The Joint Chiefs agreed and the dates were set, this time with no subsequent postponement.[33]

Nimitz's staff at Pearl Harbor could not wait for every eventuality to work itself out before beginning to make plans for Detachment. Accordingly, they went right to work upon receipt of the 3 October JCS directive, aiming for the original target date of 20 January. Because the Pacific Ocean Areas was a command made up of elements from all the services, the central planning agency under CinCPOA was a body organized along lines similar to those of the Joint Chief's Joint Staff. This latter group issued a study on 7 October 1944 that was meant to serve as the preliminary planning foundation for all subordinate commands. It was not a directive, however, so CinCPac/CinCPOA was not restricted by it to a particular course of action. Tentative as it was, the description of the purposes of Detachment contained therein was rooted in the ideas of America's top-level planners. These were: "To maintain unremitting military pressure against Japan. To extend our control over the Western Pacific. To establish a base from which we may: (1) Attack the Japanese Empire. (2) Protect our bases in the Marianas. (3) Cover our naval forces and conduct search operations in the approaches to the Japanese Empire. (4) Provide fighter escort for very long range operations."[34] As far as specific tasks were concerned, the study envisioned the following: "(a) To reduce Japanese naval and air strength and production facilities in the Empire. (b) To destroy enemy naval and air strength in the Bonins. (c) To capture, occupy, and defend Iwo Jima and develop an air base on that island."[35] The first of these specific tasks eventually

---

[33] Bartley, *Amphibious Epic,* p. 23; Garand and Strobridge, *Western Pacific Operations,* p. 465.

[34] Quote from Bartley, *Amphibious Epic,* pp. 23–24.

[35] Ibid.

would provide Spruance and Turner with a trump card in their argument with Marine planners over the amount of preliminary naval gunfire at Iwo.[36]

The CinCPOA directive for Operation Detachment came down on 9 October 1944. Nimitz designated in that document the following men to be his top-level commanders at Iwo: Operation Commander, Admiral Raymond A. Spruance; Joint Expeditionary Force Commander, Vice Admiral Richmond Kelly Turner; Commanding General Expeditionary Troops, Lieutenant General Holland M. Smith; and Second in Command Joint Expeditionary Force, Rear Admiral Harry W. Hill. All levels began operational planning at once. Spruance issued his Operation Plan No. 13–44 on 31 December 1944. Considering how Detachment would eventually unfold, it is important to know what Spruance understood—at the time—to be the ultimate objectives of the operation:

> (a) The occupation of SAIPAN, TINIAN, and GUAM has served to establish our shore based air forces in locations from which continuing air attacks are being made against enemy positions in the NANPO SHOTO. Continual reconnaissance from the MARIANAS of the sea areas in the southern approaches to the Japanese Empire is being conducted. The MARIANAS also provide bases from which long range bombers can operate against enemy positions in JAPAN. In order to operate with the greatest effectiveness and with a minimum of attrition, long range bombers should be provided with fighter support at the earliest practicable time. IWO JIMA provides three sites for airfields and is admirably situated as a fighter base for supporting long range bombers between the MARIANAS and the Empire.
>
> (b) The results of carrier attacks on PALAU, MINDANAO, the VISAYAS and LUZON have revealed a weakness of Japanese aviation in their forward areas which will permit more rapid advances. To exploit this situation it is necessary to establish ourselves in positions from which we can engage the enemy in the Empire itself.
>
> (c) Several divisions are now deployed in the South PACIFIC and the Central PACIFIC, from which positions they can be readily mounted for an assault on the NANPO SHOTO. The interval between the LUZON operation and the earliest subsequent operation of comparable size offers the possibility of sufficient time to complete an assault on the NANPO SHOTO without delaying or interfering with other scheduled operations.

[36] Bartley, *Amphibious Epic,* pp. 23–24; Garand and Strobridge, *Western Pacific Operations,* pp. 465–66.

(d) This assault will be executed in a single phase, with two divisions employed simultaneously in such a manner that the complete subjugation and occupation of the island will be quickly effected, after which all major assault troop units will be evacuated, leaving the development and defense of the island in the hands of garrison forces.[37]

There are two observations to be made here. First, Spruance concentrated his attention on the greater strategic questions concerning the operation rather than on the problems associated with taking the immediate objective. One cannot read too much into this conclusion alone, however, because Spruance himself admitted that he was a better strategist than a tactician and, also, he had operated successfully in this way in every operation prior to Detachment.[38] Second, Spruance initially believed that seizing Iwo would not be too difficult a proposition and that, consequently, Detachment would fit in neatly between the two larger operations in the Philippines and the Ryukyus. By itself, this last assumption would not be harmful. The combination of the two, however, would prove deadly to the Marines tasked with assaulting Sulfur Island because this combination would heavily influence Spruance when it came time to decide how many days of preliminary naval gunfire bombardment to provide the assault troops. Spruance did not make these decisions without being aware of how the greater strategic picture was affecting his thinking. In his report on the Iwo operation, he explained some of his decisions in these words:

> The planning for and the actual execution of the Iwo Jima operation were affected to a considerable extent by the operations in the Philippines which immediately preceded it, and by the necessity of preparing for the Okinawa operation which was to follow it.
>
> The Philippine operations necessitated last minute changes and reduced the total number of ships which had been previously allocated to the Iwo Jima operation. This applied primarily to battleships, cruisers, and destroyers for the Joint Expeditionary Force, although other forces were also affected to a lesser extent. . . .
>
> The Okinawa operation affected the Iwo Jima operation in two ways. First, it was felt that the threat of Japanese land based aircraft, while taking Okinawa, would be very great, both because of the great value of that island to us when we took it and because of its closeness to the Empire (325 miles). Therefore, anything which we could do during the Iwo Jima

[37] MCUA, Iwo Jima Project, Commander Fifth Fleet, Fifth Fleet Operations Plan, 13–44, 13 December 1944, p. B-1.

[38] Buell, *Quiet Warrior*, p. 332.

> operation to reduce Japanese air strength, either in aircraft and, even more, in aircraft production facilities, would help the Okinawa operation as well as support the Iwo Jima operation. The second way in which the Okinawa operation and the Iwo Jima operation affected each other was in the close timing of the two operations. D-day for the Iwo Jima operation was 19 February. L-day for the Okinawa operation had been set as 1 April. If the fighting ashore on Iwo Jima were prolonged, it might be difficult to carry out the plans for the Okinawa operation which called for initial carrier operations to start off Kyushu on L-minus-9 (23 March).[39]

While it is true that this is a summary written after Detachment had been completed and, therefore, can be seen as an attempt at justification after the fact, comparison of this statement with the objectives stated in Spruance's plan for the operation shows that similar ideas were uppermost in his mind from the very beginning.

All of the commanders named in Nimitz's 9 October directive received that document at the same time, and they, like Spruance, began preliminary planning based upon it and the 7 October CinCPOA study. The following table[40] details the principal commanders of the most important commands taking part in Operation Detachment:

Commander	Command
Admiral Raymond A. Spruance	5th Fleet
Vice Admiral R. K. Turner	Joint Expeditionary Force
Rear Admiral William H. P. Blandy	Amphibious Support Forces
Rear Admiral Harry W. Hill	Attack Force
Rear Admiral Bertram J. Rodgers	Gunfire and Covering Force
Lieutenant General H. M. Smith	Expeditionary Troops
Major General Harry Schmidt	Landing Force (V Amphib. Corps)
Major General Clifton B. Cates	4th MarDiv (Assault Troops)
Major General Keller E. Rockey	5th MarDiv (Assault Troops)
Major General Graves B. Erskine	3rd MarDiv (Exp. Troops Res.)
Vice Admiral Marc A. Mitscher	5th Fleet Fast Carrier Force

The largest of the commands subordinate to Spruance was TF 51, Admiral Turner's Joint Expeditionary Force. As commander of this task force, Turner coordinated Blandy's, Hill's, Rogers,' and H. M. Smith's planning and the execution of

[39] MCUA, Historical Amphibious Files (HAF), Box 11B, Folders 255, United States Navy, *Amphibious Operations: Capture of Iwo Jima, 16 February–16 March 1945* (hereinafter COMINCH P-0012), p. 1-1.

[40] Table information taken from Derrick Wright, *The Battle for Iwo Jima, 1945* (Stroud: Sutton, 1999), pp. 197–98.

those plans. Task Force 51 was comprised of 495 ships for use in the initial assault and the first garrison echelon and 75,144 men in the landing force, 70,647 of those being Marines.[41]

It was Turner's responsibility to flesh out Commander Fifth Fleet's concept of the operation. The plan he devised to accomplish this goal, ComPhibsPac No. A25–44, laid out the basic scheme of attack for 19 February 1945. Turner would wear more hats in executing the Iwo operation than he had ever had to wear at one time before. Because of the number of ships and men and the intricacies of the required command structure, he could not oversee everything personally as he would have liked. He had divided his forces before in the Gilberts, Marshalls, and Marianas because it was necessary to do so in order to take multiple objectives as part of the same operation. He preferred to command the assault at whichever objective he was present, though he had already had to give over command of part of the assault at Saipan and all of it at Tinian to Harry Hill because of the complexity of the Marianas operation. He would do the same at Iwo Jima.

Harry Hill as commander of TF 53, the Attack Force, once again would be the assault commander. Under Hill would be the transports, Landing Force troops, escorts, control vessels, and other various assigned units whose job it would be to carry out the invasion.[42] Turner kept one important tactical command for himself, however. Rear Admiral Blandy would command TF 52, the Amphibious Support Force, until a certain point in the invasion and then he would have to give over command to Turner. This is how Turner describes the change of command in his plan:

> Task Force 52 . . . , initially under the command of Rear Admiral BLANDY, comprising assigned gunfire support vessels, certain CVE's [*sic*], minesweepers, and Underwater Demolition Teams. After arrival at the objective, the operations of all aircraft and gunfire vessels from other forces, *while they are engaged in direct attack on the objective,* will also be under this command. At 0700(K) Dog Day, command of Task Force 52, (less attachments) [*sic*] will pass to Commander Task Force 51. Thereupon, Rear Admiral BLANDY will report to Commander Task Force 51 as Commander Task Group 51.19 for command of Transport and Tractor Night Retirement Groups. . . .[43]

---

[41] Dyer, *The Amphibians Came to Conquer,* Vol. II, p. 997.

[42] Isely and Crowl, *U.S. Marines and Amphibious War,* p. 435.

[43] MCUA, Iwo Jima Project, Commander Amphibious Forces (CTF 51) Operation Plan, A25–44 (Bound Book) (hereinafter CTF 51 Operation Plan), Commander Amphibious Forces (CTF 51) Operation Plan No. A25–44, Iwo Jima Operation, Annex A, pp. (A)-1–(A)-2. Emphasis in original.

This change of command will affect the use of naval gunfire on D-day because of the tactical relationship between TF 52 and TF 54. Rear Admiral Rodgers' Gunfire and Covering Force, composed of old battleships, cruisers, and destroyers, was tasked with providing cover against possible enemy surface attack as well as gunfire support of the invasion. They were to be directed by Blandy in the latter's capacity as Commander TF 52. When Turner took command from Blandy at 07.00 on the morning of D-day, he also assumed overall control of gunfire support for the assaulting troops. Thus, the man who was in command of the preliminary bombardment of the objective for almost three days prior to Turner's arrival and consequently was more familiar with the situation at the objective on the morning of 19 February was arbitrarily demoted in the command hierarchy so that Turner could be as hands-on as possible.[44]

Turner's plan for Iwo was rooted in the plans he and his staff had produced so many times before. The best sketch of what he expected to happen is in the plan itself, and the following shows how all-encompassing plans at Turner's level had to be:

> 3. Task force 53 will embark troops in the HAWAIIAN ISLANDS and hold preliminary rehearsals there. Task Group 51.1 will embark troops at GUAM. Task Force 52 will assemble for preliminary training at ULITHI. All of Task Force 51, less TG 51.1 and Defense and Garrison Groups [,] will then assemble at SAIPAN for final rehearsals prior to proceeding to the objective. TG 51.1 will not participate in SAIPAN rehearsals, but will sail from GUAM direct for the objective.
>
> 4. Naval elements of the Joint Expeditionary Force from HAWAII will move to ENIWETOK for re-supply, and then to SAIPAN. At SAIPAN, vessels other than battleships, transport types, and LST's [*sic*] will be topped off with fuel. Vessels which are not self-sustaining in water will be topped off with water as required. The movement of supply vessels will be as directed by Commander FIFTH Fleet.
>
> 5. The landing attack on IWO JIMA will be made on the southeast coast, (preferred), or on the northwest coast, (alternate plan), the landing being delayed as necessary to ensure reasonably favorable weather. The Commander-in Chief [*sic*], U.S. Pacific Fleet, has been requested to provide long-range weather forecasts. . . .
>
> 6. The Assault Troops will include selected elements of the Garrison Force. The main strength of our own shore anti-aircraft, coastal

[44] Ibid., p. (A)-2.

battery elements, and ground aircraft formations will begin to arrive at the objective one day after the initial landings. The Expeditionary Troops Reserve will be sent forward in time to arrive at the objective on Dog plus Two [marked through and "One" inserted]. The succeeding garrison echelons will begin to arrive at the objective about five days after the intial landings, on order from the Senior Officer Present Afloat at the objective. Garrison echelons, prior to proceeding to the objective, will go to ENIWETOK or SAIPAN, as directed, to await orders of the Senior Officer Present Afloat at the objective. . . .

8. Upon completion of the capture of IWO JIMA, and upon being relieved by the 147th Army Infantry Regiment (from NEW CALEDONIA), the THIRD, FOURTH, and the FIFTH Marine Divisions will be evacuated to GUAM, SAIPAN, and GUAM, respectively. Corps Troops will also be evacuated to GUAM.
9. Close cooperation must be effected between opposite numbers of the troops and the supporting elements of the Navy. Personal conferences will be held between the officers of the various services whose plans require coordination. This close personal cooperation must extend all the way from the top echelons down to and including boats' crews and troops. It is most important that Beach Party and Shore Party Commanders prepare joint plans, and engage in joint training; whenever possible, these officers and at least nucleii [*sic*] of their parties will be embarked in the same vessels. Garrison Force plans must be integrated with those of the assault troops. . . .
11. Each service embarked in a vessel is responsible to the commanding officer for guarding its own property against theft and loss. Commanding Officers of vessels and troops will ensure that effective steps are taken to prevent such loss, and immediate reports will be made in case losses occur. After debarkation of troops, Commanding Officers of ships will cause a very careful search to be made to ensure that troop property left on board is collected and safeguarded for return to the proper organizations. Disciplinary measures will be instituted where appropriate.
12. All commanders, in advance of the operation, will take steps to indoctrinate all hands against pillage and souvenir-hunting; and will assign specific responsibility for preventing pillage and souvenir-hunting.[45]

[45] Ibid., pp. (A)-2–(A)-4.

This plan provided the various elements of TF 51 with necessary guidance for their clash with the Japanese on Iwo Jima. Eventually, after more than a month of grueling, pitiless battle, the Marines of V Amphibious Corps prevailed—at the cost of 5,885 dead and 17,318 wounded and missing.[46]

The Japanese Plan for the Defense of Iwo Jima

Lieutenant General Tadamichi Kuribayashi, the newly-installed commander of the 109th Division of the Imperial Japanese Army in the Volcano Islands, was a rare example in the Imperial Japanese Army of an officer who was not averse to learning and adapting. He was given the responsibility of preparing Iwo Jima for an anticipated American invasion and he knew that it would be a difficult assignment at best. Studying the tactics Japanese forces had used in earlier Pacific island battles and paying special attention to the defense of Biak, Peleliu, Angaur, and Luzon, Kuribayashi concluded that standard Japanese doctrine would not suffice. If he were to last for more than a few days against the American juggernaut then he would have to approach his situation from a purely defensive perspective, a perspective generally abhorred by the Japanese.[47]

Having decided to throw away convention, Kuribayashi issued orders that stirred controversy among his more militarily conventional subordinates. First, he chose to establish his headquarters on Iwo rather than on the larger island of Chichi Jima. Second, all civilians on Iwo were evacuated, including "comfort girls," and all alcohol consumption was banned. Third, all facilities were moved underground and mining engineers were brought from Japan to design the necessarily extensive tunnel system needed for the implementation of the general's plan. The engineers produced a design that integrated existing caves with constructed tunnels, providing the Iwo defenders with adequate ventilation and protection from naval gunfire. Fourth, conceding that the Americans would take the landing beaches, he concentrated his defenses in the central and northern highlands of the island. This decision proved to be his most controversial. Rear Admiral Toshinosuke Ichimaru, in particular, pressured Kuribayashi to modify his plan in this regard. The general eventually bowed to the pressure and, in a compromise, ordered that 135 pillboxes be constructed along the most obvious landing beaches in the southern part of the island. As Kuribayashi foresaw, the Americans overran these pillboxes within three hours. Fifth, large-scale *banzai* attacks were strictly forbidden. This was another point of contention with his subordinates. To die a glorious death in battle when the odds were totally against success was considered

[46] Garand and Strobridge, *Western Pacific Operations*, p. 797.

[47] United States War Department, *Handbook on Japanese Military Forces* (London: Greenhill Books/Lionel Leventhal, 1991; reprint, Baton Rouge: Louisiana State University Press, 1995), p. 99 (page citations in the present volume are to the reprint edition).

every Japanese soldier's duty. Contrary to the spirit of this deeply ingrained tenet of the Japanese warrior ethos, all counterattacks were to be carefully considered and efficiently carried out. Individual glory and honor were relegated to secondary status—the defense of the island was primary. With this concept of efficient counterattack in mind, small groups of troops were to be sent out at night into the American lines to gather intelligence, damage equipment, and kill Marines.[48]

Kuribayashi issued his final defensive plan just before the battle began. His emphasis was on the maintenance of a flexible defense that would wear down the enemy. He ordered his artillery to remain silent during the preliminary bombardment of the island so as not to give their positions away too early in the battle. He stressed that he did not want the landings opposed by any of his men. Let the Americans land! Once the invading forces had come ashore and advanced up the beach approximately 500 yards, automatic weapons in the vicinity of Motoyama Airfield #2, along with automatic weapons and artillery on the high ground north of the landing beaches and around Mount Suribachi to the south, would rain concentrated fire down on them. The general's purpose was not to defeat the Americans. He knew that U.S. control of the sea, principally as a result of the effectiveness of its submarine force, ensured that he could not win.[49] Instead, he would inflict the maximum number of casualties on the American invasion force as was humanly possible. Once the artillery had done all the damage that it could do from its original positions on the high ground above the beaches, then it was to move northward to continue its mission. Infliction of casualties was the rule. If he could not win with the offensive, then maybe he could cause the Americans to lose heart and give up, or, barring that unlikely outcome, then maybe massive casualties on Iwo Jima might cause the American public to think twice about carrying the fight all the way to the Japanese Home Islands.[50]

Naval Gunfire at Iwo Jima—The "Lessons" Made Irrelevant

The battle for Iwo Jima actually began in June of 1944 when the U.S. Navy carried out the first large-scale carrier raid against the island. Regularly scheduled air strikes began taking place in August and the pre-invasion strategic bombing

[48] Bartley, *Amphibious Epic,* p. 11; Garand and Strobridge, *Western Pacific Operations,* pp. 453–59; Joseph H. Alexander, *Storm Landings: Epic Amphibious Battles in the Central Pacific* (Annapolis: Naval Institute Press, 1997), p. 132.

[49] Alexander points out on page 61 of *Storm Landings* that the U.S. submarine force was placing increasing pressure on the Japanese ability to send supplies out to its garrison forces in the Pacific. The ease with which they had been able to supply Betio would not be the norm for 1944 and 1945.

[50] Garand and Strobridge, *Western Pacific Operations,* pp. 456–57; Alexander, *Storm Landings,* pp. 131–32.

campaign against Iwo got underway on 8 December. For seventy-four consecutive days, Seventh Air Force B-24s and Marine PBJs (the Navy variation of the B-25 Mitchell bomber) based in the Marianas dropped payload after payload on islands in the Bonin and Volcano groups. Beginning 31 January 1945, air operations against Iwo entered a new phase. The number of sorties per day was increased in preparation for the beginning of the preliminary naval gunfire on 16 February. The stated purpose for the bombing was the neutralization of the airfields and other installations on the island, the destruction of gun positions and various fixed defenses, and the unmasking of additional targets for the naval gunfire ships. On 16 February, the same day on which naval gunfire preparation began, the daylight air attacks were stepped up even further and night harassing missions were thrown in for good measure. To top the whole air campaign off, fighter sweeps shot up every airplane and living thing the pilots could find on the island.[51]

Photographic reconnaissance monitored the damage done by these air strikes. A comparison of photos taken between 3 December 1944 and 10 February 1945 showed that, while appreciable damage had been done to aircraft on the ground and that the airfields had indeed been neutralized, the Japanese had not been stopped in their attempts to strengthen Iwo's defenses. A study submitted to the Chief of Staff of VAC on 9 February 1945 shows the concern of Marine Corps planners for this lack of results: "Photographic coverage of Iwo Jima to 24 January 1945 indicates that damage to installations resulting from bombing strikes between 3 December 1944 and 24 January 1945 was, on the whole, negligible. These strikes have apparently not prevented the enemy from improving his defensive position and, as of 24 January 1945, his installations of all categories had notably increased in number. The island is now far more heavily defended by gun positions and field fortifications than it was on 15 October 1944, when initial heavy bombing strikes were initiated."[52] With the air campaign not accomplishing its goals, the preliminary naval gunfire bombardment grew in importance proportionately.[53]

One of the enduring stories of the assault on Iwo is that the Americans did not know what they were up against until it was too late to do anything about it. This was not true. The above quote shows that at least some of the operational planners were very well aware of the fact that Iwo was a tough objective. The question was what to do about it. It is out of consideration of this problem that the great debate arose over how much preliminary naval gunfire bombardment to provide. Central Pacific experience and published doctrine dictated several days of slow, thorough preparation, and Nimitz's headquarters included eight days of preliminary gunfire

---

[51] Garand and Strobridge, *Western Pacific Operations,* pp. 485–86.

[52] Quote from Garand and Strobridge, *Western Pacific Operations,* p. 486.

[53] Garand and Strobridge, *Western Pacific Operations,* pp. 486–87.

support in their original plan with this in mind.[54] Spruance, strategic concerns uppermost in his mind, decided that eight days were too many given the need to coordinate Detachment with simultaneous carrier air raids on the Japanese Home Islands and with the subsequent invasion of Okinawa. There were logistical considerations as well. He would need more gunfire support ships than he could obtain at the time because of MacArthur's continuing problems in the Philippines. As Spruance himself put it in his After Action Report: "The only source from which additional gunfire support ships could be obtained was from Task Force 58 (Fast Carrier Force). In order to provide the necessary additional battleships for gunfire support, the Commander in Chief, United States Pacific Fleet, authorized the use of the North Carolina and Washington for this purpose. These two ships were, accordingly, loaded principally with bombardment ammunition, their service allowance of armor piercing ammunition being correspondingly reduced. Certain cruisers of Task Force 58 were also loaded with some additional bombardment ammunition."[55]

Another logistical consideration besides the number of ships available was how to keep the ships he could get supplied with large-caliber ammunition over the course of a long bombardment. Spruance determined that the best that could be done, given all of these problems and questions, was to bombard Iwo for three days prior to the invasion.[56]

There is other evidence besides that presented above that the top American planners were aware of at least some of the difficulties the assaulting forces would face on Iwo Jima. The following description is found in the final version of the naval gunfire annex of Turner's Operation Plan A25–44:

> IWO JIMA is a relatively small but heavily defended island presenting a series of integrated defense installations which will require a carefully coordinated scheme of fire from all attacking agencies. It must be emphasized that advanced intelligence cannot be expected to disclose more than a fraction of existing defenses. Close observation, both visual and photographic, plus imagination stimulated by a close study of the terrain, are of the utmost importance in locating others. . . . Inshore the ground rises rapidly in a series of terraces culminating in steep embankments surrounding built-up and graded portions of Airfields 1 and 2. The entire slope is covered by fire trenches, emplacements, pillboxes, rifle and machine gun pits and a few blockhouses, all of which must be destroyed or

[54] Isely and Crowl, *U.S. Marines and Amphibious War,* p. 441.

[55] COMINCH P-0012, p. 1-1.

[56] MCUA, Box 35, Folder 649, Collection of communications between parties concerning naval gunfire requirements for the invasion of Iwo Jima (hereinafter Collection of Communications).

> neutralized prior to How Hour by short range direct fire or air bursts as appropriate. The beaches are flanked on the North by cliffs and steep slopes extending South from MINAMI and on the South by SURIBACHI MOUNTAIN, both of which are brush covered and offer excellent possibilities for the usual Japanese camouflage and defense from cave positions.[57]

Joseph Alexander states that Nimitz's intelligence section was aware that Japanese defensive tactics were changing but that a bulletin from his command forecasting Iwo Jima's defenses to be more along the lines of Peleliu's than Roi-Namur's or Saipan's did not receive much attention from the planners of the Iwo assault.[58] The description of the conditions Turner expected to find on Iwo presented above indicates that someone on Turner's staff actually had given the photographic evidence and Nimitz's bulletin more than just a cursory glance.

Generals Smith and Schmidt knew from hard experience that a target as tough as Iwo Jima required massive amounts of naval gunfire preparation over several days in order to soften it up sufficiently for assault. They knew that Spruance and Turner were set on three days of naval gunfire, and they wrote numerous letters to the two admirals in a battle to get them to authorize more. In one of the first of these, dated 24 October 1944, Schmidt lists the basic assumptions from which he and his planners were working in making their determinations:

> (a) That all known defensive installations must be destroyed.
> (b) That a minimum of 50% more targets will be uncovered during preliminary bombardment and that to discover these targets it will be necessary to fire a considerable amount of ammunition for the purpose of blasting away camouflage and concealment.
> (c) That a methodical "working over" with major caliber ammunition of the slopes of the crater on the south flank and the terrain formation on the north flank will be required to uncover and destroy concealed emplacements and casemates.

[57] CTF 51 Operation Plan, Ships' Gunfire Support Plan, pp. 4–5.

[58] Alexander, *Storm Landings,* p. 129. The report was CINCPAC-CINCPOA Bulletin No. 9–45, "Iwo Jima: First Supplement to Nanpo Shoto Information Bulletin No. 122–44," dated 10 January 1945. Isely and Crowl seem to allude to the same document on p. 436, but they do not name the source. They also report on the same page that records captured in the Marianas outlined the basic defensive plan for Iwo and that aerial reconnaissance photographs showed work continuing on island defenses despite almost daily American air and periodic sea bombardment.

(d) That from one to four major caliber direct hits will be required to destroy known defensive installations and that 10% hits is the average expected occurring in direct fire.[59]

With these and other considerations taken into account, Schmidt recommended:

(a) That a minimum period of ten days be allotted for naval bombardment of (IWO Jima).

(b) In addition to the Cruiser Division now allotted, that a minimum of one division of BB's [*sic*] be added for preliminary bombardment.

(c) That a staff trained and equipped to evaluate results be present to assess the results of preliminary bombardment and to make target assignments; that this staff not only include gunfire personnel but also support air personnel and that this staff be present on SAIPAN by D-20 to study results of 7th AAF bombing.

(d) That the date of D-Day be dependent on the successful prosecution of the destruction of enemy defensive installations. . . .[60]

Smith forwarded Schmidt's request on to Turner on 26 October with his recommendation and the comment that "[i]n order to insure the quick seizure of the objective with a minimum of casualties, the increase in the duration of intensity of naval preliminary bombardment over that now contemplated is considered a necessity."[61] Turner sent his reply on 15 November. He turned Schmidt down, explaining in similar terms as Spruance would have used and offering a plan of his own:

> . . . Limitations on the availability of ships, difficulties of replenishment of ammunition and lose [*sic*] of surprise interpose serious obstacles to meeting your recommendations. However, it is felt that the following plan will accomplish all the objectives desired:
>
> (a) It is understood that (IWO Jima) will be bombarded by one Cruiser Division on or about 15 December and at irregular intervals thereafter. Bombardment will be for the purpose of accomplishing such destruction as is possible, and for establishing a flow of intelligence of target destruction supplementing that expected from air strikes during the same period.

[59] Collection of Communications, p. 1.

[60] Ibid., p. 6.

[61] Ibid., p. 8.

(b) On Dog minus three, a methodical and thorough bombardment will be instituted by the Amphibious Support Force. Competent evaluation of results and corresponding adjustments in the bombardment plan will be assured through control and coordination by an Amphibious Group Commander embarked in an AGC (with representative of your command aboard if desired). The increased number of bombardment ships and local control and evaluation of results will enable more ammunition to be delivered at the target in three days than the estimated requirements listed [in your request] for ten days. . . . It is believed that the excess of 5," 14," and 16" capabilities [in this plan] over your estimate of requirements will more than offset the apparent shortage of 6" and 8" capabilities.

(c) Emphasis will be placed on the securing and utilization of all information of target destruction.[62]

Turner, like so many Navy men before him, places the emphasis on the amount of ordnance to be put on the target. He speaks of "destruction," but he does not appear to understand, at least as far as the wording of this letter is concerned, that destruction can only occur when that massive quantity of ammunition is delivered slowly and methodically, a point the Marines will continue to make.

On 24 November, General Schmidt sent a letter to Turner in which he conceded that he would not receive the ten days he had requested, but he provided evidence to support a request for four days instead of three:

2. As has been stated in previous correspondence, the preliminary bombardment should provide for the deliberate and methodical destruction of all known or subsequently located enemy gun positions and other installations that can interfere with the successful execution of the landing. The question is whether the time now allotted is adequate for deliberate destruction. The amount of ammunition allotted appears to be adequate.

3. Since this question may be determined accurately in advance, two alternatives suggest themselves:

    (a) To provide for an additional day of bombardment prior to the landing, if it is found during the preliminary bombardment that all known targets can not be destroyed prior to D-Day. This involves obtaining early information by the Expeditionary Force Commander in order that orders could be issued in time to task forces at sea as to the postponement. Under conditions

[62] Ibid., pp. 9–10.

of radio silence, and the dispersion of forces involved, this would appear difficult. The target date in this case would be postponed one day.

(b) Allot four days for the preliminary bombardment. This would allow for more deliberate firing, particularly after necessary minesweeping has been effected [*sic*]. It theoretically would involve no increase in the expenditure of ammunition, but rather a slower rate of fire. Any increase in ammunition requirements would have to come from that allocated to call fire.

(c) It is recommended that, if consistent with other considerations, the plan outlined in paragraph 3(b) above be adopted and that the preliminary bombardment begin on D-4.[63]

General Smith, sending Schmidt's latest request on to Turner with his recommendation, added the following:

1. From lessons learned in previous operations and continued study and analysis of the proposed Operation (against IWO Jima), it is the considered opinion of this Headquarters that four (4) full days for preliminary bombardment is the absolute minimum necessary for success.
2. This objective lends itself to a strong defense with elaborate installations, and unless these defenses are destroyed or at least neutralized we may expect casualties far beyond any heretofore suffered in the Central Pacific, or possibly jeopardize the success of the entire operation. It is considered that three (3) days for preliminary bombardment are insufficient.
3. A comparison of casualties suffered on SAIPAN after an approximate three (3) days of preliminary bombardment with the casualties received on TINIAN and GUAM after many days of preliminary bombardment further convinces this Headquarters of the necessity for a minimum of at least four (4) days of preliminary bombardment. . . .[64]

Both Smith and Schmidt refer to accepted doctrine to explain why they are requesting more naval gunfire and Smith points out that the lessons learned thus far in the Pacific support this claim. The Marines are pleading with their Navy superiors upon what they believe to be irrefutable grounds.

---

[63] Ibid., p. 25.

[64] Ibid., p. 26.

It is at this point that Spruance himself weighed in on the debate. On 2 December 1944, he sent a letter to Turner refusing to allow the additional day of bombardment. He drew the greater strategic picture for Turner so that the latter could leave Schmidt and Smith with no illusions as to what the overall commander thought:

> 1. The recommendation of Commanding General, V Amphibious Corps, that surface ship bombardment of (IWO Jima) be commenced on D minus 4 Day is not approved for the following reasons:
>   (a) The initial surface bombardment must be simultaneous with the initial carrier attack upon the TOKYO area. The carrier attacks will be continued there for three days if practicable, but it may prove desirable or necessary to discontinue attacks after two days or less. If the attacks were made on D minus 4 and D minus 3 days, time would then be available to the enemy for recovery and reinforcement early enough to initiate threatening air operations at the objective by D day.
>   (b) The situation at (IWO Jima) will be different from that encountered at SAIPAN for reason that by D day the enemy personnel and fixed defenses at (IWO Jima) will have been under heavy shore based air attack for a considerable period of time. This prolonged air bombardment, which was not undertaken at SAIPAN, may be considered at least as effective as the recommended additional day of surface ship bombardment.
>   (c) The trench and pill box [*sic*] defense system at IWO Jima is strong and must be taken by assault, supported, until shore artillery can be emplaced, by intense naval gunfire on D day. There will be no early opportunity for replacement of naval ammunition, a large proportion of which must be saved for support of D day. There is a limit to the quantity of ammunition which can be made available for pre D day bombardment and no advantage is seen in delivering that quantity in four days rather than three.[65]

Spruance placed great faith in the air attacks, but, as the Marines were beginning to learn at about the time the Commander Fifth Fleet was writing this letter, the air campaign was not the equivalent of that extra day of naval gunfire.

---

[65] Ibid., p. 28.

Schmidt and Smith tried again in early January, pointing out that photographic reconnaissance was not bearing out Spruance's predictions concerning air bombing.[66] Turner, wanting to bring the debate to an end, sent one last letter to the Marine generals on 9 January in which he took them to task for sticking so closely to the "lessons" the Marines thought they had learned thus far in the Pacific war. First, as to the idea that naval gunfire ships should emphasize short-range bombardment, Turner commented:

> 4. It is not agreed that short ranges are always the most effective for destructive fire. The best experience, as clearly set forth in the PhibsPac Circular letter AL15-Rev. 1, indicates that short range [*sic*] pointed fire is best for targets that present an appreciable vertical surface. On the other hand, short range firing at flat targets wastes ammunition because so many ricochets and duds occur. Therefore, a considerable amount of long and medium range firing must be done, to take care of the many flat targets on (IWO Jima). For example, it would be quite impossible to hit any targets on the tops of the hills by means of short-range fire.[67]

While it is true that the flat trajectories of naval guns makes it exceedingly difficult for them to hit non-vertical targets, it is also true that hitting targets from longer ranges requires more firings and, therefore, more time. This would mean that Turner would have to allow more time than the three days he was willing to allot in order for the massive quantity of ordnance he stressed so heavily in his 15 November letter to be used effectively. This paradox did not seem to occur to him at the time.

Second, as to the continued attempts by the Marine generals to change the naval gunfire schedule, Turner wrote:

> 5. The firing schedules were originally prepared in collaboration with representatives of ComGenVPhibCorps [Schmidt] and ComGenFMFPac [Smith]. Then after a final check, before issue, they were completely revised at the request of representatives of ComGenVPhibCorps in order to allow every ship the maximum possible firing time. The allotment of ammunition to targets was also changed radically. More time for general targets could be allotted than as directed in the present plan if it were not considered necessary to perform UDT operations on the Alternate Beaches. If UDT reconnaissance of the Alternate Beaches shows

[66] Garand and Strobridge, *Western Pacific Operations,* p. 492.

[67] Collection of Communications, pp. 34–35.

> that no beach demolitions are necessary, then there will be more time and ammunition available for bombardment of the Preferred Beaches. However, it should be recognized that fire for covering UDT operations is *all* directed at targets that will particularly threaten troops.[68]

Schmidt and Smith could point out to Turner that their original estimates for gunfire were based on incomplete photographic reconnaissance and that their attempts to modify what they had already approved were based upon the latest evidence at their disposal, not on any wish to be obstinate. Turner was aware of the new evidence as well, but he does not show in this letter that his awareness of it is affecting his decisions. He is also not indicating that he understood that three days was not the original amount of naval gunfire projected, Nimitz's command having recommended eight days instead. In an attempt to assure Schmidt and Smith that the gunfire ships would be performing double duty and, in so doing, would be destroying targets deemed important by the Marines, Turner stresses the work of the covering ships in protecting the Underwater Demolition Teams (UDT).

Third, concerning a Marine Corps emphasis on the landing beaches, Turner added:

> 6. The concentration of more firing vessels off the Preferred Beaches as desired by ComGenVPhibCorps would result in very thin coverage of the other portions of the objective. Guns in such locations can most probably be used to fire on the Preferred Beach area after How Hour. Therefore they too should be destroyed. If the recommendations in the basic letter are approved, the coverage of the Alternate Beaches would be only about 25% of that on the Preferred Beaches, and this is believed to be too small. Most assuredly, it is not proposed to fire on coast defense batteries only on Dog minus THREE, and thereafter concentrate only on what are spoken of in [your] basic letter as "troop targets." Any such procedure would be unsound to an extreme degree. It is essential that coast defense and anti-aircraft batteries receive a great deal of attention.[69]

It is most ironic that Turner is making a point here, over a month before the beginning of the preliminary naval gunfire bombardment of the objective, which would prove accurate as to what the Marines would find upon assaulting the beaches of Iwo. This point will be discussed in greater depth presently.

---

[68] Ibid., p. 35. Emphasis in original.

[69] Ibid.

And finally, to allay any fears that Turner was placing the naval gunfire schedule on the level of Scripture, something that could not be modified under any circumstances, he asserted: "7. ComPhibGrp ONE [Blandy] as, Commander Support Force, will be in charge of the preliminary bombardment. He has been given full authority to change schedules of fire to meet eventualities as they develop. He is fully cognizant of the features brought out in the basic letter and endorsements, and has been instructed to exercise discretion in modifying schedules to get the best results as a whole from the air and ship bombardments."[70] This concession on Turner's part gave the Marines an out, an opportunity to conform the firing schedule to what they considered more appropriate based on experience and doctrine, in case the situation at the objective proved contrary to what the planners expected. They would take advantage of this option. As they saw it, they had no choice because three days was all they were going to get as far as Raymond Spruance and Kelly Turner were concerned.

Though known to be a workaholic, Turner did not produce his plans by himself. The nuts and bolts of the different sections of an invasion plan were torqued together by many different officers from many different backgrounds and specialties. One such person who had significant input in the creation of the Detachment naval gunfire support plan was Lieutenant Colonel Donald M. Weller. He served as the VAC naval gunfire officer at Iwo Jima and it was his job, in part, to work with the Navy to make sure that Marine Corps gunfire support concerns were addressed as the operation unfolded. Weller was present during the preliminary bombardment from D-3 to D-1 and he was instrumental in the making of decisions concerning the application and the altering of the original gunfire plan. His after action comments are extremely instructive because of his intimate knowledge of how and why those alterations were made. Weller reported that ships engaged targets during the preliminary bombardment according to an established priority system. The assignment of targets in this way was in line with established doctrine. Priority A targets consisted of installations that could threaten ships and aircraft of the invasion force and underwater demolition team operations. Examples included: any battery that opened fire on ships or aircraft of the invasion force, all coast defense guns, all anti-aircraft guns, all covered or open artillery emplacements where the presence of weapons was confirmed, and all anti-tank guns. Priority B targets consisted of installations that threatened the Landing Force in the ship to shore movement. Examples of these targets included: blockhouses; covered artillery; pillboxes; and various targets such as command posts, unspecified unidentified installations, earth-covered structures, machine guns, and areas of heavy growth. Priority C targets consisted of installations that could oppose troops after the landing had taken place. This was a broad category that included such targets as caves

[70] Ibid.

near the beach, radio and radar stations, ammunition storage areas, fuel dumps, and bivouac areas.[71]

Weller reports that targets were addressed according to this priority system on D-3 and D-2, but photographic assessments of damage caused by the bombardment on those two days indicated that the level of destruction that had been achieved was unsatisfactory. The weather on D-3 had limited the effectiveness of that day's bombardment and, while the weather had been good on D-2, the skillful use of camouflage by the Japanese increased the number of hits necessary to take out island installations. More hits per target meant more time, time the preliminary bombardment team did not have. These concerns caused Weller to begin thinking of what needed to be done to ensure that as adequate a bombardment as possible could be delivered in the short time left. The Japanese reaction to UDT operations on D-2 offered proof that gunfire coverage, while knocking out the obvious Priority A targets, had been woefully inadequate in other respects. Something had to be done, but what? The solution to the problem was dictated ultimately by yet another event on D-2. Weller states:

> A hitherto undiscovered four-gun battery situated in *Idaho's* area was disclosed in TA 166 VW on top of the bluff in a portion which enfiladed the entire landing beach. [This position was located to the right of the 4th Marine Division landing beaches.] This discovery of additional enemy defensive positions as well as this [*sic*] full realization of the heavy firepower the enemy was able to bear, was of paramount importance. Officers conducting the preliminary bombardment were impressed far more by this development than by negative results of photographic assessment of the day's firing; it brought home the large amount of damage yet to be inflicted on the enemy installations, and impressed all concerned with the absolute necessity of placing the bulk of the remaining fire power in the vicinity of the preferred landing beaches.[72]

To address the lack of destruction in the vicinity of the landing beaches, Weller

> . . . recommended that a maximum concentration of bombardment be placed on and near the preferred landing beaches; the recommendation was approved by the Commander, Amphibious Group 1 [Admiral Blandy]. The schedule for Dog Minus One Day was accordingly abandoned and the following plan substituted. . . . This arrangement placed

---

[71] MCUA, Iwo Jima Project, Fifth Amphibious Corps Landing Force, Volume IV, CG VAC, VAC Landing Force SAR, Annex CHARLIE, Appendix 2, 30 May 1945, Comments of Naval Gunfire Officer, pp. 7–8.

[72] Ibid., p. 12.

> the fire of four battleships and one heavy cruiser on, and in close vicinity to, the main landing beach. . . . Ships delivering this fire were directed to close the range as early as practicable and to execute maximum destruction. All unexpended ammunition allotted for the preliminary bombardment was to be expended if practicable.[73]

Weller, in other words, advised Blandy to do exactly what doctrine indicated should be done: expend ammunition on the landing beaches and adjacent areas because that is where the weapons that are most deadly to the landing force are located. This was a rule of thumb that had served the Marine Corps well for most of the war, but by following it in this situation, Donald M. Weller fell into Kuribayashi's unintended trap.[74] The Japanese commander knew that American firepower would destroy anything he put on the beach and this realization caused him to insist on a defense in depth. The weapons placed near the beach were not an integral part of Kuribayashi's plan. They represented, after all, a compromise that he was forced into by his more conservative subordinates. Placing the weapons near the beach, however, raised a merely formidable defensive scheme to the level of brilliance. The presence of these installations, afterthoughts though they were to Kuribayashi, ensured that the Americans would spend their last precious day of preliminary bombardment blasting away at the one place on Iwo Jima where such a massive expenditure of ammunition was guaranteed to do the least amount of good for the invaders—the landing beaches. The result can be gauged by comments from the division Action Reports. According to the Fifth Division report:

> The Japs did not elect to defend the beach. First troops ashore reported occasional enemy small arms fire from the base of Mount Suribachi, mortar fire from a defiladed area in that same vicinity and from the north; they also found coast defense guns on Suribachi out of action and nearly every pillbox on the beach and ground in rear of beach destroyed. The troops crossed the island in about [3½] hours. . . . [The preliminary NGF bombardment was intense and well executed, but it did not]: 1. succeed in taking out a large percentage of the enemy fortifications; 2. prevent the enemy from being able to place accurate artillery and mortar fire from prepared positions on any part of the island.[75]

---

[73] Ibid., p. 15.

[74] Isely and Crowl, *U.S. Marines and Amphibious War,* p. 470, praise Rear Admiral Blandy's decision to go with Weller's recommendation.

[75] MCUA, Iwo Jima Project, Fifth Marine Division Action Report on Iwo Jima, Volume I (Bound Book), CG 5th Marine Division, 5th Marine Division Action Report, Annex HOW, Naval Gunfire Support, pp. 4, 12, and 13.

The Fourth Division report was not so generous in its assessment:

> It is estimated that approximately [10%] of the beach defenses were knocked out and all enemy troops neutralized by scheduled bombardment in RCT 23 zone of action. Destruction was principally accomplished by heavy caliber shells. High velocity guns were not knocked out on the flanks and automatic weapons from emplacements along abutments of the airfield to the front were active. Mortars from the flanks and reverse slopes exacted heavy casualties on the beaches. Construction of emplacements, in conjunction with terrain, rendered area fires largely ineffective, although observation revealed it possible to close small caves with 5″ projectiles. . . . In RCT 25 zone of action large pillboxes on beach Blue 1 were knocked out by heavy caliber fire prior to landings. Effect of 5," rocket, and mortar fires on beaches was not visible due to the sandy nature of the beach. The rolling barrage screened initial waves sufficiently to enable them to organize on the beach but enemy riflemen had held their positions and were able to fire through the barrage from the right flank. Most emplacements observable from seaward were destroyed and the fire received came from reverse slopes and emplacements further inland.[76]

Weller states that "the Dog-Day bombardment, in conjunction with the destruction accomplished in the preliminary firing, enabled a successful landing to be made against one of the enemy's most heavily and skillfully defended possessions, with acceptable casualties."[77] The problem with this conclusion is that it does not take into account that Kuribayashi had decided to grant the landing to the invasion force before the first gunfire support shell struck Iwo on D-3—the Japanese, in other words, had adapted to the preponderance of firepower that the United States could bring to bear at the water's edge by simply conceding the beach. With the "lessons of Tarawa" and the application of those lessons in operations over the course of 1944 firmly in mind, the Navy and Marine Corps planned to fight a different battle at Iwo Jima than the one they were forced to fight. Even with photographic proof of the complexity and density of Kuribayashi's defenses before them, the naval gunfire emphasis on D-1 and on D-day was still on the landing beaches. The Marine Corps has argued that a longer pre-assault bombardment would have cut down the number of U.S. casualties. This is possibly correct,

---

[76] MCUA, Iwo Jima Project, Fourth Marine Division Report, Iwo Jima, 19 February–16 March 1945, w/encl. A-C, CG 4th Marine Division, 4th Marine Division Operation Report, Annex CHARLIE, Operations, pp. 18–19.

[77] MCUA, Iwo Jima Project, Fifth Amphibious Corps Landing Force, Volume IV, CG VAC, VAC Landing Force Report, Annex CHARLIE, Appendix 2, 30 May 1945, Comments of Naval Gunfire Officer, p. 34.

but just how much more damage could have been done given that the Japanese were underground and well concealed? American amphibious warfare planners working in the Central Pacific failed to understand fully the changes that occurred in Japanese defensive strategy and, consequently, U.S. naval gunfire doctrine failed to adapt sufficiently to address this changed strategy. In failing to adapt, it also failed in one of its most important objectives—to save lives.

Donald Weller spent much of his life after the invasion of Iwo Jima analyzing and advising on the use of naval gunfire in support of amphibious operations and, in his capacity as analyst, excusing the planning and execution anomalies that plagued that operation. Weller was not the only Marine artillery officer present during that hellish month on Volcano Island, however, and at least one of them has left a record of his opinions as to the efficacy of Weller's gunfire support decisions. Lieutenant Colonel Kenyth A. Damke served as the Executive Officer of the 13th Marines, the artillery regiment of the Fifth Marine Division, at Iwo. He took the Senior Course in the Amphibious Warfare School after the war and, as part of that course, he wrote a paper in which he analyzed the pre-D-day naval gunfire bombardment at Iwo Jima. The question he attempted to answer: did pre-D-day naval gunfire accomplish its mission in Operation Detachment? He reviewed Action Reports from several levels of command and considered everything from the stated mission of naval gunfire to the priority of targets set forth in the plans to the hydrographic conditions in the waters surrounding the island. His conclusions are as follows:

> Adopting a very strict interpertation [*sic*] of the mission of the pre-D-day bombardment of an objective by naval gunfire, as given in U.S.F. 63, the over all [*sic*] mission was not accomplished at IWO JIMA.
>
> Hundreds of targets remained; naval gunfire was capable of destroying them. At the rate of destruction achieved on D-1, another five (5) days of bombardment, under conditions similar to those existing for that day, would have been required to have reduced the fortifications.
>
> The destruction of defensive installations in the prefered [*sic*] beach areas was generally very good. A landing force had been placed ashore which had captured the island; in doing so, it had suffered a very high percentage of casualties. Who can say what the casualties might have been in this force and in other forces with in [*sic*] the theater, had the bombardment been extended until more of the enemy installations opposing the landing force had been destroyed? As in other major decisions in warfare which involves large forces in large theaters, the answer to this question will never be known. Suffice to say that insufficient time and ships were available with in [*sic*] the theater to allow additional bombardment of IWO JIMA before the landing force went ashore.[78]

[78] MCUA, Papers and Theses Collection, Kenyth A. Damke, "Was the Mission of the Pre-D-Day Bombardment by Naval Gunfire Accomplished at Iwo Jima?," pp. 12–13.

Damke, a man who was there, a man who witnessed much of the carnage wreaked upon his fellow Marines, and a man who was trained in the proper use of artillery in support of land forces, did not agree with Weller's assessment of the effectiveness of pre-D-day naval gunfire at Iwo.

Kuribayashi was successful in accomplishing the limited objectives he had set for himself. First, he made the Marines pay an extremely high price for the taking of Iwo Jima. Second, the sacrifice of himself and his command affected U.S. thinking concerning the invasion of Japan. Admiral Ernest J. King, Chief of Naval Operations and Commander-in-Chief of the U.S. Fleet, already had doubts about invading the Home Islands before the Iwo Jima operation commenced. King had agreed to preparations for an invasion as a contingency plan, believing that it was only prudent to make such plans because an invasion might prove to be necessary. It could be called off easily, however, in the event that it was not. Both King and Admiral William Leahy, personal chief of staff to President Roosevelt, preferred a plan of blockade and bombardment. This strategy was in line with the war plan the Navy had worked out during the interwar period for a conflict with Japan, the famous War Plan Orange. Chester Nimitz expressed support for Operation Olympic, the codename for the invasion of Kyushu, in a message to King on 28 April, but he withdrew his support in an "eyes only" message to King on 25 May. The heavy casualties suffered by U.S. forces at Iwo Jima, the slow progress of fighting on Okinawa, and intelligence reports of a buildup of Japanese defenses on Kyushu caused him to reconsider. King was about to make Nimitz's change of heart known to the Joint Chiefs of Staff when the dropping of the atomic bombs on Hiroshima and Nagasaki made the arguments concerning invasion moot.[79] Having accomplished his two major objectives, therefore, it can be argued that Kuribayashi's essentially hopeless defense of Iwo Jima was not in vain.

[79] Richard B. Frank, *Downfall: The End of the Imperial Japanese Empire* (New York: Random House, 1999), pp. 37, 147, 212, 276; John Ray Skates, *The Invasion of Japan: Alternative to the Bomb* (Columbia: University of South Carolina Press, 1994), pp. 21, 25–26, 29, 44–45, 54. Skates does not mention Nimitz's change of heart indicated in the Admiral's 25 May "eyes only" communication to King.

Chapter 8

Conclusions

The war against Japan ground on for another four months and nineteen days after 26 March 1945, the day on which the United States announced an end to the capture and occupation phase of Operation Detachment. The doctrine for the use of naval gunfire in support of amphibious assaults played an important part in reaching the point where, at Sulfur Island, it received its most rigorous test. Ironically, as integral to U.S. success as it had been through February of 1945, it played little direct role in the very last stages of the war. At Okinawa, Lieutenant General Mitsuru Ushijima was able to go even further than Kuribayashi in implementing the new Japanese defensive doctrine first seen at Biak. Okinawa's size allowed him the option of granting American forces four days of relative peace in getting ashore, finally contesting the American invasion from prepared inland defenses in depth instead of at the water's edge. The United States, in the end, chose a different strategy to force the Japanese to surrender than the one that had brought them essentially to the Emperor's doorstep. Rather than mounting an invasion of the Home Islands, the most massive amphibious assault contemplated by American wartime planners in either theater, a new and infinitely more powerful American technological innovation than naval gunfire—the atomic bomb—was used to bring Imperial Japan to its knees.

What, then, can be said about the effectiveness of naval gunfire in the preparation for and the execution of an assault on a well-defended beach? Did the prewar doctrine hold up without fundamental modification? In possession of an untried naval gunfire doctrine at the beginning of the war, the sea services did not get to put it to the test until November of 1943 in the Gilberts—a test it failed. The assault on Tarawa Atoll proved that naval gunfire doctrine needed some fine-tuning. American commanders made changes and implemented them in the next operation, against the Marshall Islands, in January and February of 1944. United States amphibious forces, partly because of these changes, overwhelmed Japanese resistance on Roi-Namur and Kwajalein. Rapturous praise on the part of U.S. commanders aside, however, the Marshalls were not a sufficient test of the newly-modified doctrine, and the reason for this is as follows: the Marshall atolls invaded by the Americans were not the hardened targets that Betio Island had been. The "Lessons of Tarawa" concerning naval gunfire did seem to have been absorbed and applied, however, and the Marine Corps was pleased.

The next operation would seem to show that only one naval commander, Rear Admiral Richard L. Conolly, had learned the vaunted "lessons." Saipan received only one day of bombardment from the ships whose crews had been trained in the intricacies of point fire against shore targets, the old battleships, cruisers, and destroyers of the Fire Support Task Group. Conolly, by contrast, worked over Guam for thirteen days, but he was able to do so only because the date of the invasion of that island had to be postponed due to the mushrooming problems associated with subduing the Japanese on Saipan. To his credit, however, he used the time wisely, applying the "lessons" with the precision of a master.

The assault on Peleliu suffered from failures at several levels, but the failure that cost the assaulting Marines most dearly on D-day was the ignorance of accumulated naval gunfire "lessons" exhibited by the man in command of the operation's preliminary gunfire support, Rear Admiral Jesse Oldendorf. This is particularly surprising considering that Oldendorf had participated in several preliminary bombardments prior to 15 September 1944, and that he was aware of the importance of thorough gunfire preparation for the success of an amphibious assault landing. The height of frustration for anyone perusing the records of Stalemate II is when Oldendorf declared that he had run out of targets, this before he had finished using the quota of ammunition allotted him for the bombardment. Finally, at Iwo Jima, the Marine Corps argued for ten days of preliminary bombardment but received only three. The Navy, in the persons of Raymond Spruance and Kelly Turner, cited several reasons why the recognized doctrine requiring a bombardment commensurate with the strength of the enemy's defenses should be discarded in the case of Iwo Jima. Spruance, upon inspecting Japanese fortifications after the island fell to the forces under his command, believed himself justified in limiting the bombardment to three days. Kuribayashi's defenses were so thoroughly hardened that, in his estimation, only Marines with rifles and flamethrowers could have gotten them out, regardless of the amount of aerial bombs and naval shells thrown at them.[1] For Spruance, the doctrine was irrelevant in the face of such strength and organization.

In summary, then, what were the major problems associated with the United States Navy and Marine Corps' World War II-era doctrine for the use of naval gunfire in the support of amphibious assaults? First, the doctrine's lack of clarity in its use of terms caused confusion and cost lives. Second, application of the doctrine varied too much from one commander to another and, consequently, from one operation to another. Third, the commanding officers of ships tasked with providing naval gunfire in support of amphibious operations were slow to adapt to the new mindset required of them, namely, that the lives of the Marines and soldiers going ashore and the mission they had to perform were more important than the safety of an individual ship. For the naval mind, such a thought was absolute heresy—even the captain's life counted for nothing if the continued existence of his ship was on the line. Repeatedly Turner and Conolly had to force ship commanders to put their

[1] Buell, *Quiet Warrior*, p. 366.

vessels directly in harm's way so that adequate gunfire could be brought to bear during an assault. Fourth, the amount of naval gunfire used in each operation and the way in which it was portioned out varied according to no demonstrable formula. Lack of a consistent formula resulted in inconsistent application of the doctrine. Fifth, and most important, neither the Navy nor the Marine Corps understood the extent to which the Japanese were modifying their own doctrine by mid-1944 in response to American firepower. Consequently, American commanders failed to modify in a timely manner their application of naval gunfire doctrine in reaction to Japanese doctrinal changes. This failure resulted in the loss of thousands of American lives at Peleliu and Iwo Jima and the maiming of several thousand more.

The "lesson" most often mentioned in regard to the use of naval gunfire in support of American Central Pacific amphibious assaults during World War II is that long, slow, deliberate, and precise bombardment was necessary in order to ensure the success of the assault of a well-defended beach. A survey of the operations undertaken in the Central Pacific shows quite clearly that this lesson was not followed consistently, so, either it was not learned as was claimed or it was ignored when planners considered it convenient to do so. There was, however, a lesson that was never mentioned as such but was consistently applied, and this lesson fit in well with an American trait demonstrated in the European Theater as well as the Pacific—inadequacies in doctrinal finesse were to be overcome through the application of massive firepower. Many naval commanders continued to equate tonnage of ordnance to efficacy of naval gunfire support even after the "lessons of Tarawa" supposedly demonstrated the fallacy of such a conclusion. They excused lack of precision by pointing out that they were delivering a certain amount of ordnance in a relatively short period and that surely no defender could hold up under such punishment. Repeatedly, the Japanese showed that they indeed could hold up under the tremendous pounding of American naval artillery and that they would defend their positions to the death, both of themselves and of as many Americans as they could take with them. The Japanese modified their defensive doctrine during 1944 and 1945, taking into consideration the destructive capacity of American firepower, and they found a way to negate the American advantage. While they could not meet their enemy at the water's edge and drive him back into the sea, they could hold out long enough to exact a high price for each inch of ground given up. In the end, this defensive scheme caused the Americans to pause and consider in dread the costs to be incurred in taking the Home Islands, just as Kuribayashi hoped they would.

Acknowledgments

I would like to thank those who provided help and inspiration in this journey to publication. It is not possible to list them all, but I cannot let this opportunity pass without mentioning a special few. First, I want to thank Robert von Maier, Publisher and Editor-in-Chief at Brécourt Academic. Rob offered me an outlet for my scholarly activities and, along the way, has become a good friend. Next, a deeply heartfelt thank you to First Sergeant Ray B. McKenzie, USMC (Ret.), who demonstrated for me what it meant to be a Marine. Also, I wish to express my most profound gratitude to James and Bryan Morrison who provided me with support and encouragement when I needed it most. Finally, none of this would have been possible without the love and support of my dear wife, Becky Mitchener.

Appendix

Table A.1.

Number of ships present during preliminary and pre-assault bombardments arranged according to ship types

	FBB	OBB	CA	CL	DD
Tarawa	0	3	2	2	11
Roi-Namur	3	3	2	3	11
Saipan	0	7	6	5	26
Guam	0	6	5	2	19
Peleliu	0	4	3	1	9
Iwo Jima	2	6	5	3	9

Sources: Naval Gunfire Report, Tarawa, VAC NGF Officer; Naval Gunfire Report, Roi-Namur, VAC NGF Officer; Morison, *New Guinea and the Marianas*; III MAC Operations Report, NGF Report; Expeditionary Troops Report, NGF Report, Appendix II.

Table A.2.

Size of island objectives and total number of combatants per side

	Size of Island	American Forces	Japanese Forces
Tarawa	800 × 3800 yds	17,447	4,866
Roi-Namur	Roi – 1,170 × 1,250 yds Namur – 80 × 890 yds	24,902	3,563
Saipan	5½ × 12½ miles	66,779	31,629
Guam	13½ × 33 miles	54,691	16,100
Peleliu	2 × 6 miles	28,484	10,700
Iwo Jima	4⅔ × 2½ miles	71,245	21,000

Sources: Rottman, *World War II Pacific Island Guide*; Rottman, *U.S. Marine Corps World War II Order of Battle.*

Glossary of Terms

amphibious assault—A type of amphibious operation that involves establishing a force on a hostile or potentially hostile shore.

amphibious force—An amphibious task force and a landing force together with other forces that are trained, organized, and equipped for amphibious operations.

amphibious operation—A military operation launched from the sea by an amphibious force, embarked in ships or craft with the primary purpose of introducing a landing force ashore to accomplish the assigned mission.

area fire—Gunfire delivered in a prescribed area. Area fire is generally neutralization fire.

beachhead—A designated area on a hostile or potentially hostile shore that, when seized and held, ensures the continuous landing of troops and materiel, and provides maneuver space requisite for subsequent projected operations ashore.

close-support fire—Fire placed on enemy troops, weapons, or positions which, because of their proximity, present the most immediate and serious threat to the supported unit.

continuous fire—Fire that is not stopped for spots or corrections.

D-day—The day on which a particular amphibious operation commences or is to commence.

deep-support fire—Fire directed on objectives not in the immediate vicinity of friendly forces, for neutralizing and destroying enemy reserves and weapons, and interfering with enemy command, supply, communications, and observations.

defilade—1. Protection from hostile observation and fire provided by an obstacle such as a hill, ridge, or bank. 2. To shield from enemy fire or observation by using natural or artificial obstacles.

deflection—Lateral angular correction applied to target bearing to bring fire onto a target. Most targets move, so it is necessary to "lead" them so that the projectile will arrive at their future position.

destruction fire—Fire delivered for the sole purpose of destroying material objects.

direct fire—Fire delivered on a target using the target itself as a point of aim for either the weapon or the director. Direct fire is usually used on targets that can be seen (by optics or radar) from the firing ship.

director control or director fire—A method of firing guns from a distant control station after the guns have been laid to a predetermined angle of elevation and trained upon the correct bearing. It includes equipment by which the guns can be correctly elevated and trained when the target is obscured from the gun position.

dispersion—The distance from the point of impact of a particular projectile to the MPI of the salvo. Dispersion in range is measured parallel to the line of fire and dispersion in deflection is measured at right angles to the line of fire. A Dispersion Pattern is the combining of all the impact points of a particular salvo.

doctrine—Fundamental principles by which the military forces or elements thereof guide their actions in support of national objectives. It is authoritative, but requires judgment in application.

echelon—1. A subdivision of a headquarters, i.e., forward echelon, rear echelon. 2. Separate level of command. As compared to a regiment, a division is a higher echelon, a battalion is a lower echelon. 3. A fraction of a command in the direction of depth to which a principal combat mission is assigned; i.e., attack echelon, support echelon, reserve echelon. 4. A formation in which its subdivisions are placed one behind another, with a lateral and even spacing to the same side.

elevation—Movement of a gun along the vertical axis.

enfilade—To be able to fire along or down the long axis of a formation.

estimate of the situation—A logical process of reasoning by which a commander considers all the circumstances affecting the military situation and arrives at a decision as to the course of action to be taken in order to accomplish his mission.

H-hour—For amphibious operations, the time the first assault elements are scheduled to touch down on the beach, or a landing zone, and in some cases the commencement of countermine breaching operations.

indirect fire—Fire delivered on a target that is not itself used as a point of aim for the weapons or the director. Indirect fire is always used on targets not visible from the ship. Projectiles are fired on a ballistic trajectory based upon targeting information provided by air spotting or a forward observer on the ground.

Mean Point of Impact (MPI)—The mean point around which rounds impact. The MPI should be near the center of the intended target.

neutralization fire—1. Fire that is delivered to render the target ineffective or unusable. 2. In naval war parlance it is rapid, fairly accurate fire delivered for the purpose of hampering, interrupting, or preventing enemy fire, movement, or action. The destruction of weapons and personnel is a secondary consideration. The effect of neutralization is comparatively temporary, and such fire may have to be repeated.

plunging fire—In naval warfare, plunging fire is fire that comes down upon a target at close to a ninety-degree angle so that it can best penetrate the thinner armor of a ship's decks or the roof of a bunker.

point fire—Gunfire directed at a specific material target in order to destroy that particular object.

pointer fire—A method of fire in which individual guns, mounts, or turrets are pointed and fired from pointer stations at the guns. In pointer fire, the target must be visible from the gun, mount, or turret sights, and sights must be set in range and deflection.

prearranged or scheduled fire—Gunfire that is formally planned and executed against targets of known location. Such fire is usually planned well in advance and is executed at a predetermined time or during a predetermined period of time.

suppression—Temporary or transient degradation by an opposing force of the performance of a weapons system below the level needed to fulfill its mission objectives.

Time-Sector Method—A method of naval gunfire support delivery in which the area to be covered is divided into smaller sectors, each sector being assigned to a certain ship or group of ships. The ship or ships deliver a specified number of shells on the targeted sector within a specified period of time. The goal is to provide as complete coverage as possible over the time period allotted. This method works especially well when area fire is needed.

training or deflection—Movement of a gun along the horizontal axis.

uplift—To change the elevation of naval guns so that fire impacts at a predetermined distance inland, away from friendly troops.

Selected Bibliography

Alexander, Joseph H., *Utmost Savagery: The Three Days of Tarawa* (Annapolis: Naval Institute Press, 1995; reprint, New York: Ivy Books, 1995).

Alexander, Joseph H., *Storm Landings: Epic Amphibious Battles in the Central Pacific* (Annapolis: Naval Institute Press, 1997).

Bartley, Whitman S., *Iwo Jima: Amphibious Epic* (Washington, DC: Historical Division, HQMC, 1954).

Bartlett, Merrill L. (ed.), *Assault from the Sea: Essays on the History of Amphibious Warfare* (Annapolis: Naval Institute Press, 1983).

Buell, Thomas B., *The Quiet Warrior: A Biography of Admiral Raymond A. Spruance* (Boston: Little, Brown, 1974; reprint, Annapolis: Naval Institute Press, 1987).

Burrell, Robert S., *The Ghosts of Iwo Jima* (College Station: Texas A&M University Press, 2006).

Clausewitz, Carl von, *On War*, Michael Howard and Peter Paret (eds. and trans.) (Princeton: Princeton University Press, 1976).

Clifford, Kenneth J., *Amphibious Warfare Development in Britain and America from 1920–1940* (Laurens, NY: Edgewood, 1983).

Clifford, Kenneth J., *Progress and Purpose: A Developmental History of the United States Marine Corps, 1900–1970* (Washington, DC: HQMC, 1973).

Crowl, Philip A., and Edmund G. Love, *Seizure of the Gilberts and Marshalls, United States Army in World War II, The War in the Pacific* (Washington, DC: U.S. Army Center of Military History, 1955; reprint, Harrisburg, PA: National Historical Society, 1995).

Crowl, Philip A., *Campaign in the Marianas, United States Army in World War II, The War in the Pacific* (Washington, DC: U.S. Army Center of Military History, 1960; reprint, Harrisburg, PA: National Historical Society, 1994).

Damke, Kenyth A., "Was the Mission of the Pre-D-Day Bombardment by Naval Gunfire Accomplished at Iwo Jima?," paper presented in fulfillment of 1947–48 Senior Course requirements, Amphibious Warfare School, Marine Corps Schools, Quantico, VA.

Dyer, George C., *The Amphibians Came to Conquer: The Story of Admiral Richmond Kelly Turner*, 2 vols. (Washington, DC: GPO, 1969).

Frank, Richard B., *Downfall: The End of the Imperial Japanese Empire* (New York: Random House, 1999).

Gailey, Harry, *Peleliu: 1944* (Annapolis: The Nautical and Aviation Publishing Company of America, 1983).

Gailey, Harry, *The Liberation of Guam, 21 July–10 August 1944* (Novato, CA: Presidio Press, 1988).

Garand, George W., and Truman R. Strobridge, *History of U.S. Marine Corps Operations in World War II*, Vol. IV, *Western Pacific Operations* (Washington, DC: Historical Branch, HQMC, 1971; reprint, Nashville: The Battery Press, 1994).

Hayes, Grace Person, *The History of the Joint Chiefs of Staff in World War II: The War Against Japan* (Annapolis: Naval Institute Press, 1982).

Heinl, Robert D., Jr., and John A. Crown, *The Marshalls: Increasing the Tempo* (Washington, DC: Historical Section, HQMC, 1954).

Hoffman, Carl W., *Saipan: The Beginning of the End* (Washington, DC: Historical Section, HQMC, 1950).

Hough, Frank O., *The Assault on Peleliu* (Washington, DC: Historical Section, HQMC, 1950).

Hughes, Wayne P., *Fleet Tactics: Theory and Practice* (Annapolis: Naval Institute Press, 1986).

Isely, Jeter A., and Philip A. Crowl, *The U.S. Marines and Amphibious War: Its Theory and Its Practice in the Pacific* (Princeton: Princeton University Press, 1951; reprint, Quantico: Marine Corps Association, 1988).

Jablon, Howard, *David M. Shoup: A Warrior against War* (Lanham: Rowman & Littlefield, 2005).

King, Ernest J., and Walter Muir Whitehill, *Fleet Admiral King: A Naval Record* (New York: W.W. Norton, 1952; reprint, New York: Da Capo Press, 1976).

Knox, Dudley W., "The Role of Doctrine in Naval Warfare," *Proceedings* 41 (March/April 1915), pp. 325–54.

Lodge, Orlan R., *The Recapture of Guam* (Washington, DC: Historical Branch, G-3 Division, Headquarters, USMC, 1954).

Matloff, Maurice, *Strategic Planning for Coalition Warfare, 1943–1944, United States Army in World War II, The War Department* (Washington, DC: Office of the Chief of Military History, Department of the Army, 1959).

Miller, Edward S., *War Plan Orange: The U.S. Strategy to Defeat Japan, 1897–1945* (Annapolis: Naval Institute Press, 1991).

Millett, Allan R., *Semper Fidelis: The History of the United States Marine Corps,* rev. ed. (New York: The Free Press, 1991).

Millett, Allan R., "Assault from the Sea: The Development of Amphibious Warfare between the Wars—The American, British, and Japanese Experiences," in Williamson Murray and Allan R. Millett (eds.), *Military Innovation in the Interwar Period* (New York: Cambridge University Press, 1996), pp. 50–95.

Morison, Samuel Eliot, *Aleutians, Gilberts and Marshalls: June 1942–April 1944, History of United States Naval Operations in World War II,* Vol. 7 (Boston: Little Brown, 1951).

Morison, Samuel Eliot, *New Guinea and the Marianas: March 1944–August 1944, History of United States Naval Operations in World War II,* Vol. 8 (Boston: Little Brown, 1953).

Morison, Samuel Eliot, *Leyte: June 1944–January 1945, History of United States Naval Operations in World War II,* Vol. 12 (Boston: Little Brown, 1958).

Potter, E. B. (ed.), *The United States and World Sea Power* (Englewood Cliffs, NJ: Prentice-Hall, 1955).

Potter, E. B., and Chester W. Nimitz (eds.), *Sea Power: A Naval History* (Englewood Cliffs, NJ: Prentice-Hall, 1960).

Potter, E. B., *Nimitz* (Annapolis: Naval Institute Press, 1976).

Potter, E. B. (ed.), *Sea Power: A Naval History,* 2nd ed. (Annapolis: Naval Institute Press, 1981).

Prados, John, *Islands of Destiny: The Solomons Campaign and the Eclipse of the Rising Sun* (New York: New American Library, 2012).

Rottman, Gordon L., *World War II Pacific Island Guide: A Geo-Military Study* (Westport, CT: Greenwood Press, 2002).

Rottman, Gordon L., *U.S. Marine Corps World War II Order of Battle: Ground and Air Units in the Pacific War, 1939–1945* (Westport, CT: Greenwood Press, 2002).

Roscoe, Theodore, *United States Destroyer Operations in World War II* (Annapolis: United States Naval Institute, 1953).

Russ, Martin, *Line of Departure: Tarawa* (Garden City, NY: Doubleday, 1975).

Russell, John H., "A Plea for a Mission and Doctrine," *Marine Corps Gazette* 1 (June 1916), pp. 112–16.

Shaw, Henry I., Jr., Bernard C. Nalty, and Edwin T. Turnbladh, *History of U.S. Marine Corps Operations in World War II*, Vol. III, *Central Pacific Drive* (Washington, DC: Historical Branch, HQMC, 1966; reprint, Nashville: The Battery Press, 1994).

Silverstone, Paul H., *U.S. Warships of World War II* (Shepperton: Ian Allan, 1965).

Skates, John Ray, *The Invasion of Japan: Alternative to the Bomb* (Columbia: University of South Carolina Press, 1994).

Sledge, E. B., *With the Old Breed at Peleliu and Okinawa* (Novato, CA: Presidio Press, 1981; reprint with new Introduction by Paul Fussell, New York: Oxford University Press, 1990).

Smith, Holland M., and Percy Finch, *Coral and Brass* (New York: Scribner's, 1948; reprint, New York: Bantam Books, 1987).

Smith, Robert Ross, *The Approach to the Philippines, United States Army in World War II, The War in the Pacific* (Washington, DC: Center of Military History, 1953).

Smith, S. E. (ed.), *The United States Marine Corps in World War II* (New York: Random House, 1969).

Stockman, James R., *The Battle for Tarawa* (Washington, DC: Historical Section, HQMC, 1947).

Terzibaschitsch, Stefan, *Battleships of the U.S. Navy in World War II* (New York: Bonanza Books, 1977).

Tritten, James J., *Naval Doctrine . . . From the Sea* (Norfolk: Naval Doctrine Command, 1994).

U.S. Department of Defense, *Dictionary of Military Terms* (New York: Arco, 1988).

United States War Department, *Handbook on Japanese Military Forces* (London: Greenhill Books/Lionel Leventhal, 1991; reprint, Baton Rouge: Louisiana State University Press, 1995).

Weller, Donald M., *Gunfire Support of Amphibious Operations: Past, Present, and Future* (Dahlgren, VA: Naval Surface Weapons Center, 1977).

Wright, Derrick, *The Battle for Iwo Jima, 1945* (Stroud: Sutton, 1999).

Index